J.K. LASSER'S™

1001 DEDUCTIONS AND TAX BREAKS 2007

Look for these and other titles from J.K. Lasser™—Practical Guides for All Your Financial Needs

J.K. Lasser's Strategic Investing after 50 by Julie Jason

J.K. Lasser's Small Business Taxes by Barbara Weltman

J.K. Lasser's 1001 Deductions by Barbara Weltman

J.K. Lasser's Homeowner's Tax Breaks by Gerald Robinson

J.K. Lasser's New Rules for Estate Planning and Tax by Harold Apolinsky and Stewart Welch III

J.K. Lasser's From eBay to Mary Kay: Taxes Made Easy for Your Home-Based Business by Gary Carter

J.K. Lasser's The New Bankruptcy Law and You by Nathalie Martin with Stewart Paley

J.K. LASSER'S™

1001 DEDUCTIONS AND TAX BREAKS 2007

Your Complete Guide to Everything Deductible

Barbara Weltman

BICENTENNIAL 1807 WILEY 2007 BICENTENNIAL

John Wiley & Sons, Inc.

Published by John Wiley & Sons, Inc., Hoboken, New Jersey.
Published simultaneously in Canada.

For general information on our other products and services, or technical support, please contact our Customer Care Department within the United States at 800-762-2974, outside the United States at 317-572-3993 or fax 317-572-4002.

Wiley also publishes its books in a variety of electronic formats. Some content that appears in print may not be available in electronic books.

For more information about Wiley products, visit our web site at www.wiley.com.

ISBN-13 978-0-471-78667-2
ISBN-10 0-471-78667-5

Printed in the United States of America.

10 9 8 7 6 5 4 3 2 1

Contents

Introduction

Say the word "taxes" and most people groan. There are good reasons for this response: First of all, the cost of paying your taxes annually can be a financial burden. You may feel taken to the cleaners every time you view your paycheck *after* withholding for federal income taxes (not to mention state income taxes as well as Social Security and Medicare taxes).

Second, the tax law is very complicated and changing all the time. Congress changes the tax law to a greater or lesser extent every single year—and this year is no exception! In addition, new court decisions and IRS rulings appear each day, providing guidance on how to interpret the law.

How can you combat the feeling of dread when it comes to taxes? It helps to know that the tax law is peppered with many, many tax breaks to which you may be entitled. These breaks allow you to *not* report certain economic benefits you enjoy or to subtract certain expenses from your income or even directly from your tax bill. As the famous jurist Judge Learned Hand once stated (in the 1934 case of *Helvering v. Gregory* in the Court of Appeals for the Second Circuit):

> Anyone may arrange his affairs so that his taxes shall be as low as possible; he is not bound to choose that pattern which best pays the treasury. There is not even a patriotic duty to increase one's taxes. Over and over again the Courts have said that there is nothing sinister in so arranging affairs as to keep taxes as low as possible. Everyone does it, rich and poor alike, and all do right, for nobody owes any public duty to pay more than the law demands.

So get your tax affairs in order and reduce what you pay each year to Uncle Sam!

In getting a handle on how to do this by taking advantage of every tax break you may be entitled to without running afoul of the Internal Revenue Service (IRS), there are some simple rules to keep in mind. They include:

- You must report all of your income unless a specific law allows you to exclude or exempt it (so that it is never taxed) or defer it (so that it is taxed at a later time).
- You can claim deductions only when and to the extent the law allows. Deductions are referred to as a "matter of legislative grace;" Congress doesn't have to create them and does so only for some purpose (for example, to encourage economic activity or to balance some perceived inequity in the tax law).
- Tax credits are worth more than tax deductions. A credit reduces your tax payment on a dollar-for-dollar basis; a $1,000 credit saves you $1,000 in taxes. A deduction is worth only as much as the top tax bracket you are in. Suppose you are in the 28 percent tax bracket, which means this is the highest rate you pay on at least some of your income. If you have a $1,000 deduction, it is worth $280 (28 percent of $1,000) because it saves you $280 in taxes you would otherwise have to pay.
- Even if your income is modest, you may have to file Form 1040 (the so-called "long form"), rather than a simplified return (Form 1040A or 1040EZ), in order to claim certain tax benefits.
- In a number of cases, different deduction rules apply to the alternative minimum tax (AMT), a shadow tax system that ensures you pay at least some tax if your regular income tax is lower than it would have been without certain deductions.

This book is designed to tell you how to get every tax edge you're entitled to. Knowing what to look out for will help you plan ahead and organize your activities in such a way that you'll share less of your hard-earned money with Uncle Sam.

Tax-Favored Items

There are five types of tax-advantaged items receiving preferential or favorable treatment under the tax law:

1. *Tax-free income*—income you can receive without any current or future tax concerns. Tax-free income may be in the form of exclusions or exemptions from tax. In many cases, tax-free items do not even have to be reported in any way on your return.

2. *Capital gains*—profits on the sale or exchange of property held for more than one year (long-term). Long-term capital gains are subject to lower tax rates than the rates on other income, such as salary and interest income. Ordinary dividends on stocks and stock mutual funds are taxed at the same low rates as long-term capital gains.
3. *Tax-deferred income*—income that isn't currently taxed. Since the income builds up without any reduction for current tax, you may accumulate more over time. However, at some point the income becomes taxable.
4. *Deductions*—items you can subtract from your income to reduce the amount of income subject to tax. There are two classes of deductions: Those "above the line," which are subtracted directly from gross income, and those that can be claimed only if you itemize deductions instead of claiming the standard deduction (explained later).
5. *Credits*—items you can use to offset your tax on a dollar-for-dollar basis. Usually you must complete a special tax form for each credit you claim.

This book focuses on three types of tax-favored items: exclusions (tax-free income), deductions, and credits.

Limits on Qualifying for Tax-Favored Items

In many cases, eligibility for a tax benefit, or the extent to which it can be claimed, depends on adjusted gross income (AGI) or modified adjusted gross income (MAGI).

Adjusted gross income is gross income (all the income you are required to report), minus certain deductions (called "adjustments to gross income"). Adjustments or subtractions you can make to your gross income to arrive at your adjusted gross income are limited to the following items:

Alimony payments.

Business expenses.

Capital loss deductions of up to $3,000.

Domestic production activities deduction.

Educator expenses up to $250. *(Provision expired 12/31/05. Extension expected for 2006.)*

Forfeiture-of-interest penalties because of early withdrawals from certificates of deposit (CDs).

Health Savings Account (HSA) contributions.

Individual Retirement Account (IRA) deductions.

Jury duty pay turned over to your employer.

Moving expenses.

Net operating losses (NOLs).

One-half of self-employment tax.

Performing artist's qualifying expenses.

Qualified retirement plan contributions for self-employed individuals.

Rent and royalty expenses.

Repayment of supplemental unemployment benefits required because of the receipt of trade readjustment allowances.

Self-employed health insurance deductions.

Simplified employee pension (SEP) or savings incentive match plan for employees (SIMPLE) contributions for self-employed individuals.

Student loan interest deduction up to $2,500.

Travel expenses to attend National Guard or military reserve meetings more than 100 miles from home.

Tuition and fees deduction up to $4,000. *(Provision expired 12/31/05. Extension expected for 2006.)*

Figuring AGI may sound complicated, but in reality it's merely a number taken from a line on your tax return. For example, AGI is the figure you enter on line 37 of the 2006 Form 1040, line 21 of the 2006 Form 1040A, or line 4 of 2006 Form 1040EZ.

Modified adjusted gross income is merely AGI increased by certain items that are excludable from income and/or certain adjustments to gross income. *Which* items are added back varies for different tax breaks. For example, the MAGI limit on eligibility to claim the student loan interest deduction is AGI (disregarding the student loan interest deduction) increased by the tuition and fees deduction as well as the exclusion for foreign earned income and certain other foreign income or expenses. All of these items are explained in this book.

Standard Deduction versus Itemized Deductions

Every taxpayer, other than someone who can be claimed as a dependent on another taxpayer's return, is entitled to a standard deduction. This is a subtraction from your income, and the amount you claim is based on your filing status. Table I.1 shows the standard deduction amounts for 2006.

In addition to the basic standard deduction, certain taxpayers can increase these amounts. An additional standard deduction amount applies to those age 65 and older and for blindness. For 2006, the additional amount is $1,250 for individuals who are not married and are not a surviving spouse and $1,000 for those who are married or a surviving spouse.

TABLE I.1 Standard Deduction Amounts for 2006

Filing Status	Standard Deduction
Married filing jointly	$10,300
Head of household	7,550
Single (unmarried)	5,150
Qualifying widow(er) (surviving spouse)	10,300
Married filing separately	5,150

Example

In 2006, you are single, age 68, and *not* blind. Your standard deduction is $6,400 ($5,150 + $1,250).

Instead of claiming the standard deduction, you can opt to list certain deductions separately (i.e., *itemize* them). Itemized deductions include:

Medical expenses.

Taxes.

Interest payments.

Gifts to charity.

Casualty and theft losses.

Unreimbursed employee business expenses.

Investment expenses.

Legal fees to earn income.

Gambling losses.

Estate tax payments on income in respect of decedents.

You cannot claim any additional standard deduction that applies to those 65 or older and/or blind if you choose to itemize deductions in lieu of claiming the basic standard deduction amount.

Overall Limit on Certain Itemized Deductions

Even if you meet all conditions for claiming certain itemized deductions, you may lose some of the benefit of claiming them because of a special rule currently in the law. If your income is more than a set limit, these itemized deductions are reduced by 3 percent of the excess income, subject to a two-thirds phaseout. More specifically, if your adjusted gross income (AGI) in 2006 is more than $150,500 (or $75,250 if you are married but file a separate return), your itemized deductions (other than certain ones) are reduced by 3 percent of your excess AGI. This reduction amount, however, is divided by three; only one-third of the reduction is taken into account in 2006.

Itemized deductions *not* subject to this reduction include deductions for:

- Medical expenses.
- Investment interest.
- Casualty and theft losses.
- Gambling losses.

You can use Worksheet I.1 to figure the reduction in your itemized deductions (*after* you have figured each and every one under the regular rules throughout this book).

If you use your computer to figure your taxes, your tax software or online program does this computation automatically; you aren't even aware of it. But

WORKSHEET I.1 Figuring the 3 Percent Reduction

1.	Enter your adjusted gross income for 2006.	1. ________
2.	Enter $150,500 (or $75,250 if you are married filing separately).	2. ________
3.	Subtract line 2 from line 1.	3. ________
4.	Multiply the amount on line 3 by 3 percent (0.03).	4. ________
5.	Enter your total itemized deductions (before any reduction).	5. ________
6.	Enter the total of your deductions for medical expenses, investment interest, casualty and theft losses, and gambling losses (itemized deductions not subject to reduction).	6. ________
7.	Subtract line 6 from line 5.	7. ________
8.	Multiply the amount on line 7 by 80 percent (0.80).	8. ________
9.	Enter the smaller of line 4 or line 8. *This is your disallowed amount.*	9. ________
10.	Subtract line 9 from line 5. *This is the net amount of itemized deductions you can claim for 2006.*	10. ________

WORKSHEET I.1 *(Continued)*

Example

In 2006, you are single with adjusted gross income of $160,000. Your itemized deductions (after applying various limits for them) total $30,000:

Medical expenses (after the 7.5 percent floor)	$ 500
State and local income taxes	12,000
Real estate taxes	4,000
Home mortgage interest	6,000
Charitable donations	7,000
Miscellaneous itemized deductions (after 2 percent floor)	500
Total	$30,000

All of the deductions (except the one for medical expenses) are subject to the 3 percent reduction.

1.	Enter your adjusted gross income for 2006.	1. $160,000
2.	Enter $150,500 (or $75,250 if you are married filing separately).	2. 150,500
3.	Subtract line 2 from line 1.	3. 9,500
4.	Multiply the amount on line 3 by 3 percent (0.03).	4. 285
5.	Enter your total itemized deductions (before any reduction).	5. 30,000
6.	Enter the total of your deductions for medical expenses, investment interest, casualty and theft losses, and gambling losses (itemized deductions not subject to reduction).	6. 500
7.	Subtract line 6 from line 5.	7. 29,500
8.	Multiply the amount on line 7 by 80 percent (0.80).	8. 23,600
9.	Enter the smaller of line 4 or line 8.	9. 285
10.	Divide line 9 by 3 and enter the results as a decimal.	10. 95
11.	Subtract line 10 from line 9.	11. 190
12.	Subtract line 11 from line 5. *This is the net amount of itemized deductions you can claim for 2006.*	12. $ 28,100

TABLE I.2 Average Itemized Deductions for 2004*

AGI	Medical	Taxes	Interest	Donations
Under $ 15,000	$ 7,588	$ 761	$ 6,926	$ 1,421
$ 15,001–30,000	6,229	2,761	6,664	1,969
$ 30,001–50,000	5,324	3,592	6,933	2,132
$ 50,001–100,000	6,125	5,808	8,310	2,663
$100,001–200,000	9,811	10,520	10,949	4,130
$200,001 and over	31,332	38,143	19,721	19,014

*The latest year for which statistics are available.

it's useful to know that you may not fully realize the value of the deductions you are otherwise entitled to because of the 3 percent reduction in the law.

The good news is that this reduction is being eliminated from the tax law, starting with 2006. Eventually, no one will have to go through this long computation to figure a reduction in allowable itemized deductions.

The bad news is that this elimination is phased in over a number of years (it is fully phased in by 2010). The reduction in itemized deductions is phased out by one-third in 2006 and 2007 and another one-third in 2008 and 2009, and the final one-third in 2010.

Impact of Deductions on Your Chances of Being Audited

Did you know that the IRS collects statistics from taxpayers to create profiles of average deductions? If you claim more than the average for your income range, the computer *may* select your return for further examination.

Table I.2 shows the average itemized deductions for taxpayers in various adjusted gross income (AGI) ranges.

Tax experts agree that you should claim every deduction you are entitled to, even if your write-offs exceed these statistical ranges. Just make sure to have the necessary proof of your eligibility and other records you are required to keep in case your return in examined.

How to Use This Book

The chapters in this book are organized by subject matter so you can browse through them to find the subjects that apply to you or those in which you have an interest.

Each tax benefit is denoted by an icon to help you spot the type of benefit involved:

Exclusion.

Above-the-line deduction.

Itemized deduction (a deduction taken *after* figuring adjusted gross income).

Credit.

Other benefit (e.g., a subtraction that reduces income).

For each tax benefit you will find an explanation of what it is, starting with the maximum **benefit or benefits** you can claim if you meet all eligibility requirements. You'll learn the **conditions** or eligibility requirements for claiming or qualifying for the benefit. You'll find both **planning tips** to help you make the most of the benefit opportunity as well as **pitfalls** to help you avoid problems that can prevent your eligibility. You'll see **where to claim the benefit** (if reporting is required) on your tax return and what records you must retain to support your tax position.

You'll find hundreds of examples to show you how other taxpayers have successfully taken advantage of the benefit. Over the years, taxpayers have be able to write off literally thousands of items; not every one is listed here because space does not allow it. And you'll learn what *isn't* allowed even though you might otherwise think so. There are references to free IRS publications on a variety of tax topics that you can download from the IRS web site (www.irs.gov) or obtain free of charge by calling 800-829-1040. Also included are titles of other J.K. Lasser books on various topics throughout this book.

In the appendixes you'll find a listing of items that can be adjusted each year to reflect cost-of-living changes so you can plan ahead as well as a checklist of items that are not deductible.

At the time this book went to press, there were several tax bills before Congress. Throughout the book you will find notes to alert you to other possible changes to come. For a free update on tax developments, and a free download of the Supplement to this book (available February 1, 2007), go to www.jklasser.com.

J.K. LASSER'S™

1001 DEDUCTIONS AND TAX BREAKS 2007

CHAPTER 1

You and Your Family

Do the old clichés still ring true? Can two still live as cheaply as one? Are things really cheaper by the dozen? For tax purposes, there are certain tax breaks for building a family.

This chapter explains family-related tax benefits, including:

- Personal exemption
- Dependency exemption
- Exemption for housing Hurricane Katrina victims
- Child tax credit
- Earned income credit
- Dependent care credit
- Adoption costs
- Foster care
- Child support
- Alimony

For more information on these topics, see IRS Publication 501, *Exemptions, Standard Deduction, and Filing Information*; IRS Publication 503, *Child and Dependent Care Expenses*; IRS Publication 504, *Divorced or Separated Individuals*; and IRS Publication 972, *Child Tax Credit*.

Personal Exemption

Each taxpayer (other than someone who is another taxpayer's dependent) automatically is entitled to a deduction just for being a taxpayer. The amount of the deduction, called the exemption amount, is a fixed dollar amount ($3,300 in 2006). However, if a taxpayer is considered to be a "high-income taxpayer," he or she loses some or all of this deduction.

Benefit

You can claim a deduction for yourself, called a personal exemption. In 2006, the exemption amount is $3,300 (each year it is indexed for inflation). Table 1.1 shows you the value of your personal exemption for your tax bracket in 2006 (the amount of taxes you save by claiming it).

Conditions

There are no conditions to claiming this deduction; it's yours because you are a taxpayer and the law says you are entitled to it.

Each spouse is entitled to his or her own personal exemption. On a joint return, two personal exemptions are claimed. If you are married but file a separate return, you can claim both deductions (an exemption for you and an exemption for your spouse) if your spouse has no income and is not the dependent of another taxpayer.

However, you *cannot* claim the personal exemption if you can be claimed as a dependent on another taxpayer's return. For example, a child who is the parent's dependent cannot claim a personal exemption on the child's own return.

Planning Tips

If a parent waives a dependency exemption for a child, the child can then claim the exemption on his or her own return (the child is no longer treated as a dependent). This may be advisable, for example, when the parent cannot use an education credit because the parent's income is too high, but the child can use the credit to offset his tax liability (see Chapter 3).

TABLE 1.1 Value of Your Personal Exemption in 2006

Your Top Tax Bracket	Value of Your Exemption
10%	$ 330
15%	495
25%	825
28%	924
33%	1,089
35%	1,155

High-income taxpayers may lose some or all of their deduction for exemptions as explained below (see Pitfalls). But the phaseout of personal and dependency exemptions is being eliminated. The reduction of this phaseout, which starts in 2006, is not fully in effect until 2010.

Pitfalls

You may lose some or all of the personal exemption (as well as dependency exemptions discussed later) if you are a high-income taxpayer. The write-off for exemptions is phased out for taxpayers with adjusted gross income above a set amount; once AGI reaches a set level, no write-offs are permitted. Table 1.2 shows where the phaseout of exemptions begins and the AGI level at which no exemptions can be claimed.

Once your AGI exceeds the beginning of the phaseout range, the deduction for personal and dependency exemptions is reduced by 2 percent for each $2,500 of AGI over the beginning phaseout number. However, the phaseout is reduced by one-third. Use the Worksheet 1.1 to figure your limitation, if any, on exemptions you can claim.

Example

In 2006, you are single and have AGI of $275,000. Since your AGI is over the limit of $273,000, you cannot use any of your personal exemption.

You cannot claim any personal or dependency exemption for alternative minimum tax (AMT) purposes, a shadow tax system designed to ensure that all taxpayers pay at least some tax. A large number of exemptions can substantially reduce or even eliminate any regular tax. So if you have a large number of exemptions, you may trigger or increase AMT liability. You may wish to engage in some tax planning to minimize or eliminate your AMT liability.

TABLE 1.2 Phaseout of Personal Exemption for 2006

Your Filing Status	AGI—Beginning of Phaseout	AGI above Which Exemption Fully Phased Out*
Married filing jointly	$225,750	$348,250
Head of household	188,150	310,650
Unmarried (single)	150,500	273,000
Married filing separately	112,875	174,125

*This is prior to the one-third cut explained above.

WORKSHEET 1.1 Reduction of Exemption Amount

Use this worksheet to figure the amount to enter on Worksheet 1, line 4.

1.	Multiply $3,300 by the number of exemptions you plan to claim.	1.	______
2.	Enter the amount from Worksheet 1, line 1	2.	______
3.	Enter: $150,500 if single $225,750 if married filing jointly or qualifying widow(er) $112,875 if married filing separately $188,150 if head of household	3.	______
4.	Subtract line 3 from line 2 and enter here	4.	______
5.	Is line 4 more than $122,500 (more than $61,250 if married filing separately)? ❑ Yes. Multiply $1,100 by the number of exemptions you plan to claim and enter the result here and on Worksheet 1, line 4. Do not complete the rest of this worksheet. ❑ No. Divide line 4 by $2,500 ($1,250 if married filing separately). If the result is not a whole number, increase it to the next whole number.	5.	______
6.	Multiply line 5 by 2% (.02). Enter the result as a decimal, but not more than 1.0	6.	______
7.	Multiply line 1 by the decimal on line 6.	7.	______
8.	Divide line 7 by 1.5.	8.	______
9.	Subtract line 8 from line 1. Enter the result here and on Worksheet 1, line 4.	9.	______

Where to Claim the Personal Exemption

You claim the exemption directly on your tax return in the "Tax and Credits" section of Form 1040 or the "Tax, Credits and Payments" section of Form 1040A; no special form or schedule is required. If you are filing Form 1040EZ, the exemption amount is built into the tax table (you can file this return only if you are single or married filing jointly with no dependents); you don't have to subtract it anywhere on the return.

If your AGI exceeds the beginning of the phaseout range, use a worksheet in the instructions for the return to figure the phaseout of your exemption.

Dependency Exemption

A fixed deduction ($3,300 in 2006) is allowed to every taxpayer who supports another person and meets other tests described below. The deduction is called a dependency exemption. However, if a taxpayer is considered to be a "high-income taxpayer," he or she loses some or all of this deduction.

Benefit ◉

You may be entitled to a dependency exemption for each person you support if certain conditions are met. Like the personal exemption, each dependency exemption in 2006 is a deduction of $3,300.

Conditions

There are two classes of dependents: qualifying children and all other qualifying individuals. Different conditions apply to each class of dependents.

For a qualifying child, there are four conditions:

1. Being your child.
2. Modified support test.
3. Citizenship test (see end of "Conditions" section).
4. Joint return test (see end of "Conditions" section).

BEING YOUR CHILD. For purposes of a qualifying child, your children include your natural children, stepchildren, adopted children (including those placed for adoption), and eligible foster children (those placed with you by an authorized adoption agency or court). A qualifying child also includes grandchildren and brothers and sisters (including stepsiblings). The child must be under age 19, under age 24 and a full-time student, or permanently disabled (any age).

Your child must live in your household for more than half the year. A child kidnapped by someone other than a family member continues to be treated as a member of your household until the year in which he or she would have attained age 18.

MODIFIED SUPPORT TEST. A qualifying child must not have provided more than half of his or her own support (you do not have to show you paid more than half the child's support). Amounts received as scholarships are *not* counted as support. There is no gross income test for a qualifying child as there is for a qualifying relative explained below.

Special rule for divorced or separated parents: The exemption belongs to the noncustodial parent if these conditions are met:

- The child receives more than half of his/her support from the parents.
- A decree of divorce or separation agreement between the parents states that the noncustodial parent is entitled to claim the dependency exemption

or the custodial parent signs a written declaration that he/she will not claim the exemption.

If there is no divorce decree or separation agreement with a statement on the dependency exemption for the noncustodial parent or the custodial parent fails to sign a written declaration waiving the exemption, then a so-called tiebreaker rule applies. Under this rule the exemption belongs to the parent with whom the child resided for the greater amount of time, or if equal time, then to the parent with the higher adjusted gross income. Thus, the custodial parent will usually prevail because the child is a member of the custodial parent's household for more time during the year than the child is a member of the noncustodial parent's household.

In the case of a child whose parents divorced before 1985, the dependency exemption can be claimed by the noncustodial parent as long as he/she provides at least $600 for the support of the child during the year. The fact that the noncustodial parent is behind in child support payments has no impact on claiming the exemption (as long as the $600 threshold is met).

There are five tests for claiming a dependency exemption for someone who is not a qualifiying child. You must satisfy *all* of them:

1. Relationship or member of the household test.
2. Gross income test.
3. Support test.
4. Citizenship or residency test.
5. Joint return test.

RELATIONSHIP OR MEMBER OF THE HOUSEHOLD TEST. The person you claim as a dependent must either be a relative (whether or not they live with you) or a member of your household. Relatives who do not have to live with you in order to qualify as your dependent include:

- Child, adopted child, or stepchild (other than a qualifying child).
- Grandchild (other than a qualifying child).
- Great-grandchild (other than a qualifying child).
- In-law (son, daughter, father, mother, brother, or sister).
- Parent or stepparent.
- Sibling, stepbrother or stepsister, half-brother or half-sister.
- Uncle, aunt, nephew, or niece if related by blood.

Any other individual, including, for example, a cousin, must be a member of your household for the entire year (not counting temporary absences).

GROSS INCOME TEST. The person you claim as a dependent must have gross income of less than the exemption amount—$3,300 in 2006.

Gross income means income that is subject to tax. It does not include tax-free or excluded items, such as municipal bond interest, employee fringe benefits, or gifts. Social Security benefits are gross income only to the extent they are taxable (which may be 50 percent or 85 percent, depending on the recipient's income and Social Security benefits).

SUPPORT TEST. You must provide more than half of the person's support for the year (or meet the multiple support rules discussed later). Generally, this test does not present a problem; you may be the person's only means of support.

But where the person pays some of his or her own support while receiving help from you and other sources, you need to look closely at whether you pay more than half of the person's support. "Support" is different from "income." You need to look at what is *spent* on personal living needs and not what the person *receives* in the way of income. Government benefits payable to the person, including Social Security benefits, are treated as the person's own payment of support (whether or not actually spent on personal living needs).

EXAMPLES OF SUPPORT ITEMS

Clothing.

Education expenses (If your child takes out a student loan that he or she is primarily obligated to repay, the loan proceeds count as the child's own payment of support).

Entertainment.

Food.

Lodging (If the person shares your home, support is based on the fair rental value of the room or apartment in your home, including a reasonable allowance for heat and other utilities).

Medical expenses (for details see Chapter 2).

Recreation, including the cost of a television, summer camp, dance lessons, and a wedding.

CITIZENSHIP OR RESIDENCY TEST. The person you claim as a dependent must be a U.S. citizen or national, or a resident of the United States, Canada, or Mexico.

JOINT RETURN TEST. If you are claiming an exemption for someone who is married, the person may not file a joint return with his or her spouse. However, this joint return test is not failed if a joint return is filed merely to claim a refund and both spouses have income under the exemption limit.

Example

You are supporting your married daughter. Both she and her husband are graduate students who each earned $3,000 as teaching assistants and file a joint return to claim a refund of taxes paid on these earnings. Even though your daughter files a joint return, you can still claim her as a dependent (assuming other tests are met).

Planning Tips

As described earlier in this chapter, elimination of the phaseout of the exemptions begins in 2006; by 2010, high-income taxpayers will no longer lose the benefit of personal and dependency exemptions.

MULTIPLE SUPPORT AGREEMENTS. Even if you do not provide more than half the support of another person, you may still qualify for the deduction if you contribute more than 10 percent of the person's support and, together with others, contribute more than half the person's support. Then each of the other supporters who contribute more than 10 percent must agree among themselves who claims the exemption (it cannot be prorated among the supporters).

Example

You and your two sisters support your elderly mother. You contribute 40 percent, Ann contributes 35 percent, and Betty contributes 5 percent (your mother pays 20 percent of her own support). Since you and your sisters contribute more than half of your mother's support, a multiple support agreement is warranted.

However, only you and Ann qualify since you each contribute more than 10 percent of the support. You and Ann can decide who claims the exemption—it does not matter that you paid more than Ann.

In deciding which person should claim the exemption when more than one person qualifies, the decision should be based on who would benefit more. Factors to consider include:

- Which person is in the higher tax bracket.
- Whether such person is a high-income taxpayer subject to the phaseout of personal and dependency exemptions.

If all things are equal, then rotate from year to year who claims the exemption (for example, one year you claim the exemption for a parent and the following year your sibling claims it).

Pitfalls

For rules on the phaseout of the dependency exemption for high-income taxpayers as well as the impact of the AMT, see earlier sections of this chapter.

If you support a domestic partner or lover and meet all of the tests, you can claim a dependency exemption only if the relationship does not violate local law. For example, in North Carolina, a man was prohibited from claiming the exemption for his live-in girlfriend because under North Carolina law this cohabitation was a misdemeanor. In contrast, a man in Missouri was permitted to claim the exemption for his live-in girlfriend because the relationship there was not in violation of state law.

If you can claim an exemption for a partner, you cannot claim one for the partner's qualifying child because you do not satisfy the relationship test.

Where to Claim the Dependency Exemption

You claim the exemption directly on your tax return in the "Tax and Credits" section of Form 1040 or the "Tax, Credits and Payments" section of Form 1040A; no special form or schedule is required. You cannot claim a dependency exemption if you file Form 1040EZ.

If your AGI exceeds the beginning of the phaseout range, use a worksheet in the instructions for the return to figure the phaseout of your exemption.

Exemption for Housing Hurricane Katrina Victims

Hurricane Katrina displaced more than 300,000 people in the days and weeks following the hurricane. While some have returned to their homes, many others continue to be displaced persons. Some displaced persons have found shelter with government assistance. Others have been taken in by friends, family, or even strangers. Those who opened their homes to unrelated individuals are rewarded with a special tax break.

Benefit ◉

If you gave shelter in your home to someone displaced by Hurricane Katrina, you may qualify for a special exemption in 2006. The exemption is $500 per displaced person, for a maximum deduction of $2,000 (for housing four people).

The $2,000 limit applies in total for 2005 and 2006. If you claimed an exemption amount of $1,500 in 2005 for housing three victims, your maximum allowance for 2006 is $500, even if you housed more than one victim in 2006.

Conditions

To claim the exemption, you must meet four conditions:

1. You must provide shelter to a displaced person for at least 60 consecutive days.
2. The person must *not* be a qualifying dependent or your spouse.
3. The person's main home was located in the Katrina disaster area on August 28, 2005, and the person was displaced because of the storm.
4. You must provide the person's tax identification number (Social Security number) on your return.

Planning Tips

This exemption is not subject to reduction by high-income taxpayers as is the case for other personal exemptions.

The exemption is deductible for purposes of the alternative minimum tax (AMT), even though other personal exemptions are not deductible for the AMT.

Pitfalls

There is no similar exemption for housing people displaced by Hurricane Rita or Wilma.

You cannot claim the exemption if you receive any rent or other amount from any source for housing the displaced person.

Where to Claim the Exemption

You figure the exemption amount on Form 8914, Exemption Amount for Taxpayers Housing Individuals Displaced by Hurricane Katrina. You claim the exemption in the "Tax and Credits" section of Form 1040; you cannot claim the exemption on Form 1040A or 1040EZ.

Child Tax Credit

The U.S. Department of Agriculture estimates that it costs $15,300 a year for a middle-class family to raise a child born in 2003 to age 17 (without adjustment for inflation). In recognition of this cost, you can claim a tax credit each year until your child reaches the age of 17. The credit is currently up to $1,000 per child. This credit is in addition to the dependency exemption for the child.

Benefit

You may claim a tax credit of up to $1,000 in 2006 for each child under the age of 17. If the credit you are entitled to claim is more than your tax liability, you may be entitled to a refund under certain conditions.

Generally, the credit is refundable to the extent of 15 percent of earned income over $11,300 in 2006.

If you have three or more children for whom you are claiming the credit, you are entitled to an additional child tax credit. In reality, the additional child tax credit is merely a larger refund of the credit you are ordinarily entitled to. There are two ways to figure your refundable amount (the additional child tax credit) and you can opt for the method that results in the larger refund:

1. Fifteen percent of earned income over $11,300 in 2006.
2. Excess of your Social Security taxes (plus one-half of self-employment taxes if any) over your earned income credit for the year (the earned income credit is explained in the next main section).

Conditions

To claim the credit, you must meet two conditions:

1. You must have a qualifying child.
2. Your income must be below a set amount.

QUALIFYING CHILD. You can claim the credit only for a "qualifying child." This is a child who is under age 17 at the end of the year and meets the definition of a qualifying child explained earlier in this chapter.

MAGI LIMIT. You must have modified adjusted gross income (MAGI) below a set amount. The credit you are otherwise entitled to claim is reduced or eliminated if your MAGI exceeds a set amount. MAGI for purposes of the child tax credit means AGI increased by the foreign earned income exclusion, the foreign housing exclusion or deduction, or the possession exclusion for American Samoa residents.

The credit amount is reduced by $50 for each $1,000 of MAGI or a fraction thereof over the MAGI limit for your filing status. The phaseout begins if MAGI exceeds the limits found in Table 1.3.

TABLE 1.3 Phaseout of Child Tax Credit over MAGI Limits in 2006

Filing Status	MAGI Limit
Married filing jointly	$110,000
Head of household	75,000
Unmarried (single)	75,000
Qualifying widow(er)	75,000
Married filing separately	55,000

Example

In 2006 you are a head of household with two qualifying children. Your MAGI is \$80,000. Your credit amount of \$2,000 (\$1,000 × 2) is reduced by \$250 (\$80,000 – \$75,000 = \$5,000 MAGI over the limit ÷ \$1,000 × \$50). Your credit is \$1,750 (\$2,000 – \$250).

REFUNDABLE CREDIT. If the credit you are entitled to claim is more than your tax liability, you can receive the excess amount as a "refund." The refund is limited to 15 percent of your taxable earned income (such as wages, salary, tips, commissions, bonuses, and net earnings from self-employment) over \$11,300 in 2006. If your earned income is not over \$11,300, you may still qualify for the additional credit if you have three or more children.

If you have three or more children for whom you are claiming the credit, you may qualify for a larger refund, called the additional child tax credit. You can figure your refund in the usual manner as explained earlier, or, if more favorable, you can treat your refundable amount as the excess of the Social Security taxes you paid for the year (plus one-half of self-employment taxes, if any), over your earned income credit (explained later in this chapter).

Planning Tip

If you know you will become entitled to claim the credit (e.g., you are expecting the birth of a child in 2006), you may wish to adjust your withholding so that you don't have too much income tax withheld from your paycheck. Increase your withholding allowances so that less income tax is withheld from your pay by filing a new Form W-4, Employee's Withholding Allowance Certificate, with your employer.

Pitfall

There is no downside to claiming the credit. If you are entitled to it, be sure to claim it.

Where to Claim the Credit

You figure the credit on a worksheet included in the instructions for your return. You claim the credit in the "Tax and Credits" section of Form 1040 or the "Tax, Credits and Payments" section of Form 1040A; you cannot claim the credit if you file Form 1040EZ.

If you are eligible for the additional child tax credit, you figure this on Form 8812, Additional Child Tax Credit.

Earned Income Credit

Low-income taxpayers are encouraged to work and are rewarded for doing so by means of a special tax credit, called the earned income credit. The earned income credit is the second largest program, after Medicaid, that provides assistance to low-income people. The amount of the credit varies with income, filing status, and the number of dependents, if any. The credit may be viewed as a "negative income tax" because it can be paid to taxpayers even if it exceeds their tax liability. On 2003 returns, 22 million taxpayers claimed the earned income credit, totaling $38 billion.

Benefit

If you are a working taxpayer with low or moderate income, you may qualify for a special tax credit of up to $4,536 in 2006. The amount of the credit depends on several factors, including your adjusted gross income, earned income, and the number of qualifying children that you claim as dependents on your return. Table 1.4 shows the maximum credit you may claim based on the number of your qualifying children, if any.

The credit is "refundable" because it can be received in excess of the tax owed. What's more, in some cases the credit can be received on an advanced basis—included in your paycheck throughout the year.

Conditions

To be eligible for the credit, you must have earned income from being an employee or a self-employed individual. The amount of the credit you are entitled to claim depends on several factors.

QUALIFYING CHILDREN. You may claim the credit even if you have no qualifying child. But you are entitled to a larger credit if you have one qualifying child and a still larger credit for two or more qualifying children.

To be a qualifying child, the child must:

- Be a qualifying child as defined earlier in the chapter under dependency exemption.
- Be under age 19 or under age 24 and a full-time student or permanently and totally disabled.

TABLE 1.4 Maximum Earned Income Credit for 2006

Number of Qualifying Children	Maximum Earned Income Credit
No qualifying child	$ 412
One qualifying child	2,747
Two or more qualifying children	4,536

- Live in your U.S. household for more than half the year.
- Qualify as your dependent if the child is married at the end of the year.
- Be a U.S. citizen or resident (or a nonresident who is married to a U.S. citizen and elects to have all worldwide income subject to U.S. tax).

EARNED INCOME. Earned income includes wages, salary, tips, commissions, jury duty pay, union strike benefits, certain disability pensions, U.S. military basic quarters and subsistence allowances, and net earnings from self-employment (profit from your self-employment activities). For 2006, military personnel can elect to treat tax-free combat pay as earned income for purposes of the earned income credit.

Nontaxable employee compensation, such as tax-free fringe benefits or salary deferrals—for example, contributions to company 401(k) plans—is not treated as earned income.

To qualify for the maximum credit, you must have earned income at or above a set amount. Table 1.5 shows the earned income you need to obtain the top credit (depending on the number of your qualifying children, if any).

ADJUSTED GROSS INCOME. If your adjusted gross income is too high, the credit is reduced or eliminated. Table 1.6 shows the AGI phaseout range for the earned income credit. This depends not only on the number of qualifying children, if any, but also on your filing status, as shown in the table.

JOINT RETURN. If you are married, you usually must file a joint return with your spouse in order to claim an earned income credit. However, this requirement is waived if your spouse did not live in your household for the last six months of the year. In this case, assuming you paid the household expenses in which a qualifying child lived, you qualify as head of household and can claim the earned income credit (using "other taxpayers" limits on AGI).

Planning Tips

If you have a qualifying dependent and are eligible for the credit, don't wait until you file your tax return to receive the benefit from it. Instead, file Form W-5, Earned Income Credit Advance Payment Certificate, with your employer

TABLE 1.5 Earned Income Needed for Top Credit in 2006

Number of Qualifying Children	Earned Income Needed for Top Credit
No qualifying child	$ 5,380
One qualifying child	8,080
Two or more qualifying children	11,340

TABLE 1.6 AGI Phaseout Range for the Earned Income Credit in 2006

Number of Qualifying Children	Married Filing Jointly	Other Taxpayers
No qualifying child	$ 8,740–14,120	$ 6,740–12,120
One qualifying child	$16,810–34,001	$14,810–32,001
Two or more qualifying children	$16,810–38,348	$14,810–36,348

Example

You are married and file a joint return. You and your spouse have one qualifying child. In 2006, if your AGI is less than $16,810, your earned income credit is *not* subject to any phaseout. If your AGI is $34,001 or higher, you cannot claim *any* earned income credit; it is completely phased out. If your AGI is between these amounts (within the phaseout range), you claim a reduced credit.

so that the credit is factored into your income withholding. In effect, a portion of the credit is added back to your paycheck.

The credit is based on a set percentage of earned income. However, you don't have to compute the credit. You merely look at an IRS Earned Income Credit Table for this purpose, which accompanies the instructions for your return.

You can have the IRS figure your credit for you (you don't even have to look it up in the table). To do this, just complete your return up to the earned income credit line and put "EIC" on the dotted line next to it. If you have a qualifying child, complete and attach Schedule EIC to the return. Also attach Form 8862, Information to Claim Earned Income Credit after Disallowance, if you are required to do so as explained next.

Pitfalls

You lose eligibility for the credit if you have unearned income over $2,800 in 2006 from dividends, interest (both taxable and tax-free), net rent or royalty income, net capital gains, or net passive income that is not self-employment income.

You lose out on the opportunity to claim the credit in future years if you negligently or fraudulently claim it on your return. You are banned for two years from claiming the earned income credit if your claim was reckless or in disregard of the tax rules. You lose out for 10 years if your claim was fraudulent. If you become ineligible because of negligence or fraud, the IRS issues a deficiency notice. You may counter the IRS's charge by filing Form 8862, Information to Claim Earned Income Credit after Disallowance, to show you are eligible. If the IRS accepts your position and recertifies eligibility, you don't have to file this form again (unless you again become ineligible).

If you received the earned income credit on an advance basis and it turns out to be more than you were entitled to (for example, your unearned income for the year disqualifies you for the credit), you owe the money back as unpaid taxes.

Where to Claim the Earned Income Credit

You can claim the earned income credit on *any* income tax return (Form 1040, 1040A, or 1040EZ) as follows: in the "Payments" section of Form 1040; the "Tax, Credits and Payments" section of Form 1040A; or the "Payments and Tax" section of Form 1040EZ.

You can check your eligibility to claim the credit on Schedule EIC, Earned Income Credit, which must be attached to your return.

Dependent Care Expenses

Many taxpayers must pay for the care of a child in order to work. According to the U.S. Department of Agriculture, the annual cost of child care in 2004 ranged from $9,990 to $27,960. The tax law provides a limited tax credit for such costs, called the dependent care credit. The amount of the credit you can claim depends on your income.

Benefit

If you hire someone to care for your child or other dependent to enable you to work or incur other dependent care expenses, you may be eligible for a tax credit of up to $2,100. More specifically, this credit is a percentage of eligible dependent care expenses (explained later). The credit percentage ranges from a low of 20 percent to a high of 35 percent. The maximum amount of expenses that can be taken into account in figuring the credit is $3,000 for one qualifying dependent and $6,000 for two or more qualifying dependents.

If your employer pays for your dependent care expenses, you may be able to exclude this benefit from income up to $5,000.

Conditions for the Tax Credit

There are a number of conditions for claiming the dependent care credit; you must satisfy all six of them to claim the credit:

1. Incur the expenses to earn income.
2. Pay expenses on behalf of a qualifying dependent.
3. Pay over half the household expenses.
4. File a joint return if you are married.

5. Have qualifying expenses in excess of employer reimbursements.
6. Report information about the child care provider.

INCUR THE EXPENSES TO EARN INCOME. The purpose of the dependent care credit is to enable you to work. This generally means that if you are married, you both must work, either full-time or part-time.

However, a spouse who is incapacitated or a full-time student need not work; he or she is treated as having earned income of $250 per month if there is one qualifying dependent or $500 per month if there are two or more qualifying dependents.

Example

You are a single mother and a full-time student with one child. You are treated as having earned income of $3,000 for the year ($250 × 12). You can use this income in figuring your credit, even though you didn't actually receive this income.

PAY EXPENSES ON BEHALF OF A QUALIFYING DEPENDENT. This is your child under the age of 13, your incapacitated child of any age, or your spouse who is incapacitated.

If your child has his or her 13th birthday during the year, you can take into account expenses incurred up to this birthday.

PAY OVER HALF THE HOUSEHOLD EXPENSES. You (and your spouse) must pay more than half of the maintenance expenses of the household.

FILE A JOINT RETURN IF MARRIED. Generally, to claim the credit you *must* file a joint return if eligible to do so. However, you can claim the credit even though you are still married if you live apart from your spouse for over half the year, you pay over half the household expenses for the full year, and your spouse is not a member of your household for the last six months of the year. In this case, you qualify to file as unmarried (single).

HAVE QUALIFYING EXPENSES IN EXCESS OF EMPLOYER REIMBURSEMENTS. Only certain types of child care expenses can be taken into account in figuring the credit. Qualifying expenses can be incurred in your home or outside the home (using a day care center). You cannot include amounts paid to you, your child who is under age 19 at the end of the year, your spouse, or any other person you can claim as a dependent.

EXAMPLES OF QUALIFYING EXPENSES

Baby-sitter.

Day camp, including a specialty camp such as soccer or computers (but *not* sleep-away camp).

Day care center.

Housekeeper (the portion of compensation allocated to dependent care).

Nursery school.

Private school (the costs for first grade and higher do not qualify unless the child is handicapped, provided the child spends at least eight hours per day in your home).

Transportation if supervised (so that it is part of care), such as to a day camp or after-school program not on school premises, but not the cost of personally driving a dependent to and from a dependent care center.

You do not have to find the least expensive means of providing dependent care. For example, just because your child's grandparent lives in your home doesn't mean you must rely on the grandparent for child care; you can pay an unrelated person to baby-sit in your home or take your child to day care.

The expenses you incur for dependent care must be greater than any amount you exclude as employer-provided dependent care.

REPORT INFORMATION ABOUT THE DEPENDENT CARE PROVIDER. You must list the name, address, and employer identification number (or Social Security number) of the person you pay for dependent care. No employer identification number is required if payment is made to a tax-exempt charity providing the care.

If the person has not completed Form W-4, Employee's Withholding Allowance Certificate, as your household employee, you can obtain the necessary information by asking the provider to complete Form W-10, Dependent Care Provider's Identification and Certification, or by looking at a driver's license, business letterhead, or invoice. This may seem like a lot of bother and formality for a baby-sitter, but if you want to claim the credit, you must comply with this information reporting requirement.

HOW TO FIGURE YOUR CREDIT PERCENTAGE BASED ON AGI. The amount of the credit you claim depends on your AGI. However, no matter how large your AGI, you are entitled to a minimum credit of 20 percent of eligible expenses. Table 1.7 shows you the maximum credit you may claim based on your AGI and number of dependents.

TABLE 1.7 Dependent Care Credit Limits

AGI	Credit Percentage	One Dependent	Two or More Dependents
$15,000 or less	35%	$1,050	$2,100
$15,001–17,000	34	1,020	2,040
$17,001–19,000	33	990	1,980
$19,001–21,000	32	960	1,920
$21,001–23,000	31	930	1,860
$23,001–25,000	30	900	1,800
$25,001–27,000	29	870	1,740
$27,001–29,000	28	840	1,680
$29,001–31,000	27	810	1,620
$31,001–33,000	26	780	1,560
$33,001–35,000	25	750	1,500
$35,001–37,000	24	720	1,420
$37,001–39,000	23	690	1,380
$39,001–41,000	22	660	1,320
$41,001–43,000	21	630	1,260
$43,001 and over	20	600	1,200

Example

In 2006, you have one qualifying child and adjusted gross income of $40,000. Your credit is 22 percent of your dependent care expenses up to $3,000, for a top credit of $660.

Conditions for the Exclusion

Benefits must be provided by your employer under a written plan that does not discriminate in favor of owners or highly compensated employees (for example, top executives cannot obtain greater benefits than you). The dollar limit on this benefit is $5,000 (or $2,500 if you are married and file separately).

The same limits apply to a flexible spending arrangement (FSA), which is an employer plan to which you contribute a portion of your pay to be used for dependent care expenses. This salary reduction amount is *not* currently taxable to you; it becomes tax-free income that you withdraw from the FSA to cover eligible expenses.

Planning Tip

If you have the option of making salary reduction contributions to your company's flexible spending arrangement (FSA) for dependent care expenses, decide carefully on how much to contribute each month. You can use the funds in the FSA only for dependent care expenses; you cannot, for example, use any of the funds for your medical expenses or other costs. Any funds not used up by the end of the year are forfeited; they do not carry over to the following year.

Pitfalls

If you qualify to receive an exclusion, you must reduce the amount of eligible expenses used in figuring the credit by the amount of the exclusion.

Example

You have one child and receive reimbursement from your employer's plan for the year of $2,500. In figuring your tax credit, you can use only $500 of eligible expenses ($3,000 – $2,500). In essence, once your exclusion is $3,000 for one child or $6,000 if you have two or more children, you cannot claim any tax credit.

If you participate in a dependent care FSA, distributions from the plan are treated as employer reimbursements. Like excludable benefits, distributions from FSAs reduce the amount of expenses you can use to figure the credit.

If you pay someone to care for your dependent in your home, you are the worker's employer. You are responsible for employment taxes. For more information about these employment taxes, see IRS Publication 926, *Household Employer's Tax Guide*, at www.irs.gov.

Where to Claim the Tax Credit or Exclusion

You figure the credit and the exclusion on Form 2441, Dependent Care Expenses. If you file Form 1040, the credit is then entered in the "Tax and Credit" section of your return. If you file Form 1040A, the credit is figured on Schedule 2 of the return. You may not claim the credit if you file Form 1040EZ.

If you owe employment taxes for a dependent care worker, you must file Form 1040 and complete Schedule H, Household Employment Taxes, which is attached to the return. You include employment taxes you owe in the "Other Taxes" section of your return.

Adoption Costs

Each year, about 127,000 children are adopted in the United States, with costs for some adoptions topping $40,000. Taxpayers who adopt a child may qualify for a tax credit. The amount of the credit may or may not fully offset actual costs for the adoption. If an employer pays for adoption costs, a worker may be able to exclude this fringe benefit from income.

Benefit

If you adopt a child, you may be eligible to claim a tax credit for the expenses you incur. The maximum credit is $10,960 per child in 2006. The credit is 100 percent of eligible adoption expenses up to this dollar limit.

Example

In 2006, your income is $100,000; you pay $9,000 in attorney's and adoption agency fees to adopt a child (the adoption becomes final in 2006). You can claim a tax credit of $9,000 (100 percent of your eligible costs that do not exceed $10,960).

If your employer pays or reimburses you for adoption expenses, you may exclude this benefit from your income; it is tax free to you if you meet eligibility conditions. The exclusion has the same dollar limit and income limits as the credit.

If a tax-exempt organization makes a payment to help pay adoption costs, the payment is not taxable. The payment is viewed as a gift to the recipient.

Conditions

To claim the adoption credit or exclusion, two key conditions apply.

1. You must pay qualified adoption expenses.
2. Your modified adjusted gross income cannot exceed a set amount.

QUALIFIED ADOPTION EXPENSES. Qualified expenses include any reasonable and necessary expenses related to the adoption.

EXAMPLES OF QUALIFIED ADOPTION EXPENSES

Adoption agency fees.

Attorney's fees.

Court costs.

Travel expenses while away from home (including meals and lodging).

Nonqualifying expenses include those related to your adoption of your spouse's child, expenses related to a surrogate parenting arrangement, expenses paid using funds received from a government program, and expenses that violate the law.

MODIFIED ADJUSTED GROSS INCOME LIMIT. To be eligible for the full credit or the exclusion, your modified adjusted gross income in 2006 cannot exceed $164,410. If your MAGI is over $204,410, the credit is completely phased out.

Example

You adopt a child in 2006 and your MAGI is $184,410. You can only claim a credit of up to $5,480; half of the credit limit is phased out because of your MAGI.

Modified adjusted gross income for this purpose is AGI increased by the foreign earned income exclusion; the foreign housing exclusion or deduction; and the exclusion for income from Guam, American Samoa, Northern Mariana Islands, or Puerto Rico.

Planning Tips

The amount of the adoption credit cannot be more than your tax liability for the year. Tax liability for this purpose means your regular tax, plus your tentative alternative minimum tax (without regard to the foreign tax credit), dependent care credit, credit for the elderly or disabled, education credit, child tax credit, or mortgage interest credit if any.

However, if the credit exceeds your tax liability, you can carry the excess credit forward for up to five years.

If your employer has an adoption assistance program but you aren't entitled to some or all of the exclusion (e.g., your MAGI is too high or your expenses exceeded the dollar limit), plan to pay tax on the amount your employer pays or reimburses you. The employer is *not* required to withhold income tax on these payments. Employer-paid expenses are reported on your Form W-2.

Pitfall

The year for which you are entitled to claim the credit depends on the type of child you are adopting.

CHILD WHO IS A U.S. CITIZEN OR RESIDENT. If you adopt or are adopting a child who is a U.S. citizen or resident, use Table 1.8 to see the year for which to claim the credit for payments you make.

FOREIGN CHILD. You can take the credit only if the adoption becomes final. Use Table 1.9 to see the year in which to claim the credit.

Where to Claim the Adoption Credit or Exclusion

You figure the adoption credit on Form 8839, Qualified Adoption Expenses, which is attached to your return. You can claim the credit only if you file Form 1040 or Form 1040A; you cannot claim the credit if you file Form 1040EZ.

Example

In 2005, you start the adoption process, hiring a lawyer and paying a retainer of $3,000. In 2006, the lawyer helps you work with an authorized adoption agency to which you pay a fee of $8,000 to adopt your daughter, a U.S. resident. The child is placed with you at that time. In 2007, you pay the lawyer an additional $2,000 and the adoption becomes final in this year. You may *not* claim any credit in 2005. In 2006, you may claim a credit for $3,000, the expenses paid in the prior year. In 2007, you may claim another credit of $7,960 of the $10,000 expenses paid in 2006 and 2007 ($8,000 adoption agency fee and $2,000 lawyer's fee). *Note:* If the credit limit increases above $10,960 in 2007, an additional amount may be claimed in that year.

TABLE 1.8 Year to Claim the Credit for Adoption of a U.S. Citizen or Resident Child

When You Pay Expenses	When You Claim Credit
Any year before year the adoption becomes final (or falls through)	Year after year of payment
Year adoption becomes final (or falls through)	Year adoption becomes final (or falls through)
Any year after year adoption becomes final (or falls through)	Year of payment

TABLE 1.9 Year to Claim the Credit for Adoption of a Foreign Child

When You Pay Expenses	When You Claim Credit
Any year before year adoption becomes final	Year adoption becomes final
Year adoption becomes final	Year adoption becomes final
Any year after year adoption becomes final	Year of payment

If your employer paid or reimbursed you for qualified expenses, you must also complete this form to figure excludable benefits.

Foster Care

Taxpayers who care for children in foster care and receive funds for expenses may not be taxed on the funds. Instead, they may be able to exclude the payments they receive from income.

Benefit

If you receive foster care payments to care for a child placed with you by a state or local agency or a tax-exempt foster care placement agency, you are not taxed on the payments. They are fully excludable; there is no dollar limit.

Qualified payments include payments for the provision of foster care. They also include difficulty-of-care payments to account for the additional care required for a child with physical, mental, or emotional handicap.

However, the exclusion for foster care payments is limited to payments received for five qualifying individuals who are over age 18. The exclusion for difficulty-of-care payments is limited to payments received for 10 qualifying individuals who are over age 18). There are no limits on the number of children age 18 or under for whom the exclusion may be claimed.

Condition

Foster care payments include only those made by a state or local government or qualified foster care placement agency for the care of a qualified foster child or a difficulty-of-care payment.

Planning Tip

If you are a foster care parent dealing with a private agency, make sure the placement entitles you to exclude payments received for the care of the child.

Pitfall

Payments received from private agencies that are not tax-exempt entities, even though licensed by the state, are not excludable from income.

Where to Claim the Exclusion

Foster care payments are not reported on the return if they are excludable. If you care for more than the allowable number of children over age 18, you must include the payments in income. Report this as "other income" on your return.

Child Support

Divorced or separated parents may be ordered by a court to make support payments for a child of the marriage. Even an unwed parent may be instructed to support his or her child. The recipient of child support payments, who is typically the parent with whom the child resides, is not taxed on these payments. (The parent making the payments cannot deduct them, but paying for a child support may entitle the parent to other tax write-offs discussed throughout this chapter, such as the dependency exemption.)

Benefit

Child support payments are not taxable to the child, nor to the parent who receives them on behalf of the child. There is no dollar limit to this benefit.

Conditions

Payments for child support should be fixed. If they are set by a decree of divorce or separate maintenance or a separation agreement, they are considered to be fixed.

In addition, if payments that are made to a parent will be reduced or terminated upon a contingency related to the child, then those payments are treated as being fixed for child support. Contingencies for this purpose include:

- Reaching the age of majority (generally age 18 or 21, depending on the law in your state).
- Leaving school.
- Marrying.
- Entering military service.
- Moving out of the custodial parent's home.
- Starting to work and/or attaining a set income level.

Planning Tip

If a parent is required to pay both alimony and child support but makes a single payment that is less than the total amount due, the first dollars are considered tax-free child support.

Example

Ed owes his former spouse $1,000 each month to cover alimony of $600 and child support of $400. In March 2006, Ed pays only $500. Of this amount, $400 is treated as child support; $100 is treated as alimony.

Pitfalls

The parent who makes child support payments cannot deduct them. They are not considered to be part of deductible alimony payments (explained in the next section).

If a reduction in child support payments to a parent is not specifically tied to the child's age of majority but is scheduled to occur within six months before or after such date, the reduction is treated as if it was tied to the child. This means that the amount subject to reduction is viewed as child support and not as deductible alimony. The same rule applies if you are making payments on behalf of more than one child and there are at least two reductions, each of which is within one year of a child's reaching the age of majority.

If you are due a refund of federal income tax because you overpaid it through withholding or estimated taxes, you won't receive it if you are delinquent on your child support payments. The IRS is authorized to divert your refund to the parent owed the child support payments as long as the state provides notice to you and a procedure you can follow to contest this action.

Where to Claim the Exclusion

Child support payments received need not be reported on the return.

Alimony

Taxpayers who are required by a court to make payments to a spouse or former spouse can deduct such payments. The payments may be called alimony, support, or spousal maintenance, depending on state law (called "alimony" here for convenience). The tax law in most cases imposes symmetry on the treatment of alimony so that the government effectively comes out even; the spouse receiving the payments reports them as income while the spouse making the payments gets to deduct them.

Benefit

If you make payments to a spouse or former spouse for alimony, support, or spousal maintenance, you can deduct the payments if certain conditions are met. There is no dollar limit on this deduction. The deduction is claimed as an adjustment to gross income; you do not have to itemize your other deductions to write off alimony payments you make.

Conditions

There are four conditions that must be met for payments made to a spouse or former spouse to be considered alimony.

1. Amounts must be paid pursuant to a legal requirement, such as a court decree.
2. Payments must be made in cash.
3. You must live apart from your spouse or former spouse.
4. Your responsibility to make payments must terminate on the death of your spouse or former spouse.

Typically, alimony that is deductible by the payer is taxable to the recipient—the government effectively nets no additional tax revenue from the arrangement. But this symmetry is not required. If you meet all of the conditions, you can deduct your alimony payments even if your former spouse is not required to pay tax on them (for example, your former spouse lives abroad where alimony is exempt income).

PAYABLE UNDER A COURT DECREE. You can't deduct alimony if you voluntarily make payments. You must either be ordered to do so under a decree of divorce, legal separation, or support or agree to make payments under a written separation agreement.

If the marriage is annulled and you are ordered to make payments, they can be treated as alimony if the other conditions are satisfied.

CASH PAYMENTS. You can deduct only payments made in cash. But you don't necessarily have to make these payments directly *to* your spouse or former spouse. Payments made *on behalf of* your spouse or former spouse qualify for the deduction if required by the divorce decree or separation agreement. For example, if you are ordered to pay your former spouse's rent with a check directly to the landlord, you can treat the payment as alimony if the other conditions are met.

If you continue to own the home in which your former spouse resides (i.e., own it by yourself or jointly with your former spouse) and you pay the mortgage and other expenses, only some of these expenses qualify as deductible alimony—even if you are required to make the payments under the terms of a divorce decree or separation agreement. If you own the home, you benefit from the payment of the mortgage, real estate taxes, and other maintenance on the property and cannot deduct these payments. If you own the home jointly, only one-half of your payments can be treated as alimony because only one-half benefits your spouse or former spouse. (Of course, you can deduct mortgage interest and real estate taxes as itemized deductions as explained in Chapter 4.)

LIVING APART. You and your spouse or former spouse must not live in the same household. This means separate residences; merely having separate bedrooms in the same home is not good enough for payments to be treated as alimony.

However, payments made while you are preparing to leave can be deducted. There is a one-month limit so that only payments made within one month prior to your departure can be treated as alimony. If it takes you longer to move out, your earlier payments are not deductible.

PAYMENT RESPONSIBILITY ENDS ON DEATH. Your responsibility to make payments to your spouse or former spouse must end if that person dies. If your obligation to make payments continues beyond the recipient's death (for example, you must continue to pay until total payments reach a set amount), you cannot treat *any* of the payments as alimony (even those made before death).

Generally, the divorce decree should state that your obligation to make payments ends on the recipient's death. But this isn't necessary as long as this condition is part of the law in your state.

The fact that your estate continues to be liable for payments after your death does not prevent you from treating your payments as alimony.

Planning Tip

Don't voluntarily increase your payments. If you want to ensure that increased payments qualify as deductible alimony, you need to amend the court order or separation agreement to incorporate the change.

Pitfalls

Payments made to someone who was never legally your spouse cannot be treated as alimony. For example, if you make payments to a domestic partner, you cannot deduct them even though they otherwise have all the earmarks of alimony.

If you make payments that are reduced in the third year by $15,000 or more, you may lose some of the deductions you've already claimed. This reduction is viewed as front-loading—trying to make a property settlement appear to be alimony so that you can deduct it (a property settlement isn't deductible).

In effect, deductible payments in year one and year two are recaptured in the third year if payments decline by more than $15,000. The recipient removes them from income and you lose your deductions, and this is reported on the return for the third year (you don't go back and amend the returns in years one and two).

Where to Claim the Deduction

The deduction for alimony payments is claimed on Form 1040 in the section labeled "Adjusted Gross Income." You cannot deduct alimony if you file Form 1040A or Form 1040EZ.

There is no separate form or schedule to complete when deducting alimony. However, you *must* include the recipient's Social Security number on your return (to allow the IRS to cross-check whether the recipient reported the alimony as income).

CHAPTER 2

Medical Expenses

The cost of health care continues to escalate faster than the rate of inflation. Insurance premiums are soaring (15 percent per year increases are not uncommon), and, in many cases, employer coverage is declining. About 46 million Americans now have no health insurance at all. The bottom line is that it's probably costing you more to pay your medical bills. What can you do? Fortunately, the tax law provides you with some relief by allowing you to treat your medical expenses in special tax-advantaged ways.

This chapter covers:

- Itemized medical expenses
- Self-employed health insurance deduction
- Health insurance credit for eligible recipients
- Long-term care coverage
- Flexible spending arrangements for health care
- Health reimbursement arrangements
- Health Savings Accounts (HSAs)
- COBRA coverage
- Medicare
- Continuing care facilities and nursing homes

- Accelerated death benefits
- Decedent's final illness

To learn more about medical and dental expenses, see IRS Publication 502, *Medical and Dental Expenses* and IRS Publication 969, *Health Savings Accounts and Other Tax-Favored Health Plans*.

Itemized Medical Expenses

Medical care for most Americans today is very costly. Even those with insurance still pay out-of-pocket for many things, including co-payments, noncovered procedures, and, often, the insurance premiums themselves. More than 45 million Americans have *no* medical coverage. The tax law recognizes that medical costs, even though they are personal expenses, should be deductible if they exceed a set percentage of your income.

Benefit

If you itemize deductions (instead of claiming the standard deduction), you can write off medical expenses that are not covered by insurance, employer payments, or government programs to the extent they exceed 7.5 percent of adjusted gross income.

Example

Your adjusted gross income is $100,000. You have $8,000 of medical costs that are not covered by insurance. You can deduct $500—the first 7.5 percent ($7,500) is nondeductible.

There is no dollar limit on what you can deduct for medical expenses (once you pass the 7.5 percent of AGI threshold).

Conditions

To be treated as qualified medical expenses, payments must be for the diagnosis, cure, mitigation, treatment, or prevention of disease or any treatment that affects a part or function of your body.

Deductible expenses include those paid not only for yourself but also for a spouse and dependents. A dependent, for this purpose, includes not only someone for whom you claim a dependency exemption but also someone you could have claimed the exemption for except for the fact that the person has gross income in excess of the exemption amount ($3,300 in 2006).

Example

In 2006, you provide more than half of your mother's support, including the payment of all her medical expenses. Her gross income is $12,000 so you cannot claim her as a dependent. You can, however, include your payment of her medical expenses with yours when figuring your medical expense deduction.

Examples of Deductible Medical Expenses

PROFESSIONAL SERVICES

Chiropodist.

Chiropractor.

Christian Science practitioner.

Dermatologist.

Dentist.

Gynecologist.

Neurologist.

Nurse, including board, wages, and employment taxes on wages.

Nurse's aide for an elderly person in need of supervision and assistance.

Obstetrician.

Ophthalmologist.

Optician.

Optometrist.

Osteopath.

Pediatrician.

Physician.

Physiotherapist.

Plastic surgeon for medically necessary surgery.

Podiatrist.

Practical nurse.

Psychiatrist.

Psychoanalyst.

Psychologist.

Registered nurse.

Surgeon.

DENTAL SERVICES

Artificial teeth.

Cleaning teeth.

Dental X rays.

Extracting teeth.

Filling teeth.

Gum treatment.

Oral surgery.

Orthodontia.

EQUIPMENT AND SUPPLIES

Abdominal supports.

Arches.

Artificial eyes and limbs.

Autoette.

Back supports.

Blood sugar test kit.

Braces.

Braille books and magazines.

Contact lenses.

Crutches.

Elastic hosiery.

Eyeglasses.

Hearing aids.

Heating devices.

Home exercise equipment for doctor-prescribed weight loss.

Invalid chair.

Iron lung.

Orthotics and orthopedic shoes (but only the excess over the cost of regular shoes).

Oxygen or oxygen equipment to relieve breathing problems caused by a medical condition.

Reclining chair if prescribed by a doctor.

Repair of special telephone equipment for someone who is hearing impaired.

Sacroiliac belt.

Seeing-eye dog and its maintenance.

Splints.

Telephone-teletype costs and television adapter for closed-caption service for someone who is hearing impaired.

Television adapter to display the audio part of programs as subtitles for the hearing impaired.

Truss.

Wheelchair.

Wig advised by a doctor as essential to the mental health of a person who lost all hair from disease.

HOME IMPROVEMENTS[1]

Air conditioner where necessary for relief from an allergy or for relieving difficulty in breathing.

Cost of installing stair-seat elevator for a person with a heart condition.

Fluoridation unit.

Lead-based paint removal to prevent a child with lead poisoning from eating the paint (but not the cost of repainting the scraped area).

Ramps for wheelchair access.

Swimming pool.

INSURANCE

Blue Cross and Blue Shield.

Contact lens replacement insurance.

Health insurance premiums you pay to cover hospital, surgical, and other medical expenses (health insurance paid by your employer is not deductible by you, but you aren't taxed on this benefit).

Long-term care insurance to the extent permitted for your age (explained later in this chapter).

Medicare Part B (and Medicare Part A for those not covered by Medicare).

Medicare Part D.

[1]The amount of home improvements treated as a deductible medical expense usually is limited to the extent they do not increase the home's value. However, this limitation does not apply to improvements necessary to cope with a disability (e.g., a ramp or railing for someone who is wheelchair-bound).

Medigap (supplemental Medicare insurance).

Membership in a medical service cooperative.

Student health fee.

MEDICINE AND DRUGS

Birth control pills.

Insulin.

Prescription drugs.

Viagra if medically prescribed.

TESTS

Blood tests.

Cardiograms.

Metabolism tests.

Spinal fluid tests.

Sputum tests.

Stool examinations.

Urine analyses.

X-ray examinations.

TREATMENTS AND PROGRAMS

Abortion.

Alcoholism inpatient's treatment at a therapeutic center.

Acupuncture.

Blood transfusion.

Breast reconstructive surgery following a mastectomy.

Childbirth classes for expectant mothers.

Childbirth delivery.

Clarinet lessons advised by a dentist for the treatment of tooth defects.

Convalescent home—for medical treatment only.

Diathermy.

Drug treatment center—inpatient care costs.

Egg donor fees (including legal fees for preparation of a contract between the taxpayer and the donor).

Electroshock therapy.

Fertility treatments, including in vitro fertilization and surgery to reverse prior sterilization.

Health institute fees for exercises, rubdowns, and so on that are prescribed by a doctor as treatments necessary to alleviate a physical or mental defect or illness.

Hearing services.

Hospitalization.

Hydrotherapy.

Kidney donor's or possible donor's expenses.

Laser eye surgery or keratotomy.

Lifetime care (see "Continuing Care Facilities and Nursing Homes" section later in this chapter).

Long-term care costs for someone who is chronically or terminally ill.

Navajo healing ceremony ("sings").

Organ transplant (including the costs of a donor or prospective donor).

Prenatal and postnatal visits.

Psychotherapy.

Radium therapy.

Remedial reading for someone with dyslexia.

Special school for a mentally or physically impaired person if the main reason for attendance is to use its resources for relieving the disability.

Sterilization.

Stop-smoking programs.

Surgery to remove loose skin following 100-pound weight loss.

Tutoring for severe learning disabilities.

Vaccines.

Vasectomy.

Weight-loss program to treat obesity, high blood pressure, or other condition.

TRAVEL

Ambulance hire.

Autoette (auto device for handicapped person).

Bus fare to see doctors, obtain treatment (including attendance at AA meetings), or pick up prescriptions.

Cab fare to see doctors, obtain treatment (including attendance at AA meetings), or pick up prescriptions.

Car use to see doctors, obtain treatment (including attendance at AA meetings), or pick up prescriptions at 18 cents per mile.

Conference expenses (travel costs and admission fees) for medical conferences on an illness or condition suffered by you, your spouse, or dependent.

Lodging to receive outpatient care at a licensed hospital, clinic, or hospital-equivalent facility, up to $50 per night ($100 per night if you accompany a sick child).

Train fare to see doctors, obtain treatment (including attendance at AA meetings), or pick up prescriptions.

Planning Tips

Payments by credit card are deductible in the year of the charge (not in the year of paying the credit card bill), so year-end charges for unreimbursed expenses (such as prescription sunglasses) are deductible in the year of the purchase.

If you don't expect your medical expenses to be sufficient to exceed the 7.5 percent floor this year, hold off on elective procedures until next year. Then you can effectively bunch expenses (this year's and next year's) into one year to exceed the 7.5 percent floor.

Pitfalls

Not every expense of a medical nature is deductible. Here is a listing of instances where no deduction was allowed by the IRS:

- Antiseptic diaper services.
- Bottled water purchased to avoid the city's fluoridated water.
- Burial, cremation, and funeral costs.
- Child care so a parent can see a doctor.
- Cosmetic surgery (*unless* it is medically necessary). For example, a nose job to improve appearance is not a qualified medical expense, but one done following a car accident to repair a nose broken in the accident is a qualified expense.
- Ear/body piercing.
- Hair transplant.
- Health club and gym memberships for maintaining general good health or appearance.
- Illegal drugs and controlled substances (e.g., laetrile) in violation of federal law.
- Marijuana, even if prescribed by a doctor in a state permitting the prescription (it is contraband under federal law).
- Marriage counseling fees.
- Massages recommended by a doctor to relieve stress.
- Maternity clothes.

- Nicotine patches and gums.
- Nutritional supplements, including vitamins, and herbal supplements.
- Over-the-counter medicines.
- Premiums on policies guaranteeing a specified income each week in the event of hospitalization.
- Scientology fees (but see Chapter 6).
- Sex change operation.
- Special foods or beverage substitutes (in lieu of what is normally consumed).
- Tattooing.
- Teeth-whitening treatment.
- Toothpaste.
- Weight-loss program to improve general good health or appearance.

Medical expenses are deductible for purposes of the alternative minimum tax (AMT) *only* to the extent they exceed 10 percent of AGI.

Where to Claim the Deduction for Medical Expenses

Itemized medical expenses are reported in the first part of Schedule A of Form 1040. You cannot deduct medical expenses if you file Form 1040A or Form 1040EZ.

RECORDKEEPING. Retain all canceled checks, doctors' statements, receipts, and other evidence of medical expenses you paid. If you are deducting car mileage for medical-related travel, keep a detailed record of the date and distance of each trip in a diary, logbook, or other record keeper.

Self-Employed Health Insurance Deduction

Self-employed individuals (and more-than-2-percent S corporation shareholders) cannot deduct their health insurance costs from their business income. This means that health insurance costs do not reduce net earnings from self-employment. But these individuals are permitted to deduct premiums as an adjustment to gross income even if they do not itemize other deductions.

Benefit

Self-employed individuals and shareholders owning more than 2 percent of S corporations can deduct all of their health insurance directly from gross income. Thus, the write-off can be taken even if other deductions are not itemized.

This deduction includes not only payments for normal medical care, but also long-term care insurance. There is no dollar limit on this deduction.

Conditions

To qualify for this write-off, you and your spouse may not have any employer-subsidized coverage. This condition applies on a month-by-month basis.

Example

If you (or your spouse) are eligible for employer-subsidized coverage in January but opt to pay your own coverage that month, you do not qualify for the deduction. But if, in February, you are no longer qualified under the employer plan, you can deduct your premium for this month.

Also, the deduction cannot exceed the net earnings from the business in which the medical insurance plan is established. These earnings may not be aggregated with earnings from other businesses. For S corporation shareholders, the deduction cannot be more than wages from the corporation (if this was the business in which the insurance plan was established).

Planning Tips

You can claim the deduction whether you buy the insurance through the business or individually, as long as you meet the conditions explained earlier.

If you are paying for your medical insurance, you may wish to combine this with a Health Savings Account (explained later in this chapter).

Pitfalls

The deduction does not offset business expenses. Thus, it does not reduce self-employment income subject to self-employment tax.

In the case of S corporation shareholders, the policy must be purchased by the corporation for the owners to deduct premiums above the line. If the shareholders buy the policy in their personal names, premiums can only be deducted as an itemized medical expense. This is so even though state law bars a single-owner corporation from purchasing a policy.

Where to Claim the Self-Employed Health Insurance Deduction

The deduction is claimed in the "Adjusted Gross Income" section on Form 1040 (whether or not you itemize other medical expenses).

You cannot claim the self-employed health insurance deduction if you file Form 1040A or Form 1040EZ.

Health Insurance Credit for Eligible Recipients

Certain individuals may be casualties of trade agreements or changing economic situations that shift jobs offshore. In recognition of this fact, Congress has created a special tax credit designed to help pay for certain types of health insurance for affected workers.

Benefit

If you qualify, the government pays 65 percent of your health insurance premiums for COBRA (Consolidated Omnibus Budget Reconciliation Act of 1986) continuation coverage or insurance through a state-run program (through a tax credit to which you are entitled); you pay the balance of the premiums from your own pocket. There is no dollar limit on the credit you can claim or any restrictions on claiming the credit because of your income level.

Example

If your annual premium is $6,000, your tax credit is $3,900 (65 percent of $6,000).

Conditions

To claim the credit, you must meet two conditions:

1. You are an eligible recipient ("eligible individual").
2. You pay for certain health care coverage ("qualifying health insurance").

ELIGIBLE INDIVIDUAL. To be an eligible individual, you must fall within either of two categories:

1. You are a worker who lost your job due to foreign trade competition. You must be treated as someone eligible to receive a trade adjustment allowance (TAA) or an alternative TAA (or who would have received a TAA but you have not exhausted your unemployment benefits).
2. You are a retiree age 55 or older receiving benefits from the Pension Benefit Guaranty Corporation (you are called a PBGC pension recipient). This means that to claim the credit for 2006, you must have been born before 1951.

You can claim the credit if your spouse or dependent is an eligible individual. If you file a joint return, only one spouse has to meet eligibility conditions. You cannot claim the credit if you can be claimed as another taxpayer's dependent.

Eligibility is determined on a month-by-month basis. You are eligible in a month if, as of the first day of the month, you meet eligibility requirements. You may, for example, only be entitled to a credit for a portion of the year (the months in which you are an eligible individual).

You do not qualify if you are imprisoned under federal, state, or local authority.

As a practical matter, you don't have to determine whether you're an eligible individual; the government does this for you. It will send you Form 8887,

Health Insurance Credit Eligibility Certificate, stating that you are an eligible TAA, alternative TAA, or PBGC pension recipient.

QUALIFYING HEALTH INSURANCE. Even if you are an eligible individual, you do not qualify for the credit if you have health coverage under Medicare Part A, Medicare Part B, Medicaid, State Children's Health Insurance Program (S-CHIP), Federal Employees Health Benefit Plan (FEHBP), Tricare (for certain military personnel and their families), or any coverage if at least 50 percent is paid by your (or your spouse's) employer.

EXAMPLES OF QUALIFYING HEALTH INSURANCE

Certain state-sponsored health insurance if the state elects to have it apply.

COBRA (see later in this chapter).

Coverage under a group plan available through the employment of your spouse.

Coverage under individual health insurance, provided you were covered during the entire 30-day period that ends on the date you separated from the employment that makes you an eligible individual.

Planning Tips

You can include as part of the credit any distributions taken from an Archer Medical Savings Account or a Health Savings Account (discussed later in this chapter) to pay qualified health insurance coverage.

You can claim the credit in advance of filing your tax return and are entitled to it even if you don't owe any taxes. As long as you obtain the proper certification, you pay only 35 percent of your health insurance premiums and the federal government pays the other 65 percent. Certification is made by obtaining Form 8887, Health Insurance Credit Eligibility Certificate.

Of course, you cannot claim a tax credit on your tax return if the credit has been obtained on an advance basis by means of government payment of your health insurance. The amount of the credit you claim on your return is reduced by the amount of the credit you receive in advance.

Pitfalls

Even if you are an eligible individual, not all health insurance qualifies for the credit. Examples of nonqualifying health insurance (in addition to those listed earlier) include:

Accident and/or disability insurance.

Automobile medical insurance.

Coverage for on-site medical clinics.

Coverage only for a specified disease or illness.

Coverage under a flexible spending arrangement (FSA).

Credit-only insurance.

Hospital indemnity or other fixed indemnity coverage.

Liability insurance or a supplement to liability insurance.

Medicare supplemental insurance ("Medigap").

Tricare supplemental insurance (for military personnel and their families).

Workers' compensation or similar insurance.

Check for enrollment requirements. State programs can require eligible individuals to enroll within a reasonable period after becoming qualified and deny enrollment for failure to make timely payments (and can restrict eligibility to state residents).

If you claim the credit, you cannot include the same premiums in determining your itemized medical deduction on Schedule A, your self-employed health insurance deduction, or tax-free distributions from any medical or health savings account.

Where to Claim the Credit

There are two ways to obtain the credit: by registering in advance so that a portion of the credit is applied toward your premiums (register by calling toll free 866-628-4282) or by claiming it on your return.

You figure the credit on Form 8885, Health Insurance Credit for Eligible Recipients. You claim the credit as "Other Credits" on Form 1040.

You cannot claim the credit on Form 1040A or Form 1040EZ.

Long-Term Care Coverage

Individuals who are suffering from chronic conditions such as Alzheimer's disease or are merely elderly and incapable of self-care (such as feeding and bathing themselves) require long-term care, either in their own homes or in nursing homes. According to a Metlife survey in 2005, the average annual cost of a nursing home stay in a private room is now about $74,000 (over $64,000 for a semiprivate room); it is about $200,000 in Alaska. This cost generally is *not* covered by Medicare or supplemental Medicare insurance. Only special insurance, called long-term care insurance, pays for this type of care. The tax law allows a portion of this special medical insurance to be deductible.

Benefit

You can deduct a portion of long-term care insurance premiums as a qualified medical expense (based on your age).

Benefits received under a long-term care policy generally are treated as tax-free income (the benefits are an exclusion from income).

Conditions

Since there are two benefits—a deduction for the payment of long-term care insurance premiums and an exclusion from income for benefits received under the policy—different conditions apply for each.

CONDITIONS FOR THE DEDUCTION. You can deduct only a portion of premiums based on your age. For 2006, the deduction is limited to the amounts shown in Table 2.1.

The premium limit is a per-person basis.

Example

Both you and your spouse carry long-term care insurance. You are age 55 and your spouse is age 52. Your annual premium is $2,200 and your spouse's premium is $1,800. You can treat $2,120 ($1,060 for you and $1,060 for your spouse) of your total $4,000 premiums as a deductible medical expense.

CONDITIONS FOR THE EXCLUSION. The exclusion applies only to qualified long-term care services provided to a person who is chronically ill and that are necessary for medical or personal care and are provided under a plan of care prescribed by a licensed health care practitioner. You are chronically ill if a licensed health care practitioner certifies that within the past 12 months you meet *either* of these conditions:

- You are unable for at least 90 days to perform at least two activities of daily living without substantial assistance, due to loss of functional capacity. Activities of daily living include eating, toileting, transferring, bathing, dressing, and continence.

TABLE 2.1 Deductible Long-Term Care Premiums for 2006

Age by Year-End	Deduction Limit
Age 40 or younger	$ 280
Age 41–50	530
Age 51–60	1,060
Age 61–70	2,830
Age 71 or older	3,530

- You require substantial supervision for your safety due to severe cognitive impairment.

If the policy pays your long-term care expenses, you can exclude these payments.

Benefits paid under an indemnity-type contract are fully excludable to the extent they cover long-term care expenses. If you receive benefits under a per diem contract, there is a per-day dollar limit on what you can exclude. For 2006, the exclusion is $250 per day.

Planning Tips

Since the average annual cost of a nursing home now exceeds $74,000 ($64,000 for a semi-private room), you might want to carry long-term care coverage to pay some or all of this cost if it arises. The younger you are when you purchase the policy, the smaller your annual premiums will be (they are fixed at the time of purchase and generally do not increase thereafter).

Long-term care insurance may be available as an employee fringe benefit under your company's cafeteria plan. If you opt for this coverage, you are not taxed on this benefit.

States may provide their own benefit for long-term care insurance. In New York, for example, there is a 20 percent tax credit, with no age or dollar limitations.

Pitfall

Since long-term care insurance usually pays a fixed dollar amount and, hopefully, you won't need long-term care for many years to come, it can be difficult to know how much insurance to carry. Consider including a cost-of-living rider to adjust your dollar coverage for inflation.

Where to Claim the Deduction and/or Exclusion

The deduction for long-term care insurance premiums is treated like other deductible medical expenses. Generally, they are included with your other itemized medical expenses (up to your allowable dollar limit). However, if you are self-employed, you can include this amount with your other medical insurance claimed as part of the self-employed health insurance deduction, which is an adjustment to gross income.

If you receive benefits under a long-term care policy that are fully excludable, you do not have to report anything on your return. But if you are limited in what you can exclude (as explained earlier), excess benefits are reported as "Other Income" on Form 1040.

Flexible Spending Arrangements for Health Care

Companies are increasingly forced to make employees pay for some or all of their medical expenses. But they can assist them by creating special arrangements, called flexible spending arrangements, that enable employees to pay for medical expenses on a pretax basis. This means employees can dedicate some of their wages to special accounts used for medical expenses. Amounts put into these accounts are not currently taxed. Contribution limits are not fixed by the tax law; they are set by the terms of the companies' plans.

Benefit

Businesses can set up flexible spending arrangements (FSAs) to allow employees to pay for expenses not covered by insurance on a pretax basis. At the start of the year employees agree to a salary reduction amount as their contribution to the FSA. These amounts are not treated as taxable compensation and are not subject to Social Security and Medicare (FICA) taxes. Employees then use these amounts anytime during the year to pay for medical costs, including health insurance premiums or other expenses not covered by insurance, such as orthodontia and prescription eyeglasses.

For purposes of health FSAs, reimbursable medical expenses include over-the-counter medications (such as antacids, pain relievers, allergy medications, and cold remedies), but not items used for general good health (such as dietary supplements).

Conditions

The plan (not the IRS) sets the limits on how much you can commit to the FSA each year. It may be fixed as a percentage of your compensation (e.g., up to 6 percent). Ask your plan administrator for details on your contribution limits and the deadline for signing up each year (just because you were in the FSA this year does not automatically cover you for next year; you may be required to complete the same paperwork all over again).

Planning Tips

You can tap into your annual contribution at any time during the year (even before you have fully paid into the FSA).

Example

In January you agree to contribute $1,800 for the year, which is $150 each month, to your company's FSA. In February, when you have contributed only $300, you pay a dental bill of $1,500 that is not covered by insurance. You submit the paid bill to your plan administrator and receive the full reimbursement of $1,500.

Decide carefully how much you wish to contribute for the year. You generally cannot change your monthly salary reduction during the year. If you fail to use up all of your contribution during the year or by the end of the plan's grace period (if any), you lose this money forever. You generally cannot carry it over to next year or withdraw the unused amount as cash. You may see this referred to as the "use it or lose it" rule (but see grace period below). Your medical expenses for the previous year may give you an idea of what your needs will be so you can set your salary reduction amount at a rate that you expect to fully utilize.

Your employer can adopt an IRS-approved grace period of up to two and a half months. If so, you have up to March 15, 2007, to incur medical expenses that can be reimbursed out of your 2006 FSA amounts.

Example

In 2006, you contribute $200 per month to your FSA. At the end of December you have used up only $2,000 of this amount. Assuming your employer adopted the IRS grace period, you have until March 15, 2007, to incur additional medical expenses of $400 so you can use up your account. If you incur $600 of medical expenses between January 1, 2007, and March 15, 2007, the first $400 is applied against your 2006 FSA contributions; the balance is applied against your 2007 FSA contributions (assuming you have agreed to these contributions).

Pitfalls

As just mentioned, FSAs operate on a use-it-or-lose-it basis. If you contribute more than your covered medical expenses for the year and cannot use it up in the contribution year or grace period (if applicable), you can't get the money back. Don't agree to a salary reduction amount in excess of what you reasonably expect to use for medical expenses.

FSAs cannot pay for any expenses that would not qualify as a deductible medical expense. For example, FSAs cannot be used to pay for cosmetic surgery (unless it is medically necessary—for example, to correct a birth defect).

Where to Claim the Benefit

Since this benefit is an exclusion from income, you do not have to report anything on your return. Compensation reported on your Form W-2 is reduced to the extent of your FSA contributions.

However, you are required to account to the FSA administrator in order to receive payments from the plan. For example, you may be asked to submit a paid bill for prescription sunglasses in order to receive reimbursement from the FSA, and the bill must be submitted within a certain period after incurring the expense. Talk to your plan administrator for rules on how to obtain reimbursements from the plan.

Health Reimbursement Arrangements

Companies are continually looking for ways to reduce their health care costs for employees. Within the past few years, a new type of plan, called a health reimbursement arrangement, has been created under which companies set aside a fixed dollar amount for each employee (employees do not pay anything toward these plans). An employee can use funds in his or her account within the plan to pay for medical costs without being taxed when funds are contributed or when they are withdrawn for approved medical expenses.

Benefit

Employers may set up health reimbursement arrangements (HRAs) to allow employees to pay for unreimbursed medical expenses without any cost to them. Here's how they work. The company sets up accounts for each employee and contributes a flat dollar amount. You are not taxed on employer contributions. Similarly, when you use funds in your account to cover your medical costs, you are not taxed on withdrawals. There is no dollar limit on employer contributions on your behalf, nor on amounts you can withdraw tax free to pay for medical expenses.

Condition

Your company (not the IRS) sets any and all participation requirements, so talk with the HRA administrator about anything you must do to participate in and receive reimbursements from the HRA.

Planning Tip

You can use the funds in your account whenever you need to within the year. Any amounts remaining in the account at year-end automatically carry over to the next year and can be used to cover your future medical expenses.

Pitfall

There are no pitfalls for participating in your company's HRA. You are receiving a tax-free fringe benefit to the extent you use the coverage under the HRA.

Where to Claim the Benefit

Since this benefit is an exclusion from income, you do not have to report anything on your return.

However, you are required to account to the HRA administrator in order to receive payments from the plan. For example, you may be asked to submit a paid bill for prescription sunglasses in order to receive reimbursement from the HRA. Talk to the plan administrator for rules on how to obtain reimbursement.

Health Savings Accounts

Individuals who are covered by health insurance policies with high deductibles may be eligible to contribute money to a special savings account, called a Health Savings Account (HSA). About 46 million Americans are currently uninsured, and HSAs may be a way for them to obtain needed health coverage on an affordable basis. In fact, as of May 2006, more than 3.3 million people had already opted for HSAs, and predictions put the number at 24 million by 2010. Some estimate that 23 percent of small businesses offering health coverage will use HSAs by 2007.

Contributions to the account are tax deductible. Earnings on the account are not subject to immediate tax. If withdrawals are made to pay for medical expenses, they are fully tax free. Otherwise withdrawals are taxable and subject to a 10 percent penalty unless taken when age 65 or older or disabled. Spouses who inherit an account can roll over the funds tax free.

Benefit

If you have a "high-deductible" health insurance policy (defined in "Conditions" section), you can contribute to a special savings account. Benefits to HSAs include:

- Contributions within set limits are deductible as an adjustment to gross income (you do not have to itemize deductions to claim this benefit). See Table 2.2 for 2006 limits. The limits for those under age 55 will be indexed for inflation after 2006; the additional contribution limits for those age 55 and older increase in $100 increments to $1,000 by 2009.
- Interest or other earnings in the account are tax deferred.
- Withdrawals used to pay medical costs are tax free.

Conditions

To contribute to an HSA, you must meet two conditions:

1. You are not covered by Medicare.
2. You are covered by a high-deductible health insurance policy.

MEDICARE. HSAs are designed to cover individuals who do not qualify for Medicare. Therefore, you are ineligible for an HSA once you are covered by Medicare. Since determination of eligibility is made month-by-month, you may

TABLE 2.2 Health Savings Account Contribution Limits for 2006

Your Age	Self-Only Plan	Family Plan
Under age 55	$2,700	$5,450
55 or older	$3,400	$6,150

be qualified for a deduction for the portion of the year before you are covered by Medicare.

QUALIFYING HIGH-DEDUCTIBLE HEALTH INSURANCE. You must have a high-deductible health insurance policy. This can be one that you have obtained personally or coverage provided by your employer. The determination of whether you have such coverage is made on the first day of the month.

A high-deductible policy is one that falls within certain limits. (See Table 2.3.). These limits will be indexed for inflation after 2006.

You cannot have any other health coverage, other than accident insurance, dental care, disability coverage, disease-specific coverage (such as cancer insurance), long-term care, vision care, and workers' compensation.

Like individual retirement accounts (IRAs), contributions to HSAs can be made up to the due date for the return (without extensions). For example, contributions for 2006 can be made up to April 16, 2007.

Tax-Free Withdrawals

Only account distributions used to pay qualified medical expenses are tax free. Qualified medical expenses include:

- Any expense that could be claimed as an itemized medical deduction (see the section earlier in this chapter).
- COBRA premiums.
- Over-the-counter medications.
- Premiums for long-term care insurance.
- Periodic health evaluations, such as annual physicals.
- Routine prenatal and well-child care.
- Child and adult immunizations.
- Tobacco cessation programs.
- Obesity weight-loss programs.
- Screening services, such as those listed.

TABLE 2.3 2006 High-Deductible Policy Limits

	Self-Only Coverage	Family Coverage
Annual deductible at least	$1,050	$ 2,100
Limit on expenses	$5,250	$10,500

Examples of Screening Services Treated as Medical Expenses for HSAs

CANCER SCREENING

Breast cancer (e.g., mammogram).

Cervical cancer (e.g., Pap smear).

Colorectal cancer.

Oral cancer.

Ovarian cancer.

Prostate cancer (e.g., prostate-specific antigen [PSA] test).

Skin cancer.

Testicular cancer.

Thyroid cancer.

HEART AND VASCULAR DISEASES SCREENING

Abdominal aortic aneurysm.

Carotid artery stenosis.

Coronary heart disease.

Hemoglobinopathies.

Hypertension.

Lip disorders.

INFECTIOUS DISEASES SCREENING

Bacteriuria.

Chlamydial infection.

Gonorrhea.

Hepatitis B virus infection.

Hepatitis C.

Human immunodeficiency virus (HIV) infection.

Syphilis.

Tuberculosis infection.

MENTAL HEALTH CONDITIONS AND SUBSTANCE ABUSE SCREENING

Dementia.

Depression.

Drug abuse.

Family violence.

Problem drinking.

Suicide risk.

METABOLIC, NUTRITIONAL, AND ENDOCRINE CONDITIONS SCREENING

Anemia, iron deficiency.

Dental and periodontal disease.

Diabetes mellitus.

Obesity in adults.

Thyroid disease.

MUSCULOSKELETAL DISORDERS SCREENING

Osteoporosis.

OBSTETRIC AND GYNECOLOGIC CONDITIONS SCREENING

Bacterial vaginosis in pregnancy.

Gestational diabetes mellitus.

Home uterine activity monitoring.

Neural tube defects.

Preeclampsia.

Rh incompatibility.

Rubella.

Ultrasonography in pregnancy.

PEDIATRIC CONDITIONS SCREENING

Child developmental delay.

Congenital hypothyroidism.

Lead levels in childhood and pregnancy.

Phenylketonuria.

Scoliosis, adolescent idiopathic.

VISION AND HEARING DISORDERS SCREENING

Glaucoma.

Hearing impairment in older adults.

Newborn hearing.

Planning Tips

It is up to you to keep track of medical costs so that you can prove withdrawals from your HSA were used to pay qualified expenses. The financial institution with which you have your account won't ask you for any substantiation on your part. Neither will your employer if the account is set up through your company.

Funds in the account can be used for retirement savings. Since there is no tax on earnings that the account is building up, the healthier you stay (and the less you need to use account funds for medical bills), the more you'll have in retirement to use for any purpose. While the withdrawals will be taxed, there is no penalty on withdrawals for nonmedical purposes once you reach age 65.

Pitfalls

If you take withdrawals to pay nonmedical expenses, the distribution is taxed as ordinary income, regardless of your age. In addition, if you are under age 65, you are also subject to a 10 percent penalty (unless you are disabled). There is no 10 percent penalty on distributions because of the account owner's death.

If you have a separate prescription drugs benefit plan that has no deductible (only co-payments for each prescription), you cannot be an eligible individual for HSA purposes.

If you inherit an HSA and are not a surviving spouse of the account owner, you must take a complete distribution of the account and include all of the funds in your income. Check to see if you qualify for a deduction for federal estate tax on the HSA (see Chapter 16).

Where to Claim the Benefits

The deduction is figured on Form 8889, Health Savings Accounts (HSAs). The deduction is then claimed as an above-the-line deduction in the "Adjusted Gross Income" section of Form 1040. You cannot claim the deduction if you file Form 1040A or 1040EZ.

If your employer contributes to an HSA on your behalf, this is a tax-free fringe benefit; no reporting is required.

Archer Medical Savings Accounts *(Provision expired 12/31/05. Extension expected for 2006.)*

Self-employed individuals and small employers can set up Archer Medical Savings Accounts (MSAs) to save money for their health insurance costs by combining a "high-deductible" medical insurance policy with this special savings plan. If they have a policy that falls within parameters set by the tax law, then they (or their employees) can contribute a fixed amount to an IRA-like account. Contributions are deductible, earnings are not currently subject to tax, and withdrawals for medical purposes are tax free (i.e., contributions and earnings on contributions used to pay medical costs are never taxed). Archer MSAs are an alternative to HSAs for eligible taxpayers.

Benefit

If you are self-employed or an employee of a small employer with a "high-deductible" health insurance policy (defined in "Conditions" section), you can contribute to a special savings account that can be tapped to cover unreimbursed medical expenses. There are several benefits to Archer Medical Savings Accounts (MSAs):

- Contributions within set limits are deductible (or tax free if made by your employer).
- Interest or other earnings in the account are tax deferred.
- Withdrawals used to cover medical expenses are tax free.

Conditions

You must be self-employed or an employee of a "small employer" covered by a "high-deductible" health insurance policy. A small employer is an employer who had on average 50 or fewer employees during either of the two preceding calendar years. If the business is new, then the employer is treated as a small employer if it reasonably expects to employ 50 or fewer workers. If a business made contributions to an Archer MSA this year, it can continue to be treated as a small employer as long as it had no more than 200 employees each year after 1996.

A high-deductible policy is one that falls within certain limits on deductibles and out-of-pocket expenses required to be paid (other than premiums) before the policy kicks in. (See Table 2.4.)

Example

In 2006, you are self-employed and have a self-only health insurance policy with an annual deductible of $2,000 and a limit on out-of-pocket expenses of $3,000. Assuming you meet other conditions, you have a high-deductible plan and can fund an Archer MSA in 2006.

You (or your spouse) cannot have any other health plan that is not a high-deductible plan. But coverage under certain other health plans will not prevent you from being able to fund an Archer MSA. Other coverage you may have *in addition* to a high-deductible plan includes insurance covering accidents, disability, dental care, vision care, long-term care, benefits related to worker's compensation, a specific illness or disease, or a fixed amount per day or other period of hospitalization.

Assuming you meet the conditions for claiming a deduction, the amount is limited to 65 percent of your annual deductible for self-only coverage or 75 percent of your annual deductible for family coverage.

TABLE 2.4 2006 Limits on Deductibles and Out-of-Pocket Expenses

Type of Coverage	Minimum Annual Deductible	Maximum Annual Deductible	Maximum Annual Out-of-Pocket Expenses
Individual (self-only policy)	$1,800	$2.700	$3,650
Family	$3,650	$5,450	$6,650

Example

In 2006, you are self-employed and have a health insurance policy for family coverage with a $4,000 annual deductible. In 2006, you can contribute $3,000 to an Archer MSA ($4,000 × 75%).

If you have coverage for only part of the year, you must prorate the deduction.

Example

Same facts as in the preceding example but you start coverage on July 1, 2006, and maintain it for the balance of the year. You can contribute $1,500 to an Archer MSA ($4,000 × 75% ÷ 12 months × 6 months).

Contributions for 2006 must be made no later than December 31, 2006. Even though the account resembles an HSA, you do not have until tax time to fund the account.

Planning Tips

You can roll over funds in an Archer MSA tax free to a Health Savings Account. This may be advisable because of the extensive availability of financial institutions offering HSAs compared with limited Archer MSA options.

You can use an Archer MSA to provide retirement income. Money can be withdrawn for any purpose penalty-free after attaining age 65.

Pitfalls

If you are self-employed, you cannot contribute more than your net earnings from self-employment. Thus, if you have a loss year, you cannot fund an Archer MSA.

Example

You are 65 years old and, because you have stayed healthy, the funds in your account have accumulated to $10,000. You can withdraw this money to take a vacation. While you'll owe income tax on the withdrawal (because you are not using the funds for medical reasons), you are not subject to the 15 percent penalty (explained next).

If you withdraw funds from an Archer MSA for other than medical expenses before attaining age 65, the funds are subject to a 15 percent penalty unless you are disabled (or die).

WHEN YOU DIE. If you have an Archer MSA, you can name your spouse as the beneficiary of the account. Your spouse becomes the owner of the account when you die. If you designate any other person as your beneficiary, the account ceases to be an Archer MSA on your death and the funds remaining in the account are taxable to the beneficiary as income. If there is no designated beneficiary, the balance of your account is included as income on your final tax return.

Where to Claim the Benefits

The deduction is figured on Form 8853, Archer MSAs and Long-Term Care Insurance Contracts. The deduction is then claimed as an above-the-line deduction in the "Adjusted Gross Income" section of Form 1040. Enter the amount of your deduction on the dotted line next to line 36 and identify it with the notation "MSA." You cannot claim a deduction if you file Form 1040A or 1040EZ.

If your employer contributes to an Archer Medical Savings Account on your behalf, this is a tax-free fringe benefit; no reporting is required.

REPORTING INCOME. Withdrawals are reported to you (and the IRS) on Form 1099-SA, Distributions from an HSA, Archer MSA, or Medicare Advantage MSA. Funds withdrawn for anything other than medical expenses are taxable as ordinary income. Report the income on Form 1040 as other income.

If you owe a 15 percent penalty on withdrawals for nonmedical purposes before age 65, you report the penalty in the section for "Other Taxes" on Form 1040.

COBRA Coverage

The Consolidated Omnibus Budget Reconciliation Act of 1986, or COBRA for short, imposed a new requirement on certain employers who maintain health insurance coverage for workers: allow workers who leave the job to continue their company coverage for a period of time (at the workers' expense). The opportunity to continue under the company's health plan means that terminated workers and other eligible people pay for medical insurance at group rates.

Benefit

Under federal law, if you work for a company that regularly employs 20 or more workers and has group health insurance, you are entitled to continue under the employer's group plan even if you leave employment (voluntarily or are laid off for any reason other than gross misconduct) or your hours are reduced below the level entitling you to employer-paid coverage. This is referred to as COBRA continuation coverage or simply COBRA. Your state may have its own "mini-COBRA" law, which may expand your rights (contact your state insurance department for details). For example, Massachusetts mini-COBRA requires employers with 2 to 19 employees to offer continuation coverage. And there is a special second COBRA election period for certain qualifying individuals.

Being eligible for and electing COBRA coverage gives you two key benefits:

1. Health insurance at an affordable group rate.
2. A deduction for premium payments if you itemize your medical expenses.

You can continue COBRA coverage for up to 18 months or until you become eligible under a new employer's plan, you qualify for Medicare, or you fail to make your COBRA payments (usually there's a 30-day grace period). The coverage period can be extended to 29 months if you become disabled within the first 60 days of COBRA coverage. Your family can retain COBRA coverage for up to 36 months if their eligibility results from your death.

You must pay the cost of the coverage, plus up to 2 percent as an administrative fee (102 percent of the premiums). But you enjoy the group term rates, which may be less than what you could purchase on your own. Your payment of premiums under COBRA is a deductible medical expense (explained earlier).

If you are a displaced worker, you may be able to claim a tax credit for your COBRA premiums, as explained earlier in this chapter.

Conditions

If your employer is subject to COBRA, you must notify the employer about a qualifying event and opt for coverage within 60 days of that event (no extensions are granted). A qualifying event includes:

- You terminate employment (voluntarily or involuntarily, as long as you are not terminated for fraud or other gross misconduct).
- Your parent has health insurance through his or her employer and you attain the age at which you no longer qualify (generally age 21 or upon graduation from college).
- Your spouse has health coverage through his or her employer and you divorce your spouse.

SECOND COBRA ELECTION PERIOD. To qualify, you must be receiving trade adjustment allowance (TAA) benefits (or would be but for the requirement that you first exhaust unemployment benefits), you lost health coverage because of termination of employment that resulted in TAA eligibility, and you did not elect COBRA during the regular COBRA election period.

Planning Tip

Before opting for COBRA, see if there are less costly health insurance options. For example, if your spouse is working, his/her employer may offer less expensive health coverage. Or you may be able to buy coverage through a professional or trade association that is less expensive than COBRA.

Pitfalls

You can reduce your current level of coverage, but you can't increase it. For example, if you had dental coverage but now wish to eliminate it (and the expense) under COBRA, you can do so. But if you didn't have dental coverage, you can't add it under COBRA.

COBRA does not apply to long-term care insurance. You may be able to pick up the long-term care policy individually when you leave employment, but your employer is not required to offer you this coverage through COBRA.

Where to Claim the Deduction for COBRA Payments

COBRA payments are treated as a deductible medical expense (see earlier in this chapter).

Medicare

In 1965, Congress introduced a federally sponsored health insurance program as part of the Social Security Act. This program, called Medicare, is designed primarily to provide those age 65 and older with affordable comprehensive health coverage. Today, the program has grown to afford seniors various types of coverage options, from fee-based services to managed care programs. More than 40 million Americans are now covered by Medicare. At the time this book went to press Congress was working out details on expanding Medicare to offer prescription drug options.

Benefit

If you are age 65 or older, are under age 65 and disabled for at least two years, or have end-stage renal disease, you are entitled to participate in the federal government's health insurance program called Medicare. Your monthly premiums (whether paid directly by you or withheld from your Social Security benefits check), as well as your co-payments and deductibles under Medicare, are qualified medical expenses that are deductible as miscellaneous itemized deductions to the extent your total exceeds 7.5 percent of adjusted gross income (see the general rules on deducting medical expenses, including medical insurance, discussed earlier in this chapter). You are not taxed on the benefits you receive through Medicare.

Part A, which covers hospitalization, is free (those who did not work sufficient quarters can pay for this coverage). Part B, which covers doctors' charges and certain other expenses, requires you to pay a monthly premium. The premium is subtracted from your Social Security benefits if you are collecting benefits. Both Part A and Part B have certain co-payments or deductibles for your covered medical expenses.

There is a new Medicare prescription drug plan called Part D. Certain low-income beneficiaries qualify for additional assistance to pay for prescription drugs called the Extra Help program. To be eligible, beneficiaries must have an income in 2006 below $14,700 if single or $19,800 if married and not be eligible for any other prescription drug coverage (including outpatient prescription drug coverage through Medicare managed care plans). Details on the Medicare drug program can be found at www.medicare.gov.

Conditions

To be eligible for free coverage under Part A, you (or your spouse) must have at least 40 quarters of Medicare-covered employment. If you don't have the necessary quarters, you can pay for this coverage.

Part B is available to just about anyone age 65 or older (there are no minimum work requirements).

Part D is available to all Medicare beneficiaries.

Planning Tips

Medicare coverage generally isn't automatic; you must apply for it if you haven't yet applied for Social Security benefits. You should contact your local Social Security office to apply for Medicare three months before the date you reach your full retirement age so that coverage can start on time.

If you have been collecting Social Security benefits before your full retirement age (e.g., starting at age 62), you do not have to apply when you near full retirement age; enrollment in Medicare Part A (hospitalization insurance) in this case is automatic and free; however, you must then decide whether to also elect Medicare Part B (health insurance).

If you opt for traditional fee-for-service Medicare (rather than some managed care program within Medicare), you may want to purchase supplemental Medicare insurance ("Medigap" coverage). Medigap premiums are deductible as a qualified medical expense (explained earlier in this chapter).

Pitfalls

If you claim the standard deduction (including the additional amount for being age 65 or older), you cannot deduct your Medicare Part B payments since you do not itemize deductions.

If you wait too long to apply for Medicare Part B, your monthly premium will be increased. To obtain the lowest possible premium, you *must* apply either within a seven-month window extending from three months before to four months after your 65th birthday, or, if still employed and covered at work, within eight months after that ends.

If you did not sign up for Medicare Part D but were eligible to do so, and you do not have other "creditable coverage" (e.g., employer or other coverage that is at least as good as Medicare), you are penalized 1 percent per month for each month you delay. For example, if you wait 15 months to sign up beyond the deadline, you pay 15 percent of the premium as a penalty when you enroll. If the premium is normally $40 per month, you'd paid $46 per month ($40 plus 15 percent penalty). The penalty percentage continues for the rest of your life.

Where to Claim the Deduction

You deduct premiums as well as your co-payments and deductibles as itemized medical expenses (see earlier in this chapter). You must complete Schedule A and attach it to Form 1040.

Continuing Care Facilities and Nursing Homes

Elderly and infirmed individuals may require round-the-clock care because of their age or condition. Comprehensive programs in special living arrangements are now used to care for these individuals. A portion of the cost may qualify as a deductible medical expense.

Benefit

Advanced age and/or chronic illness may require ongoing daily treatment. Payments for nursing homes, convalescent homes, and sanitariums may be treated as deductible medical expenses. The deduction generally is not limited to the portion covering medical care; it also includes lodging and meals if confinement is primarily for the purpose of medical treatment.

If the main reason for admission is not medical care, you can still treat the portion of monthly fees allocable to medical care as a deductible medical expense. Typically, this applies to fees to continuing care facilities—the portion of the fees for medical care is deductible but the portion covering lodging and meals is not.

Conditions

Admission to the facility must be *primarily* for medical treatment to deduct all charges and fees. You can prove this by showing that:

- Entry was on or at the direction of a doctor.
- Attendance or treatment at the facility has a direct therapeutic effect on the condition suffered by the patient.
- Attendance at the facility is for the treatment of a specific ailment and not merely for general good health.

Planning Tip

Generally, prepayments for future care are not currently deductible medical expenses. However, you can claim a current deduction if you can show there is

Example

You and your spouse enter a retirement home that requires the payment of an entrance fee of $50,000, plus monthly payments of $1,000, to cover your accommodations, meals, and medical care for life. The home estimates for you that 10 percent of the entrance fee and 15 percent of the monthly fee are used for medical care. If you leave the home, you are entitled to a refund of a portion of the founder's fee. On these facts, you can treat 10 percent of the entrance fee and 15 percent of the monthly fee paid in the year as deductible medical expenses.

a current obligation to pay and you can establish the portion of the prepayment allocated to medical care.

Pitfall

If you claim the standard deduction (including the additional amount for being age 65 or older), you cannot deduct your payments for continuing care facilities or nursing homes since you do not itemize deductions. As a practical matter, however, if you are a resident in such a facility for a full year, the cost will generally result in a large enough medical deduction to warrant itemizing your deductions in lieu of claiming the standard deduction, even with the additional amount for age.

Where to Claim the Benefit

See itemized medical expenses earlier in this chapter.

Accelerated Death Benefits

Whoever thought that life insurance could be beneficial to the person insured? Today, policies intended to provide death benefits to heirs may be used for lifetime assistance to the insured under special circumstances. Congress has acted in the wake of AIDS to allow proceeds from life insurance policies that are tapped during the insured's life to receive the same tax-free treatment as death proceeds in certain circumstances.

Benefit

If you own a life insurance policy with cash value and become terminally or chronically ill, you may be able to tap into that cash value on a tax-free basis to pay medical and other personal expenses.

There are two ways in which to use a life insurance policy to provide you with current cash on a tax-free basis:

1. Tap into the policy's cash surrender value under an accelerated death benefit clause if the policy contains such an option.
2. Sell the policy to a viatical settlement company (a company in the business of buying policies under these conditions).

Conditions

You must be terminally or chronically ill to qualify for the exclusion. You are considered to be terminally ill if a physician certifies that you suffer from an illness or physical condition that is reasonably expected to result in death within 24 months of the date of certification.

You are considered to be chronically ill if a licensed health care practitioner certifies that within the past 12 months you meet *either* of these conditions:

- You are unable for at least 90 days to perform at least two activities of daily living without substantial assistance, due to loss of functional capacity. Activities of daily living include eating, toileting, transferring, bathing, dressing, and continence.
- You require substantial supervision for your safety due to severe cognitive impairment.

LIMITS FOR THE CHRONICALLY ILL. While *all* payments received by someone who is terminally ill are fully excludable (whether or not such amounts are used for medical care), limits apply to those who are chronically but not terminally ill. The same limits for benefits received under a long-term care policy apply for this purpose. Thus, if accelerated death benefits are not more than the daily dollar limit ($250 in 2006) and do not exceed actual long-term care costs, they are fully excludable. But any excess amounts are taxable.

Planning Tip

To the extent you use accelerated death benefits for medical expenses, you reap a double tax benefit: The funds are tax-free income to you, and you can treat the payments you make as deductible medical expenses if you itemize your deductions.

Pitfall

To the extent you use your life insurance policy while you are alive, there is that much less for your beneficiaries after your death. If you have other options to cover your expenses, you might weigh your current needs against your beneficiaries' needs after your death in deciding whether to use accelerated death benefits.

Where to Claim the Benefit

If benefits are fully excludable, they need not be reported. However, if a chronically ill person receives benefits in excess of the limit ($250 per day in 2006), such amounts are reported as other income on Form 1040.

Decedent's Final Illness

There are no special deductions for someone who dies. But the tax law provides opportunities on the timing of deductions for the deceased. Those handling the affairs of a person who has died can choose how to handle medical deductions for optimum tax savings.

Benefit

Payments of medical expenses for a deceased spouse or dependent can be deducted as a medical expense in the year they are paid, even if this is before or after the person's death.

A decedent's personal representative (executor, administrator, etc.) has a choice of how to treat medical expenses—as an itemized deduction on the decedent's final income tax return (to the extent provided) or as a deduction on the estate tax return. Of course, if the decedent's estate is too small to require the filing of an estate tax return, there is no real choice; the deduction should automatically be treated as a deduction on the decedent's income tax return.

If the personal representative of a decedent's estate pays medical expenses within one year of death, an election can be made to treat the expenses as if they were paid by the decedent in the year the services were provided rather than the year in which they were paid. This may entitle the personal representative to file an amended return for the decedent for a prior year.

Example

In 2005, the decedent received treatment for a condition that eventually resulted in her death on May 1, 2006. At the time of death, payment for this treatment was outstanding. Assuming her personal representative pays any of her unreimbursed cost in February 2007, the personal representative may file an amended return for the decedent for 2005 to include the payment along with the decedent's other deductible medical expenses.

Condition

The decision on when and where to claim the decedent's medical expenses is made by the personal representative—the executor, administrator, or other person empowered by a court to act for the estate. This person can override a decision by a surviving spouse.

Planning Tip

Generally, if the decedent leaves an estate large enough to be subject to estate tax, it usually is preferable to claim the deduction on the estate tax return. The top estate tax rate in 2006 is 46 percent compared with a top individual income tax rate of only 35 percent. What's more, *all* of the medical expenses can be deducted on the estate tax return; there is no 7.5 percent floor for this purpose.

Pitfall

If the personal representative opts to deduct medical expenses on the decedent's income tax return, the 7.5 percent portion that is not deductible cannot be claimed on the estate tax return.

EXAMPLES OF NONDEDUCTIBLE EXPENSES FOR A DECEDENT

Burial fees.

Cremation costs.

Funeral expenses.

Perpetual care for a grave or mausoleum.

Where to Claim the Benefit

If the personal representative opts to deduct the medical expenses on the decedent's income tax return, a statement must be attached to the return agreeing *not* to claim the expenses as a deduction on the decedent's estate tax return.

CHAPTER 3

Education Costs

No one doubts the importance of education—for ourselves, our children, and our grandchildren—but obtaining it can be pricey. According to the College Board, the average cost of one year in a private college today is over $30,000 (most of the top schools are about $40,000 annually), and the cost of higher education is increasing at about 5 percent annually (compared with an overall inflation rate of under 3 percent). Fortunately, the tax law provides many incentives to help you save for education and to pay for it on a tax-advantaged basis.

This chapter explains education-related tax benefits, including:

- Employer-paid courses
- Scholarships, fellowships, and grants
- Hope credit
- Lifetime learning credit
- Credit for attendance in schools within the Katrina Gulf Opportunity Zone
- Job-related education
- Tuition and fees deduction
- Student loan interest
- Interest on U.S. savings bonds
- Coverdell education savings accounts (ESAs)

- Qualified tuition programs (529 plans)
- Seminars
- Educational travel
- Cancellation of a student loan
- Penalty-free withdrawals from IRAs

For more information, see IRS Publication 970, *Tax Benefits for Education*.

Employer-Paid Courses

Companies want an educated workforce. Some are willing to underwrite the cost of additional education for their employees. The tax law not only allows companies to deduct the costs they pay on behalf of workers for higher education, but also workers can enjoy this fringe benefit tax free up to a set dollar amount each year.

Benefit

If your employer pays or reimburses you for the cost of higher education, you are not taxed on payments up to $5,250 annually. If the courses are job-related, there is no dollar limit to the exclusion from income for this employer-paid fringe benefit. This fringe benefit is not subject to Social Security and Medicare (FICA) taxes.

If you work for an educational institution and receive tuition reductions, such benefit may be excludable (see Conditions, next).

Conditions

Different conditions apply to employer-paid education under an education assistance plan and tuition reduction if you work for a college or university.

EMPLOYER-PAID EDUCATION. Employer-paid education must be furnished under an employer's education assistance plan that does not discriminate in favor of owners or highly paid employees.

The courses need *not* be job-related to qualify for the limited exclusion of $5,250 annually. For example, if you are currently a programmer and your employer pays for accounting courses, you can still exclude the benefit.

There is no dollar limit on the amount you can exclude from income if you meet the following three conditions:

1. The courses relate to your current job.
2. The courses do not qualify you for a new profession.
3. You have already met the job's minimum education standards.

For example, if you are a programmer who takes more programming courses, the value of this benefit is fully excludable.

TUITION REDUCTION. If you work for an educational institution, you are not taxed on tuition reductions for you, your spouse, and your dependents (as well as widows or widowers of deceased or former employees) if:

- The courses are undergraduate courses. However, if you are a graduate student who is a teaching or research assistant, you aren't taxed on tuition reduction as long as it is in addition to regular pay for your teaching or research activities.
- The benefit is *not* payment for teaching or other services. However, if you receive a scholarship under the National Health Services Corps Scholarship Program or the Armed Forces Health Professionals Scholarship Program, you can exclude any reduction despite your service requirements.

If you are eligible for tuition reduction, the benefit is not limited to courses taken at the school in which you work. You can exclude from your income the value of courses you take at any school covered by a tuition reduction agreement (area colleges and universities typically have reciprocal class agreements).

Planning Tip

If you are seeking a job and plan to pursue college or graduate courses while working, look for a company with an educational assistance plan. The value of this benefit can be substantial to you if you use it fully and should be factored into the salary being offered for the position.

Example

You are in the 28 percent tax bracket and in 2006 your employer pays for courses totaling $5,000. If you had to pay for these courses yourself, you would need to earn an additional $6,944 in income to have the funds to pay for the courses yourself (assuming you can't deduct them).

Pitfalls

Generally, you must attain a certain course grade for your employer to pay for the education. Make sure you understand what you must do to obtain reimbursement or have your course fully paid by your employer.

You cannot use any benefit received under an employer's plan as the basis for claiming a second tax benefit. For example, if your employer pays $2,000 for a course you take, you cannot claim an education credit for this amount.

Where to Claim the Exclusion

If employer-provided education is excludable from income, it is not reported on your return. You may find the amount of employer-paid education benefits reported on your Form W-2 for information purposes only; it is not added to your compensation.

Scholarships, Fellowships, and Grants

There are over 20 million scholarships worth more than $1 trillion available each year. This money is available through government programs, nonprofit organizations, and corporations that support education. Grants are made on the basis of need, scholastics, or special talents (such as athletics or music). The tax law enables you to receive this money on a tax-free basis under certain circumstances.

Benefit

If you are enrolled in a degree program at a school and receive a scholarship, fellowship, or grant, you can fully exclude it from income. There is no dollar limit on this exclusion.

If you are not enrolled in a degree program (for example, you take only two courses in a semester), you can exclude the portion of the grant for tuition, course-related fees, books, supplies, and equipment.

If you receive a Fulbright award, it is fully taxable (unless you can claim the foreign earned income exclusion explained in Chapter 14).

Condition

For tax-free treatment to apply, the grant must be for study in a degree program. A degree program includes:

- Primary and secondary school.
- College or university degree programs.
- Full-time or part-time scholarships for study at a school that provides an education program acceptable for full-time credit toward a degree or offers a program of training to prepare students for employment in a recognized occupation.

Planning Tip

For education planning purposes, obtaining a scholarship, fellowship, or grant is the best way to finance learning. The award doesn't cost you anything and doesn't have to be repaid. Explore carefully any grants to which you, a spouse, or a dependent may be entitled.

Pitfalls

If you are a graduate student who receives payment (a stipend) for teaching, doing research, or providing other services as a condition of the grant, you are taxed on the payment. Such amount is reported on Form W-2 and is subject to income tax withholding.

Generally, no exclusion can be claimed if receipt of a federal grant is conditioned on your performing services in the future. For example, if you receive a scholarship that requires you to teach for at least three years as a condition of the grant, you cannot exclude this grant from your income.

Where to Claim the Exclusion

If the grant is excludable from income, you do not have to report it on your return.

If the grant is partially taxable (for example, you are not a degree candidate and so are taxed on the portion of the grant for housing), you report this as other income in the "Income" section of Form 1040 or Form 1040A. If you are a graduate student receiving a stipend for services, such amounts are reported as wages on your return, regardless of which type of return you file.

Hope Credit

The tax law allows you to claim a limited tax credit, called the Hope credit, when you pay for higher education. The credit applies whether you pay out-of-pocket from savings or borrow the money. You may claim the credit each year you qualify for it.

Benefit

There are two tax credits related to higher education expenses: the Hope credit and the lifetime learning credit. If you meet certain conditions, you can claim the Hope credit for higher education costs of up to $1,650 per student (100 percent of the first $1,100 of costs, plus 50 percent of the next $1,100 of costs). Thus, for example, if you have twins who are freshmen in college, you can qualify for a credit of up to $3,300.

The credit limit is doubled for students in colleges and universities within the region hit by Hurricane Katrina (including counties in Alabama, Louisiana, and Mississippi), as explained later in this chapter.

Conditions

To claim the Hope credit, you must meet all five of these conditions:

1. Payments relate to the first two years of higher education.
2. Payments are made on behalf of an eligible student.
3. Payments are made to an eligible institution.
4. Payments cover qualified higher education costs.
5. Your modified adjusted gross income is not above a set limit.

FIRST TWO YEARS OF HIGHER EDUCATION. The credit applies for only the first two years of college or other postsecondary school. In effect, you can claim the credit only twice for the same student—for year one and for year two. This is so even if the student has not completed two full years (as measured by credits required for such completion).

Example

Your child starts college in September 2005, attending both the fall and spring semesters. Your child again enrolls in September 2006 for the fall and spring semesters. You may claim a credit for 2005 based on tuition for the fall semester (essentially half the year) and a credit in 2006 for the spring semester of your child's freshman year and the fall semester of his sophomore year (a full year). You cannot claim the Hope credit for tuition paid for the spring semester in 2007.

ELIGIBLE STUDENT. The credit may be claimed for you, your spouse, or your dependent for whom you claim an exemption on your return. The student must be enrolled for at least one academic period (a semester, trimester, or quarter) during the year.

No credit may be claimed if the student has a federal or state felony drug conviction on his or her record.

ELIGIBLE EDUCATIONAL INSTITUTION. Only payments to an eligible institution entitle you to claim the credit. This includes any accredited public, nonprofit, or proprietary postsecondary institution eligible to participate in the student aid programs administered by the U.S. Department of Education. Ask your school if it is eligible, or check www.studentaid.ed.gov.

Enrollment must lead to a degree, certificate, or other recognized educational credential.

QUALIFIED HIGHER EDUCATION COSTS. Qualified expenses include *only* tuition and related fees. Related fees can include, for example, a student activity fee paid to the institution if it is required for all students and no portion of it covers personal expenses. Hobby or sports courses and noncredit courses do not qualify for the credit *unless* they are part of the student's degree program.

The following costs do *not* qualify for the credit:

- Room and board (even if they are required to be paid to the institution as a condition of enrollment).
- Books and supplies (unless they are required to be purchased directly from the institution).

- Medical expenses.
- Transportation.
- Insurance.
- Personal living expenses.

As a practical matter, the institution furnishes the student with an information return showing the payment of qualified tuition and related expenses for the year. The return, Form 1098-T, Tuition Payments Statement, for 2006 is issued by January 31, 2007.

If you prepay expenses for an academic period that begins within the first three months of 2007, you can include this amount when figuring your 2006 credit.

Example

In December 2006 you pay tuition for your child for the semester beginning February 2007. You can include the tuition payment as part of qualified expenses in figuring your 2006 credit.

MAGI LIMIT. The ability to claim the credit depends on your modified adjusted gross income (MAGI). MAGI for this purpose is adjusted gross income increased by the foreign earned income exclusion and other foreign items.

If your MAGI is below a phaseout range, then the full credit can be claimed; a partial credit is allowed for those with MAGI within the range. No credit can be claimed if MAGI exceeds the range. The phaseout range is adjusted annually for inflation. Table 3.1 shows the phaseout ranges for 2006.

Example

In 2006, you are single, with MAGI of $50,000. Your top credit is limited to $825 (one half of the maximum credit of $1,650), since you are midway in the MAGI phaseout range. If your MAGI is $40,000, you can claim a credit up to $1,650; if your MAGI is over $55,000, you cannot claim any credit.

TABLE 3.1 2006 MAGI Phaseout Range for Hope Credit

Filing Status	MAGI
Married filing jointly	$90,000–110,000
Other filing status*	$45,000–55,000

*No credit may be claimed for married filing separately.

Planning Tips

You can claim the credit even though eligible expenses are paid with the proceeds of a loan. You can also claim the credit if eligible expenses are paid by someone other than you, your spouse, or your dependent, such as the student's grandparent. The payment is treated as having been made by the student, and as your dependent, this entitles you to claim the credit if you are otherwise eligible to do so.

As the parent, if you pay the expenses but your MAGI is too high to permit you to claim the credit, you can waive your right to do so. This will allow your child to claim the credit on his or her own return (assuming the child has tax liability and can benefit from the credit). Your child can claim the credit even though you pay the expenses.

To allow your child to claim the credit you must forgo the dependency exemption for your child. To make the waiver, you do not have to file any special waiver forms or attach any statements to your return or to the child's return.

If your child cannot use the credit, consider taking the above-the-line deduction for tuition and fees if you are qualified to do so (explained later in this chapter). The tuition and fees deduction has a higher MAGI limit so you may qualify for this benefit even though your MAGI prevents you from claiming the credit.

You may file for a tax refund if you were eligible to claim double the credit in 2005 with respect to a student in a college or university within the region hit by Hurricane Katrina but failed to do so. The larger credit can be claimed for a student who attended a school in the region in the spring of 2005 as well as one who enrolled in the fall but did not return after the storm.

Pitfalls

The credit must be coordinated with other education tax benefits you may be qualified to use. You can claim the credit in the same year in which you receive distributions from a Coverdell education savings account (ESA) or 529 plan. However, the expenses on which you base the credit cannot be the same expenses used to figure the tax-free portion of the distributions.

Example

Your child's college tuition bill for the year is $15,000. You pay $5,000 of this amount from a 529 plan. For purposes of figuring the credit, you can only take $10,000 of eligible expenses into account ($5,000 is used as a tax-free distribution from the 529 plan).

If you claim a credit and in a later year (after you have filed the return and claimed the credit) receive a refund of an amount that was used to figure the credit, you must recapture some or all of the credit. This means you must repay

Example

In 2006, you take a Hope credit of $1,650 based on $2,500 of tuition costs. In 2007, your child receives a grant reimbursing him for tuition of $1,000. You must recapture $500 (50 percent of $1,000). You report this recapture as "other income" on your 2007 return.

some or all of the credit. You treat the recaptured amount as additional tax liability for the year of recapture. Do not amend the return on which the credit was claimed.

You may not claim the Hope credit if you claim an above-the-line deduction for tuition and fees for a student (discussed later in this chapter). You must choose which write-off gives you the greater benefit, assuming you qualify for each.

Example

You are a single parent with MAGI in 2006 of $40,000 and pay $5,000 in tuition for your child. You can claim a Hope credit of $1,650, which gives you a tax savings of $1,650. Or you can claim an above-the-line deduction for tuition of $4,000, which gives you a tax savings of $1,000 if you are in the 25 percent tax bracket ($4,000 × 25%). In this case, you'd choose the credit alternative.

You cannot claim the credit for expenses that are paid by tax-free scholarships, fellowships, grants, veterans' educational assistance, or employer-provided educational assistance.

Where to Claim the Credit

The Hope credit is figured on Form 8863, Education Credits. The credit is then entered in the "Tax and Credits" section of Form 1040, or in the "Tax, Credits, and Payments" section of Form 1040A.

You may not claim the credit if you file Form 1040EZ.

Lifetime Learning Credit

The tax law allows you to claim a limited tax credit, called the lifetime learning credit, when you pay for higher education. The credit applies whether you pay out-of-pocket from savings or borrow the money. You may claim the credit each year you qualify for it.

Benefit

If certain conditions are met, you can claim a credit of up to $2,000 on your return for the payment of qualified higher education costs for you, your spouse, or your dependent. In contrast to the Hope credit, which is a per student credit, the lifetime learning credit is per taxpayer. So if you have three children in college, your lifetime learning credit for the year is limited to $2,000 (assuming you qualify to claim it).

Unlike the Hope credit, which applies only for the first two years of higher education, the lifetime learning credit can be claimed for any higher education, including graduate-level courses.

But like the Hope credit, the lifetime learning credit is doubled for students in colleges and universities within the region hit by Hurricane Katrina (see details later in this chapter).

Conditions

Most of the conditions for the lifetime learning credit are the same as those for the Hope credit detailed earlier, unless otherwise noted here. Thus, the same MAGI limits apply to the lifetime learning credit, and the same planning tips and pitfalls also apply.

ELIGIBLE STUDENT. There is no ban on claiming the lifetime learning credit for a student who has a felony drug conviction on his or her record, as there is for claiming the Hope credit.

HIGHER EDUCATION. Unlike the Hope credit, which can be claimed only for courses leading to a degree, the lifetime learning credit can be claimed for one or more courses at an eligible educational institution that are part of a postsecondary degree program or part of a nondegree program taken to acquire or improve job skills. In other words, the student does not need to be pursuing a degree or other recognized educational credential.

There is no limit on the number of years for which the lifetime learning credit may be claimed.

Planning Tip

Since the lifetime learning credit cannot be claimed for a student for whom a Hope credit is claimed, decide which credit produces the greater tax savings. As a general rule, assuming that either credit could be claimed, you will probably be better off taking the lifetime learning credit if qualifying expenses exceed $7,500; if expenses are below this amount, then the Hope credit may be the better choice.

Pitfalls

The same pitfalls applicable to the Hope credit apply to the lifetime learning credit.

Where to Claim the Credit

The lifetime learning credit is figured on Form 8863, Education Credits. The credit is then entered in the "Tax and Credits" section of Form 1040, or in the

"Tax, Credits, and Payments" section of Form 1040A. You may not claim the credit if you file Form 1040EZ.

Credit for Attendance in Schools within the Katrina Gulf Opportunity Zone

To encourage students to enroll in colleges and universities within the area designated by Congress as the Katrina Gulf Opportunity Zone, the education credits are increased.

Benefit

For 2006, the Hope credit and lifetime learning credit are expanded for students in schools in the area affected by Hurricane Katrina. The expanded credits include:

- Hope credit limitation increases to $3,300 (instead of $1,650).
- Lifetime learning credit limitation increases to $4,000 (instead of $2,000).
- Room and board expenses can qualify for the credits.

Conditions

The expanded credits apply only to students attending colleges and universities within the area designated as the Katrina Gulf Opportunity Zone, which includes designated counties in Alabama, Louisiana, and Mississippi. These breaks apply to both returning students as well as new students who enroll in schools within the area.

Planning Tip

The credit applied in 2005 as well and could have been claimed, even for students who did not complete their normal school term because of the hurricane.

Pitfall

The expanded education credits do not apply to students attending schools in the areas affected by Hurricanes Rita and Wilma.

Where to Claim the Credit

The credit is reported on Form 8863, Education Credits. The credit is then entered in the "Tax and Credits" section of Form 1040, or in the "Tax, Credits, and Payments" section of Form 1040A. You may not claim the credit if you file Form 1040EZ.

Job-Related Education

Americans are always trying to better themselves. Whether you are a teacher taking courses toward an advanced degree or a data processor learning the latest technology, you may be eligible to deduct your education costs.

Benefit

If you pay for education related to your current line of work, you may be able to deduct your expenses.

If you qualify for the deduction by meeting all of the conditions, you claim the deduction as a miscellaneous itemized deduction if you are an employee or as a business expense if you are self-employed. This means that if you are an employee, you can take the deduction only if your miscellaneous itemized deductions exceed 2 percent of your adjusted gross income. There is no dollar limit on this deduction.

Conditions

To deduct education expenses, you must meet all five of these conditions:

1. You are an employee or self-employed.
2. You already meet the minimum job requirements for your work (as set by your employer or state law).
3. The courses maintain or improve your skills or you are required by your employer or by law to take the course to keep your current salary or position.
4. The courses do not lead to a new line of work.
5. You pay for eligible education expenses.

EMPLOYED OR SELF-EMPLOYED. You cannot deduct the cost of courses taken before you start to work.

MINIMUM JOB REQUIREMENTS. Minimum job requirements are based on a review of your employer's standards, the laws and regulations of your state, and the standards of your profession or business. Just because you are currently employed doesn't automatically mean you meet minimum job requirements. You may be hired provisionally on the condition that you complete certain courses.

If job requirements change after you enter the job market or profession, any courses you take to meet the new standards are deductible.

Example

You graduated from college with a degree in physical therapy and start to work in your chosen occupation. Then state law is changed to require physical therapists to complete at least one year of graduate school to retain certification. You can deduct the cost of the additional year of schooling because you had already met your initial minimum job requirements.

MAINTAIN OR IMPROVE SKILLS OR REQUIRED BY EMPLOYER OR BY LAW. General education courses are not deductible. The courses must be designed to keep you up-to-date and qualified.

Courses that give you a specialty *within* your current line of work are deductible.

EXAMPLES OF DEDUCTIBLE COURSES

- Attorney in practice who takes LLM courses to obtain a master's degree in taxation.
- Continuing education courses by professionals.
- Dentist who takes courses in orthodontics. This postgraduate schooling improves professional skills as a dentist.
- Practicing psychiatrist who takes courses at an accredited psychoanalytic institution.
- Psychiatrist who takes personal therapy sessions.
- Salesperson who is encouraged by his or her employer to pursue an MBA degree in order to move up in the company because the degree merely enhances his skills.
- Teachers may deduct courses taken for job changes within the teaching profession (e.g., elementary to secondary school, one classroom subject to another, classroom teacher to guidance counselor, and classroom teacher to principal).

NOT A NEW LINE OF WORK. If the courses enable you to follow a new line of work, they are not deductible.

EXAMPLES OF NONDEDUCTIBLE COURSES

- Law school (even by someone who intends to continue in his or her original line of work, such as accounting).
- Nurse who takes courses that qualify him to become a physician's assistant.

ELIGIBLE EDUCATION EXPENSES. If you qualify for the deduction, it is not limited to the cost of tuition and fees as is the case with many other types of education tax breaks. The deduction applies not only to the cost of courses but also to:

- Books and supplies.
- Local transportation expenses to and from the course, including bus, subway, or train fares. If you use your car, you can deduct mileage at the rate of 44.5 cents per mile, plus parking and tolls.

- Lodging, meals, and transportation. If you attend courses out of town, you can deduct away-from-home expenses. The deduction for meals is limited to 50 percent of actual cost.

Planning Tip

Check to see whether education expenses qualify for an education credit or the above-the-line tuition and fees deduction, which may provide a greater tax benefit than an itemized deduction subject to the 2 percent floor.

Pitfalls

As a practical matter, even if your costs for taking courses are eligible for the deduction, you may not achieve any meaningful tax benefit from claiming them. First, as mentioned earlier, the deduction is limited to amounts exceeding 2 percent of your adjusted gross income. Thus, if your AGI is $50,000, your total miscellaneous itemized deductions must exceed $1,000 to claim any write-off; you lose the first $1,000 of deductions.

Second, claiming miscellaneous itemized deductions can trigger or increase the alternative minimum tax (AMT). The reason: Miscellaneous itemized deductions are *not* deductible for AMT purposes.

Where to Claim the Deduction

You must file Form 1040 to claim the deduction; you cannot claim the deduction if you file Form 1040A or 1040EZ.

If you are an employee, you complete Form 2106, Employee Business Expenses, or 2106-EZ, Unreimbursed Employee Business Expenses, to figure your unreimbursed employee expenses that are then deducted on Schedule A.

If you are self-employed, you deduct the expenses directly as a business expense on Schedule C.

Tuition and Fees Deduction *(Provision expired 12/31/05. Extension expected for 2006.)*

The tax law allows you to claim a limited deduction when you pay for higher education. The deduction applies whether you pay out-of-pocket from savings or borrow the money. You may claim the deduction each year you qualify for it.

Benefit

If you pay tuition and fees for higher education for you, your spouse, or a dependent, you may be able to deduct up to $4,000 in 2006 as an adjustment to gross income, even if you don't itemize your other deductions.

Conditions

To claim the deduction for tuition and fees, you must meet all five of these conditions:

1. Be an eligible taxpayer.
2. Make payments to an eligible educational institution.
3. Pay qualified expenses.
4. Have MAGI below a set amount.
5. You do not claim an education credit.

ELIGIBLE TAXPAYER. You can claim the deduction for you, your spouse, or your dependent for whom you claim an exemption on your return.

You may not claim the deduction if you are married filing separately. You may not claim the deduction if you can be claimed as a dependent on another taxpayer's return.

ELIGIBLE EDUCATIONAL INSTITUTION. Only tuition and fees paid to an eligible educational institution qualify for the deduction. An eligible educational institution includes any college, university, vocational school, or postsecondary institution eligible to participate in the financial aid programs of the U.S. Department of Education.

QUALIFIED EXPENSES. The same expenses that qualify for the Hope credit discussed earlier qualify for the tuition and fees deduction. Student activity fees and even the cost of books can be treated as deductible fees if the cost is paid to the eligible educational institution. As a practical matter, the institution furnishes the student with an information return showing the payment of qualified tuition and related expenses for the year. The return, Form 1098-T, Tuition Payments Statement, for 2006 is issued by January 31, 2007.

Qualified expenses do not include any amounts paid by tax-free scholarships, tax-free distributions from Coverdell education savings accounts or 529 plans, and excludable interest from the redemption of U.S. savings bonds.

Qualified expenses paid directly to the educational institution under a court-approved divorce decree are treated as paid by the student (not by the person making the payments), so only the student is eligible to claim the deduction. Remember that the student can claim the deduction only if he or she cannot be claimed as the dependent of another taxpayer.

The same treatment applies to qualified expenses paid by someone else (such as a grandparent). Again, the student is treated as making the payment, and the student is eligible to claim the deduction only if he or she cannot be claimed as the dependent of another taxpayer.

MAGI LIMIT. You can claim the deduction only if your MAGI is no more than the limit found in Table 3.2. MAGI for this purpose is adjusted gross income increased by the foreign earned income exclusion, income from Puerto Rico or American Samoa, or the foreign housing exclusion or deduction.

Example

You are married and file a joint return with your spouse. If your MAGI is:

- **No more than $130,000, your deduction is $4,000.**
- **More than $130,000 but not more than $160,000, your deduction is $2,000.**
- **Over $160,000, your deduction is zero.**

NO EDUCATION CREDIT. You cannot claim the deduction for a student's expenses for which you claim a Hope credit or lifetime learning credit (education credits). If you qualify for both the tuition and fees deduction and an education credit, you must choose the write-off that provides the greater benefit; generally this will be a credit.

Planning Tip

Compare the tax savings from claiming the deduction with the savings from an education credit. Remember that the amount of a credit equals the amount of your tax savings from claiming it. Usually the tax credit provides the greater benefit. Use the following worksheet to compare your tax savings:

Tuition and Fees Deduction		Education Credit	
Amount of deduction	$______________	Amount of credit	$______________
× your tax bracket	$______________		
Tax savings	$______________	Tax savings	$______________

TABLE 3.2 2006 MAGI Limits for Tuition Deduction

Filing Status*	MAGI Limit for $4,000 Deduction	MAGI Limit for $2,000 Deduction
Married filing jointly	Not more than $130,000	More than $130,000 but not more than $160,000
Other taxpayers	Not more than $65,000	More than $65,000 but not more than $80,000

*You cannot claim the deduction if you are married filing separately.

Example

You are single and your MAGI permits you to claim either a $4,000 tuition and fees deduction or a $2,000 lifetime learning credit. You are in the 25 percent tax bracket. The deduction provides you with a $1,000 tax savings ($4,000 × 25%). The credit provides you with a $2,000 tax savings. But if your MAGI limited your lifetime learning credit to less than $1,000 (e.g., your MAGI is $50,000), you would reap a greater tax savings by claiming the deduction.

Pitfall

Even one dollar over the MAGI limit prevents you from claiming a deduction. There is no phaseout of this deduction, as there is with many other deductions.

Where to Claim the Deduction

The deduction is claimed on Form 1040 or 1040A in the section called "Adjusted Gross Income." No special form or schedule is required. You cannot claim the deduction if you file Form 1040EZ.

Student Loan Interest

Millions of students must borrow money to pay for their education. Repayment of student loans runs between 5 and 30 years. Fortunately, the tax law allows interest on student loans to be deductible each year within limits.

Benefit

If you pay interest on student loans, you may be able to deduct up to $2,500 of interest as an adjustment to gross income (if your actual interest payment is more than $2,500, your deduction is limited to that amount). There is no limit on the number of years you can claim this deduction; as long as you continue to pay off the loan, you can deduct your interest if eligible to do so.

If the loan is canceled, you may qualify for tax-free treatment on the debt forgiveness (explained later in this chapter).

Conditions

There are a couple of conditions for claiming a deduction for student loan interest as an adjustment to gross income. You must meet both:

1. The loan must be a qualified loan.
2. Your modified adjusted gross income cannot exceed a set limit (there is a partial deduction allowed if MAGI falls within a phaseout range).

LOAN QUALIFICATIONS. To be treated as a student loan for which interest is deductible, the loan must have been taken out solely to pay qualified education expenses. Qualified education expenses relate to a qualified educational institution (virtually all accredited public, nonpublic, and proprietary postsecondary institutions are eligible educational institutions). Qualified education expenses include:

- Tuition and fees.
- Room and board.
- Books, supplies, and equipment.
- Other necessary expenses (including transportation to and from school).

You cannot deduct interest on a loan from a related person or made under a qualified employer plan. Related persons include:

- Spouses.
- Siblings and half-siblings.
- Parents.
- Grandparents.
- Children.
- Grandchildren.
- Certain corporations, partnerships, trusts, and exempt organizations.

The loan must be for you, your spouse, or your dependent (in the year you take out the loan). The loan must be taken for an eligible student, who is enrolled at least half-time in a degree program.

You must be legally obligated to make payments on the loan. For example, if your child took out the loan and you are now helping her make the payments, you cannot deduct the interest because you are not the borrower (you are not legally responsible for the loan).

If the loan is a revolving line of credit (e.g., credit card debt), interest qualifies as student loan interest only if funds on the line are used solely to pay qualified education expenses.

MAGI LIMITS. You can claim the full deduction if your modified adjusted gross income is below the phaseout range. A partial deduction is permitted if your MAGI is within the phaseout range. No deduction can be claimed if your MAGI exceeds the phaseout range, which is adjusted annually for inflation. Table 3.3 shows the 2006 phaseout ranges for claiming the student interest deduction.

Example

You are single and graduated from college in May 2006. You start to pay back your loans, paying interest in 2006 of $800. You can deduct this amount in full if your MAGI is under $50,000. If, however, you landed your dream job and earned $70,000 in just seven months remaining in 2006, you cannot deduct *any* of your student loan interest because your MAGI is above the limit for your filing status.

TABLE 3.3 2006 Phaseout Ranges for Student Interest Deduction

Filing Status*	MAGI
Unmarried (single), head of household, and surviving widow(er)	$ 50,000–65,000
Married filing jointly	$105,000–135,000

*You cannot claim the deduction if you are married filing separately.

Planning Tip

If you have been paying off a qualified loan for many years but stopped claiming interest deductions after five years, you may now resume deducting your interest. The old 60-month limit on interest no longer applies after 2001.

Pitfall

You cannot claim a double benefit for the same interest deduction. For example, if you take out a home equity loan to pay your child's college expenses, you cannot claim a student interest deduction if you deduct the mortgage interest as an itemized deduction. It is, of course, more favorable to treat the interest as student loan interest to the extent possible.

Where to Claim the Deduction

The deduction is claimed on Form 1040 or 1040A in the section called "Adjusted Gross Income." No special form or schedule is required. However, you can use a worksheet in the instructions to your return to figure your allowable deduction if your MAGI falls within the phaseout range.

You cannot claim the deduction if you file Form 1040EZ.

Interest on U.S. Savings Bonds

The first savings bonds, series A, were issued in 1935 at 75 percent of face value in denominations of $25 to $1,000, paying 2.9 percent accrued interest, and were sold through the U.S. Post Office. Since then savings bonds have become a permanent investment vehicle. Americans purchase an average of $8 million in U.S. savings bonds per week. If you happen to be holding these bonds and decide to cash them in to pay for higher education costs, you may be eligible to receive the interest tax free.

Benefit

If you redeem U.S. savings bonds to pay for qualified higher education costs or to contribute to a 529 plan or Coverdell education savings account, you are not taxed on the interest as long as your modified adjusted gross income is below a set amount. There is no dollar limit to this benefit; if you qualify you can exclude from income all of the interest received on the redemption of the bonds.

Conditions

Assuming you have not been reporting interest on the savings bonds annually but deferring it, you can claim the exclusion if you meet all four of these conditions:

1. Eligible bonds.
2. Eligible taxpayer.
3. MAGI limit.
4. Qualified use of redemption proceeds.

ELIGIBLE BONDS. The exclusion applies only to series EE bonds issued after 1989 or series I bonds. You cannot claim the exclusion when redeeming older EE bonds or E bonds.

ELIGIBLE TAXPAYER. You must be the purchaser of the bond and hold it in your name or the joint name of you and your spouse. You must have been at least 24 years old when you purchased the bonds.

No exclusion can be claimed for interest on bonds held in the child's name or in the joint name of you and your child.

If you are married, you must file jointly to claim the exclusion.

MAGI LIMIT. To claim a full or partial exclusion you cannot have modified adjusted gross income (MAGI) over a fixed dollar limit (which is adjusted annually for inflation). MAGI for this purpose means AGI increased by the redeemed interest, the deductions for tuition and fees and for student loan interest, foreign earned income exclusion and other foreign items, and the exclusion for employer-paid adoption.

Table 3.4 shows the phaseout range for 2006. If your MAGI is below the start of the phaseout range, you can claim a full exclusion. If your MAGI is over the phase-

TABLE 3.4 2006 Phaseout Ranges for Savings Bond Interest Exclusion

Filing Status	MAGI
Unmarried (single) and head of household	$63,100–78,100
Married filing jointly and surviving widow(er)	$94,700–124,700

out range, no exclusion can be claimed, even if all of the other conditions are met. If your MAGI is within the phaseout range, you can claim a partial exclusion.

Example

In 2006, you are married filing jointly with MAGI of $109,700. You redeem bonds with interest of $5,000, and you use all of the redemption proceeds for qualified higher education expenses. You can exclude $2,500 of the $5,000 interest because your MAGI is in the middle of the phaseout range.

QUALIFIED USE OF REDEMPTION PROCEEDS. The proceeds must be used only for a qualified purpose:

- Paying higher education costs (tuition and fees for a college, university, or vocational school that meets federal financial aid standards). The higher education expenses can be for you, your spouse, or a dependent.
- Funding a 529 plan or a Coverdell education savings account.

If the proceeds from the redemption exceed the amount used for a qualified purpose, you can exclude a portion of the interest based on the ratio of expenses (or funding) to the redemption amount.

Example

In 2006, you redeem bonds worth $10,000, using $5,000 to pay your child's qualified higher education costs. Interest on the bonds is $3,000. Since half of the proceeds were used for qualified expenses, half of the interest, or $1,500, is eligible for the exclusion (assuming the other conditions are met).

Planning Tips

If you are holding EE or I savings bonds and want to know how much they are worth today, you can check their redemption values at www.savingsbonds.gov.

The U.S. Treasury has changed the way in which interest on Series EE bonds is computed. Rather than adjusting the interest semiannually, these bonds now pay a fixed rate until redemption or maturity. As a result, Series I bonds may be a better option because their interest rate still adjusts semiannually for inflation.

Pitfalls

You cannot use this exclusion to pay college expenses for your grandchild *unless* the grandchild is your dependent in the year in which the bonds are redeemed.

You cannot claim the exclusion if you are married and file a separate return from your spouse.

Where to Claim the Exclusion

If you claim the exclusion, you must complete Form 8815, Exclusion of Interest from Series EE and I Bonds Issued after 1989, and attach it to your return.

Coverdell Education Savings Accounts

Is the high cost of a prep school or college in your child or grandchild's future? If you decide to help save for this expense, consider doing so using a tax-advantaged savings account, called a Coverdell education savings account (ESA), designed for this purpose.

Benefit

You may be able to contribute up to $2,000 annually to a savings account for each beneficiary. The account is called a Coverdell education savings account (ESA) (it used to be called an education IRA). The account can have multiple contributors, but no more than $2,000 can be placed in the account for any one year.

Earnings on contributions accumulate tax deferred. If withdrawals from the account are used to pay qualified education expenses, the earnings become tax free.

Conditions

There are a couple of conditions for funding a Coverdell education savings account as well as for taking tax-free distributions.

1. For purposes of contributions, they can be made only on behalf of an eligible beneficiary (defined next) by a contributor whose modified adjusted gross income does not exceed set limits. Contributions must be made in cash, not property.
2. For purposes of tax-free distributions, funds must be used only for eligible expenses.

ELIGIBLE BENEFICIARY. Generally, a beneficiary is a person who is under the age of 18 at the time the contribution is made. Thus, for example, if a beneficiary attains the age of 18 on July 1, 2006, contributions can be made through June 30, 2006.

A beneficiary can also be a special needs person over the age of 18. A special needs beneficiary is one who requires additional time to complete his or her education because of a physical, mental, or emotional condition. This would include, for example, a person with a learning disability.

MAGI FOR CONTRIBUTORS. There is no familial requirement for contributors. Anyone can make a Coverdell education savings account contribution on behalf of an eligible beneficiary, as long as the contributor meets MAGI limits. Contributions can even be made by the beneficiary herself.

In order to contribute the full $2,000 to a Coverdell education savings account, your modified adjusted gross income cannot be more than a set limit. MAGI for this purpose means adjusted gross income increased by the foreign earned income exclusion, the foreign housing exclusion or deduction, the exclusion for income from American Samoa, or the exclusion for income from Puerto Rico.

A reduced contribution limit applies if your MAGI falls within a phaseout range. No contribution can be made if your MAGI exceeds the phaseout range, which is adjusted annually for inflation. The MAGI phaseout range for Coverdell ESA contributors in 2006 may be found in Table 3.5.

Example

In 2006, you are a single parent with MAGI of $80,000. You can make a $2,000 contribution on behalf of your 12-year-old child. But if your MAGI is between $95,000 and $110,000, only part of the $2,000 may be contributed (you figure the limit using a worksheet provided in IRS Publication 970).

CASH CONTRIBUTIONS. Contributions must be made in cash; you cannot contribute property to a Coverdell ESA. If you own stocks or mutual funds, you must sell the property and invest the proceeds. You may incur a capital gain on the sale of property.

TABLE 3.5 **2006 MAGI Phaseout Ranges for Coverdell ESA Contributors**

Filing Status	MAGI Phaseout Range
Married filing jointly	$190,000–220,000
Other taxpayers	$ 95,000–110,000

ELIGIBLE EXPENSES. Unlike most other education tax breaks that are restricted to higher education, Coverdell education savings accounts can be used for education in grades K–12 and/or for higher education. Primary and secondary school can be public, private, or religious school.

The range of eligible expenses for which tax-free withdrawals can be made is quite broad. Just about anything related to education is a qualified expense.

EXAMPLES OF ELIGIBLE ELEMENTARY AND SECONDARY SCHOOL EXPENSES

Academic tutoring.

Books.

Computer and peripheral equipment; software only if it is predominantly educational in nature.

Extended day programs required or provided by the school.

Internet access.

Special services for a special needs beneficiary.

Supplies.

Transportation.

Uniforms.

EXAMPLES OF ELIGIBLE HIGHER EDUCATION EXPENSES

Books, supplies, and equipment.

Room and board.

Tuition and fees.

Planning Tips

You can open a Coverdell education savings account at any bank or other financial institution that has received IRS approval to offer Coverdell ESAs. You can then select the investments you prefer, from certificates of deposit to stocks and mutual funds (to the extent available from the institution you select).

Just like IRA contributions, contributions to Coverdell ESAs can be made up to the due date of the return for the year to which they relate. However, obtaining a filing extension does not extend the deadline for making contributions.

Example

Contributions for 2006 may be made up to April 16, 2007, even if the contributor and/or the beneficiary has obtained a six-month filing extension.

You can turn taxable custodial accounts into tax-free Coverdell education savings accounts by using the funds in the custodial account for contributions. However, only cash contributions are permitted to a Coverdell education savings account, so investments in the custodial accounts must first be sold so that the proceeds can be contributed.

Example

Junior has $5,000 in a custodial account that owns shares in a mutual fund, the earnings from which are reported annually as taxable income to Junior. He can opt to sell $2,000 from the mutual fund in his custodial account each year and contribute the proceeds to a Coverdell education savings account of which he is the designated beneficiary (assuming he meets the age and MAGI limits). The account can own shares in the same mutual fund, but now the earnings become tax deferred and, if funds are withdrawn for qualified expenses, they become tax free.

You can change accounts from one financial institution to another by means of a tax-free rollover. You may not be satisfied with the service or investment options you have at one financial institution and can switch by means of a rollover to another financial institution.

You can move money in a Coverdell ESA between certain beneficiaries on a tax-free basis. The amount withdrawn from a Coverdell ESA can be rolled over to the same or a new designated beneficiary who is a member of the original beneficiary's family (listed in the next section). The rollover must be completed within 60 days. There are no tax consequences to naming a new designated beneficiary (as long as such beneficiary is permissible).

Pitfalls

If you contribute more than $2,000 on behalf of a beneficiary within one year, the excess amount is subject to a 6 percent excise tax. The penalty is paid by the beneficiary (not the contributor). But the penalty can be avoided by with-

Example

In 2006, Aunt Mary contributes $2,000 to a Coverdell ESA for Amy. Unaware of Aunt Mary's contribution, Uncle Ed also contributes $2,000 to a Coverdell ESA for Amy in 2006. Amy can avoid the 6 percent excise tax on the excess $2,000 contribution by withdrawing it, plus any earnings, by May 31, 2007. (Whether she chooses to give it back to Aunt Mary or Uncle Ed or split it between them is up to Amy.)

drawing the excess contribution, plus any earnings on the contribution, before the beginning of the sixth month following the year of the contribution (e.g., by May 31, 2007, for 2006 contributions).

The 6 percent excise tax continues to apply each year in which excess contributions (and earnings on excess contributions) remain in the Coverdell ESA.

Taxable distributions, which are withdrawals made to pay for noneligible expenses, are not only taxed as ordinary income but are subject to a 10 percent additional tax. However, the 10 percent penalty does not apply to distributions that meet any of these conditions:

- Distributions are made to a beneficiary or to the estate of a designated beneficiary on or after the death of a designated beneficiary.
- Distributions are made because the designated beneficiary is disabled.
- Distributions are made because the designated beneficiary received a tax-free grant or educational assistance allowance that equals or exceeds the distribution.
- Distributions are taxable only because the qualified expenses are reduced by expenses taken into account in figuring an education credit.

Withdrawals from a Coverdell ESA can be made in the same year in which an education credit is claimed. However, the same expenses cannot be used for both benefits.

Withdrawals from both a Coverdell ESA and a 529 plan are permitted in the same year. But if total withdrawals exceed qualified higher education expenses, the expenses must be allocated between the Coverdell ESA and 529 plan to figure the taxable portion of the withdrawals. Generally, the allocation is based on the ratio of the Coverdell ESA withdrawals to the total withdrawals.

Example

In 2006, Henry begins college and withdraws \$800 from a Coverdell ESA and \$3,200 from a 529 plan to pay \$3,000 of eligible expenses. Of the \$800 withdrawn, \$600 is tax free: \$800 Coverdell ESA withdrawal ÷ \$4,000 total withdrawals = 0.2; 0.2 × \$3,000 qualified expenses = \$600.

Funds remaining in the account become taxable to the beneficiary within 30 days of attaining age 30 (or within 30 days of death if the beneficiary dies before age 30). The 30-year age limit does not apply to a special needs beneficiary (defined earlier).

However, tax on the earnings in the account can be avoided if the balance in the account is transferred to another eligible beneficiary within 60 days of attaining age 30 (or death if earlier). An eligible beneficiary for this purpose includes members of the beneficiary's family:

- Spouse.
- Child or stepchild.
- Grandchild.
- Brother, sister, half-brother, or half-sister.
- Niece or nephew.
- Parent or stepparent.
- Grandparent.
- In-laws and the spouses of any of the listed relatives.

Where to Claim the Exclusion

Contributions to a Coverdell education savings account are not reported on the return of the contributor or the beneficiary. Similarly, withdrawals that are not taxable are not reported on any return.

If contributions are subject to the 6 percent excise tax, the beneficiary figures the excise tax in Part V of Form 5329, Additional Taxes on Qualified Plans (Including IRAs) and Other Tax-Favored Accounts, and report it as "Other Taxes" on Form 1040.

If withdrawals from a Coverdell ESA are taxable, they are reported on the beneficiary's return as "other income" on the return on Form 1040 or in the "Income" section on Form 1040A. If they are also subject to the 10 percent additional tax, this amount is figured in Part II of Form 5329, Additional Taxes on Qualified Plans (Including IRAs) and Other Tax-Favored Accounts.

Qualified Tuition Programs (529 Plans)

You can help save for the higher education expenses of your child or grandchild using a tax-advantaged account called a 529 plan. The 529 plan is a qualified tuition program offering federal (and in some cases state) tax incentives for savings.

Benefit

There are two types of qualified tuition programs (QTPs): a prepayment plan under which payments are guaranteed to cover (or partially cover) tuition, regardless of tuition increases, and a savings-type plan in which the funds you will have available to pay for higher education depend on the investment performance of your account. From a tax perspective, however, both types of plans are governed by the same tax rules under Section 529 of the Internal Revenue Code (hence the name "529 plans"), and both types of plans have the same benefits and conditions.

While contributions to qualified tuition programs do not generate a federal income tax deduction or credit, the long-term benefits are considerable:

- Earnings within the plan are tax deferred.
- If funds in the plan are used to pay qualified higher education costs, they are tax free (the earnings on the contributions are never taxed in this case).
- Unused amounts can be transferred tax free to another beneficiary if the original beneficiary does not go to college or otherwise need the funds.

There may be state income tax breaks for the contributions to qualified tuition programs as well. For example, if you are a resident in New York, you can deduct contributions to the New York 529 College Savings Program up to $5,000 per taxpayer per year on your New York state income tax return.

Conditions

Most conditions and requirements are fixed by each state's own 529 plan. However, for tax purposes, there are a couple of key conditions to obtaining all of the benefits under a qualified tuition program.

1. Contributions can be made only to qualified tuition programs. There are no federal tax limits on annual or total contributions to a 529 plan. These limits are fixed by each state's unique program.
2. Distributions can be withdrawn only for qualified expenses.

QUALIFIED TUITION PROGRAMS. Contributions can be made only to state plans and IRS-approved private college/university plans. A personally devised plan, even one that mimics the investment strategies of the state plans, does not entitle you to these benefits.

At present, all states offer savings-type plans and nearly two dozen have prepaid tuition plans.

QUALIFIED EXPENSES. For distributions from qualified tuition programs to be tax free, they must be used only to pay for qualified expenses. These include tuition for higher education, fees, books, supplies, and room and board (if the student is enrolled at least half time).

There is no set dollar limit on these expenses, including room and board. Thus, any reasonable amount for room and board (including expenses of off-campus housing) can qualify.

Planning Tips

The terms and conditions of qualified tuition programs vary considerably from state to state. You can learn about the investment options, fees, and other rules on state 529 plans at www.savingforcollege.com. For details on the private 529 plan created by a consortium of private colleges and universities (nearly 250 schools now participate), go to www.independent529plan.org.

If you plan for your child to attend your alma mater on a legacy basis, ask the school whether it offers or plans to offer a tuition prepayment plan.

Qualified tuition programs can be used effectively for estate planning purposes. For example, a wealthy grandparent can reduce the size of his or her estate while funding an education savings plan for a grandchild with little or no gift tax cost. If you plan to make sizable contributions in one year, you can elect to treat the contributions as made equally over five years. This will entitle you to apply the annual gift tax exclusion five times to avoid or reduce gift tax.

Example

In 2006, when the annual gift tax exclusion is $12,000 per beneficiary, you contribute $60,000 (or $120,000 per couple) to a state savings plan for your grandchild. Since you can treat the $60,000 as having been made ratably over five years, there is no taxable gift in this transfer. The transfer is fully offset by the annual gift tax exclusion ($12,000 × 5).

If the contribution exceeds this limit, the excess amount is treated as a gift in the year the contribution is made.

Amounts in a 529 plan can be transferred to a new beneficiary or rolled over tax free within 60 days of a distribution. There is a limit of one transfer or rollover per year. However, a beneficiary can be changed without making a transfer or rollover; the new name is substituted for the old one on the same account. This option applies only if the new beneficiary is a member of the old beneficiary's family, which includes:

- Child or grandchild.
- Stepson or stepdaughter.

- Sibling or stepsibling.
- Parent or grandparent.
- Stepparent.
- Aunt or uncle.
- Niece or nephew.
- Son-in-law, daughter-in-law, father-in-law, mother-in-law, brother-in-law, or sister-in-law.
- The spouse of any relative listed above.
- First cousin.

In the case of a savings-type 529 plan, if the account declines in value from the amount contributed, the loss can be recognized when all of the funds in the account are distributed. The IRS says that the loss is claimed as a miscellaneous itemized deduction on Schedule A of Form 1040, which is deductible to the extent total miscellaneous itemized deductions exceed 2 percent of adjusted gross income. Some tax experts believe that the loss is simply claimed as an ordinary loss. This theory has yet to be tested in court.

Pitfalls

If funds are withdrawn from a 529 plan and *not* used for qualified education expenses, earnings on the distribution are taxable. For example, if part of a distribution is used for spending money or travel expenses, the earnings on this portion of the distribution are taxable. The cost of a computer may or may not be a qualified education expense.

Example

If $25,000 is withdrawn and $20,000 is used for qualified expenses while $5,000 is used for spending and travel money, earnings on the $5,000 portion of the distribution are taxable.

In addition, the portion of the distribution representing earnings on contributions is subject to a 10 percent penalty.

Withdrawals from a 529 plan can be made in the same year in which an education credit is claimed, but the same expenses cannot be used for both benefits.

If withdrawals are made from a 529 plan and Coverdell ESA in the same year and the total withdrawal exceeds qualified education expenses, a portion of the withdrawal is taxable. How to figure the taxable portion was explained earlier in the Coverdell Education Savings Accounts section, under "Pitfalls."

Where to Claim the Exclusion

Contributions to qualified tuition programs need not be reported on the return of the contributor or the return of the beneficiary.

Distributions from qualified tuition programs need not be reported if they are tax free. To figure the tax-free portion of distributions, you can use a worksheet for this purpose in IRS Publication 970. For any year in which distributions are made, the 529 plan must send you (and the IRS) an information return, Form 1099-Q, Qualified Tuition Program. For distributions in 2006, the return must be issued no later than January 31, 2007.

Seminars

You've seen the ads: Attend a seminar to learn all about this subject or that. While some seminars are free of charge, others can cost hundreds or even thousands of dollars. From a tax standpoint, the cost of seminars is deductible only under limited circumstances.

Benefit

Job-related seminars may be deducted if the conditions for job-related education discussed earlier in this chapter are met.

No deduction can be claimed for seminars on self-improvement that are not job-related. No deduction can be claimed for investment seminars.

Where on the Return to Claim the Deduction

See job-related education discussed earlier in this chapter.

Educational Travel

Saint Augustine said, "The world is a book, and those who do not travel read only a page." Taxwise, the cost of travel usually is a nondeductible personal expense. But there are exceptions for which the cost of travel may be deductible.

Benefit

They say travel is broadening (a century ago, wealthy young men and women used to "take the grand tour" as a coming-of-age lesson). From a tax perspective, however, a deduction for educational travel is extremely limited. As a general rule, no deduction can be claimed for educational travel. However, this ban does not apply to overseas courses and lectures, the cost of which may qualify for a job-related education deduction.

Conditions

To be deductible as job-related education, travel must meet all of the conditions discussed earlier in this chapter.

Planning Tip

Overseas courses need not be taken for credit to qualify for a deduction. For example, an English teacher who took a course on Greek myths in Greece taught by university professors was allowed a deduction for her travel expenses and course registration fees even though she did not take the courses for credit.

Pitfall

No deduction can be claimed for travel that is merely beneficial. For example, an architect who travels to Europe to view cathedrals there cannot deduct the cost of the trip as an education expense.

Where to Claim the Deduction

See job-related education earlier in this chapter.

Cancellation of a Student Loan

If you are facing mountains of debt from student loans and have opted to get out from under by taking a particular job, you may be able to not only have your loans canceled, but have them canceled without any tax cost to you.

Benefit

Normally, the cancellation of a loan results in income to the borrower. But under certain conditions, the cancellation of a student loan can be tax free. There is no dollar limit to this benefit.

Example

You take out a government loan to obtain your teaching license. The loan is forgiven if you work for five years as a teacher on a Native American reservation. This debt forgiveness is *not* income to you if you complete the required years of work.

Conditions

You can exclude the debt forgiveness on your student loan from income if you are required to work for a set period of time in a certain profession for any of a broad class of employers.

The loan must have been made by a qualified lender, which includes:

- The government (federal, state, or local government or an agency of the government).
- A tax-exempt public benefit corporation.
- An educational institution if the loan is made under an agreement with the government or a tax-exempt public benefit corporation or under a program designed to encourage students to serve in occupations or areas with unmet needs.

Planning Tip

Make sure you fully understand your work obligation in order to secure tax-free treatment for cancellation of your student loan.

Pitfall

If you satisfy only part of the required work and a portion of the loan is forgiven anyway, you must include that portion in income.

Where to Claim the Benefit

If the loan forgiveness is tax free you do not report anything on your return. If cancellation of your student loan is not tax free, you must include the debt forgiveness in income on your return. Report it as "other income." Generally, debt forgiveness that is not tax free is reported to you (and to the IRS) on Form 1099-C, Cancellation of Debt.

Penalty-Free Withdrawals from IRAs

Distributions can be taken from an IRA before age 59½ if the funds are used to pay qualified higher education costs for yourself, your spouse, or dependent. The Tax Court has said that funds used to buy a computer are *not* a qualified expense where its use is not required for any course and access to computer-posted course syllabi can be done through school computers in the library.

Withdrawals must be taken only in the year in which you pay the expenses.

CHAPTER 4

Your Home

Home ownership is part of the American dream. According to the U.S. Department of Housing and Urban Development, about 70 percent of Americans now own their own homes. There are many reasons that we want to own rather than rent a home—for example, homes have proved to be the one bright spot in our recently poor economy. But there are also sound tax reasons favoring home ownership. Certain expenses of home ownership are deductible. And when you sell your home, some or all of your profit may be tax free.

This chapter explains:

- Mortgages
- Mortgage interest tax credit
- Home equity loans
- Points
- Refinancing
- Prepayment penalties
- Late payment penalties
- Penalty-free IRA withdrawals for home-buying expenses
- District of Columbia homebuyer credit
- Real estate taxes
- Cooperative housing

- Minister's rental allowance
- Home sale exclusion
- Moving expenses
- Energy improvements

Casualties and disasters that can befall your home, and the deductions you can claim for them, are explained in Chapter 13. The home office deduction for using a portion of your home for business is explained in Chapter 15.

For more information, see IRS Publication 521, *Moving Expenses*; IRS Publication 523, *Selling Your Home*; IRS Publication 530, *Tax Information for First-Time Homeowners;* and IRS Publication 936, *Home Mortgage Interest Deduction*. See also *J.K. Lasser's Homeowner's Tax Breaks* by Gerald Robinson.

Mortgages

Mortgages are a way to leverage yourself into home ownership: The bank or other lender (called the mortgagee) lends you the funds needed to buy your home over and above your out-of-pocket investment. You become the mortgagor and each month repay a portion of the principal (the money you borrowed), plus interest. While your repayment of principal is *never* deductible, you may be able to deduct your interest payments.

Benefit

Interest on your home mortgage may be fully deductible as an itemized deduction. There is no dollar limit on the amount of interest you can deduct annually, but there are limits on the size of the mortgage on which the interest is claimed. The mortgage interest rule applies to both fixed and adjustable rate mortgages.

You may deduct interest on so-called "acquisition indebtedness" up to $1 million (or any amount for loans obtained before October 14, 1987). In addition, you can deduct interest on home equity debt up to $100,000 (discussed later in this chapter). Thus, you can deduct interest on total home debt up to $1.1 million. And you can use this rule for your main home plus one additional residence of yours that you designate as your second home.

Conditions

For interest to be fully deductible, you must meet four conditions:

1. Acquisition indebtedness (which is usually a mortgage used to buy or build your home) cannot exceed $1 million. However, this dollar limit does not apply to a mortgage obtained before October 14, 1987.
2. The debt must be secured by the residence.
3. You deduct interest on no more than two residences.
4. You are personally obligated for repayment of the debt.

ACQUISITION INDEBTEDNESS. Acquisition indebtedness is usually a mortgage obtained to buy, build, or substantially improve a home (subject to the two residence limit). If you use the funds to construct your home, only interest paid during the 24-month period starting with the month in which construction begins is deductible. Interest paid before or after this 24-month period is not acquisition indebtedness; it is treated as nondeductible personal interest.

Example

In May 2005, you buy land to build your dream home and obtain a construction loan in June. Construction begins in September 2005, and the home is completed in June 2006. You may deduct interest on the loan starting with interest in September 2005, the month in which construction began. Since the home is completed within 24 months, interest through the end of construction is deductible.

If a loan is taken out within 90 days after construction is completed, it may still qualify in full as acquisition indebtedness. It qualifies as acquisition indebtedness to the extent of construction expenses incurred within the last 24 months before the completion of the home, plus expenses through the date of the loan.

Example

Same as the preceding example, except that in July 2006 you refinance the loan. Since the loan is obtained within 90 days after building completion, it qualifies as acquisition indebtedness and interest is deductible.

How much renovation is required to be considered a substantial improvement to the home? There is no clear rule. Generally, if you add a room, convert an attic, garage, or basement to living space, or renovate a kitchen, you can safely treat interest on the loan as acquisition indebtedness. Just about any type of capital improvement that adds to the basis of your home constitutes a substantial improvement; a repair is not a capital improvement, and a loan to make repairs is not acquisition indebtedness.

A home for this purpose isn't limited to a single-family dwelling. It also includes a condominium or cooperative unit, houseboat, mobile home, or house trailer as long as it has sleeping, cooking, and toilet facilities.

The $1 million limit applies to total acquisition indebtedness; it does not apply on a per-home basis.

DEBT SECURED BY THE HOME. The loan must be secured by your main or second home in order for interest on the loan to be deductible. "Secured" means that the loan is recorded in your city, town, or county recording office or the loan satisfies similar requirements under your state's law that gives the lender the right to foreclose against your home if you fail to repay the loan.

TWO-RESIDENCE LIMIT. A deduction for mortgage interest is limited to two residences: your main home and a second residence. If you have more than two homes, you can select which of the additional homes to designate as your second residence for interest deduction purposes. Obviously, it pays to designate the home with the larger interest payments. You can change your designation from year to year.

If a married couple files jointly, they can designate a second residence as a home even if it is owned or used by one of them. But if they file separately, each spouse generally may deduct interest on debt secured by one home unless they agree in writing to allow one spouse to deduct interest on the main home plus a second residence.

If you rent out a home during the year but use it for personal (nonrental) purposes for more than 14 days or 10 percent of the rental days, you can treat the home as a personal residence for which the interest is deductible. In counting rental days, include any days that the home is held for rental. In counting personal days, include any days your home is used by close family members.

Example

In addition to your main home, you own a beachfront condominium that you rent out through a rental agency two weeks each year at the start of the summer season. You spend the balance of the summer at your unit, so your personal use is sufficient for your home to be treated as a personal residence despite the rental. You can designate your condo as your second residence and deduct interest on the mortgage on the condo.

PERSONAL LIABILITY. To deduct interest on a home mortgage you must be personally obligated for its repayment. If, for example, you are financially unable to obtain a mortgage so your parents help you out by obtaining the loan, you cannot deduct mortgage interest (even if you pay the lender directly rather than repaying your parents). Only they can deduct the interest.

One case did allow a homeowner to deduct interest on a loan obtained by a brother because the homeowner had a poor credit rating, but the facts in the case were unique; the homeowner was contractually obligated to his brother to pay off the mortgage.

Planning Tips

Think hard about the type and amount of mortgage you want to take out when you buy your home. Once you have purchased your home, additional financing generally doesn't qualify as acquisition indebtedness.

When you sell your home, look at the settlement papers to determine the interest charged up to the date of sale so that you don't overlook any interest deduction you may be entitled to claim.

Pitfalls

You cannot deduct your interest if you claim the standard deduction; you must itemize deductions to claim this benefit.

You cannot deduct mortgage fees that you paid to obtain the loan, such as the cost of an appraisal, a credit report, or loan assumption fees. But points paid to obtain the mortgage may be deductible, as discussed later.

You cannot deduct interest on mortgage assistance payments made on your behalf under Section 234 of the National Housing Act.

Where to Claim the Deduction

You deduct home mortgage interest on Schedule A of Form 1040. You cannot claim the deduction if you file Form 1040A or Form 1040EZ. The amount of mortgage interest is reported annually to you by the lender on Form 1098, Mortgage Interest Statement.

Mortgage Interest Tax Credit

The government's policy is to encourage home ownership. To help low-income people become homeowners, the government offers certain assistance, including the opportunity to claim a tax credit for mortgage interest.

Benefit

Even better than deducting your mortgage interest, you may be eligible for a tax credit of up to $2,000 of home mortgage interest paid through mortgage interest certificates. These certificates are issued to certain homeowners as a means of encouraging home ownership. The credit may be claimed regardless of whether you itemize your personal deductions or claim the standard deduction.

If you received a mortgage credit certificate from your state or local government in connection with the purchase or renovation of your main home, you may be entitled to claim a tax credit with respect to your mortgage interest. The amount of the credit is the percentage shown on your mortgage credit certificate multiplied by the lesser of:

- Interest you paid during the year on your actual loan amount.
- Interest you paid on the loan amount shown on your mortgage credit certificate.

The credit cannot be more than $2,000 if the percentage shown on your mortgage credit certificate is 20 percent or more.

You must reduce your deduction for home mortgage interest by the amount of any credit you claim.

Conditions

You can claim this tax credit only if you meet two conditions:

1. You have received a mortgage credit certificate from your state or local government ("qualified mortgage credit certificate").
2. Your home meets certain requirements ("qualified home").

QUALIFIED MORTGAGE CREDIT CERTIFICATE. You qualify for the credit only if you receive a qualified certificate. Qualified mortgage interest certificates are issued by a state or local government or agency under a qualified mortgage credit certificate program. Certificates issued by the Federal Housing Administration, the Department of Veterans Affairs, and the Farmers Home Administration as well as Homestead Staff Exemption Certificates do not qualify.

QUALIFIED HOME. The home must be your main home. The value of your home cannot exceed a certain value:

- A value of 90 percent of the average area purchase price.
- A value of 110 percent of the average area purchase price in certain targeted areas.

Planning Tips

If you are thinking about buying a home but do not know if you can afford the payments, you may be able to swing a deal if you qualify for this type of government assistance. For information about special financing programs, visit the U.S. Department of Housing and Urban Development at www.hud.gov/buying/insured.cfm.

To find out whether you are eligible for a mortgage credit certificate, contact your local housing or redevelopment agency or ask your local real estate agent for information.

If you qualify for the credit and it exceeds your tax liability without regard to other tax credits, you do not lose the credit. Instead, you can carry the excess amount forward to be used in a future year if you are also eligible for the credit in that year.

If you refinance your mortgage, you do not lose your eligibility to claim the credit if your certificate is reissued and the reissued certificate meets five conditions:

1. It must be issued to the original holder of the existing certificate for the same property.
2. It must entirely replace the existing certificate (you cannot retain any portion of the outstanding balance of the existing certificate).
3. The certified indebtedness on the reissued certificate cannot be more than the outstanding balance on the existing certificate.
4. The credit rate of the reissued certificate cannot be more than the credit rate of the existing certificate.
5. The reissued certificate cannot result in a larger amount of interest than is otherwise allowable under the existing certificate for any year.

Pitfalls

You must reduce your deduction for home mortgage interest by the amount of the credit.

If you own your home jointly with a person who is not your spouse, you must divide the credit between the two of you according to your respective ownership interests. If you each own a 50 percent interest in the home, then you are each entitled to one-half of the credit.

If you buy a home using a mortgage credit certificate and sell it within nine years, you may have to repay some of the credit.

Where to Claim the Credit

You figure the credit on Form 8396, Mortgage Interest Certificate, and enter the amount of the credit in the "Tax and Credits" section of Form 1040.

You cannot claim the credit if you file Form 1040A or 1040EZ.

If you are subject to recapture of the credit because you sold your home within nine years of using the mortgage credit certificate, you must complete Form 8828, Recapture of Federal Mortgage Subsidy. You report the recaptured amount in the "Other Payments" section of Form 1040. You must file Form 1040 and cannot file Form 1040A or 1040EZ.

Home Equity Loans

Equity is the amount of money you would receive, over and above any outstanding mortgage, if you were to sell your home today. Equity is built up in two ways: by paying down a mortgage on the home and by appreciation in property values. As your equity increases, you may be able to tap into it *without* selling the home by using a home equity loan. This loan may be the only loan on the property or it may be a second or even third loan in addition to any other home mortgage. The tax law allows interest on home equity loans to be deductible under certain conditions.

Benefit

You may deduct interest on home equity loans up to $100,000 if you itemize your deductions. There is no dollar limit on the amount of interest you can deduct (the limit applies to the amount of borrowing).

The rules for deducting interest on home equity loans apply to any type of home equity loan: a fixed home equity loan or a home equity line of credit with an adjustable interest rate. The deduction applies regardless of how you spend the proceeds (i.e., you don't have to use them for the home and can spend them in any way you desire, including paying off credit card debt).

Conditions

The same four conditions discussed for mortgage interest earlier (except for a smaller maximum amount) apply to deducting interest on home equity loans in full.

1. Total home equity debt cannot exceed $100,000. In measuring the $100,000 limit, take into account only the amount you've borrowed, not your potential borrowing under a home equity line of credit loan. The $100,000 home equity limit is figured separately from the $1 million home acquisition limit discussed earlier in this chapter, so that interest is deductible on total borrowing up to $1.1 million ($1 million acquisition debt and $100,000 home equity debt).
2. The debt must be secured by the residence.
3. The debt can apply to your main or second home.
4. You are personally obligated for repayment of the debt.

Planning Tips

If the amount of a home equity loan exceeds the $100,000 limit, you treat the interest on the first $100,000 as fully deductible mortgage interest. Interest on the balance of the debt may still be deductible under a tax rule other than home mortgage interest. The treatment of this portion of interest depends on what you use the proceeds for:

- If you use the proceeds to pay personal expenses (e.g., a vacation or credit card debt), it is nondeductible.

- If you use the proceeds to purchase investments (other than tax-exempt securities), you can treat it as investment interest. The rules on deducting investment interest are explained in Chapter 8.
- If you use the proceeds for your business, interest may qualify as fully deductible business interest, as explained in Chapter 15.

Pitfalls

In the case of a reverse mortgage, where a homeowner who is at least age 62 borrows against the equity in the home to pay personal living expenses and does not make mortgage payments (the lender recoups what is owed when the homeowner sells the home or dies), interest is deductible only when the loan is repaid. No deduction can be taken as the interest accrues each month on the outstanding loan.

While interest on home equity debt up to $100,000 is fully deductible for regular tax purposes regardless of what the loan proceeds are used for, such interest is deductible for purposes of the alternative minimum tax only if the proceeds are used to improve your main or second home.

Where to Claim the Deduction

You deduct interest on home equity debt on Schedule A of Form 1040. The amount of mortgage interest is reported annually to you by the lender on Form 1098, Mortgage Interest Statement.

You cannot claim the deduction if you file Form 1040A or Form 1040EZ.

Points

"Points" are additional charges for acquiring a loan. Each point is 1 percent of the loan amount. In general, the more points you pay, the lower your interest rate on the loan. Points generally are deductible; the only question is *when* they can be deducted.

Benefit

When you take out a mortgage, you may pay points to the lender. Points paid to obtain a home mortgage are deductible as part of your itemized interest deduction. However, points in some cases are deductible in full in the year in which they are paid while in other cases they must be amortized (deducted ratably) over the term of the loan.

Conditions

First determine whether the payment qualifies as "points" (defined next). Then see if the points can be deducted in full in the year of payment or must be deducted over the term of the mortgage.

IMMEDIATE DEDUCTIBILITY. If the loan is taken to buy, build, or substantially improve your main home, you may deduct the points in the year of payment if you meet the following conditions:

- Points are charged for interest and not for services performed by the lender. The designation of the payment, as points, loan origination fees, or otherwise, is not controlling of the tax treatment; it is the purpose for which the money is charged that governs whether you can treat points as interest.
- The loan is secured by your main home. If the loan relates to a second home, you cannot fully deduct the points in the year of payment.
- The charging of points is an established business practice in the geographical area in which you are located.
- The amount of points is computed as a percentage of the loan and specifically earmarked on the loan closing statement as points, loan origination fees, or loan discount.
- You pay the points directly to the lender. Points withheld from the loan proceeds used to buy your main home are treated as having been paid directly to the lender. Points withheld from loan proceeds used to substantially improve your main home are not immediately deductible; you must pay the points with other funds to secure a full deduction in the year of payment. Points paid by the seller are not treated as paid directly to the lender but rather are viewed as an adjustment to the purchase price of the home.

DEDUCTIBLE OVER THE TERM OF THE LOAN. As long as the payments meet the definition of points and are not fees for services performed by the lender but cannot be deducted in full in the year of payment, they are deducted over the term of the loan.

Example

In 2006, you pay points of $3,600 to obtain a 30-year mortgage for your vacation home. You must amortize the points over 360 months and can deduct $10 per month each year until you've deducted all of the points or pay off the mortgage.

The following are situations in which you amortize the points rather than fully deduct them in the year of payment:

- To buy a second home.
- To substantially improve your main home but the points are withheld from the mortgage.

- To refinance an existing mortgage.
- To buy your main home but you elect to amortize the points.

Planning Tips

If you pay points to buy your main home, you are not required to deduct them in full in the year of payment. You can opt to amortize them over the term of the loan. You may wish to make this election if you can't benefit from the deduction in the year of payment. This might occur if you buy your home late in the year and your total itemized deductions do not exceed your standard deduction amount.

When you are financing a mortgage and faced with the option of paying higher interest with little or no points or a lower interest rate but some or substantial points, which option should you select? The answer usually depends on how long you plan to remain in the home (how long you will be paying the mortgage). To help you make this decision based on your circumstances, use a mortgage points calculator (you can find one at www.dinkytown.net/java/MortgagePoints.html).

Pitfall

If you refinance your loan with a new lender and have been amortizing points over the term of a previous loan (for example, this is your second or third refinance), be sure to deduct the remaining balance of the unamortized points.

Example

In January 2002, when rates had declined below your original mortgage rate, you refinanced your outstanding balance for a new 15-year mortgage, paying $1,800 in points. In July 2006, you refinance again. On your 2006 return, be sure to deduct the unamortized points of $1,260: $1,800 ÷ 180 months = $10 per month; 4 years, 6 months × $10 = $540; $1,800 – $540 = $1,260.

Where to Claim the Deduction

You deduct points along with your home mortgage interest on Schedule A of Form 1040. There is a separate line on Schedule A to list your points if they are not included on Form 1098 with your other home mortgage interest.

You cannot claim the deduction if you file Form 1040A or Form 1040EZ.

Refinancing

When interest rates decline or a personal credit rating improves, homeowners with existing mortgages can obtain more favorable terms by refinancing. Generally, this means getting a new mortgage to replace the old one. But you may borrow more than you owe on your old loan if the equity in your home allows for such borrowing—to add a room, pay off credit card debt, fund a child's education, or take a vacation. Under the tax law, the treatment of interest depends on what you use the excess funds for.

Benefit

With interest rates low, refinancing is a highly popular strategy to reduce monthly mortgage payments or obtain additional cash for various purposes. If your home has appreciated in value and/or you have paid down your mortgage, you may be sitting on substantial equity that you can tap by refinancing. You are not taxed on the equity you receive when you refinance your mortgage—the proceeds are tax free.

Example

You bought your home 10 years ago for $100,000, using an $80,000 mortgage, which you've paid down to $72,000. Today your home is worth $225,000. If you refinance for $175,000 and use $72,000 of the proceeds to pay off the old mortgage, you can put $103,000 in your pocket tax free.

Whether and when interest on refinanced debt, as well as points to obtain the new loan, are deductible depend on the purpose of the refinancing (these rules are explained next).

Conditions

Your purpose in refinancing the outstanding debt on your home determines the tax treatment of the interest.

If you refinance your existing acquisition indebtedness, the new loan continues to be treated as acquisition indebtedness so that the interest is fully deductible (assuming the mortgage does not exceed $1 million). It does not matter whether you shorten or lengthen the term of the loan.

If you refinance your existing mortgage to take out equity you've built on in your home, deductibility of the interest on a new mortgage depends on what you do with the proceeds in excess of amounts used to simply refinance the existing debt.

If you use the excess proceeds to pay off credit card debt or other personal expenses, this portion of the debt is treated as home equity debt subject to the $100,000 limit. If the excess debt used for personal purposes exceeds this amount, a portion of your interest is nondeductible.

Example

Your home today is worth $500,000 and the remaining balance of your old mortgage is $200,000. If you refinance for $350,000 and use $50,000 of the proceeds to buy a personal car, take a vacation, and pay off some credit card debt, you can deduct interest on only $300,000 ($200,000 of acquisition indebtedness and $100,000 of home equity debt).

If you use the excess proceeds to substantially improve your home, such as remodel the kitchen or add a family room, interest on this portion of the debt, as well as the portion used to pay off the existing mortgage, is treated as acquisition indebtedness, which is fully deductible if the total does not exceed $1 million.

Example

Same as the preceding example except you use the $50,000 to add a family room to your home. Now you can deduct all of the interest on the new loan ($250,000 of acquisition indebtedness and $100,000 of home equity debt).

Planning Tip

If this is a subsequent refinancing (you've already refinanced your original acquisition indebtedness at least once), points paid on the prior refinancing become fully deductible in the year of your latest refinancing.

Example

In January 2002, you refinanced your original mortgage and paid $3,600 for a 30-year loan. In January 2006, when interest rates have again declined, you refinance the outstanding balance of the 2002 loan. Of the points paid in 2002, you have already deducted $480 ($120 for 2002, 2003, 2004, and 2005). On your 2006 return you can deduct $3,120, the remaining amount of points on your 2002 refinancing.

Pitfall

If you refinance, consider what term you want for the new loan. If, for example, you have been paying off a 30-year mortgage and have only 22 years remaining, when you refinance do you want to start the clock over again with a new 30-year mortgage? Maybe the answer is yes just to keep monthly payments as low as possible. But you may opt for a shorter term, such as 15, 20, or 25 years, so that you will pay off the mortgage at or about the same time as you had originally planned.

Where to Claim the Benefits

Since the equity you receive on refinancing for more than your old mortgage is not taxable income, you do not have to report it on your return.

You deduct home mortgage interest (including home equity debt and points) on Schedule A of Form 1040. The amount of mortgage interest is reported annually to you by the lender on Form 1098, Mortgage Interest Statement.

You cannot claim the deduction if you file Form 1040A or Form 1040EZ.

Prepayment Penalties

It costs a lender money to make a loan, which it expects to recoup through interest collected during the term of the loan. But if a borrower pays off a loan within a short time of obtaining it (generally under two years), the lender has not had time to recoup its lending costs. To protect the lender against a quick payoff, prepayment penalties may be owed. The prepayment penalties are spelled out in the mortgage note at the time of obtaining the mortgage. From the borrower's perspective, the tax law looks favorably on prepayment penalties, allowing them to be deductible if certain conditions are met.

Benefit

If you pay off your mortgage or home equity debt before you are required to, there may be a prepayment penalty as specified in your mortgage papers. Prepayment penalties are treated as deductible interest—they are a set amount of interest—for example, six months of interest on 80 percent of your outstanding loan balance) if you pay off the mortgage before a set term (usually one to two years). For the rules on deducting interest on your home or second home, see earlier in this chapter.

Conditions

There are no special conditions to meet for deducting prepayment penalties. Simply refer to the rules discussed earlier in this chapter on how to treat mortgage interest.

Planning Tip

Think ahead. When taking out a mortgage, check whether there are any potential prepayment penalties. You may be able to get the lender to delete these from the loan agreement. This is important because you may have to relocate before you had planned and do not want to incur this needless cost.

Pitfall

Don't sign any mortgage loan agreement before finding out if there are prepayment penalties. One common scam by unscrupulous lenders is nondisclosure of prepayment penalties, which can run as much as six months of interest on up to 80 percent of the outstanding loan balance. Such a high penalty can keep you locked into a mortgage when you otherwise could have refinanced for a lower mortgage rate.

Where to Claim the Deduction on Your Return

Assuming that the prepayment payment penalty is deductible, you claim it with your home mortgage interest on Schedule A of Form 1040. The amount of mortgage interest is reported annually to you by the lender on Form 1098, Mortgage Interest Statement.

You cannot claim the deduction if you file Form 1040A or Form 1040EZ.

Late Payment Penalties

Under the terms of a loan, if a payment is late for any reason the borrower may owe additional amounts called late payment penalties. There are different types of late payment penalties: a flat fee, such as $25, charged without regard to the amount of the late payment or how long it is outstanding, and a percentage fee, fixed with regard to the late payment. The percentage fee continues to be accessed each month that a payment remains delinquent. Only late payment penalties qualifying as "interest" may be deductible.

Benefit

If you are late in making a payment, you may be charged a penalty by the lender. Generally, penalties for delinquent payments are treated as deductible interest, which can be written off if you itemize your deductions.

Example

Your monthly mortgage payment is $1,000, which is subject to a 2 percent late payment penalty. Due to unexpected financial reverses, you fail to make your payment for June, July, and August. In September, you're back on your feet and pay up all outstanding amounts, including the late payment penalties of $120 (June payment: 2% of $1,000 × 3 months; July payment: 2% of $1,000 × 2 months; August payment: 2% of $1,000 × 1 month). Since the late payment penalties are an interest charge, they are deductible.

Condition

Late payment penalties are treated as deductible interest as long as they are not imposed for a specific service provided by the lender. If they are a flat charge imposed regardless of how late the delinquency may be, they are viewed as a nondeductible service charge rather than as deductible interest.

Planning Tip

Even though late payment penalties can be deductible, you should try to avoid them if possible. The deduction does not fully offset your payment. One way to do so is to arrange for mortgage payments to be debited automatically from your checking account.

Pitfall

Being late on making your mortgage payments can cost you more than late payment penalties. Being late can adversely affect your credit rating and hurt your ability to obtain a loan or even get a job within two years or so of the late payment. Usually if your payment is no more than 30 days late, it will not show up on your credit report. But anything later will be reported by the lender to the major credit reporting bureaus and can affect your creditworthiness for about two years.

Where to Claim the Deduction on Your Return

Assuming that the late payment penalty is deductible, you claim it with your home mortgage interest on Schedule A of Form 1040. The amount of mortgage interest is reported annually to you by the lender on Form 1098, Mortgage Interest Statement.

You cannot claim the deduction if you file Form 1040A or Form 1040EZ.

Penalty-Free IRA Withdrawals for Home-Buying Expenses

If you thought IRAs were for retirement only, you'd be wrong. The tax law lets you tap into your IRA for certain special reasons without incurring any penalty (although withdrawals are subject to tax). One of those reasons is to buy a home.

Benefit

You may be able to use money in your IRA toward the cost of buying a home without incurring an early distribution penalty from your IRA. The withdrawal is subject to regular income tax, but you avoid the 10 percent early distribution penalty on withdrawals before age 59½.

Condition

You can only withdraw up to $10,000 free from penalty from your IRA. This is a once-in-a-lifetime opportunity. If you have already used this break to buy a previous home, you can't use it again.

You must spend the $10,000 on qualified first-time home-buying expenses, such as a down payment to purchase a home. These are expenses used to buy, build, or rehabilitate a main home for yourself, your spouse, child, grandchild, or ancestor (parent or grandparent) of you or your spouse. Such person cannot have had an ownership interest in a principal residence within two years before the purchase, construction, or renovation of the new home.

Planning Tip

Use this tax break only as a last resort. Once you withdraw the funds from the IRA and spend them on home-buying expenses, you cannot replace the funds in your retirement savings account. In effect, you lose the opportunity to build up your retirement savings.

Pitfall

If you take a withdrawal from your IRA with the intention of using the money to buy a home but the sale falls through, you become taxed on the money unless you redeposit it back in the IRA. You have 120 days from your initial withdrawal to take this action. For victims of Hurricanes Katrina, Rita, and Wilma, funds withdrawn after February 28, 2005, could have been recontributed before March 1, 2006 to avoid the penalty.

When a couple is buying a home together, each must be a first-time home-buyer for the penalty exception to apply.

Where to Claim the Benefit

If you take money from your IRA, you must file Form 5329, Additional Taxes on Qualified Plans (Including IRAs) and Other Tax-Favored Accounts. You report total early distributions from your IRA. You can then subtract those exempt from the 10 percent penalty because you used them for qualified first-time home-buying expenses. You must indicate on the appropriate line on the form which exception to the 10 percent penalty you are relying on (a number is assigned to each exception, and these numbers are listed in the instructions to this form).

Since you do not have any penalty on the distribution, you do not report anything in the section of Form 1040 for "Additional Taxes."

If you take money out of your IRA, you *must* file Form 1040 even if you are not subject to a penalty; you cannot file Form 1040A or 1040EZ.

District of Columbia Homebuyer Credit

(Provision expired 12/31/05. Extension expected for 2006.)

The District of Columbia may be the seat of the federal government, but it is also home to more than 575,000 residents. To encourage home ownership in our nation's capital, the federal government offers a special incentive: a one-time tax credit for those qualifying as first-time homebuyers within D.C.

Benefit

You can claim a tax credit of up to $5,000 ($2,500 if married filing separately) for the purpose of buying a home in the District of Columbia if certain conditions are met.

Conditions

To claim the credit you must meet two conditions:

1. You must be a first-time homebuyer in the District of Columbia.
2. Your modified adjusted gross income cannot exceed set limits.

FIRST-TIME HOMEBUYER. Being a first-time homebuyer doesn't mean you've *never* owned a home. To qualify as a first-time homebuyer, you (and your spouse) must not have owned a home in the District of Columbia within one year preceding the date of the purchase of your D.C. home.

The credit applies only to the purchase of your main home; you cannot use the credit for the purchase of a second home.

MAGI LIMIT. The amount of the credit you can claim, if any, depends on your modified adjusted gross income (MAGI). MAGI for this purpose is adjusted gross income increased by the foreign earned income exclusion and certain other foreign items.

You can claim a full credit only if your modified adjusted gross income is below the phaseout range found in Table 4.1. You can claim a partial credit if your MAGI is within the phaseout range; no credit may be claimed if your MAGI exceeds the phaseout range.

Planning Tip

If the amount of credit exceeds your tax liability (reduced by certain other credits), you don't lose the credit. Instead, you can carry over the unused credit to succeeding tax years.

Pitfall

The credit is a one-time credit, so if you claimed this credit before, you cannot use it again, even if you meet eligibility conditions.

Example

You bought a D.C. home in December 1998 and sold it in 2001. You rented a home until you bought a new main home in the District of Columbia in May 2006. Since you claimed the credit on your 1998 return, you cannot claim the credit again for your purchase in 2006, even though you otherwise meet the conditions of a first-time homebuyer.

TABLE 4.1 Phaseout Ranges for the District of Columbia Homebuyer Credit

Filing Status*	MAGI
Joint return	$110,000–130,000
Unmarried	$70,000–90,000

*You cannot claim the credit if you are married filing separately.

Where to Claim the Credit

You figure the credit on Form 8859, District of Columbia First-Time Homebuyer Credit, and enter the credit amount in the "Tax and Credits" section of Form 1040.

You cannot claim this credit if you file Form 1040A or 1040EZ.

Real Estate Taxes

Property owners are charged real estate taxes to cover government services related to the property. Local property taxes may include city, town, and/or county taxes; school taxes; and even other charges (such as fire or sewer district taxes). Fortunately, the tax law allows property owners to deduct these taxes.

Benefit

Your burden of paying local property taxes, including city, town, and/or county taxes and school taxes, can be eased somewhat by deducting your payments.

You can deduct real estate taxes you pay on your main home and any other home you own. There are no limits on the dollar amount of real estate taxes you can deduct. There are no limits on the number of homes for which you can claim the deduction. The deduction for real estate taxes on your residence and vacation homes is claimed as an itemized deduction (you cannot use this benefit if you claim the standard deduction).

If you pay real estate taxes on a rental property, it is deductible against your rental income, regardless of whether you itemize your personal deductions.

Conditions

You must be the owner of the home so that you are obligated for the payment of the tax. If you buy the property at a tax sale, you cannot start to deduct property taxes until you receive title to the property under state law (typically following a redemption period).

If you pay the seller's unpaid back taxes when you purchase the home, you cannot deduct this payment as your taxes. You can add the payment to your basis in the home used for figuring gain or loss when you sell it.

In the year that property is sold, real estate taxes must be allocated between the buyer and the seller. (Generally this allocation is reflected in your closing papers.)

- The seller can deduct taxes for the portion of the year through the day before the date of sale.
- The buyer can deduct taxes for the portion of the year commencing with the date of sale.

Generally if you rent rather than own your home, you cannot deduct the portion of the rent that the landlord uses to pay the property taxes. However, in Hawaii you can do so if the lease runs for 15 years or more. Also, as a tenant in California you can deduct your payments if you have your name placed on the tax rolls and agree to pay the tax directly to the taxing authority.

Planning Tip

Consider prepaying an upcoming tax bill before the end of the year to increase your current deductions. For example, pay your January 2007 property tax bill in December 2006 to increase your deductions for 2006.

Pitfalls

If you make payments to the lender that are held in escrow and disbursed to the taxing authority, you can only deduct real estate taxes when the lender makes the disbursements (not when you pay the lender).

If title to your home is in the name of one spouse and the other spouse pays the real estate tax bill, the deduction can be claimed only if you file a joint return. Since the party paying the tax isn't the legal owner of the home, the tax may not be deducted on a separate return.

Special assessments by homeowners associations for the purpose of maintaining common areas or special assessments by municipalities for certain government services (water, sewage, or garbage collection) are not deductible as real estate taxes.

Do not prepay real estate taxes if you are subject to the alternative minimum tax. Since taxes are not deductible for AMT purposes, prepaying them can trigger or increase your AMT liability. Effectively you lose the benefit of claiming the deduction.

Where to Claim the Deduction

You deduct your payment of real estate taxes on your residence and vacation homes as an itemized deduction on Schedule A of Form 1040. You deduct real estate taxes on rental properties on Schedule E of Form 1040.

You cannot deduct property taxes on a personal residence or rental property if you file Form 1040A or 1040EZ.

In the year you sell property, if your share of real estate taxes is paid in advance by the buyer, the lender or real estate broker will generally include this information on Form 1099-S, Proceeds from Real Estate Transactions. But this form is not required to be filed for all sales, so you should keep track of this information (check your settlement papers).

Each year that you own property you do *not* receive any official information return notifying you of the amount of taxes you paid during the year. As a practical matter, if you make payments to a commercial lender to cover real estate taxes, your annual tax payments will be detailed in a year-end statement sent to you by the lender.

Cooperative Housing

Cooperative housing, also called a co-op, is a form of home ownership. You become a tenant-stockholder in a cooperative housing corporation (CHC) that owns and runs a multiunit housing complex. Your shares entitle you to exclusive use of your housing unit, plus access to common areas. There are tax breaks unique to this form of home ownership.

Benefits

You may experience two levels of deductions—one that is allocated to you from the CHC and the other that you obtain through your direct payments. For example, you may incur two interest deductions—one for your share of interest on debt of the CHC (e.g., for common areas) and one for the purchase of your unit that you financed through a bank. This section discusses only your allocated deduction; deductions for your direct payments are included in other sections of this chapter (e.g., home mortgage interest).

Condition

The only condition for claiming a deduction for CHC expenses allocated to you is ownership of shares in the CHC.

Planning Tip

Tenant-stockholders in cooperative housing corporations are treated the same in the tax law as homeowners of condominiums and single-family homes.

Pitfall

While a tenant-shareholder of an apartment in a cooperative housing corporation can deduct his/her share of the co-op's real estate taxes, a federal appeals court has decided that these taxes are *not* deductible for purposes of the alternative minimum tax (AMT). Even though the AMT rules do not specifically bar a deduction, these taxes are treated in the same manner as if the taxes had been paid directly by the owner of a single-family home.

Where to Claim the Deduction

You claim a deduction for your share of the CHC's mortgage interest and real estate taxes allocated to you on Schedule A of Form 1040 as a "Miscellaneous Itemized Deduction." This deduction is not subject to the 2 percent of AGI limitation.

You cannot deduct your allocated mortgage interest and real estate taxes if you file Form 1040A or 1040EZ.

The CHC should provide you with Form 1098, Mortgage Interest Statement, to show your share of these expenses.

Minister's Rental Allowance

Members of the clergy of any recognized faith or denomination who receive assistance with their housing costs, through free use of a home or payments toward these living costs, may qualify for a tax break: Their housing allowance may be a nontaxable fringe benefit of their job.

Benefit

You are not taxed on the rental value of a home provided to you by your religious institution—this is tax-free income to you. If you receive an allowance for housing, you can exclude the amount used to pay rent, make a down payment to buy a house, or make mortgage payments, or for utilities, real estate taxes, or repairs to the home. There is no dollar limit on this exclusion.

Conditions

You must be a duly ordained minister and acting in that capacity. A rabbi or cantor is treated as a minister for purposes of this exclusion. Retired ministers can qualify for the exclusion if the housing allowance is made in recognition of past services. A minister acting as a teacher or an administrator of a parochial school or seminary qualifies for the exclusion if the school is an integral part of a church organization.

Church officers who are not ordained cannot qualify for the exclusion. Ordained ministers who are working as executives of nonreligious organizations cannot claim the exclusion even if they perform religious duties. For example, a minister-administrator of an old age home not under church authority could not claim the exclusion.

The religious institution (e.g., church or local congregation) must designate the part of your compensation that is the housing allowance. This designation must be made in advance of the payments to you. Designation can be made in an employment contract, minutes, a resolution, or a budget allowance.

Planning Tip

If you pay mortgage interest and/or real estate taxes, you can claim deductions for these payments even if you finance them with the tax-free housing allowance. You must itemize your deductions to write off mortgage interest and real estate taxes on your home, as explained in this chapter.

Pitfalls

Even though the housing exclusion is not subject to income tax, it is treated as self-employment income for purposes of Social Security and Medicare taxes. If you use a church-provided home tax free, figure the rental value for purposes of self-employment taxes at what you would pay for similar quarters in your area, including utilities and garage or parking space if any.

Claiming the housing allowance can have an adverse impact on your business deductions. The portion of business deductions allocable to the tax-free housing allowance is not deductible.

Example

Your salary as a minister is $25,000. You also receive a $25,000 housing allowance. Your work-related expenses are $6,000. You can deduct only $3,000. Since half of your income is tax free, only half of the expenses are deductible.

Where to Claim the Exclusion

If you can exclude the benefit, you do not have to report anything on your return. If you receive an allowance in excess of the amounts used for housing expenses, you must include the excess as part of your salary reported on your income tax return. You can do so on Form 1040, 1040A, or 1040EZ.

Home Sale Exclusion

Homeowners are highly favored under the tax law. Not only can they deduct certain costs of home ownership, such as mortgage interest and property taxes, but they can also receive tax-free income when they sell their homes. A special rule permits a limited amount of gain from the sale of a main home to escape federal income tax. And this tax break can be used over and over again.

Benefit

If you sell your home for a profit, you may avoid tax on some or all of your gain as long as you meet certain conditions. More specifically, you do not pay any tax on gain up to $250,000 from the sale of your home ($500,000 on a joint return) if you owned and used the home as your main residence for at least two of the five years preceding the date of sale. The amount you exclude is tax-free income to you.

Conditions

To be eligible to use the *full* exclusion amount of $250,000 ($500,000 on a joint return), you must meet all three conditions:

1. The home must be your main home ("principal residence").
2. You owned your home for at least two years prior to the sale.
3. You used your home as your main home for at least two years prior to the sale.

If you acquired your home in a tax-free exchange, the ownership and use periods must be five full years (instead of two of five years) before qualifying for the exclusion.

MAIN HOME. Your main home is the one in which you primarily dwell. If you own two or more homes, you must determine which one is your primary residence. This determination is usually based on which one you live in for the greater part of the year. However, this isn't a bright line test; you can use other factors to show that the home you used less of the time is your main home. Such factors include:

- Where you work or own a business.
- Where your family members reside.
- The address you use for your federal and state income tax returns.
- The address you use for your bills and correspondence.
- Where you have your driver's license and voter registration.
- The location of religious institutions and clubs you belong to.

Your main home isn't limited to a single-family dwelling. You can treat as your main home a mobile home, trailer, houseboat, or condominium apartment used as your primary residence. Even stock in a cooperative housing corporation is subject to this rule as long as you live in the cooperative apartment or house as your main home.

If you change the title to your home, you don't necessarily lose the opportunity to claim the exclusion.

- If you transfer ownership of your home to a grantor trust, one in which you are treated as the owner of the trust and report all of the trust's income on your personal tax return, the trust can use the exclusion provided you meet the ownership and use tests.
- If you transfer ownership of your home to a one-member limited liability company, again, the LLC can use the exclusion provided you meet

the ownership and use tests. The LLC is treated as a "disregarded entity" for tax purposes so you report all of the LLC's income on your personal tax return.

- If you divorce and title to the home is changed from your spouse's name or joint name to your name alone, you can include the period of your spouse's ownership in meeting the ownership test.
- If you are a surviving spouse, you can use the $500,000 exclusion amount if you sell the home in the year of your spouse's death. But if you sell in a later year, you are limited to the $250,000 exclusion.

OWNERSHIP TEST. You must own your home for at least two years in the aggregate prior to the date of sale. This means that you owned the home for a full 24 months or 730 days (365 × 2) during the five-year period that ends on the date of sale. The periods of ownership and use need not be continuous or identical.

If you are married and file a joint return, only one spouse is required to meet the ownership test to qualify for the exclusion as long as both satisfy the use test.

USE TEST. You must use your home as your primary residence for at least two years in the aggregate prior to the date of sale. This means that you lived in the home for a full 24 months or 730 days (365 × 2) during the five-year period that ends on the date of sale. The periods of ownership and use need not be continuous or identical.

Example

In November 2003, you purchased your home and lived there until September 2004 when you took a one-year sabbatical overseas. You returned to your home in September 2005 and lived there until you sold the home in December 2006. You meet the ownership test because you lived in your home for 26 months (10 months before the sabbatical and 16 months after it).

Temporary absences (for example, a three-week vacation) are ignored. This is true even if you rent out your home while you are away.

If a homeowner becomes incapacitated before meeting the two-year use test and resides in a licensed care facility, the full home sale exclusion can be used as long as the homeowner used the home for at least one year prior to moving from the home and meets the two-year ownership test.

PARTIAL EXCLUSION. Even if you sell before meeting the full two-year ownership and use tests, you may be eligible to use a prorated exclusion amount for the period of your ownership and use. A partial exclusion is allowed if you sell early because of:

- *Change in jobs.* If you relocate for a new job or a new business (if self-employed), you automatically are treated as having a qualified change in jobs if the distance test used for the moving expense deduction (explained later in this chapter) is met. The distance between your new job location and your former home must be at least 50 miles greater than the distance between your old job location and your former home. If your spouse, co-owner, or person who resides with you has a change of jobs, you can qualify for the exclusion.
- *Health reasons.* The change must be medically motivated (for example, your doctor recommends a change so you can receive medical or personal care for an illness or injury. A change that is merely beneficial to your health (for example, moving to a warmer climate) isn't viewed as a health reason for purposes of using the partial exclusion. Again, the health of your spouse, co-owner, or person who resides with you can be taken into account in determining your eligibility for the partial exclusion.
- *Unforeseen circumstances.* If you are forced to sell because of events beyond your control, you can use the partial exclusion. Such events include, but are not limited to: Your home is destroyed through acts of war or terrorism, someone in your household dies or goes on unemployment benefits, you become unable to pay basic living expenses because of a change in employment or self-employment, there is a legal divorce or separation, you have multiple births resulting from the same pregnancy, you must have a larger home to meet adoption agency requirements, you received death threats at the current address, you must leave a senior retirement home so your young grandchild can live with you, you must move to a home that can accommodate your paralyzed mother's disability, or you are forced to sell because of pressure from neighbors.

Planning Tips

If you have owned your home for a long time and paid down the mortgage, your gain may exceed your exclusion amount. You can minimize your gain by adding to the basis of your home any capital improvements you've made to it.

EXAMPLES OF CAPITAL IMPROVEMENTS

Addition of a deck, garage, porch, or room.

Appliances.

Duct work.

Fencing.

Heating and cooling systems.

Kitchen and bathroom modernization.

New roof.

Paving the driveway.

Satellite dish.

Security system.

Storm doors and windows.

Wiring upgrade.

If you subdivide your property, selling off vacant land separately from the parcel on which the home is situated, you can claim the exclusion for the sale of the vacant land and the sale of the home provided they occur within two years of each other. However, only one exclusion amount applies to both sales.

Example

You are single in 2006 and subdivide your property and sell the vacant land for a profit of $100,000 (you must allocate the basis in your home between the vacant land and the parcel with the home to determine your gain on the sale of each parcel). You can exclude this gain on your 2006 return. In 2007, you sell the parcel containing your home for a profit of $200,000. You can exclude $150,000 of this $200,000 gain on your 2007 return (you already used $100,000 of the exclusion on your 2006 return). You must report and pay tax on the remaining $50,000 profit.

If you have been claiming a home office deduction for a portion of the home, you can still apply the exclusion to the home office portion as long as both the personal and business portions are part of the same dwelling.

You can use the exclusion over and over again. As long as you meet the two-year ownership and use tests for each residence, you can avoid tax on gains from each one. One exclusion can be claimed every two years.

You aren't required to use the exclusion. You may wish to waive it by reporting your gain if you expect to sell another home shortly at a more substantial profit and wish that home to qualify for the exclusion.

Example

You own two homes, a house in New Jersey and a condominium in Arizona. You've owned each home for many years. In 2006, you sell your New Jersey home to relocate full-time to Arizona. You can use the exclusion for gain from the sale of the New Jersey home in 2006. In 2007, you build a house in Arizona and place your condominium on the market. You sell it in 2008 and can use the exclusion for any gain from the sale of your condominium.

Pitfalls

If you have been claiming a home office deduction for a portion of your home, you must recapture depreciation you have claimed for the office after May 6, 1997. This is so even though you can use the exclusion for gain on this part of the home. "Recapture" means you pay tax on all the depreciation claimed after May 6, 1997, at the rate of 25 percent (assuming your tax bracket is at or above this rate). Home office deduction rules are discussed in Chapter 15.

You must reduce the basis of your home by the amount of any energy credit claimed. For example, if you claim a $200 tax credit in 2006 for installing new storm doors, you must subtract $200 from the basis of your home.

Where to Claim the Exclusion

If your gain is fully excludable, you do not have to report the sale of your home on your return. If, however, some of the gain is taxable because it exceeds the exclusion amount (or all of your gain is taxable because you opt *not* to use the exclusion), you report the sale on Schedule D of Form 1040.

You can use a worksheet in IRS Publication 523 to figure your gain and whether any portion of the gain is excludable.

Moving Expenses

According to the U.S. Census Bureau, 40 million Americans moved during 2002 and 2003; individuals will move 11.7 times during their lives. The cost of a move may be high—$10,000 and up in some cases. From a tax perspective, deductibility of moving costs depends on the reason for the move and satisfying certain conditions.

Benefit

When you sell your home and move your things to a new residence because of a change in your work location, you may be able to deduct moving expenses as an adjustment to gross income, even if you don't itemize your other deductions. There is no dollar limit on this benefit.

Deductible amounts include amounts paid to pack, crate, and move your household goods and personal effects. Storage and insurance costs can be treated as deductible expenses for any period within 30 days after the items were moved from your old home but before they were delivered to your new home. If you move overseas, there is no limit on storage and insurance costs while you work at your overseas location. The cost of connecting or disconnecting household appliances is a deductible moving expense, but the cost of installing a telephone in your new home is not deductible.

Deductible amounts also include travel expenses for you and members of your household.

EXAMPLES OF DEDUCTIBLE TRAVEL EXPENSES FOR THE MOVING DEDUCTION

- Lodging en route from the old home to the new home. Include the cost of lodging before you depart for one day after your old residence is unusable as well as lodging for the day of arrival at your new location before you move into your home. However, the cost of meals is not deductible.
- Transportation from the old home to the new home. You and members of your household do not have to travel together; simply add up the costs for each person.
- Your car expenses at 18 cents per mile for 2006, or your actual out-of-pocket costs for oil, gas, and repairs, if any, for the move. You can also deduct parking and tolls, regardless of which deduction method you use.

If your employer pays to relocate you, reimbursements or employer payments on your behalf are not income if you would have been able to deduct the expenses had you paid for them yourself (i.e., you meet the deduction conditions given next). Such reimbursement need not be included on your Form W-2 if the benefit is excludable. Of course, reimbursements for nondeductible expenses, such as premove house-hunting expenses, are reported on your W-2 and taxable to you as income.

Conditions

To be treated as a deductible expense (or to qualify as a tax-free fringe benefit if paid by the employer), the expense must meet two tests:

1. A distance test
2. A time test

DISTANCE TEST. The distance from your new workplace must be at least 50 miles farther from your old home than your old workplace was. If you relocate to a distant city or across the country, there's no question that you satisfy the distance test. But if you relocate within the same general area, make sure that the move meets the distance test.

Example

Your old workplace was five miles from your old home. Your new workplace is 75 miles from your old home. Since the difference is more than 50 miles, you meet the distance test.

If you are a member of the armed forces, you do not have to meet the distance test if the move is due to a permanent change of station. A permanent change of station includes a move in connection with retirement or termination of active duty if it is within one year of such retirement or termination.

TIME TEST. If you are an employee, you must work full-time in the area of your new workplace for at least 39 weeks during the 12-month period following your move. If you change from being self-employed to being an employee, you must meet the 39-week test as an employee and cannot use any weeks of self-employment for this purpose.

If you are self-employed, you must work full-time in the area of your new workplace for 78 weeks during the 24-month period following your move. If you change from being an employee to being self-employed, you can include any weeks of employment for purposes of the 78-week test.

On a joint return, only one spouse is required to meet the time test.

If you expect to satisfy the time test, you can claim the deduction on your return even though you have not yet satisfied it.

Example

You move in August 2006 to a job in another state. By the end of 2006 you have completed only 20 weeks of full-time work in your new workplace. You can deduct your moving expenses on your 2006 return as long as you anticipate staying on the job for at least another 19 weeks.

If you don't claim the deduction in the year of the move, you must then file an amended return to claim the moving expense deduction. But if you claim the deduction on your return for the year of the move but later fail to satisfy the time test, you can either:

- Amend your return, eliminating the deduction you had claimed.
- Report as income in the year you should have met the time test but didn't the deduction you claimed on the earlier return.

If you expected to meet the time test, you don't have to report the deduction as income if the failure was due to:

- Disability that results in job termination.
- Job termination because you are laid off or fired for a reason other than willful misconduct.
- A permanent change of station if you are in the armed forces.
- Being a retiree or survivor of a person living outside the United States. If your old workplace and old home were both outside the United States, a move home is deductible (you don't have to meet any time test). Similarly, if you are the spouse or dependent of someone whose principal workplace was outside the United States at the time of his or her death, your moving costs are deductible without regard to the time test if the move begins within six months of the death and you lived with the person at the time of his or her death.
- Death. In other words, if someone claimed a moving expense deduction but died before meeting the time test, there is no income recapture of the benefit.

Planning Tip

Even though you can deduct your moving costs, it still makes sense to keep them as low as possible. When planning a move, to get a rough idea of moving costs, use The Moving Calculator from Realtor.com (www.homefair.com/homefair/calc/moveclacin.html). Be sure to get several binding quotes from reputable moving companies before contracting with one of them. Finally, put everything you agree to in writing and include adequate insurance for loss, breakage, and other damage.

Pitfalls

You cannot claim a moving expense deduction if you are relocating because of retirement (other than in the case of the armed forces). For example, if you sell your business in New York and retire to Florida, the cost of the move is a nondeductible personal expense.

You cannot deduct the costs of a move to start your first job after you've completed your education, even if you've held summer or part-time jobs during school. For example, if you graduate from college in California in June 2006 and accept a position in Washington, D.C., you cannot deduct your moving expenses; you don't have an old workplace from which to measure your move.

Not every move-related expense is deductible.

EXAMPLES OF NONDEDUCTIBLE MOVING EXPENSES

- Any part of the purchase price of a new home.
- Car registration tags.
- Driver's license.
- Expenses of buying or selling a home.
- Expenses of getting or breaking a lease.
- Home improvements to sell your home.
- Losses from disposing of club memberships.
- Meal expenses.
- Mortgage penalties (but they may be deductible as an itemized mortgage interest expense as explained earlier in this chapter).
- Premove house-hunting expenses.
- Real estate taxes (but they may be deductible as an itemized expense).
- Refitting of carpets and draperies.
- Security deposits forfeited.
- Storage charges except those incurred in transit and for foreign moves.
- Temporary living expenses.

Where to Claim the Deduction

If your employer pays your moving costs and you are eligible to exclude this benefit from your income, you do not report them on your return.

If you deduct your expenses, figure the deduction on Form 3903, Moving Expenses, which you attach to your return. Enter the deductible amount in the "Adjusted Gross Income" section of Form 1040.

You cannot claim a moving expense deduction if you file Form 1040A or Form 1040EZ.

Energy Improvements

The Energy Tax Incentives Act of 2005 created tax credits for homeowners who make certain energy-saving improvements in 2006 and 2007. In view of currently high energy costs, which are expected to remain high (at least for some time), consider taking advantage of tax breaks to save money on taxes and energy costs.

Benefit

There are several tax credits that a homeowner may claim for making certain energy improvements to the home. These include a 10 percent credit for adding qualified energy efficiency improvements and a 30 percent credit for solar energy and fuel cell power plants.

Conditions

The law requires that these improvements meet certain energy-saving standards and cannot exceed certain dollar limits. Different requirements apply to energy improvements and to solar energy and fuel cell power plants.

ENERGY IMPROVEMENTS. To qualify for the 10 percent credit, energy improvements must meet or exceed the criteria established by the 2000 International Energy Conservation Code (including supplements) and must be installed in your main home in the United States.

ELIGIBLE ITEMS. These include:

- Insulation systems that reduce heat loss/gain.
- Exterior windows (including skylights).
- Exterior doors.
- Metal roofs treated with special paint (meeting applicable Energy Star requirements).
- Advanced main air circulating fan (up to $50).
- Qualified natural gas, propane, or oil furnace or hot water heater (up to $150).
- Each item of qualified energy-efficient property (up to $300).

LIMITATIONS. In addition to the dollar limits listed, the maximum credit for all taxable years is $500. No more than $200 of the credit can be attributable to expenses for windows.

SOLAR POWER AND FUEL CELLS. To qualify for the 30 percent credit, solar panels, solar water heating equipment, or a fuel cell power plant must be added to your main home in the United States.

In general, a qualified fuel cell power plant converts a fuel into electricity using electrochemical means, has an electricity-only generation efficiency of more than 30 percent, and generates at least 0.5 kilowatts of electricity.

You can claim one credit equal to 30 percent of the qualified investment in a solar panel up to a maximum credit of $2,000, and another equivalent credit for investing in a solar water heating system.

Additionally, you are allowed a 30 percent tax credit for the purchase of qualified fuel cell power plants. The credit may not exceed $500 for each 0.5 kilowatt of capacity.

Planning Tip

The credit applies only to improvements made in 2006 and 2007. If you have not yet taken advantage of this credit opportunity, consider doing so before it's too late.

Pitfalls

Not every energy-saving measure qualifies for a credit. For purposes of the energy improvements credit, siding does not qualify (although anyone who purchased it on the dealer's certification before December 1, 2006, may rely on this to claim the credit). For purposes of the solar or fuel cell power plant credit, no part of either system can be used to heat a pool or hot tub.

You must reduce the basis of your home by the amount of any energy credit claimed. For example, if you claim a $200 tax credit in 2006 for installing new storm doors, you must subtract $200 from the basis of your home.

Where to Claim the Credits

You figure the credit on Form 5965, Residential Energy Credits. The credit is then entered in the "Tax and Credits" section of Form 1040, or in the "Tax, Credits, and Payments" section of Form 1040A. You may not claim the credit if you file Form 1040EZ.

CHAPTER 5

Retirement Savings

Your Social Security benefits alone, or even retirement benefits derived from employer contributions to retirement plans on your behalf, won't provide you with the financial security you want for your retirement years. You need to save up so that you'll have the assets to generate income for you after you stop working. Fortunately, the tax law provides important incentives to encourage your personal savings in special retirement accounts. You may be able to write off your savings (contributions) as well as qualify for special treatment when you start drawing from these savings.

This chapter explains:

- Traditional IRAs
- Roth IRAs
- IRA rollovers
- 401(k) and similar plans
- Self-employed retirement plans
- SEPs
- SIMPLEs
- Special rules for hurricane victims
- Retirement saver's credit
- Custodial/trustee fees
- Employer-paid retirement planning advice
- Charitable transfers of IRA distributions

If you are an employer, you may be eligible for a tax credit for starting a qualified retirement plan for your business. This credit is explained in Chapter 15.

For more information see IRS Publication 560, *Retirement Plans for Small Business*; IRS Publication 575, *Pension and Annuity Income*; and IRS Publication 590, *Individual Retirement Arrangements (IRAs)*. Also see *J.K. Lasser's Your Winning Retirement Plan* by Henry K. Hebeler, *J.K. Lasser's Winning with Your 401(k)* by Grace Weinstein, and *J.K. Lasser's Winning with Your 403(b)* by Pam Horowitz.

Traditional IRAs

The Employee Retirement Income Security Act of 1974 created individual retirement accounts (IRAs) to enable taxpayers to save for their own retirement largely because company pensions could no longer be relied upon for retirement income. With an IRA, the government effectively contributes to your retirement savings by permitting a tax deduction for contributions if certain conditions are met. The tax savings are the government's contribution. For example, if you are in the 33 percent tax bracket, the government contributes almost one-third of your contributions to a traditional (deductible) IRA—your tax savings from the total contribution amount; you only have to come up with about two-thirds of the contribution.

Benefit

If you work as an employee or have net earnings from self-employment, you can contribute to an IRA. The contribution limit for 2006 is $4,000, or $5,000 if you are age 50 or older by the end of 2006, as long as you earn at least this dollar amount.

Example

If you are under age 50 and earn at least $4,000, you can make a full contribution. If you work part-time and earn only $2,000, your contribution is limited to $2,000.

If you have a spouse who does not work for compensation, you can contribute to an IRA for your spouse based on your own earnings. The same dollar limit of $4,000 (or $5,000 if age 50 by the end of 2006) applies to a spousal IRA. This means that if you have sufficient earnings and both you and your spouse are under age 50, you can contribute up to $8,000 ($4,000 for yourself and $4,000 for your spouse) for 2006.

If you do not participate in another qualified retirement plan, such as a 401(k) plan, or if you do participate but your income is below a set amount, you can deduct your contributions. The deduction is claimed as an adjustment to gross income; you claim it regardless of whether you itemize your other deductions.

Earnings on IRA contributions build up on a tax-deferred basis (no tax is owed annually on the earnings of an IRA). However, you are required to take certain withdrawals from the IRA starting at age 70½. If you fail to take these required amounts (called required minimum distributions, which are not discussed further in this book), you may be subject to a whopping 50 percent penalty of the amount you should have taken.

Conditions for Making Contributions

There are three conditions for making a contribution:

1. Earned income
2. Under age 70½
3. Cash contributions

EARNED INCOME. Earned income for purposes of making IRA contributions means taxable wages (including tips, commissions, bonuses, and jury duty fees) and net earnings from self-employment. Earned income also includes taxable alimony.

You must earn the income. If you live in a community property state where one-half of your spouse's earnings is viewed as income, you cannot use your share of your spouse's income as the basis for making your IRA contribution.

Earned income does not include:

- Deferred compensation, pensions, or annuities.
- Investment income, such as dividends or interest.
- Income earned abroad for which the foreign earned income exclusion has been claimed.
- Unemployment compensation.

UNDER AGE 70½. There is no *minimum* age requirement for making an IRA contribution. Thus, if your 12-year-old child has a newspaper delivery route, he or she can make IRA contributions based on earnings from this job.

However, no contributions are permitted starting for the year in which you turn age 70½.

Example

You were born in March 1936. Since you attain age 70½ in 2006, no IRA contributions can be made for 2006. If you were born in September 1936, you attain age 70½ in 2006, so you can still make an IRA contribution for 2006.

If you continue to work past this age, you may still contribute on behalf of a nonworking spouse who is under age 70½.

CASH CONTRIBUTIONS. All contributions must be made in cash (which includes payments by check). If you currently own investments that you want to use as your contributions, you must first liquidate them. Your IRA account can then reacquire the same investments (provided they are not prohibited investments discussed later).

Condition for Claiming a Deduction

Just because you meet all the conditions for making an IRA contribution does not mean that you can claim a deduction for the contribution. Even if you qualify to make contributions, there is an additional condition in order to deduct your contributions.

To deduct contributions you must not participate in another qualified retirement plan or if you are an active participant in a qualified retirement plan, your modified adjusted gross income (MAGI) cannot exceed a phaseout range. The deduction amount phases out for MAGI within the phaseout range. No deduction can be claimed if MAGI exceeds the phaseout range. MAGI for this purpose is adjusted gross income, increased by exclusions for interest on U.S. savings bonds used for higher education, employer-paid adoption assistance, and foreign earned income as well as deductions for interest on student loans and higher education tuition and fees. Table 5.1 shows the phaseout ranges for 2006.

Example

You are single, age 42, and participate in your company's 401(k) plan. If your AGI is $38,000, you can fully deduct your IRA contributions. If your AGI is $55,000, your basic deduction is limited to $2,000 (one-half of $4,000). If your AGI is $62,000, you cannot deduct your IRA contributions.

TABLE 5.1 **MAGI Phaseout Range in 2006 for Active Participants Deducting IRA Contributions**

Filing Status*	MAGI
Married filing jointly	$75,000–85,000
Other taxpayers (other than married filing separately)	$50,000–60,000

*A married person filing a separate return has a zero limit so that no deduction can be claimed if the person is an active participant.

Planning Tips

You have until April 15 of the following year to make an IRA contribution. For example, you have until April 16, 2007 (April 15 is a Sunday), to make an IRA contribution for 2006. But even if you obtain a filing extension, you do not gain any additional time to make your annual contribution.

Just because you have more time to act doesn't mean it's a good idea to delay. The earlier in the year you make your contribution, the sooner you begin to earn tax-deferred income. For example, if you make your 2006 contribution on January 15, 2006, rather than on April 16, 2007, you gain an additional 15 months of tax-deferred investment buildup in the IRA.

You can help your child jump-start his or her retirement savings by providing the funds for an IRA contribution. As long as your child has earned income (e.g., from a part-time or summer job), you can make a gift of the contribution amount to your child.

Example

Your child earns $1,800 from a summer job and uses her earnings as spending money for the year. You can give your child $1,800 to make an IRA contribution.

Under a new law, military personnel can base IRA contributions on tax-free combat pay and make back contributions for 2004 and 2005 through May 28, 2009 (see Chapter 14).

Looking ahead, the contribution limits are scheduled to increase as detailed in Table 5.2. After 2008, the basic limit will be increased for inflation in $500 increments. The additional limit for those age 50 and older remains at $1,000.

Also, the AGI phaseout range for determining whether active participants can deduct their IRA contributions also increases as detailed in Table 5.3.

TABLE 5.2 IRA Contribution Limits

Year	Basic Limit	Limit for Those Age 50 and Older
2006	$4,000	$5,000
2007	4,000	5,000
2008	5,000	6,000

TABLE 5.3 MAGI Phaseout Ranges for Active Participants Deducting IRA Contributions

Year	Married Filing Jointly	Single
2006	$75,000–85,000	$50,000–60,000
2007 and later	$80,000–100,000	$50,000–60,000

Pitfalls

IRAs are designed to be long-term investments for you. Don't make contributions if you know you'll need the funds within a short time (say, this year or next); early withdrawals may trigger a tax penalty and possibly an investment-related penalty (such as bank charges for cashing in a certificate of deposit before maturity) (early distribution penalties and the exceptions to them are discussed next).

Also, use care in figuring how much you can put into the IRA each year and how much you may be required to withdraw annually. Again, there are penalties for putting in too much or taking out too little under certain circumstances (discussed later).

You cannot treat reinvestments in your IRA account as additional contributions and claim a deduction for them. Dividend reinvestments are merely investment returns on your contributions.

EARLY DISTRIBUTION PENALTIES. If you need funds from your IRA before you retire, you may be subject to a 10 percent early distribution penalty. This penalty applies if you take money out before age 59½, unless you meet one of the following exceptions to the penalty:

- You become disabled (or die and your heirs take out the money).
- You take the money in a series of substantially equal periodic payments. This essentially means you take withdrawals in even amounts for at least five years or until you attain age 59½, whichever is later.

- You use the money to pay medical expenses exceeding 7.5 percent of your adjusted gross income.
- You are unemployed and receiving unemployment benefits for at least 12 consecutive weeks (or if you had been self-employed, you would have received such benefits due to lack of work).
- You use the money to pay higher education expenses (this exception to the 10 percent penalty is explained more fully in Chapter 3).
- You take out no more than $10,000 and use it to pay first-time home-buying expenses (this exception to the 10 percent penalty is explained more fully in Chapter 4).
- The IRS places levies on your IRA for back taxes.

Alert: At the time this book went to press Congress was considering the addition of a new penalty-free option for victims of Hurricane Katrina.

EXCESS CONTRIBUTIONS PENALTY. If you contribute to an IRA but later determine that your income prevents you from claiming the IRA deduction reported on your return (for example, you are an active plan participant and a later IRS audit increases your MAGI above the phaseout range), you are subject to a 6 percent excise tax, called an excess contributions penalty. This tax continues to apply every year in which the excess contribution (and earnings on such contribution) remains in the IRA.

You can, however, designate that the excess contribution be treated as your IRA contribution in a subsequent year.

Example

In 2006, you deduct your $4,000 IRA contribution on your return. In 2008, the IRS audits your return and increases your MAGI to an amount that makes your contribution nondeductible. You were not eligible for a deductible contribution in 2007 but can make a fully deductible contribution in 2008. Designate the 2006 contribution as your 2008 deductible contribution to limit the 6 percent penalty to 2006 and 2007.

INVESTMENT LIMITATIONS. You can invest your IRA contributions in a wide array of investment vehicles, including certificates of deposit, stocks, bonds, and mutual funds. You can even invest in real estate if you avoid self-dealing and other prohibited transaction rules.

However, the law places certain limits on the types of things you can invest in. If you opt to invest in a prohibited vehicle, you are treated as having taken a distribution; you are taxed on the amount and, if under age 59½, subject to a 10 percent penalty. You are prohibited from putting your IRA money into collectibles, which include:

- Antiques.
- Art works.
- Coins (other than state-issued coins or certain U.S. minted gold, silver, or platinum coins).
- Gems.
- Guns.
- Metals (other than gold, silver, platinum, or palladium bullion held by your IRA trustee).
- Stamps.

Also, even though there is no law preventing you, it makes no sense to put IRA money into tax-exempt municipal bonds. Since the IRA is already tax-deferred, you don't gain any benefit from the tax-free interest on the bonds. And when you take distributions from the IRA, they will all be treated as ordinary income (even though the underlying investment producing the earnings was tax-exempt bonds).

BORROWING LIMITATIONS. You are prohibited from borrowing from your IRA or using it as collateral for a loan. If you do so, the amount borrowed or used as collateral is treated as a taxable distribution to you (and can be subject to penalty if you are under age 59½).

But you can have access to the funds for a short time without any adverse tax consequences. You can take a distribution and use it for 60 days; as long as the funds are replaced by the end of 60 days, there is no taxable distribution.

ACCOUNT LOSSES. If your investments turn out to be unsound and you lose money, you generally can't deduct the loss. For example, if you put $5,000 of your IRA money into a technology mutual fund that declines in value to $800, you cannot deduct your $4,200 loss, even if the IRA sells the fund.

The only way to deduct a loss with respect to an IRA is if you made nondeductible IRA contributions and then liquidate all of your IRAs or spend all of the funds. In this case, if the total amount you receive is less than you contributed to the nondeductible IRA, you can claim a loss on your return for the year of liquidation or account depletion.

Where to Claim the IRA Deduction

You deduct your IRA contributions in the "Adjusted Gross Income" section of Form 1040 or 1040A. No special form or schedule is required to report your deductible contribution. You cannot claim an IRA deduction if you file Form 1040EZ.

If you are treating the contribution as a nondeductible IRA, you must complete Form 8606, Nondeductible IRAs. The purpose of this form is to help you keep track of your contributions so that when distributions are later taken, you won't pay tax on these after-tax contributions.

If you are subject to the 10 percent penalty on early withdrawals from the IRA, you must file Form 5329, Additional Taxes on Qualified Plans (including IRAs) and Other Tax-Favored Accounts, and enter the penalty in the "Other Taxes" section of Form 1040; you cannot file Form 1040A if you are subject to this penalty.

Roth IRAs

Roth IRAs (named after U.S. Senator William Roth, who sponsored the law) are an alternative personal retirement savings account that debuted in 1998. While these accounts offer no immediate tax break since contributions are not deductible, they offer long-term tax savings.

Benefit

You can contribute a limited amount to a special type of retirement savings account that allows you to build up tax-free income. (Contribution limits for Roth IRAs are the same as for deductible IRAs discussed earlier in this chapter.) While there is no current tax deduction for your contributions, you have access to your contributions and can withdraw them at any time tax free (after all, you made those contributions with after-tax dollars). But you can also withdraw earnings on those contributions tax free after five years if certain conditions discussed later are met.

CONVERSION. You can also convert your existing traditional IRA to a Roth IRA; there is no dollar limit on the amount you can convert. You must pay income tax on the account, just like you would if you had taken a distribution. But there's no 10 percent early distribution penalty if you are under age 59½ as long as the funds remain in the Roth IRA for at least five years.

Conditions for Making Roth IRA Contributions

To be eligible to make contributions to a Roth IRA, you must meet two conditions:

1. You must have earned income (as explained earlier under traditional IRAs).
2. Your modified adjusted gross income (MAGI) cannot exceed a set limit.

MAGI LIMIT. Your MAGI cannot be more than $95,000 if you are unmarried, or $150,000 if you are married filing jointly. A partial contribution is allowed if your MAGI is between $95,000 and $110,000 if you are unmarried, or $150,000 and $160,000 if you are married filing jointly. No contribution is permitted if

Example

You are single, age 40, with MAGI of $75,000. You can contribute up to $4,000 to a Roth IRA in 2006. If your MAGI is over $110,000, no contribution is allowed, even if your company doesn't have any qualified retirement plan. If your MAGI falls within the phaseout range, you can make a partial contribution. You figure your allowable limit using Worksheet 5.1, adapted from IRS Publication 590.

WORKSHEET 5.1 Reduced Roth IRA Contribution Limit

1.	Enter your MAGI.	1. ________
2.	Enter: • $150,000 if you file a joint return or are a qualifying widow(er). • $0 if you are married filing a separate return and you live with your spouse at any time during the year. • $95,000 for all other taxpayers.	2. ________
3.	Subtract line 2 from line 1.	3. ________
4.	Enter: • $10,000 if you file a joint return or are a qualifying widow(er). • $15,000 for all other taxpayers	4. ________
5.	Divide line 3 by line 4. Enter the result as a decimal (carried to three places). If the result is 1.000 or more, enter 1.000.	5. ________
6.	Enter the lesser of: • $4,000 ($5,000 if 50 or older), or • Your taxable compensation.	6. ________
7.	Multiply line 5 by line 6.	7. ________
8.	Subtract line 7 from line 6. Round the result up to the nearest $10. If the result is less than $200, enter $200.	8. ________
9.	Enter contributions for the year to other IRAs.	9. ________
10.	Subtract line 9 from line 6.	10. ________
11.	Enter the lesser of line 8 or line 10. *This is your reduced Roth IRA contribution limit.*	11. ________

your MAGI exceeds $110,000 if you are unmarried, or $160,000 if you are married filing jointly.

This MAGI limit applies whether or not you participate in another qualified retirement plan.

One important condition that applies to traditional IRAs does not apply to Roth IRAs: There is no age limit for making contributions. If you continue to work past age 70½, you can continue to put money into a Roth IRA (assuming your MAGI is below the limit).

Conditions for Converting a Traditional IRA to a Roth IRA

If you want the opportunity for your retirement savings to build up on a tax-free basis, consider converting your existing IRA to a Roth IRA. But you are permitted to make the conversion only if your modified adjusted gross income is below $100,000 (MAGI has the same meaning as it does for making Roth IRA contributions, explained earlier). If you are married, you must file jointly.

Example

In 2006, you are single with MAGI of $75,000. You are permitted to convert your existing traditional IRA to a Roth IRA. But if your MAGI is $120,000 (which is over the $100,000 limit), you cannot make the conversion this year. If your MAGI falls below the limit next year, you can consider making the conversion at that time.

You do *not* have to include in MAGI any income resulting from required minimum distributions (RMDs) taken from IRAs (in the past, RMDs from IRAs were included in MAGI).

Looking ahead: In 2010, you will be eligible to convert a traditional IRA to a Roth IRA without regard to your MAGI. (You can choose to convert some or all of your IRAs at that time.) The income from a conversion made only in 2010 is reported 50 percent in 2011 and 50 percent in 2012. Alternatively, you can opt to report all of the income in 2010.

Conditions for Tax-Free Income Withdrawals

You can withdraw earnings on your contributions tax free after five years if you meet *any* of the following three conditions:

1. You are over age 59½.
2. You become disabled.
3. You withdraw no more than $10,000 and use the money for qualified first-time home-buying expenses. (Qualified first-time home-buying expenses are explained in Chapter 4.)

The five-year period runs from the first day of the year to which your contributions relate. For example, if you contribute $4,000 to a Roth IRA for 2006 on April 16, 2007, the five-year period commences on January 1, 2006.

Example

In 2000, you contributed $2,000 to a Roth IRA. If you are at least 59½ in 2006, you can now withdraw the earnings you have built up in the account completely tax free—no income tax and no early distribution penalty.

Planning Tips

Assuming your income gives you the option of choosing between making a deductible IRA contribution or a nondeductible Roth IRA contribution, which alternative makes more sense for you? In most cases, choosing to make the Roth IRA contribution is wiser because the value of the IRA deduction you are forgoing is much smaller than the value of receiving tax-free income from the Roth IRA in the future.

Example

You are eligible to make either a deductible IRA contribution or a Roth IRA contribution. Assuming you are in the 28 percent tax bracket, a $4,000 deduction to a deductible IRA would save you $1,120 this year. But let's also assume that a $4,000 contribution can quadruple in the next 25 years to $16,000 (of which $12,000 is earnings on your contribution). If you opt for the Roth IRA, then when you withdraw the funds (assuming you are over age 59½), you won't pay any income tax on the earnings—a $4,480 tax savings if you are still in the 28 percent tax bracket.

Assuming you are eligible, should you convert an existing traditional IRA to a Roth IRA? There is no fixed answer; it depends on your situation. Factors to consider are your age (the younger you are, the longer you will have to build up tax-free income, but there is no age limit on making a conversion); your income (the more modest your income, the less the tax on the conversion); and whether you have the funds to pay the tax resulting from the conversion.

Contributions you make to a Roth 401(k) plan have no impact on your ability to contribute to a Roth IRA. For example, say in 2006, you contribute $15,000 to a Roth 401(k) through your employer's plan. You can also contribute $4,000 to a Roth IRA (assuming your income does not exceed the limits).

This decision to convert isn't an all-or-nothing proposition. You can convert part of your IRA to a Roth IRA. In fact, you can do this every year in which you are eligible to make a conversion.

Pitfalls

You should have the cash on hand to pay the tax resulting from the conversion. If you convert part of an IRA and use part of it to pay the tax, the portion used to pay the tax cannot later be placed in the Roth IRA. In effect, you lose out on an important retirement savings opportunity. What's more, if you are under age 59½, the portion used to pay the tax is subject to a 10 percent penalty.

Example

In 2006, when you are 40 years old, you opt to convert your $100,000 IRA to a Roth IRA. Assuming you are in the 28 percent tax bracket, the conversion costs you $28,000. If you use $28,000 of the $100,000 to pay the tax, then you only have $72,000 in your Roth IRA. And the $28,000 not converted to the Roth IRA is subject to a 10 percent penalty, for an additional tax of $2,800.

Before making a conversion, be sure that your MAGI is under $100,000. If it turns out that you exceed this limit, you may be subject to a 6 percent excise tax on excess contributions (and earnings on these contributions). This tax continues to apply every year in which the excess contributions (and earnings on them) remain in the Roth IRA.

Example

In 2006, you are single and your MAGI is $75,000. You convert your traditional IRA to a Roth IRA. In 2008, the IRS audits you and increases your MAGI by $30,000. Since you are now over the $100,000 MAGI limit for eligibility for making a conversion, your converted account is viewed as an excess contribution and all of it, including the earnings since the conversion, is subject to the 6 percent excise tax. (If eligible, you may opt to treat part of the conversion amount as a current Roth IRA contribution and avoid penalties on this portion of the conversion.)

You can avoid the excise tax by withdrawing the funds from the Roth IRA, but you can't put them back into the traditional IRA that they came from (it's well beyond the 60-day rollover period explained later in this chapter).

Don't confuse a Roth IRA with a Roth 401(k). Contributions to a Roth 401(k) are separate and distinct from contributions to a Roth IRA.

Where to Claim the Benefit

You do not report contributions you make to a Roth IRA on your return (remember, they are not deductible). It does not matter which income tax return—Form 1040, 1040A, or 1040EZ—you file.

If you convert your traditional IRA to a Roth IRA, you must report the income resulting from the conversion in the "Income" section of Form 1040 or Form 1040A. You cannot file Form 1040EZ to report a conversion. If you use a portion of your IRA to pay the tax on the conversion and are subject to the 10 percent penalty on this amount, you must file Form 5329, Additional Taxes on Qualified Retirement Plans (Including IRAs) and Other Tax Favored Accounts and enter the penalty in the "Other Taxes" section of Form 1040; you cannot file Form 1040A if you are subject to this penalty.

If you make excess contributions to the Roth IRA (by contribution or conversion), you are subject to a 6 percent excise tax and must file Form 5329, Additional Taxes on Qualified Plans (Including IRAs) and Other Tax-Favored Accounts. Enter the excise tax in the "Other Taxes" section of Form 1040; you cannot file Form 1040A if you are subject to this tax.

IRA Rollovers

IRAs are highly portable—they can be transferred from one investment company to another with no immediate tax consequences if certain conditions are met. This allows taxpayers to move accounts from a bank to a mutual fund or from one brokerage firm to another.

Benefit

You can transfer funds from one IRA to another without any current tax. There are no dollar limits on the amount you can roll over each year.

There are two ways in which to make the transfer:

1. *Direct transfers*. You can instruct the custodian or trustee of your IRA to transfer funds directly to the custodian or trustee of another IRA.
2. *Distribution and reinvestment*. You can take a withdrawal of funds from your IRA and replace the funds within 60 days.

Conditions

The transfer method you use determines the conditions you must meet to achieve tax-free treatment.

DIRECT TRANSFERS. You instruct the custodian or trustee of your IRAs to complete the action; you cannot receive any funds that are part of the transfer. There is no time requirement for your fiduciaries to complete the transaction. There is no limit on the number of direct transfers you can make each year.

DISTRIBUTION AND REINVESTMENT. You must complete the transaction within 60 days. Generally, the IRS cannot extend this period. But you may qualify for a hardship exception in limited circumstances detailed later under "Pitfalls."

You are permitted to make only one rollover per calendar year. This rollover limit applies separately to each IRA account. So, for example, if you have three IRAs, you potentially have the opportunity to make three separate rollovers in the same year.

Note: Regardless of which method you select, rollovers are handled separately from annual contributions to IRAs and Roth IRAs. Thus, for example, you may make a rollover even if you also make a deductible IRA contribution for the year.

Planning Tip

You can use funds in your IRA as a short-term loan. While borrowing against an IRA is not permitted, you can take a distribution and avoid current tax if you replace the funds within 60 days.

Pitfalls

If you take a distribution and plan to reinvest within 60 days, make sure to watch the calendar closely. If you miss the deadline by even one day, the entire distribution becomes taxable to you.

If you try to complete the rollover on time but outside events prevent you from doing so, you may obtain an extension to the 60-day limit. The limit is automatically extended if the account is frozen, if you are serving in a combat zone, or if the President declares your area a disaster area or a terrorist or military action. But the IRS can also extend the deadline for hardship cases. It will automatically extend the deadline if the following three conditions are met:

1. The funds are received by the financial institution within the 60-day period but the institution fails to complete the transaction by this deadline.
2. You follow all of the financial institution's requirements for a rollover but due to its error the rollover is not completed in time.
3. The funds are actually deposited in the rollover account within a year of the start of the 60-day period.

The IRS will consider granting an extension for hardship cases under other circumstances that include:

- Disability.
- Mourning period for a spouse.
- Hospitalization.
- Postal error.
- Error by the financial institution other than one already mentioned.

For this discretionary extension, you must request a private letter ruling. In deciding whether to grant your request, the IRS will take into account the facts and circumstances of your situation, including the length of the delay in completing the rollover and whether you cashed a distribution check.

Where to Claim the Benefit

IRA rollovers that are distributed to you are reported to you (and the IRS) on Form 1099-R, Distributions from Pensions, Annuities, Retirement or Profit-Sharing Plans, IRAs, Insurance Contracts, Etc.

You must report the distribution on your return, but if you successfully completed the transfer within 60 days, enter only zero on the income line for IRA distributions in the "Income" section of Form 1040 or Form 1040A. You cannot file Form 1040EZ in this case.

401(k) and Similar Plans

Pensions used to be the responsibility of employers, but for the past quarter of a century that responsibility has shifted to employees. To make it easier for employees to pay for their own retirement savings, the tax law has created special retirement plans. Companies set up the plans, but employees fund them (in whole or in part) by contributing a portion of their salary each year. Employees decide how their contributions are to be invested by selecting from a menu of investment options provided by the employer. The tax law encourages employee contributions by allowing them to escape immediate taxation.

Benefit

If you are eligible to participate in your employer's 401(k) or similar plan, you can agree each year to contribute a portion of your salary as your contribution to the plan. You can change your contribution from year to year; you may also be able to reduce it within a year.

Your contribution is called an elective deferral or salary reduction amount. This amount is *not* treated as compensation to you for the year; you do not pay income tax on your elective deferral. For example, if your wages this year are $45,000 and you contribute $8,000 to your company's 401(k) plan, only $37,000 of your wages is reported on your Form W-2; you're only taxed on $37,000 this year.

Note: Contributions to a Roth 401(k) are not treated as elective deferrals; they must be made with after-tax contributions.

Conditions

Eligibility requirements to make elective deferrals are spelled out in your company's plan. You should receive a summary of the plan from your employer and be given an opportunity to designate your elective deferrals for the year (typically within a month or so before the start of a new year or upon becoming eligible to participate in your company's plan).

ELECTIVE DEFERRAL LIMITS. The law fixes the *maximum* elective deferral limits for each year. Your plan may place other restrictions or limits on how much you can contribute annually to the plan.

The law allows you to contribute up to 100 percent of your earnings to the plan, up to a dollar limit on contributions. For 2006, the dollar limit is $15,000 (or $20,000 if you are age 50 or older by the end of 2006).

Example

In 2006, you are 28 years old and earn $30,000. Your maximum contribution is $15,000 (although your plan may restrict contributions to a percentage of your compensation).

Planning Tips

If you are pressed for funds and find it difficult to take full advantage of the elective deferral opportunity, at least contribute what is necessary to obtain your employer's matching contribution if available. Your employer's matching contribution is, in effect, "free money" to you, and it would be unwise to ignore it.

Example

In 2006, you are permitted under the plan to contribute $15,000 through elective deferrals. Your employer will match 50 percent of your contributions up to 6 percent of your compensation. If you earn $30,000, you must contribute at least $3,600 to obtain your employer's top contribution on your behalf of $1,800.

Starting in 2007, the basic limit and the limit for those age 50 and older will be adjusted annually for inflation.

If you are self-employed and have no employees, you can set up a solo 401(k) to maximize your retirement plan contributions. You effectively make both employee and employer contributions (even though you are self-employed). This means you can contribute a total of up to $44,000 ($49,000 if you are age 50 or older by the end of 2006).

401(k) plans can offer a Roth 401(k) option. If your plan allows it, you can choose to make after-tax contributions to a Roth 401(k) account so that withdrawals can become tax free (like withdrawals from Roth IRAs). Contributions to a traditional and/or Roth 401(k) cannot exceed the annual limit (which is $15,000, or $20,000 for those age 50 or older by December 31, 2006). You can choose to split your contribution between a regular 401(k) and a Roth 401(k) —for example, $10,000 to a regular 401(k) and $5,000 to a Roth 401(k); total contributions cannot exceed annual limits.

Pitfalls

Once you have made your elective deferral contributions, access to your money is limited by the terms of the plan and the tax law. Generally, you can't receive the funds until you retire from the company.

Even though you are not taxed on your elective deferral amount (it is subtracted from your taxable compensation), such amount is still subject to Social Security and Medicare taxes, which are withheld from your pay.

Where to Claim the Benefit

You do not have to report anything on your tax return. You will note that your elective deferral amount is subtracted from your pay so that only the reduced amount is reported as taxable compensation to you on Form W-2, which you then report as wages on whichever tax return you file (Form 1040, 1040A, or 1040EZ).

Self-Employed Retirement Plans

In 1962, self-employed individuals for the first time were given the opportunity to set up tax-qualified retirement plans similar to those available to corporations. Initially referred to as HR 10 plans (after the number of the tax bill creating them) or Keogh plans (after the senator sponsoring the bill), these plans have evolved over the years into the same retirement savings plans as are open to corporations. The tax law today calls them self-employed retirement plans.

Benefit

If you are a sole proprietor or independent contractor and have a profitable year, you can contribute to a qualified retirement plan. There are two main types of plans:

1. *Defined contribution plan.* The funds you have on retirement are based solely on what you've contributed and how well your investments have performed. A profit-sharing plan is a defined contribution plan.
2. *Defined benefit plan.* At retirement you receive a pension based on your earnings (each year before retirement your contribution is determined by an actuary to be sufficient to pay this pension at a specific age, assuming a certain return on your investments).

You claim a deduction for your contribution. For a defined contribution plan in 2006, you can deduct 25 percent of compensation or $44,000, whichever is less. However, for self-employed individuals, net earnings from self-employment (the figure on which contributions are based) must be reduced by the contribution itself, so that the effective contribution rate is only 20 percent (not 25 percent). Also, you must reduce your net earnings from self-employment by one-half of your self-employment taxes. It may sound complicated to figure your allowable deduction, but you can use Worksheet 5.2, adapted from IRS Publication 560, to guide you.

For a defined benefit plan, your deduction is based on what is actuarially required to fund the promised pension. You need the actuary to tell you what your contribution is, based on plan assumptions (e.g., what age you expect to retire at).

Conditions

There are many conditions for starting and maintaining a qualified retirement plan. Some are highly complex and well beyond the scope of this book. But here are some things to watch out for:

- The plan must be set up before the end of the year. Even though you have until the due date of your return (including extensions) to make contributions, the plan must be in existence (you must sign the paperwork) before the end of the year.

Example

In 2006, you are self-employed and profitable. You want to contribute to a profit-sharing plan for the year. You must set up the plan by December 31, 2006. You have until April 16, 2007 (or later if you obtain a filing extension) to actually put your contribution into the plan.

- You must cover employees if they meet certain requirements. This raises the cost of having a plan. But you deduct contributions on behalf of your employees from your business income, reducing your net earnings from self-employment.
- You *may* have to file an annual information return with the U.S. Department of Labor. Generally, all qualified plans must file an information return, even if you are the only plan participant. However, if assets within the plan are no more than $100,000 (and have not exceeded this figure after 1993), you don't have to file anything if you (or you and your spouse) are the only participants. For plan years starting in 2007 (with returns due in 2008), no filing is required if plan assets for a one-participant plan are $250,000 or less at the end of the year. A simplified annual return will be used for plans covering fewer than 25 participants.

WORKSHEET 5.2 Figuring Your 2006 Contribution to a Defined Contribution Plan

1. Enter your net earnings from self-employment.	1.	______
2. Enter your deduction for self-employment tax (which is one-half of the tax).	2.	______
3. Subtract line 2 from line 1.	3.	______
4. Enter your effective contribution rate (no more than 20 percent).	4.	______
5. Multiply line 3 by line 4.	5.	______
6. Multiply $220,000 by your actual contribution rate (no more than 25 percent).	6.	______
7. Enter the smaller of line 5 or line 6.	7.	______
8. Contribution dollar limit.	8.	$44,000
9. Enter the smaller of line 7 or line 8. *This is your contribution.*	9.	______

Example

In 2006, you have net earnings from self-employment (your profits on Schedule C) of $80,000 and your plan sets a contribution limit of 25 percent. Your contribution for 2006 on your behalf is $14,776, figured as follows:

1. Enter your net earnings from self-employment.	1.	$80,000
2. Enter your deduction for self-employment tax (which is one-half of the tax).		6,120
3. Subtract line 2 from line 1.	3.	73,880
4. Enter your effective contribution rate (no more than 20 percent).	4.	20%
5. Multiply line 3 by line 4.	5.	$14,776
6. Multiply $220,000 by your actual contribution rate (no more than 25 percent)	6.	55,000
7. Enter the smaller of line 5 or line 6.	7.	14,776
8. Contribution dollar limit.	8.	$44,000
9. Enter the smaller of line 7 or line 8. *This is your contribution.*	9.	$14,776

Planning Tip

You may want to consult with a benefits expert to help you decide which type of retirement plan is best for you, based on your profitability, age, the nature of your business, and other factors, including your desire to optimize contributions.

Pitfalls

Having a qualified retirement plan means you are subject to annual reporting requirements referred to earlier; the government wants to know some details about your plan.

Generally, for the 2006 plan year, you must file Form 5500-EZ, Annual Return of One Participant (Owners and Their Spouses). But you are exempt from filing if you have a one-participant plan (you are the only participant) and plan assets of $100,000 or less at the end of every year beginning after 1993.

If you are required to file, you cannot download the form from the Internet like most other tax forms because Form 5500-EZ is a scannable form that must be obtained by mail or at an IRS office. Usually it is sent to you automatically if you have filed one in the past; otherwise, you can request one from the IRS by calling 800-829-FORM.

This form is *not* filed with the IRS. Instead it is filed with the Employee Benefits Security Administration (formerly called the Pension and Welfare Benefits Agency) of the U.S. Department of Labor (www.dol.gov/ebsa). It can be filed by mail or EFAST (electronic filing through a tax professional). It is due by the last day of the seventh month following the close of the plan year (e.g., July 31, 2007, for the 2006 year of a calendar-year plan).

Where to Claim the Benefit

You deduct contributions to the plan for your employees on Schedule C (such contributions are a business expense). You deduct your own contributions in the section for "Adjusted Gross Income" on Form 1040. No special form or schedule is required for figuring your deduction.

You cannot deduct contributions if you file Form 1040A or 1040EZ.

SEPs

A simplified employee pension (SEP) is a type of IRA that any business, whether self-employed or incorporated, can use for retirement savings. It is "simplified" because it is easy to set up and there are few administrative requirements (for example, there is no annual reporting to the government as is the case with most other company-sponsored retirement plans). The business sets up the plan and makes tax-deductible contributions to participant accounts.

Benefit

If you are self-employed (sole proprietor, independent contractor, partner, or limited liability company member) and have a profitable year, you can make deductible contributions to a simplified employee pension plan or SEP. This is a type of IRA to which you can contribute more than to a traditional IRA. The same rules that apply to sole proprietors also apply to partners and LLC members.

You claim a deduction for the contribution on your behalf as an adjustment to gross income (not as a business expense). For 2006, the top deduction is 25 percent of your compensation or $44,000, whichever is less. Compensation if you are self-employed means your net earnings from self-employment, reduced by one-half of self-employment tax and by the contribution for yourself; your effective percentage rate becomes 20 percent in this case.

Example

In 2006, you are a consultant (sole proprietor) and have net earnings from self-employment of $50,000 (after reduction for one-half of self-employment tax). Your maximum deductible contribution is $10,000 ($50,000 × 20%).

Unlike qualified retirement plans, there is no annual reporting requirement for SEPs.

Conditions

You must meet two conditions to deduct your SEP contributions:

1. You must have profits if you are self-employed or receive a salary if you are an S corporation.
2. You must include your employees within the plan if they (1) are at least age 21, (2) earn more than $450 in 2006, and (3) have worked for you at least three of the past five years. If they are included in the plan, you must make contributions on their behalf based on their compensation.

Even though a SEP is a type of IRA, you can continue to make contributions on your behalf beyond the age of 70½ as long as you continue to work. However, you must still commence your required minimum distributions at age 70½ (even though you are still working). You cannot postpone taking distributions until retirement because you own more than 5 percent of the business.

Planning Tips

If you failed to set up a qualified retirement plan by the end of the year, you can still set up and contribute to a SEP up to the extended due date of your return.

Example

You are an independent contractor in 2006 but did not set up a profit-sharing plan before the end of the year. You can set up and make your contributions to a SEP through April 16, 2007, or if you obtain an automatic six-month filing extension for your 2006 return, to October 15, 2007.

You can convert a SEP to a Roth IRA if you meet the eligibility requirements discussed earlier in this chapter. Conversion allows all future earnings on the money to become tax free when you take withdrawals from the Roth IRA (but you must pay now a tax on the converted amount).

Pitfall

You cannot contribute to a SEP if you also have a self-employed qualified retirement plan; you must choose which plan is more favorable to you. Excess contributions are subject to the same penalties discussed earlier under IRAs.

Where to Claim the Benefit

You deduct contributions to the plan for your employees on Schedule C (such contributions are a business expense). You deduct your own contributions in the section for "Adjusted Gross Income" on Form 1040. No special form or schedule is required to figure your deduction.

You cannot deduct contributions if you file Form 1040A or 1040EZ.

SIMPLEs

Savings incentive match plans for employees, or SIMPLEs, are a type of retirement plan that allows businesses to share the cost of funding retirement savings. The company sets up the plan and employees are given the option of contributing within set limits a portion of their salaries to the plan. The company must make certain contributions according to a formula fixed by the tax law. The reason this type of retirement plan is SIMPLE lies in the ease of setting it up and administering it.

Benefit

If you are self-employed or a shareholder in a corporation, the business can set up a retirement plan SIMPLE plan that allows you (and your employees) to make elective deferrals (salary reduction contributions) to the plan. Such amounts are excluded from your income. As an employer, you must contribute a set amount for each plan participant; you deduct your employer contribution as a business expense.

Whether you are the owner of the business or merely a rank-and-file employee, you can make elective deferral contributions to the plan. Like 401(k) plans discussed earlier, the portion of your compensation that you treat as your elective deferral is not included in your income for the year. (Limits on elective deferrals and required employer contributions are explained next under "Conditions").

Earnings on contributions build up on a tax-deferred basis.

A SIMPLE can be set up as either a SIMPLE-IRA or a SIMPLE-401(k) plan. For purposes of the following discussion, only the SIMPLE-IRA, the more popular type, is examined.

Conditions

There are only two key conditions for setting up a SIMPLE plan:

1. You must be a "small employer." You must have had 100 or fewer employees who received $5,000 or more in compensation from you in the preceding year. If you set up the plan but in a later year exceed the 100-employee limit, you have two more years to continue the SIMPLE plan; after two years you no longer qualify for a SIMPLE plan because you are not a small employer. You can also set up a plan if you are self-employed (even though you don't have any employees).
2. You do not maintain any other qualified plan. If, for example, you already have a profit-sharing plan, you can't also have a SIMPLE plan.

ELECTIVE DEFERRAL LIMIT. Whether you are the owner of the business or just an ordinary employee who is eligible to participate, you can agree to contribute a portion of your annual compensation to the SIMPLE plan. Your contribution, or elective deferral amount, is limited in 2006 to $10,000, or $12,500 if you are age 50 or older by the end of 2006. However, your contribution cannot exceed 100 percent of your compensation.

Example

In 2006, you are under age 50; you can contribute $10,000 whether your wages are $10,000, $30,000, or even $100,000. You can contribute up to 100 percent of your compensation, but no more than $10,000.

REQUIRED EMPLOYER CONTRIBUTION. Like other retirement plans, you must meet certain nondiscrimination requirements; your plan cannot favor you as the owner and other highly paid employees. However, SIMPLE plans don't have any complicated nondiscrimination formulas. Instead, if you make the required employer contribution on behalf of each employee who is eligible to participate, your plan is viewed as nondiscriminatory.

You must adopt one of these two contribution formulas and make contributions accordingly:

1. Employer matching contribution on a dollar-for-dollar basis.
2. Nonelective contributions of 2 percent of compensation.

In an employer matching contribution arrangement, you match employee contributions on a dollar-for-dollar basis up to 3 percent of employee compensation. If an employee does not make an elective deferral, you do not have to contribute anything on behalf of the employee.

Example

Your employee makes an elective deferral contribution to the SIMPLE of $5,000. Her annual compensation is $40,000. You must contribute $1,200 on behalf of this employee (matching her contribution of $5,000 up to 3 percent of $40,000).

Example

You make an elective deferral of $10,000, the maximum permitted in 2006. Your compensation is $350,000. Your matching contribution in this case is $10,000 (matching your contribution of $10,000, which is smaller than 3 percent of $350,000, or $10,500).

If the formula requires nonelective contributions of 2 percent of compensation these contributions must be made without regard to any employee elective deferrals. Thus, even if the employee makes no elective deferral, you must still contribute 2 percent on the employee's behalf if the employee is eligible to participate in the SIMPLE plan. No more than $220,000 of compensation can be taken into account in figuring nonelective contributions.

Example

Your employee makes an elective deferral contribution to the SIMPLE of $5,000. Her annual compensation is $40,000. You must contribute $800 (2 percent of $40,000).

Example

You make an elective deferral of $10,000, the maximum permitted in 2006. Your compensation is $280,000. Your nonelective contribution in this case is $4,400 (2 percent of $220,000).

Planning Tips

SIMPLEs may enable you to make the largest contribution possible (compared with self-employed retirement plans and SEPs) if your self-employment income is modest. SIMPLEs may also be the most cost-effective plan to use if you have employees. Discuss your retirement plan options with a benefits expert.

If you have made contributions to a SIMPLE-IRA, you can convert it to a Roth IRA (see earlier in this chapter). But you must wait at least two years following the contribution to make the conversion or be subject to a 25 percent early distribution penalty if you are under age 59½.

The basic limit ($10,000) and the limit for those age 50 and older will be adjusted annually for inflation.

Pitfalls

Distributions from SIMPLE-IRAs before age 59½ are subject to a higher early distribution penalty than the penalty imposed on traditional IRAs. Instead of the usual 10 percent early distribution penalty, you may be subject to a penalty of 25 percent for distributions within two years of SIMPLE-IRA participation if you are under age 59½.

Where to Claim the Deduction

You deduct contributions to the plan for your employees on Schedule C of Form 1040 (such contributions are a business expense). You deduct your own contributions in the section of Form 1040 marked "Adjusted Gross Income." You do not have to complete any form or schedule to claim the deduction.

You cannot deduct contributions to a SIMPLE if you file Form 1040A or 1040EZ.

Special Rules for Hurricane Victims

In the wake of Hurricanes Katrina, Rita and Wilma, various relief provisions affecting retirement plans have been enacted for individuals in affected areas. While none of the special rules increase the permissible size of contributions or otherwise change the basic rules discussed throughout this chapter, they do provide some important relief. Here is roundup of the special rules.

QUALIFIED HURRICANE WITHDRAWALS. These withdrawals from a qualified retirement plan up to $100,000 (called a qualified distribution) before January 1, 2007, are exempt from the 10 percent early distribution penalty for those under age 59½. Excess withdrawals (amounts above $100,000) do not enjoy special treatment.

The income resulting from the withdrawal can be spread equally over three years to minimize the impact of the income.

The penalty on the distribution can be avoided if the funds are rolled over within three years of the withdrawal (instead of the usual 60-day rollover period).

Form 8915, *Qualified Hurricane Katrina Retirement Plan Distributions and Recontributions*, is used for reporting qualified distributions and repayments.

LOANS FROM RETIREMENT PLANS. Loans from qualified retirement plans can be made up to the lesser of $100,000 or 100 percent of the account balance (up from the usual limits of $50,000 and 50 percent, respectively). A loan of $10,000 is permissible even if this exceeds the account balance.

IRA WITHDRAWALS. IRA withdrawals made by someone under age 59½ to purchase a first home are not subject to the 10 percent early distribution penalty if the home was in the disaster area and funds are timely recontributed to the IRA. More specifically, if the purchase or construction of the home was canceled because of the storm, the penalty is avoided if funds were withdrawn from the IRA after February 28, 2005, and before August 29, 2005, and are recontributed during the period from August 25, 2005, through February 28, 2006.

Retirement Saver's Credit

A worker's wages just don't seem to stretch far enough to pay the bills *and* save for retirement. The tax law tries to encourage those having the most difficulty—low-income taxpayers—to make retirement plan contributions by offering a special tax credit. Those qualifying for this credit also enjoy other tax benefits from making the contributions, such as a deduction for IRA contributions. At the end of the road, taxpayers taking advantage of these breaks have not only enjoyed current tax savings but also built up their personal retirement savings.

Benefit

If you contribute to a retirement plan through your company or to an IRA, you may be eligible to claim a tax credit of up to 50 percent of contributions up to $2,000, for a top credit of $1,000. This credit is in addition to any other benefit to which you may be entitled, such as salary reduction for a 401(k) plan contribution or a deduction for an IRA contribution.

Conditions

There are three conditions for claiming the retirement saver's credit. In order to claim the credit you must:

1. Have qualified retirement savings contributions for the year.
2. Be an eligible individual.
3. Have adjusted gross income below a set amount.

QUALIFIED RETIREMENT SAVINGS CONTRIBUTIONS. Retirement savings can come from several sources; you total your contributions to all of the following:

- IRA contributions (whether they are deductible or nondeductible).
- Roth IRA contributions.
- Elective deferrals (salary reduction contributions) to 401(k) plans, 403(b) annuities, or 457 plans.
- Voluntary contributions to any qualified retirement plan of your employer.

You must reduce your qualified contributions and elective deferrals by distributions included in your income that you receive from any qualified retirement plan of your employer or from a deferred compensation plan of your employer (if your employer is a state or local government or tax-exempt organization). You must also reduce your qualified contributions and elective deferrals by distributions from Roth IRAs during the five years following your contributions to such accounts or from a rollover to a Roth IRA. You must include not only distributions in the current year, but also those made in the two preceding years and in the period after the year for which you are figuring the credit up to the due date of the return (including extensions).

Example

You want to claim the retirement saver's credit for 2006. In determining your eligible contributions and elective deferrals for 2006, you must look to distributions taken in 2004 and 2005, plus any distributions you take in 2006 and up to April 16, 2007 (assuming you file your return by this deadline).

You don't have to reduce your qualified contributions and elective deferrals by the following distributions:

- Amounts treated as loans from a qualified plan.
- Excess contributions.
- Deductions for dividends paid on certain employer securities.

- Contributions returned to you before the due date of your return.
- IRA accounts rolled over to a Roth IRA.

ELIGIBLE INDIVIDUAL. To be eligible to claim the credit you must:

- Be at least 18 years old by the close of the year. Thus, even though someone who is 14 can contribute to an IRA, he or she isn't old enough to claim this credit.
- Not be claimed as a dependent on another taxpayer's return.
- Not be a full-time student (someone who is enrolled full-time for at least five calendar months during the year).

MAGI LIMIT. To claim the top credit, your modified adjusted gross income must be below a set amount. If your MAGI is more modest, you may be entitled to a smaller credit. No credit can be claimed if your MAGI exceeds a set limit, detailed in Table 5.4. MAGI for this purpose is your adjusted gross income increased by the foreign earned income exclusion, the foreign housing exclusion, or the exclusion for income from U.S. possessions or Puerto Rico.

Example

In 2006, you are single with MAGI of $22,000. Your elective deferral to your company's 401(k) plan for the year is $3,000. You may claim a tax credit of $200 (10 percent of $2,000, the maximum contribution taken into account in figuring the credit).

TABLE 5.4 MAGI Limits for Retirement Saver's Credit

Modified Adjusted Gross Income						
Joint Return		Head of Household		All Others		Applicable Percentage
Over	Not Over	Over	Not Over	Over	Not Over	
$ 0	$30,000	$ 0	$22,500	$ 0	$15,000	50%
30,000	32,500	22,500	24,375	15,000	16,250	20
32,500	50,000	24,375	37,500	16,250	25,000	10
50,000		37,500		25,000		0

Planning Tip

The retirement saver's credit is one of the very few times that the tax law allows you to "double dip." The credit can be claimed in addition to other benefits that contributions entitle you to. For example, even though you excluded your 401(k) plan contributions from income, you can still claim the credit with respect to those same contributions. Similarly, even though you deducted your IRA contributions, you can also base the credit on the same contributions.

Pitfalls

Even though you meet all conditions for claiming the credit, you may lose out on the opportunity to use it if you claim certain other credits that offset your tax liability. The retirement saver's credit cannot be in excess of your regular tax liability, plus your alternative minimum tax liability, reduced by the sum of all credits to which you may also be entitled other than the child tax credit, the adoption credit, and the foreign tax credit. You cannot receive a refund from the retirement saver's credit, and you cannot carry forward the unused amount to a future year.

Lower-income individuals who qualify for the 50 percent credit may not have sufficient tax liability to use the entire credit. For example, a married couple with MAGI of $25,000 is entitled to a maximum credit of $1,000 (50% of $2,000). However, their tax liability cannot be more than $860 (10% of [$25,000 MAGI – $10,000 standard deduction – $6,400 exemptions]).

Where to Claim the Credit

To claim the retirement saver's credit, you must file Form 1040; you cannot claim this credit if you file Form 1040A or Form 1040EZ.

You figure the credit on Form 8880, Credit for Qualified Retirement Savings Contributions, which you attach to the return. You enter the amount of your credit in the "Tax and Credits" section of Form 1040.

Custodial/Trustee Fees

Having an IRA isn't necessarily free—there may be charges for maintaining an account with a brokerage firm or mutual fund that acts as the IRA's custodian or trustee. For example, a brokerage firm may charge $10 or more each year just for keeping an IRA with the firm. Fortunately, these fees may be deductible if certain conditions are met.

Benefit

You can deduct your payments of custodial or trustee fees to maintain your IRA. There is no dollar limit on what you can deduct.

This deduction is claimed as a miscellaneous itemized deduction, which is subject to a 2 percent floor (only miscellaneous expenses over 2 percent of your adjusted gross income are deductible). You cannot claim this deduction if you use the standard deduction.

Conditions

You must pay the custodial or trustee fees directly. You cannot have them debited from your IRA account.

Planning Tip

Since you must pay the custodial or trustee fees directly, talk to your custodian or trustee to make sure the fees are separately billed to you and not automatically debited from the account. Payment by check will ensure that you have adequate proof for your deduction.

Pitfall

As a practical matter, you may not obtain any tax benefit from the payment of custodial or trustee fees. If your miscellaneous itemized deductions, including the one for payment of IRA custodial fees, are not more than 2 percent of your adjusted gross income, then you cannot use the deductible expense.

Where to Claim the Deduction

You claim the deduction as a miscellaneous itemized deduction on Schedule A of Form 1040. Note in the "Miscellaneous Deductions" section of Schedule A (or on a separate statement attached to the schedule) that your expense is "custodial/trustee fees." You do not have to complete any other form or schedule to claim this deduction.

You cannot claim the deduction for custodial fees if you file Form 1040A or Form1040EZ.

Employer-Paid Retirement Planning Advice

Retirement planning is a difficult and confusing subject. Employees nearing the end of their careers often must make important decisions regarding their company retirement plans and their personal retirement savings in order to maximize their retirement income and minimize their taxes. Companies may step in to assist these employees by bringing in outside professional assistance to provide retirement planning advice. Employees taking advantage of this expertise may enjoy the fringe benefit tax free.

Benefit

You are not taxed on the value of retirement planning advice you (and your spouse) receive through your employer. You can exclude this benefit from your income. There is no dollar limit on what you can exclude.

Conditions

This fringe benefit must be provided to you by your employer on a nondiscriminatory basis (i.e., the benefit cannot be limited to owners and highly paid employees). Whether the benefit is discriminatory is something determined by your employer, not by you.

The tax-free benefit is limited to employer-paid retirement education services that you can use to make more informed investment decisions for your retirement plan contributions as well as decisions regarding distributions upon termination of employment. You may not exclude the value of related services, such as tax-preparation, accounting, legal, or brokerage services.

Planning Tip

Many companies are now offering free online investment information related to their retirement plans; take advantage of any advice offered.

Pitfall

There is no downside to taking full advantage of any advice and information your employer offers you. If, however, you believe the advice you have received is not suitable or helpful, then talk to your own retirement-planning adviser.

Where to Claim the Benefit

Since the benefit is not included in your income, you do not have to report it on your return or complete any form or schedule to claim it.

Charitable Transfers of IRA Distributions

There is a special break for those age $70\frac{1}{2}$ and older during 2006 and 2007. They can make direct transfers (rollovers) of distributions from their IRAs to a public charity and avoid any income tax on such distributions. No charitable contribution deduction can be claimed for this rollover. There is an annual limit of $100,000 on this break.

CHAPTER 6

Charitable Giving

Americans are very generous people. Aside from the good feeling you get from following your philanthropic nature, the tax laws reward you for making donations. Americans donated $260.53 billion to charities in 2005 (according to estimates by the Giving USA group).

This chapter explains:

- Cash donations
- Appreciated property donations
- IRA payouts to charity
- Used clothing and car donations
- Intellectual property donations
- Real estate donated for conservation purposes
- Bargain sales
- Volunteer expenses
- Tickets to fund-raisers, raffles, and sporting events
- Membership fees to nonprofit organizations
- Student exchange program
- Special inventory donations
- Appraisal fees and other costs

This chapter also contains a record keeper that you can use to track your cash contributions throughout the year.

For more information, see IRS Publication 526, *Charitable Contributions;* IRS Publication 561, *Determining the Value of Donated Property;* IRS Publication 1771, *Charitable Contributions—Substantiation and Disclosure Requirements;* and IRS Publication 4303, *A Donor's Guide to Vehicle Donations.*

Cash Donations

Donations by cash, check, or credit card to charities or government bodies are deductible within set limits if certain conditions are met. The impact of this deduction is that Uncle Sam becomes your partner in making contributions. For example, if you are in the 33 percent tax bracket, the government is effectively making almost one-third of your contribution through the tax savings you enjoy from the donation.

Benefit

You can deduct the cash donations you make to tax-exempt organizations and the government. Generally, you can write off annually your cash donations up to 50 percent of your adjusted gross income (AGI) if you itemize your deductions. There is no dollar limit on your annual deduction; you are merely limited by your AGI.

Donations in excess of 50 percent of your AGI can be carried forward for up to five years.

Example

If your AGI is $30,000, you can deduct cash donations of only $15,000. If you actually donated $20,000, you can deduct $15,000 this year and carry the $5,000 excess amount forward to next year (if it is deductible next year, depending on your AGI).

Conditions

To claim a deduction for your cash contributions to charity, you must meet all three conditions:

1. Donations must be made to a qualified charity.
2. You cannot deduct donations exceeding 50 percent of your adjusted gross income.
3. You must have proof of your donations.

QUALIFIED CHARITY. Just because a charity calls itself one does not mean it is tax-qualified; it must receive IRS approval to be a tax-exempt organization to which contributions are tax deductible. The charity must be a domestic nonprofit organization, trust, community chest, fund, or foundation that is operated exclusively for one of the following purposes:

- Charitable purposes.
- Fostering amateur sports competition.
- Prevention of cruelty to children or animals.
- Religious purposes.
- Scientific, literary, and educational purposes.

Other organizations or places to which you can make tax-deductible contributions are:

- Domestic fraternal groups operating under a lodge system.
- Domestic nonprofit veterans' organizations or auxiliary units.
- Legal services corporations set up under the Legal Services Corporation Act.
- Nonprofit cemetery and burial companies (as long as voluntary contributions benefit the whole cemetery and not merely your plot).
- U.S. government; government of a U.S. possession, state, city, or town; or Indian tribal government.

Certain well-known charities, such as the American Red Cross, the United Way, the Boy Scouts and Girl Scouts, and the Salvation Army, are clearly authorized to accept tax-deductible contributions. But if you have any question about an organization's status, ask about its status or check with the IRS, which maintains an online database in IRS Publication 78, *Cumulative List of Organizations*, at www.irs.gov/article/0,,id=96136,00.html.

AGI LIMIT. Your deduction generally is limited to 50 percent of your adjusted gross income (AGI), which is explained more thoroughly in the introduction to this book. While cash donations made in the wake of Hurricane Katrina after August 27, 2005, and before January 1, 2006, were fully deductible (and not subject to the 50 percent limitation), contributions in 2006 are subject to the AGI limit, even if donations of funds are made to hurricane relief efforts.

Note: There are some organizations to which donations are limited to 30 percent, but this is not the usual case. To find out more about so-called "30 percent charities," see IRS Publication 526, *Charitable Contributions*, at www.irs.gov.

SUBSTANTIATION. You must have proof of your donations in the event your return is questioned. The tax law is very specific about the type of proof (called substantiation in the tax law) that is recognized by the IRS.

If you make a donation of $250 or more, you must obtain an acknowledgment from the organization to which you made the donation. If you make smaller gifts to one charity throughout the year, they are not totaled for purposes of the $250 limit; each gift stands alone (unless you intentionally make them separately to avoid the dollar limit).

Example

You donate $200 each month to your church. You do not need any acknowledgment from the church to claim a total deduction of $2,400.

Get this written statement for a donation of $250 or more by the time you file your return. Your canceled check or credit charge statement is not sufficient substantiation of your donation. However, a pay stub or Form W-2 showing withholding from pay for a charitable contribution is treated as a valid receipt; you do not need a separate written acknowledgment.

If the donation is more than $75 but less than $250 *and* you receive a benefit, get a disclosure statement from the charity stating the value of the benefit. More details on this statement may be found later in this chapter.

EXAMPLES OF DEDUCTIBLE CONTRIBUTIONS

- Checks payable to charity.
- Collection plate contributions.
- Credit card donations.
- Rebates applied through credit card programs.
- Withholding from wages for charitable purposes.

Planning Tips

If you give weekly to your church collection plate, keep track of your cash donations on a calendar or diary so you don't overlook this write-off. You can also use the record keeper at the end of this chapter for this purpose.

TIMING ISSUES. You can deduct contributions made up to the last day of the year. In making year-end contributions, keep these points in mind:

- Contributions by credit card are deductible in the year you charge them, not in the year you pay your credit card bill. If you charge the gift by December 31, 2006, it is deductible in 2006 even though you pay the credit card company in 2007.

- Contributions by check that are mailed before December 31 are deductible in the year of mailing even though the charity receives the check and cashes it in the following year.
- A pledge to make a charitable contribution is not deductible until you pay the pledge.
- Contributions made through a pay-by-phone bank account are not deductible when you make the call but rather as of the payment date on the bank statement.

If you have not received a written acknowledgment from the charity by the April 15 deadline for filing your return, obtain a filing extension. This will allow you to meet substantiation requirements.

AGI PLANNING. Generally tax planning dictates that you try to *reduce* your adjusted gross income to boost your deductions for medical and miscellaneous expenses as well as eligibility for certain exclusions and credits. But if you make sizable donations, you may not want or need to adopt strategies to reduce your AGI. By claiming your charitable deduction, you effectively reduce or eliminate the tax on your income.

Example

In 2006, you donate $25,000. Your AGI is $60,000. You can try to reduce your AGI, but don't do so below $50,000 (the AGI that entitles you to fully deduct your contribution this year).

Pitfall

Despite your generous nature and good intentions, you can easily slip up on technicalities that can prevent you from claiming a deduction. For example, an owner of a nationally well-known tax preparation company donated stock to charity. Since the value of the donation was never in question, he never bothered to obtain a qualified appraisal as required by the tax law. This tax-savvy taxpayer lost out on a sizable deduction for his stock donation because he overlooked a basic requirement for claiming it and the IRS caught him.

NONQUALIFIED ORGANIZATIONS. An organization may seem like a charity and still not be one. Don't assume that a hospital or school is automatically qualified to accept deductible donations. If it is operated for profit, your contributions are not deductible.

You may not deduct donations to foreign charities unless allowed by international treaties (for example, donations to charities in Mexico and Canada can be deductible). However, a domestic charity set up to distribute funds abroad may be a qualified organization under the rules discussed earlier.

Other organizations that are nonqualified include:

- Sororities and fraternities.
- Civic leagues, chambers of commerce, business leagues, or labor unions. However, you may be able to treat contributions to these organizations as deductible business expenses (see Chapter 15).
- Professional associations of attorneys, doctors, and accountants. However, some unrestricted gifts to state bar associations may be deductible (the bar association reports to you the portion of annual dues treated as charitable contributions).
- Communist and communist-front organizations.

OVERALL LIMIT ON ITEMIZED DEDUCTIONS. Even if you meet the conditions for fully deducting your cash contributions, you may still lose out on a portion of your itemized deductions for donations. Charitable contribution deductions are subject to an overall 3 percent reduction of itemized deductions if your income exceeds a set limit explained in the introduction to this book. For 2006, the limit is $150,500 (or $75,250 if you are married but file a separate return). However, one-third of the reduction does not apply in 2006; only two-thirds of the reduction is taken into account.

EXPIRATION OF CARRYOVER. Unlike other carryovers in the tax law that run indefinitely, the carryover of excess charitable contributions is limited to five years. If you have such carryovers, don't let the five years expire causing you to waste potential write-offs. Consider realizing sufficient income to allow you to use up your carryovers.

Where to Claim the Deduction

If you itemize your deductions, report your charitable deduction for your cash donations on Schedule A of Form 1040. If you make only cash donations, you do not need any additional form or schedule other than Schedule A to report your charitable contributions. You cannot claim a deduction for donations if you file Form 1040A or Form 1040EZ.

Appreciated Property Donations

The government encourages donations of appreciated property held for more than one year by allowing tax deductions at the property's value (rather than limiting them to the donor's cost or other tax basis) as long as certain conditions are met. Even though cuts in the tax rates diminish the value of such contributions from a tax-savings perspective, philanthropic-minded individuals can still enjoy considerable tax breaks while benefiting their favorite causes.

Benefit

You can claim a charitable contribution deduction *and* avoid capital gains by donating appreciated property to charity. As long as the property has been held for more than one year, the charity is qualified, and other conditions are met, the donation is based on the property's value.

Example

You own stock you bought years ago for $2,000 that is now worth $10,000. If you donate it to a tax-exempt organization, you can claim a charitable contribution deduction of $10,000, the current value of the stock. What's more, you don't have to pay capital gains tax on your $8,000 of appreciation ($10,000 – $2,000), which would have cost you $1,200 ($8,000 × 15%). If you are in the 28 percent tax bracket, your deduction saves you $2,800 in taxes ($10,000 × 28%). Your total savings from your generosity is $4,000 ($1,200 capital gains tax saved plus $2,800 tax savings from the deduction).

Donations of appreciated property are limited to 30 percent of your adjusted gross income for the year, in most cases. Donations in excess of this limit can be carried forward for up to five years.

Donations of appreciated property that do not meet the conditions listed next are deductible only to the extent of your cost. In the case of donations of tangible personal property that do not meet the conditions, donations are based on basis (generally cost) rather than value, but can be claimed up to 50 percent of your adjusted gross income.

Conditions

To claim a deduction for the value of the property you donate to charity, you must meet all four conditions:

1. The property must be held long-term ("holding period").
2. If the property is tangible personal property, such as artwork, cars, and equipment, the charity must put the property to use in its exempt purpose ("tangible property used in the charity's exempt purpose").
3. The property cannot be "ordinary income property" (which is property that would generate ordinary income rather than capital gain if it were sold instead of donated).
4. You must comply with substantiation requirements.

Remember that donations to only a qualified charity produce a tax deduction for you. Which organizations are qualified charities, and which are not, is discussed earlier in the chapter under "Cash Donations."

HOLDING PERIOD. To meet the long-term holding period, you must own the property for more than one year prior to the date of the donation.

TANGIBLE PROPERTY USED IN THE CHARITY'S EXEMPT PURPOSE. If you give property other than securities or real estate, you are giving tangible personal property. Items commonly donated in this category include works of art, books, antiques, furniture, equipment, and collectibles.

Use of the property in the charity's exempt purpose means that the use serves a function related to the charity's exemption. For example, if you donate art to a school and the school displays the work in the library or school museum so that students can study it, the property is being used in the charity's exempt purpose.

If the charity sells the property you donate, you don't meet the related use test even though the proceeds certainly serve the charity's exempt purpose. The tax law treats the sale as an unrelated purpose (see "Planning Tips" for protection).

PROPERTY IS NOT ORDINARY INCOME PROPERTY. If you donate appreciated property that would produce ordinary income if it were sold rather than donated, you cannot deduct the property's value; your donation is limited to cost. Examples of ordinary income property include inventory, stock in trade, farm crops, and works of art, books, and memoranda donated by the person who created them.

Note: C corporations that donate their inventory to certain types of charities, and computers and peripherals to schools or libraries can claim an enhanced deduction. This special rule does not apply to individuals.

(Provision expired 12/31/05. Extension expected for 2006.)

SUBSTANTIATION REQUIREMENTS. If the total deduction claimed for your property donations is more than $500, you *must* attach Form 8283, Noncash Charitable Contributions, to your return.

If you make a donation exceeding $5,000 (one item or a collection), you must obtain a written appraisal for your donation. The appraisal is summarized on the form.

You do not need a written appraisal if the donation is:

- Publicly traded securities—you simply use the market value on the date of the donation.
- Nonpublicly traded stock (stock in a private corporation) if valued at $10,000 or less. You do need an appraisal if the value exceeds this amount.

In addition to obtaining the appraisal, the charity must acknowledge on Form 8283 that it received your donation (so leave enough time to obtain this acknowledgment before filing your return).

If you donate art valued at $20,000 or more, you must attach the written appraisal to the return, along with a color photo or slide if the IRS asks for it.

If you are required by the tax law to obtain an appraisal for your property donation, you must use a qualified appraiser (a person with the right credentials). Obtain the appraisal no earlier than 60 days before you make the donation. You must have the appraisal in hand by the time you file your return (including extensions).

Planning Tips

If you are concerned that the charity may sell the tangible property you donated, which would limit your deduction to your cost, ask the charity for a letter stipulating that it has no immediate intentions of selling. Increasingly, charities are reluctant to give this guarantee, but may comply in order to receive your donation. If it does so, your deduction for the value of the property would be protected even if the charity later changes its intentions and sells your donation.

Donations of collectibles can yield even greater tax savings than donations of securities. The reason: Gain on a sale of collectibles is taxed up to 28 percent, compared with a top 15 percent rate on gain from a sale of securities. Donations avoid the capital gains tax entirely.

ELECTION TO CHANGE AGI LIMIT. If you qualify to deduct the market value of your property, you can elect to reduce the gift by its appreciation and instead use the 50 percent AGI limit (instead of the 30 percent AGI limit that is usually required). This election makes sense when there is little appreciation on the property and opting to reduce the deduction by appreciation still gives you a greater write-off.

Example

You donate stock valued at $100,000 that cost you $90,000. Your AGI is $180,000. If you do nothing, your deduction for your $100,000 is limited to $54,000 (30 percent of $180,000). But if you make the election to reduce the deduction by its appreciation so that it is limited to your cost of $90,000, you can deduct it in full; your limit in this case is 50 percent of AGI or $90,000.

You make the election simply by attaching your own statement to your return explaining that you are making the election; no special IRS form or schedule is required. But you can't change your mind later unless your election was based on a material mistake; you can't change your mind simply because you later reconsider the situation and prefer to carry forward the unused deduction that you could have claimed.

IRS APPRAISAL. If you are donating very expensive works of art valued at $50,000 or more, you can protect your deduction from IRS questioning by obtaining an advance valuation of the art from the IRS. If the IRS agrees to give you this advance valuation, you'll receive an IRS Statement of Value (SOV) that you attach to your return to support your deduction. There is a fee of $2,500, which covers SOVs for up to three items, and obtaining it can take as long as a year. The good news is that an SOV avoids hassles with the IRS over valuation later on. But the bad news is that if you don't agree with the SOV, you are left with no alternative but to litigate the issue (you still must attach it to your return, even if you claim a higher deduction than the SOV).

Pitfalls

Donations of appreciated property can produce important tax savings for you, but here are some things to watch out for.

PENALTY FOR OVERVALUATIONS. Valuing property isn't an exact science. When making charitable donations you hope that the property is valued as highly as possible to boost your deduction. But don't be too generous in your estimations; substantial overvaluations of charitable donations resulting in a tax underpayment exceeding $5,000 can lead to a penalty.

- If the value claimed is 200 percent or more of the correct value (and results in an underpayment exceeding $5,000), the penalty is 20 percent of the underpayment.
- If the value claimed is 400 percent or more of the correct value (and results in an underpayment exceeding $5,000), the penalty is 40 percent of the underpayment.

Example

You donate an oil painting to charity and estimate that its value is $35,000. In truth, it is actually worth only $10,000. Since the value claimed is more than 200 percent of the correct value and your valuation results in your underpaying tax by more than $5,000, you are subject to a 20 percent penalty of the resulting underpayment of tax. In this case, for example, if you had been in the 28 percent tax bracket, there would have been a $7,000 underpayment ([$35,000 – $10,000] × 28%) so your penalty would be $1,400 ($7,000 × 20%). If you had valued the painting at $50,000, your penalty would have been 40 percent of the underpayment.

The penalty is applied on an item-by-item basis. So, for example, if you donate two objects, overvaluing one item and undervaluing the other, you cannot offset the undervaluation by the overvaluation.

You can protect yourself from the overvaluation penalty by obtaining a qualified appraisal of the item. If you reasonably rely on the appraisal of an expert, no penalty will be imposed (the appraiser may be subject to penalty if he or she knowingly overvalues property).

DONATIONS OF PROPERTY THAT HAS DECLINED IN VALUE. If you donate property that meets all of the conditions discussed, your tax deduction is based on the value of the property, even if you paid more for it. In effect, you get no benefit from the loss in value.

Unless the charity has a specific need for your item, it is advisable to sell the property rather than donate it if you can claim a tax deduction for your loss (for example, the property is investment property on which a capital loss can be claimed). You can then donate the proceeds so that the charity receives the same benefit. But selling the property will allow you to take a tax loss on the sale.

Example

You own stock you paid $10,000 for years ago. It is now worth $2,000. If you donate the stock, your deduction is limited to $2,000. If you sell the stock and donate the proceeds, the charity receives the same $2,000. However, you can claim a tax loss of $8,000 ($10,000 – $2,000). You can use this loss to offset your capital gains and then up to $3,000 of your ordinary income; excess capital losses can be carried forward indefinitely and used in future years.

This strategy, however, does not apply to personal (noninvestment or nonbusiness) items, such as your personal car, because you cannot take a capital loss deduction on their sale.

Where to Claim the Deduction

Like cash donations, you report property donations on Schedule A of Form 1040; you cannot claim the deduction if you file Form 1040A or 1040EZ.

But you may also have to complete Form 8283, Noncash Charitable Contributions, as explained earlier under "Substantiation."

Used Clothing and Car Donations

Clothing that no longer fits, appliances, and sporting equipment that are no longer used, and cars being replaced may be of great benefit to someone else. The tax law rewards donations of these items to charities that can put them to continued good use by permitting a tax deduction if certain conditions are met.

Benefit

Your old clothing, linens, toys, cars, and other items can be of benefit to others. Consider donating them to charity and taking a tax deduction for your efforts. A deduction of these items generally is subject to the 50 percent of adjusted gross income limit. This means that donations of these items are included along with your cash contributions to determine your annual limit.

Conditions

The items must be donated to a qualified charity (see the explanation of a qualified charity under "Cash Donations" earlier in this chapter).

You cannot claim a deduction if you donate items directly to an individual, no matter how much in need that person may be. For example, if a fire destroys a neighbor's home and you provide your neighbor with clothing and other items, you cannot claim a charitable contribution deduction for your generosity.

For donations of used clothing and household items after August 17, 2006, no deduction can be claimed unless the items are in "good used condition or better." However, if a single item is appraised at over $500, it can be deducted even though it is not in good used condition (although condition certainly affects its value).

Special substantiation rules apply to donations of cars, boats, and planes valued at over $500. You must obtain a written acknowledgment, Form 1098-C, Contributions of Motor Vehicles, Boats, and Airplanes, within 30 days of the date of contribution or the date that the organization sells the vehicle without using it in any significant way (e.g., driving a car to deliver meals to the needy for one year). If the organization sells the vehicle without using it in a significant way in its charitable activities or making any improvements to the vehicle, your donation is limited to the sale proceeds that the organization receives from a sale. Information about the sale is provided to the IRS.

If you value a car over $250 but not over $500 and the charity sells it, you can deduct the actual fair market value (you are not limited to the sales proceeds). But if you value the car over $500 and the charity sells it for less than $500, your maximum deduction is $500. For example, if you value the car at $650 and the charity sells it for $450, you can deduct $500.

Planning Tips

Don't know what your used items are worth? Here are some resources you can turn to for help:

- Used cars: Kelley Blue Book at www.kbb.com provides free online prices for used cars, based on the vehicle's mileage, condition, and other factors.
- Used clothing: TurboTax It's Deductible at www.itsdeductible.com is an online program you can use to find values for your items (there is a charge for this).
- Used computers: UsedComputer.com at www.usedcomputer.com provides values for old PCs.

In one case, a court allowed a donation for used clothing valued at $25 per bag.

Pitfalls

Don't expect the charity to provide you with a valuation of your donation. It's up to you to assess the value of the items you donate; the charity merely confirms that you actually made the donation.

Don't include in the amount of your charitable contribution any appraisal fees or the cost of packing and shipping you incur when making property donations. These costs are separately deductible as a miscellaneous itemized deduction (see later in this chapter).

Where to Claim the Deduction

For information about where to claim a deduction for your donation, see the rules under "Appreciated Property Donations" earlier in this chapter, including the rules on substantiation and filing Form 8283, Noncash Charitable Contributions. Also attach Form 1098-C, Contributions of Motor Vehicles, Boats, and Airplanes, if you donated such an item valued at over $500.

Intellectual Property Donations

If you give a patent, a certain copyright, or other intellectual property to charity, you can not only deduct the initial contribution, but can also claim deductions in future years for a percentage of the income that the charity derives from the property.

Benefit

You can claim an itemized deduction for donations of intellectual property to charity of:

- The fair market value of the donation in the year of the donation for intellectual property that you did not create (or, for self-created property, the amount that would have been ordinary income had you sold it rather than donated it).
- A percentage of the income derived from the property for up to 10 years following the year of the donation. The percentage is based on Table 6.1.

Conditions

At the time of the donation, you must tell the charity that you intend to claim the additional deductions. This is done by providing the charity with your personal written statement of your intention to treat the contribution as a qualified intellectual contribution. This statement must also describe the property and the date of the donation.

TABLE 6.1 Deduction for Income from Intellectual Property Donations

Year Ending after Date of Contribution	Applicable Percentage
1st	100%
2nd	100
3rd	90
4th	80
5th	70
6th	60
7th	50
8th	40
9th	30
10th	20
11th	10
12th	10

Planning Tip

The additional deduction applies to all types of intellectual property donated after June 3, 2004. This includes not only patents and certain copyrights, but also trademarks, trade names, trade secrets, know-how, certain software, and certain applications or registrations of this property.

Pitfalls

The additional deductions can be claimed only for up to 10 years following the year of the intellectual property donation.

If the life of the property is shorter than 10 years, you cannot claim additional deductions beyond this life.

The additional deduction does not apply to donations of intellectual property to a private foundation other than an operating private foundation.

Where to Claim the Deduction

Each year the charity informs you (and the IRS) of the income derived from your donation on Form 8899, Notice of Income from Donated Intellectual Property.

To claim a charitable contribution deduction, complete Schedule A of Form 1040. You may also have to complete Form 8283, Noncash Charitable Contributions, as explained earlier in this chapter under "Substantiation Requirements" for appreciated property donations.

You cannot claim the initial or additional deductions if you file Form 1040EZ or 1040A.

Real Estate Donated for Conservation Purposes

Real estate development has gobbled up open spaces and turned them into houses, shopping malls, and office buildings. But the government wants to encourage the maintenance of green spaces and does so by permitting tax deductions for donations of certain property interests for this purpose.

Benefit

Certain donations of partial interests in real property to government agencies or publicly supported charities for exclusively conservation purposes may entitle you to a deduction. Such donations include:

- Your entire interest in real property other than retained rights to subsurface oil, gas, or other minerals. For example, you own land and donate it to your town, retaining these mineral rights.
- A remainder interest in real property. For example, you own land. You keep the right to use it for the rest of your life, giving your town the remainder interest in the property. You do this by deeding the remainder interest to the town.
- An easement, restrictive covenant, or similar property restrictions granted in perpetuity. For example, you own property but give your town an easement limiting the use of a portion of it for a bird sanctuary forever. Even if you later sell the property, the new owner must continue to respect the easement and keep the use as a bird sanctuary.

Conditions

Only donations for qualified conservation purposes entitle you to a deduction. Qualified conservation purposes include:

- The preservation of land areas for outdoor recreation, education, or scenic enjoyment.
- Preservation of historically important land areas or structures.
- Protection of plant, fish, and wildlife habitats or similar natural ecosystems.

Planning Tips

To make the donation of an easement on your property, you may need to pay an attorney to handle the legal work involved. Donations in 2006 and 2007 can be claimed up to 50 percent of the contribution base (which is essential adjusted gross income), instead of the usual 30-percent limit (provided the use of the donated property does not prevent farming or ranching). Unused contributions because of this limit can be carried forward for up to 15 years.

Pitfall

Once you give away this interest, you can't change your mind and get it back.

Where to Claim the Deduction

For information about where to claim a deduction for your donation, see the rules under "Appreciated Property Donations," earlier in this chapter, including the rules on substantiation and filing Form 8283.

Bargain Sales

Taxpayers can have their cake and eat it, too—recoup their investments in property while obtaining tax deductions to boot—by making bargain sales of property to charity. It's a bargain because the charity is paying only a portion of the property's actual value, typically the donor's original cost for the property. It's a sale because the donor is receiving payment for the transaction and not merely donating the entire value of the property. Even so, a partial tax deduction is permitted under certain conditions.

Benefit

If you have appreciated property, you can recoup your investment while obtaining a tax deduction when you make a bargain sale to charity. In effect, the donation is viewed as two transactions: part sale and part gift.

You figure your gain on the sale by allocating the basis between the sale and the gift part as follows:

Step 1: Divide the sales proceeds by the fair market value of the property (include any outstanding debt as sales proceeds).

Step 2: Apply the percentage in Step 1 to the adjusted basis of the property to find the portion of the basis allocated to the sale.

Step 3: Subtract the resulting basis of Step 2 from the sales proceeds to find your gain.

Example

You sell property to your favorite charity for what you paid for it ($12,000). At the time of the donation it is worth $20,000. Under Step 1, divide $12,000 by $20,000, which is 0.6 or 60 percent. Apply 60 percent to the adjusted basis of $12,000, which is $7,200, the basis allocated to the sale. Your gain is $4,800, the difference between your sales proceeds of $12,000 and this basis of $7,200. By making the donation, you have obtained a charitable contribution deduction of $8,000 (the appreciation on the property), while recouping your initial investment, so you are out-of-pocket nothing. Had you sold the property to someone other than a charity, you would have paid capital gains tax on the gain of $8,000 ($20,000 – $12,000), or $1,200 at a 15 percent capital gain rate.

Conditions

The same conditions apply to bargain sales as to other charitable contributions (for example, the charity must be an IRS-approved organization). For conditions, see earlier in this chapter.

Planning Tip

A bargain sale can enable you to recover your cost (investment in the property) while also obtaining a deduction for any increased value in the property. Donating the property through a bargain sale saves you the time and expense of selling it to a third party in order to raise the funds to make the donation you would make if you keep your initial investment.

Pitfall

If the property you donate is not the type of property that entitles you to a donation of the appreciation (for example, you didn't own it for more than one year), then the bargain sale doesn't produce any charitable contribution deduction. Of course, the charity still obtains the item at a bargain price.

You must allocate the basis of the property on a bargain sale even if the annual AGI limit prevents you from claiming a charitable contribution deduction.

Where to Claim the Deduction

You report the bargain sale on two schedules on Form 1040: Use Schedule D to report the sale portion and Schedule A to report the gift portion.

Details on reporting gifts of appreciated property are explained earlier in this chapter.

Volunteer Expenses

The U.S. Department of Labor, Bureau of Labor Statistics, says that between September 2003 and September 2004 about 64.5 million Americans did some volunteer work. While individuals bear the burden of the time and effort they put in, the government helps defray any actual out-of-pocket costs through a deduction that can be claimed if certain conditions are met.

Benefit

If you incur out-of-pocket expenses in serving your favorite charity, you can deduct these costs as part of your itemized deduction for charitable donations.

If you use your vehicle for charitable purposes, including attending meetings of organizations you serve, you can deduct your actual vehicle expenses for gas and oil or mileage at the rate of 14 cents per mile. Volunteers providing Katrina relief can deduct their mileage in 2006 at the rate of 32 cents per mile. Whichever method you select, you can also write off parking and tolls.

Conditions

As long as you incur out-of-pocket costs for a qualified charity (explained earlier in this chapter under "Cash Donations"), your costs are deductible.

EXAMPLES OF DEDUCTIBLE UNREIMBURSED EXPENSES

Materials and supplies you furnish (e.g., stamps).

Related costs of hosting a fund-raiser (e.g., invitations, food, and beverages).

Telephone calls.

Travel expenses, including meals and lodging for overnight trips away from home to serve as an official delegate to a convention of a church, charitable, veteran, or other similar organization.

Travel expenses to work for a charitable organization (such as Habitat for Humanity).

Uniforms required in serving the organization.

Planning Tips

Keep track of your mileage and out-of-pocket expenses on behalf of the charity. In a diary or logbook, note the odometer readings for every charity-related trip for which your car is used.

Katrina relief volunteers who are reimbursed for their car mileage are not taxed on the reimbursement. However, they cannot double dip; they can only exclude the reimbursement and not claim a deduction for this amount.

Pitfall

Just because you are not compensated by the charity for your efforts doesn't automatically mean that every cost you incur on behalf of the charity is deductible. You *cannot* deduct:

- The value of your time and energy. Even if you perform work for the charity, you cannot deduct what you would have charged for your expertise.

Example

You are an attorney who does pro bono work for a local charity. You cannot deduct your usual hourly rate for the time spent on this charitable activity.

- The rental value of your home or vacation home that you allow the charity to use in its fund-raising activities.

Example

You own a vacation home and let the charity raffle off a one-week stay there. You cannot deduct the fair rental value of that one week's use of your vacation home.

- Baby-sitting expenses you paid to enable you to put in time for your charity.
- Travel costs to attend a convention for a nonprofit organization if you are not a delegate.
- Travel costs to work on a project for a nonprofit organization if there is a significant element of personal pleasure, recreation, or vacation involved.

Where to Claim the Deduction

To claim a charitable deduction for your unreimbursed expenses, you must complete Schedule A of Form 1040. You cannot deduct donations if you file Form 1040A or Form 1040EZ.

Tickets to Fund-Raisers, Raffles, and Sporting Events

Who hasn't bought a ticket to a fund-raising event or activity, such as a raffle dinner dance, to benefit a charity? Just because the check is written out to a charity doesn't automatically entitle taxpayers to a deduction. Special rules govern the extent, if any, to which the cost of fund-raising tickets may be deductible.

Benefit

You can deduct the purchase price for raffle tickets and charity-sponsored events in excess of the regular admission price or other benefit you receive.

Example

You pay $100 for a ticket to an evening sponsored by your favorite charity that includes dinner and a show. The value of the dinner and show (what you would have paid regularly) is $75. You can deduct $25 (the excess cost over the regular price).

SPECIAL LIMIT FOR TICKETS TO SCHOOL ATHLETIC EVENTS. If you contribute to a public or nonprofit college or university and receive the right to buy preferential seating at the school's athletic facilities, your deduction is fixed at 80 percent of your contribution. The cost of the tickets themselves is not deductible. If you receive a ticket when you make your donation, first reduce the contribution by the price of the ticket and then apply the 80 percent limit.

Example

You make a sizable donation to your alma mater and receive season's tickets worth $250. Subtract $250 from your donation and then multiply the result by 80 percent to find your deduction amount.

Condition

If you pay more than $75, the charity must supply you with a written explanation of the value of the benefit you receive so that you can figure your deduction, if any.

Planning Tip

If your donation entitles you to a ticket to a charity event but you do not want to attend, you can refuse to accept the ticket. In this case you can deduct your entire contribution (provided you meet other conditions such as substantiation). Make sure that an acknowledgment you receive from the charity reflects your refusal to accept the ticket.

Pitfall

You cannot deduct any of the cost of Girl Scout cookies you buy for your own consumption. The cost of the cookies is treated as their fair market value so you haven't made any gift. But if you leave the cookies with the troop, you may treat your payment as a deduction. Similarly, if you donate the cookies to a charity, you can deduct your cost (not the estimated retail value).

Where to Claim the Deduction

To claim a charitable deduction for your donations in connection with tickets, raffles, or other fund-raisers, you must complete Schedule A of Form 1040. You do not have to attach the written explanation for your donations to your return; save them for your records with the copy of your return.

If you do not make donations of property, you do not need any additional form or schedule other than Schedule A to report your charitable contributions.

You cannot deduct your donations if you file Form 1040A or Form 1040EZ.

Membership Fees to Nonprofit Organizations

Anthropologist Margaret Mead said, "Never doubt that a small group of thoughtful, committed citizens can change the world. Indeed it is the only thing that ever has." Perhaps that's why so many Americans belong to organizations of all kinds, including religious, civic, and fraternal organizations. Belonging is rewarded taxwise to a certain extent by permitting the cost of dues to be deductible within certain limits.

Benefit

If you pay dues to nonprofit organizations, you can treat the payments as cash contributions subject to the rules discussed earlier in this chapter. Examples of membership fees that are deductible include payments to religious organizations (e.g., your church) and fraternal organizations operating under a lodge system (e.g., Elks Club).

You must reduce your deduction, however, by the value of any benefits (other than token amounts) you receive, such as monthly journals.

Example

You donate $100 to your local public broadcasting station during its annual fund drive. You receive a videocassette of one of its programs. Your deduction is limited to the donation in excess of the value of the videocassette (the station should supply you with this information).

You do *not* have to reduce your donation by these tokens distributed by the charity in gratitude for your gift:

- Items costing no more than $8.60 if your gift is at least $43 in 2006 (these figures are adjusted annually for inflation).
- Items worth no more than $1.72 (2 percent of $86) in 2006, regardless of the amount of your gift.

If you pay $75 or less for membership that entitles you to benefits, you can fully deduct your dues if either of these alternatives applies:

- You receive membership privileges that can be exercised frequently (e.g., free or discounted parking or admission) or discounts on gift shop or mail order items.
- Your membership entitles you to admission to members-only events and the cost of each event is no more than $8.60 in 2006.

If you pay more than $75, you can exclude only those benefits that you would have excluded had you paid $75 or less; more expensive benefits are not excludable.

Student Exchange Program

Individuals who open their homes to students, serving as hosts under special programs, may be eligible for a tax break that helps to defray the cost of hospitality. To claim this tax benefit, however, certain conditions must be met.

Benefit

If you support a student in your home, you may deduct up to $50 per month as a charitable contribution deduction as long as you itemize your deductions and meet certain conditions. If the student is in your home for at least 15 days of a month, you can treat it as an entire month.

Conditions

To claim a deduction for supporting a student in your home, you must meet all three of these conditions:

1. The student must be in elementary or high school.
2. The placement in your home must be arranged under an educational program by a charitable organization and is documented by a written agreement.
3. You have records showing what you spend on the student's food, clothing, medical care, schooling, and recreation.

Planning Tip

Supporting a student in your home may entitle your child to spend time in another family's home. For example, if you accept a foreign exchange student into your home, you may not only obtain a tax deduction for that foreign student, but in addition your child may be able to go abroad and there is no tax cost to this benefit—to you or to your child. While you may have to pay out-of-pocket for airfare, your child's living expenses abroad may be provided for free.

Pitfall

You usually cannot deduct any payments made where you receive money from the charity for the student's maintenance. For example, if the charity reimburses you for medical expenses you pay for the student, you cannot deduct the medical expenses you paid. However, you are permitted to deduct your prepayment of a one-time expense, such as a medical bill or vacation for the student at the request of the student's parents or sponsoring organization for which you are later reimbursed for part of the cost.

Where to Claim the Deduction

See under "Cash Donations" earlier in this chapter.

Special Inventory Donations

Business owners may enjoy an enhanced charitable contribution deduction for special inventory donations in 2006 and 2007 only. The deduction is the lesser of (1) the item's basis in inventory plus one-half of its appreciation, or (2) two times the item's basis. This rule applies to:

- Food inventory donations by sole proprieters and any other businesses to public charities. The food must be apparently wholesome and meet all federal quality and labeling standards.
- Book inventory donations to public schools by C corporations (no other businesses qualify for this break).

Appraisal Fees and Other Costs

When donating property, how can one know how much to deduct? The answer for certain donations depends on what the property is worth, and it's not always easy to determine this value. You may want, or in some cases need, the assistance of a professional appraiser to determine property value. The fees paid to appraisers may be deductible under certain circumstances. Similarly, you may pay packing, shipping, and insurance costs to send donated items to a charitable organization. These costs may also be deductible.

Benefit

When you donate property to charity, you may pay appraisal fees to determine the property's value. You may also pay to pack up and ship a painting or other item donated to charity. You may deduct these fees and costs incurred for the purpose of claiming a charitable contribution deduction as a miscellaneous itemized deduction. You do *not* include them as part of the donation.

The deduction is part of miscellaneous itemized expenses, which are deductible only to the extent the total exceeds 2 percent of your adjusted gross income.

Conditions

There are no specific conditions to meet in order to deduct your appraisal fees and other costs. Simply retain proof of this cost (keep it with copies of your tax return).

Planning Tip

Find the right appraiser for the item you are donating. For example, those qualified to appraise real estate may not be the best choice if you are donating art or closely held stock.

TABLE 6.2 Record Keeper for Your Cash Donations

Date	Name of Charity	Amount of Donation
		$
		$
		$
		$
		$
		$
		$
		$
		$
		$
		$
		$

In general, to find a qualified appraiser, see:

- American Society of Appraisers (www.appraisers.org).
- International Society of Appraisers (www.isa-appraisers.org).

Pitfall

If your miscellaneous itemized deductions do not exceed 2 percent of your adjusted gross income, you do not receive any benefit from the write-off of appraisal fees. In effect, the deduction is lost forever.

Where to Claim the Deduction

You claim the deduction for appraisal fees and other costs as a miscellaneous itemized deduction on Schedule A of Form 1040. You cannot claim the deduction if you file Form 1040A or 1040EZ.

Record Keeper for Your Charitable Giving

Use the record keeper in Table 6.2 to note cash contributions you make throughout the year. Include in this record your weekly donations in the church plate and similar donations.

CHAPTER 7

Your Car

Americans love their cars. According to the U.S. Census Bureau there are more than 230 million cars on the road in this country today. Cars can be expensive to buy or lease and to operate, especially with high fuel prices. But the tax law provides some relief for your car use by way of tax write-offs.

This chapter explains:

- Business use of your personal car
- Employer-provided car
- Vehicle registration fees
- Car accidents and other car-related problems
- Donating your car
- Hybrid vehicle credit
- Electric car credit

Deducting the use of your car for medical-related travel is discussed in Chapter 2. Deducting the use of your car for a job-related move is discussed in Chapter 4. Deducting the use of your car when working as a volunteer for charity is discussed in Chapter 6.

For more information, see IRS Publication 463, *Travel, Entertainment, Gifts, and Car Expenses*; IRS Publication 535, *Business Expenses*; IRS Publication 547, *Casualties, Disasters, and Thefts (Business and Nonbusiness)*; and IRS Publication 584, *Casualty, Disaster, and Theft Loss Workbook (Personal-Use Property)*.

Business Use of Your Personal Car

According to the U.S. Department of Energy, Americans drive their cars on average just under 12,000 miles each year. The cost of driving can be high when you factor in gasoline, insurance, and other costs. But the tax law lets a portion of the cost of this mileage be deductible under certain circumstances.

Benefit

If you use your personal car for business and do not receive any reimbursement for such use by your employer or you are self-employed, you can deduct expenses related to the business use of your car.

There is a choice of methods for claiming your deduction: You can deduct your actual expenses, including an allowance for depreciation if you own your car or lease payments if you lease it ("actual expense method"), or you can claim the IRS standard mileage rate.

The IRS standard mileage rate is 44.5 cents per mile for business driving in 2006. Whichever method you select, you can also deduct parking and tolls.

There is no dollar limit on what you can deduct for your car use each year. However, if you own your car and use the actual expense method, there are dollar limits on how much you can deduct for depreciation or first-year expensing (unless your car weighs more than 6,000 pounds).

If your employer reimburses you for business use of your car under an "accountable plan," you do not have to report the reimbursements as income (the reimbursements are not even included on your Form W-2). But you cannot claim a deduction for your car use. Ask your employer if reimbursements are made under an accountable plan, or check your W-2 form.

If your employer reimburses you for business use of your car under a nonaccountable plan, such reimbursement is treated as additional compensation to you; it is included on your Form W-2. You can then deduct business use as a miscellaneous itemized deduction (subject to a 2 percent-of-AGI floor).

Conditions

To claim write-offs for business use of your personal car you merely have to keep good records as explained later. However, *what* you can deduct may be limited by certain conditions.

STANDARD MILEAGE RATE. You can use the IRS standard mileage rate whether you own or lease your car. The standard mileage rate takes the place of separately deducting gas, oil, repairs, new tires, vehicle registration fees, insurance, and depreciation if you own the car, or lease payments if you lease the car.

However, you cannot base your car deduction on the standard mileage rate if you have depreciated your car or claimed first-year expensing. This would have occurred if you owned your car in a previous year and claimed the actual expense method.

DEPRECIATION. If you own your car and use the actual expense method, you can claim an allowance for depreciation or elect first-year expensing. Cars are treated as five-year property; for depreciation purposes they have a five-year recovery period. Because of a special rule, however, a part of the depreciation allowance is limited in the first year so that the balance must be claimed in a sixth year if you still own the car at that time. (Remember, you apply depreciation to only the business portion of the car, and you can use accelerated depreciation only if the car is used more than 50 percent for business; if business use is 50 percent or less, you are limited to straight-line depreciation.)

If you use accelerated depreciation (and are not subject to a special rule called the midquarter convention, which applies if you place more than 40 percent of all of your depreciable property in service in the last quarter of the year), your depreciation rates are:

- Year one (the year the car is placed in service): 20%
- Year two: 32%
- Year three: 19.2%
- Year four: 11.52%

Example

In January 2006, you buy a new car for $28,000 and use it 60 percent for business and 40 percent for personal purposes. You do not use first-year expensing. Assume that your business-personal use percentages remain constant so that the business portion of the car for depreciation purposes is $16,800 ($28,000 × 60%). Here is your depreciation amount for each year (subject to the dollar limits discussed later).

Year one: $3,360

Year two: $5,338

Year three: $3,226

Year four: $1,935

Year five: $1,935

Year six: $968

- Year five: 11.52%
- Year six: 5.76%

Instead of depreciating the business portion of your car, you can elect to expense it in the year it is bought and placed in service. However, like depreciation, this option may be restricted to a dollar limit, explained next.

DOLLAR LIMIT. Unless your car weighs more than 6,000 pounds, your allowance for depreciation or first-year expensing is limited to a dollar amount fixed by the IRS. Table 7.1 shows the dollar limits for gas-powered cars (higher limits not included here apply to electric vehicles).

Example

In November 2006, you buy a new car and use it 60 percent for business and 40 percent for personal purposes. Your dollar limit is $1,776 (60 percent of $2,960).

The full amount of the dollar limit on depreciation applies only if the car is used 100 percent for business. If the car is used partly for business, you must allocate the dollar limit.

If the vehicle weighs more than 6,000 pounds but not more than 14,000 pounds, as is the case for a heavy SUV used in business, you can elect to expense its cost up to $25,000; the dollar limits in Table 7.1 do not apply in this case. In addition, you can claim normal depreciation for the vehicle without applying the dollar limits. Normal depreciation rates are 20 percent for the first year, 32 percent for the second year, 19.2 percent for the third year, 11.52 percent for the fourth and fifth years, and 5.76 percent for the sixth year.

Example

In 2006, you purchase an SUV weighing 6,500 pounds for a cost of $55,000. You use it 100 percent for business. Your expensing/depreciation deduction for 2006 is $31,000 ($25,000 expensing, plus 20% of [$55,000–$25,000]).

Special dollar limits applies to light trucks and vans (those weighing 6,000 pounds gross weight or less). For these limits, see IRS Publication 463, *Travel, Entertainment, Gift, and Car Expenses.*

Vans and trucks that are not suitable for personal use (e.g., they have permanent shelving, a front jump seat, or a permanent business sign) can be depreciated or expensed without any dollar limit. The maximum amount of first-year expensing for 2006 is $108,000.

TABLE 7.1 Dollar Limit on Depreciation of Passenger Cars

Date Car Placed in Service	1st Year	2nd Year	3rd Year	4th and Later Years
2006	$2,960	$4,800	$2,850	$1,775
2005	2,960	4,700	2,850	1,675
2004	10,610*	4,800	2,850	1,675
2003	10,710+	4,900	2,950	1,775
2002	7,660#	4,900	2,950	1,775

*$2,960 if the car did not qualify for bonus depreciation (i.e., it was a used car).
+$7,660 if the car was acquired before May 6, 2003; $3,060 if the car does not qualify for bonus depreciation.
#$3,060 if the car did not qualify for bonus depreciation.

SUBSTANTIATION. You *must* keep good records to back up your deduction for business use of your car. If you fail to do so, you can lose some or all of your deduction. Here's what your records should show:

- Mileage (your odometer reading at the start and end of each trip for business purposes). A court has indicated that you cannot merely note the length of the trip (e.g., 10 miles) but must record the actual odometer readings for the trip.
- Date, destination, and purpose for the trip (when you used your car, the customers or clients you visited, and the reason for taking the trip).
- Costs for gas, oil, and other car-related expenses. ***Note:*** If you claim the standard mileage rate, you do not have to keep track of these costs.

Planning Tip

At the start and end of the year, note your odometer reading in your records. Then use a diary, logbook, handheld computer, or other device to record your business mileage throughout the year. Knowing your annual mileage and what part of it represents your business mileage will allow you to properly allocate your car expenses.

You can simplify your recordkeeping for car use with a method called "sampling." This allows you to keep records for only a part of the year and then extrapolate the business mileage for the entire year. You can use this method *only* if the portion of the year in which you kept records (e.g., the first quarter of the year) is representative of car use throughout the year.

Special dollar limits not discussed here apply to light trucks and vans. For details, see Revenue Procedure 2006-18, IRB 2006-12, 645.

For more details and strategies for deducting the expenses of using your car for business, see *J.K. Lasser's Small Business Taxes 2007*.

Pitfalls

If you own your car and you want to use the IRS standard mileage rate, you must elect to do so in the first year of use. Otherwise you are limited to deducting your actual expenses. For example, if you bought and used your car for business in 2005 and used the actual expense method for claiming a deduction for business use, you cannot use the IRS standard mileage rate in 2006 for this car.

If you lease your car and claim a deduction under the actual expense method, you may have to include a phantom amount in income. This is called the inclusion amount and is designed to equate write-offs for leased cars with those that are purchased. The inclusion amount generally is a modest figure that you take from an IRS table for this purpose. You include only the portion of the inclusion amount related to your car use. For example, if you use your car only 25 percent for business, you include only 25 percent of the applicable inclusion amount. Table 7.2 shows you some sample inclusion amounts for gas-powered cars (different inclusion amounts not included here apply for electric cars).

Inclusion amounts for cars leased prior to 2006 can be found in IRS Publication 463, *Travel, Entertainment, Gifts, and Car Expenses*.

Where to Claim the Benefit

Where you claim write-offs for business use of your personal car depends on whether you are an employee or a self-employed person.

EMPLOYEE. If you use your own car for business and are not reimbursed for such use by your employer, you can deduct your car use as a miscellaneous itemized deduction on Schedule A of Form 1040.

TABLE 7.2 Sample Inclusion Amounts for Cars First Leased in 2006

Fair Market Value		Tax Year during Lease				
Over	Not Over	1	2	3	4	Later
$15,200	$15,500	$ 4	$ 6	$ 10	$ 10	$ 16
17,500	18,000	19	41	61	71	80
19,500	20,000	32	70	103	122	139
24,000	25,000	63	138	204	243	279
29,000	30,000	96	209	311	371	426
34,000	35,000	129	281	417	498	574
39,000	40,000	161	353	523	626	721
44,000	45,000	194	424	630	753	869
49,000	50,000	227	496	736	881	1,016

You must complete Part II of Form 2106, Employee Business Expenses, or Part II of Form 2106-EZ, Unreimbursed Employee Business Expenses, to figure the deduction for car use. Be sure to answer the questions about whether you have written evidence of your car use. ***Note:*** If you opt to use Form 2106-EZ, you are limited to using the standard mileage rate; you cannot claim depreciation on the vehicle.

SELF-EMPLOYED PERSON. If you use your car for both business and personal purposes, you can deduct expenses related to your business use on Schedule C of Form 1040.

If you own your car and are required to file Form 4562, Depreciation and Amortization (you are claiming depreciation on property placed in service in 2006), complete Part V of the form. Be sure to answer the question about whether you have written evidence of your claimed use.

If you are not required to file Form 4562, you must answer the questions about your car use in Part IV of Schedule C or in Part III of Schedule C-EZ. These questions concern your mileage for business and personal use and whether you have written evidence to support your deduction.

Since you are self-employed, you must file Form 1040; you cannot use Form 1040A or 1040EZ.

Employer-Provided Car

Perhaps one of the most helpful employee benefits is the so-called company car, which means that the business pays for a car you are allowed to use not only for business travel but also for personal purposes. The extent, if any, to which you are taxed on use of a company car depends on several factors, including *how* you are using the car.

Benefit

If you use a company-owned car *only* on company business, you are not taxed on this use of the company car because it is for business (it is tax-free income to you). Similarly, if you use a certain type of company vehicle for personal use, you are not taxed on this benefit because the IRS views you as having limited personal use (it is tax-free income to you). Such vehicles include: ambulances; hearses; flatbed trucks; dump, garbage, and refrigerated trucks; one-passenger delivery trucks (even if there is a folding jump seat); tractors and other farm equipment; and forklifts. The same exclusion from income applies to vehicles where personal use is restricted or authorized only by a government authority: school buses, passenger buses, moving vans, and police and fire vehicles (including unmarked cars).

If you are given unfettered use of a company-owned car and it is not used only for business but also for personal purposes, you are taxed on your personal use. The tax can be figured in several ways (a complete discussion of which is beyond the scope of this chapter). One way is by reference to an IRS table on the annual lease value of the car (determined by the fair market value of the car). But the income resulting from personal use of a company car may be substantially less than it would cost you to own or lease a car for your personal use. Thus, even though you may have income from using the company car, it is still a tax benefit because of your out-of-pocket savings (what you would have had to pay if the company had not provided you with a car for personal use).

Example

In 2006, your employer allows you to use a company car for personal purposes and you do so 25 percent of the time the car is used (the rest of the use is strictly for business). Assuming the car's value is $20,000, your employer includes in your income $1,400 ($5,600 annual lease value of the car × 25%). If you are in the 28 percent tax bracket, this added income results in additional tax of $392. In effect, it costs you just $392 to use your company's car for personal purposes for the year.

Your employer must figure the value of your personal use of a company car using one of several alternatives and report this amount to you on your Form W-2. However, your employer may opt to report the full value of the car's use for the year (not merely your personal use); this is based on the car's lease value. In this case, you may deduct your business use of the company car as an unreimbursed employee business expense (explained earlier in this chapter) if you itemize your deductions.

If you are a full-time car salesperson who is allowed to use demonstration cars for personal use, you are not taxed on this benefit (it is tax-free income to you), provided there are restrictions on personal use. For example, personal use after normal business hours might be restricted to a 75-mile radius of the dealer's sales office or you might not be allowed to drive family members or use the car for vacation trips.

Condition

To fully exclude the value of using a company car, your personal use must be restricted or the company vehicle must be one of those listed earlier.

Planning Tip

Your employer is *not* required to withhold income taxes on your personal use of a company car. If there is no withholding for car use and you have not paid enough taxes throughout the year by means of withholding or estimated tax payments, you may wind up owing taxes at the end of the year. You may wish to voluntarily increase your withholding if you know that your employer will not withhold taxes for your car use to avoid the problem.

Pitfalls

As mentioned earlier, your employer is not limited to reporting as income only your personal use of the company car; your employer may opt to include *all* use—both business and personal—as income to you. The amount of this income may be figured by reference to the car's annual lease value, which is a figure taken from an IRS table based on the car's fair market value (or some other IRS-approved method for valuing car use).

Example

Your employer opts to report as income to you all use of a company car valued at $20,000. The annual lease value from the IRS table is $5,600, so this amount is reported as income to you.

If your employer reports the full value of the car as income on your W-2 form (as in the preceding example), you can claim a deduction for your business use (as explained earlier in this chapter). However, your deduction is subject to the 2 percent of AGI floor. This means that if you don't have other miscellaneous itemized deductions, you effectively lose write-offs equal to 2 percent of your adjusted gross income and are taxed on business use of the company car.

Where to Claim the Benefit

If you are not taxed on using the company car (i.e., your employer does not report it on your Form W-2), you do not have to report anything on your return.

If your employer reports only the actual value of your personal use of a company car, again you do not have to do anything on your return. This income is included in your compensation and reported as such on your return, whichever type of return you file.

If your employer reports 100 percent of the car's lease value as income to you on your Form W-2 and you used the car part of the time for business, you must complete Part II of Form 2106, Employee Business Expenses, or Part II of Form 2106-EZ, Unreimbursed Employee Business Expenses, to figure the deduction for car use. Be sure to answer the questions about whether you have written evidence of your car use. ***Note:*** If you opt to use Form 2106-EZ, you are limited to using the standard mileage rate; you cannot claim depreciation on the vehicle.

You then report the deductible amount of unreimbursed employee business expenses as a miscellaneous itemized deduction on Schedule A of Form 1040. You cannot claim a deduction if you file Form 1040A or 1040EZ.

Vehicle Registration Fees

One way in which states raise revenues is through the fees they charge for certain activities, including registering cars and other vehicles. The cost of registration, however, may be deductible under certain conditions.

Benefit

The state registration fees you pay for your vehicle may be deductible. If your car is used only for personal purposes, you can deduct auto registration fees based on the value of the car as a state personal property tax if certain conditions are met. You must itemize your deductions to be able to deduct this expense.

Conditions

To deduct auto registration fees as a state personal property tax, you must meet all three requirements:

1. The fee is an ad valorem tax. This means the fee is based on a percentage of the car's value, for example, 1 percent of the value. Table 7.3 lists the states that satisfy this requirement.
2. The fee is imposed on an annual basis, even though it is collected more or less frequently.
3. The fee is imposed on personal property.

If the tax or fee is based on weight, model, year, or horsepower, it is not deductible. But if the tax is based on *both* value and another factor, the portion based on value is deductible.

TABLE 7.3 States with Ad Valorem Taxes

Alabama	Massachusetts
Arizona	Minnesota
California	Mississippi
Colorado	Montana
Connecticut	Nebraska
Georgia	Nevada
Indiana	New Hampshire
Iowa	Oklahoma
Kentucky	Washington
Maine	Wyoming

Example

Your vehicle registration fee is 1 percent of the car's value, plus 40 cents per hundredweight. You can deduct the 1 percent portion as a personal property tax.

Planning Tip

If you have questions about whether your state's registration fee is deductible in whole or in part, contact your state tax authority.

Pitfall

There is no downside to deducting auto registration fees as a personal property tax if you are eligible to do so.

Where to Claim the Benefit

If you are deducting auto registration fees on your personal car as a state personal property tax, you must file Schedule A of Form 1040.

You cannot claim the deduction if you file Form 1040A or 1040EZ.

Car Accidents and Other Car-Related Problems

In 2003, the latest year for which statistics were available, there were over 6.3 million car accidents in the United States. Whether a car is partially damaged or totaled, an owner may have out-of-pocket costs. These may be limited to the deductible or may be a greater amount. The tax law may allow for a write-off, even if the car is used exclusively for personal reasons and not at all for business.

Benefit

If your personal car is damaged or destroyed in an accident and the damages are not fully covered by insurance or other reimbursement, you can deduct your loss as a casualty loss, provided you itemize your deductions. The same rules apply if your car is stolen.

There is no dollar limit on how much you can deduct.

Conditions

To claim a deduction for your loss arising from a car accident or other car-related problems, you must meet four conditions:

1. Prove that the loss arose from a casualty or theft.
2. Establish the amount of your loss.
3. Reduce your loss by $100 if your car is used for personal purposes.
4. Reduce your total losses for the year by 10 percent of your adjusted gross income if your car is used for personal purposes.

CASUALTY EVENT. Unless stolen, you must show that the damage to your car resulted from a casualty, which is a sudden, unexpected event such as an accident. Generally, this does not pose any problem since car accidents are clearly casualty events. Similarly, if a tree falls on your car during a hurricane or the car is washed away during a flood, the damage can be viewed as arising from a casualty because the triggering event is sudden and unexpected.

However, you cannot treat damage resulting from your failure to winterize your car as a casualty. The damage in this case results from your personal neglect and not from an accident or another destructive force.

ESTABLISH THE AMOUNT OF LOSS. Just because an accident has occurred does not mean you have any loss. You must show that a loss occurred and that you didn't receive compensation from insurance or another source.

You measure your loss by comparing the value of the car before and after the casualty. However, your loss for tax purposes cannot exceed your basis in the car.

Example

You paid $8,000 for a used car that you purchased from a friend who gave you a break (the car was actually worth $9,000). Shortly thereafter the car is totaled in an accident that is not covered by insurance. The value of the car before the accident is $9,000 and its value after the accident is scrap of $500, for a difference of $8,500. However, your loss for tax purposes cannot exceed $8,000, which is your adjusted basis in the car.

You can use the cost of repairs to the car to show your loss if the cost is not excessive and the repair merely restores the car to its preaccident condition.

Example

You bought your car new for $20,000 a few years ago. In 2006, it is damaged in a collision that is not covered by your insurance. You pay the repair shop $3,000 to fix the damage. You can treat this amount as your loss (assuming that this amount is not excessive and the repair only fixes the damage).

You must reduce your loss by any insurance or other reimbursement you receive. For example, if your car is hit by another driver who prefers to pay you rather than go through his insurance company, this is a reimbursement and you must reduce your loss by the amount you receive.

APPLYING THE $100 FLOOR. If your car is for personal use, you must reduce your loss for tax purposes by $100 per occurrence. If, by some bad twist of fate, your car is in two accidents within the same year, you would have to subtract $100 from each loss (for a total of $200 for the year).

If your car is used exclusively for business, you do not apply the $100 floor to your loss.

TEN PERCENT OF AGI FLOOR. You can deduct casualty and theft losses for the year only to the extent that total losses are more than 10 percent of your adjusted gross income.

Example

In 2006, you suffer a $6,000 loss in a car accident and have a $12,000 theft loss from your home (after reducing each occurrence by $100), for total losses of $18,000. Your adjusted gross income is $70,000. Your deduction for 2006 is limited to amounts in excess of $7,000 (10 percent of $70,000), which in this case is $11,000—you can never deduct the first 10 percent, or $7,000.

If your car is used exclusively for business, you do not apply the 10 percent of AGI floor to your loss.

Planning Tips

Retain proof of the accident to support your deduction. Helpful proof includes:

- Appraisals of the car's value before the accident. You can rely on automotive "blue books" for this purpose (e.g., Kelley Blue Book at www.kbb.com).
- Canceled checks, bills, receipts, and vouchers for expenses of restoring the car to its condition before the accident.
- Photos of the damaged car (yours or newspaper clippings of the accident).

If you are married and one spouse owns the car that is damaged, consider filing separate returns rather than filing jointly. If the owner-spouse has the lower income, that spouse may be able to deduct a greater portion of the loss because of the AGI floor. However, there are other situations that benefit from filing jointly, so it is advisable to run the numbers using both filing statuses and choose the one that results in the lower overall tax.

Since the tax deduction for your car accident will not fully compensate you for your loss, it is advisable that you carry enough car insurance to cover any future accidents. While many financial experts advise against continuing collision coverage after the car is old, you must weigh the cost of insurance against what you could lose if your car is damaged, even through no fault of your own.

Pitfalls

You may not deduct your loss if damage resulted from your willful conduct. For example, if you crash your car while under the influence of alcohol, you cannot claim a tax loss for your car damage.

Certain car accidents and related costs are *not* deductible. These include:

- Costs you pay for damaging another person's vehicle. However, if the damage arose in the course of your business (for example, you were driving between two business locations), then the loss is deductible as a business loss.
- Legal fees or court costs you may pay to defend an action resulting from your negligence in operating the car for personal purposes (including commuting to or from work).
- Personal injuries to you or other people arising out of the accident.
- Towing charges.

Where to Claim the Deduction

You must complete Form 4684, Casualties and Thefts, to figure your loss. The form takes you line-by-line through the process, including how to apply the $100 limit and 10 percent of AGI floor to a loss on your personal car.

You report your deduction on Schedule A of Form 1040. You cannot claim a loss if you file Form 1040A or 1040EZ.

Donating Your Car

If you donate your car to a tax-exempt organization, you may be entitled to claim a deduction for the car's fair market value. For more details, see Chapter 6.

Hybrid Vehicle Credit

A hybrid car is a clean-fuel vehicle that runs on a combination of gasoline and electricity. Typically, the car starts in the gas mode and then runs on electricity, continually recharging itself. The federal government, as a way of encouraging these fuel-efficient vehicles, permits a tax credit to be claimed for their purchase, whether the car is used for personal or for business purposes.

Benefit

If you buy a special clean-fuel vehicle powered by both gas and electricity, called a hybrid vehicle, you may qualify for a tax credit in 2006 of up to $3,400. The one-time credit applies only in the year in which you purchase the vehicle.

Conditions

Your car must receive special certification from the IRS that it is eligible for this credit. To be eligible for the credit, manufacturers must adhere to the standards that are set by the IRS. Doing so means that different models entitle you to different tax credits. Applying these standards, the follow models and their credits at this time include:

- Toyota Prius (2005 and 2006 models)—$3,150
- Toyota Highlander Hybrid (2006 model)—$2,600
- Toyota Camry Hybrid (2007 model)—$2,600
- Mercury Mariner 2WD (2006 model)—$2,600
- Ford Escape Hybrids 2WD (2006 and 2007 models)—$2,600
- Lexus RX400h 2WD and 4WD (2006 model)—$2,200
- Honda Civic Hybrid CVT (2006 model)—$2,100
- Mercury Mariner Hybrid 4WD (2006 and 2007 models)—$1,950
- Ford Escape Hybrid 4WD (2006 and 2007 models)—$1,950
- Honda Civic Hybrid CVT (2005 model) and MT (2005 model)—$1,700
- Lexus GS 450h (2007 model)—$1,550
- Honda Insight CVT (2005 and 2006 models)—$1,450
- Honda Accord Hybrid AT (2005 and 2006 models)—$650
- GMC Sierra, four-wheel drive, hybrid pickup truck (model years 2006 and 2007)—$650
- Chevrolet Silverado, four-wheel drive, hybrid pickup truck (model years 2006 and 2007)—$650
- Saturn Vue Green Line (model year 2007)—$650
- GMC Sierra, two-wheel drive, hybrid pickup truck (model years 2006 and 2007)—$250
- Chevrolet Silverado, two-wheel drive, hybrid pickup truck (model years 2006 and 2007)—$250

The IRS may add additional models when they qualify, so check with the manufacturer when shopping for a new vehicle this year.

Planning Tips

If you are planning on buying a new car, factor in the credit for hybrid cars when weighing the purchase price of cars under consideration. The write-off is designed to offset the incremental cost of the clean-fuel feature (it costs more to make a clean-fuel vehicle than an ordinary gas-powered one).

Also factor in the savings you will realize year in and year out when running a hybrid car. Some models get more than 60 miles to the gallon because they also run on electric power.

Pitfalls

You cannot claim the credit if you lease a hybrid car; it applies only for purchases.

If you are thinking about buying a hybrid vehicle, do so sooner rather than later. The full credit applies only for the first 60,000 vehicles sold by a manufacturer (it is *not* model-sensitive). The credit is reduced for additional sales starting in the second calendar quarter that the manufacturer achieves this sales target. For example, if the 60,000th vehicle limit is reached in June 2006, the credit will be reduced to 50 percent of the amount otherwise allowed in the second and third quarter (i.e., starting in October 2006), 25 percent in the fourth and fifth quarters following the 60,000th vehicle, and no credit in the sixth quarter (i.e., October 2007). Regardless of the number of vehicles sold, no credit can be claimed after 2007 unless Congress extends the law.

The credit may be lost by those subject to the alternative minimum tax.

Where to Claim the Credit

You enter details about the vehicle on Form 8910, Alternative Motor Vehicle Credit. There is nothing to compute since you are limited to the dollar amount of the credit fixed for the vehicle you purchased (subject to any phaseout percentage). You claim this deduction in the "Tax and Credits" section of Form 1040.

You cannot claim this deduction if you file Form 1040A or 1040EZ.

Electric Car Credit

Some vehicles run exclusively on electricity—the battery must be recharged for continued use. But these cars are environmentally friendly, and their owners may qualify for a special tax credit for buying an electric car.

Benefit

If you purchase a car powered entirely by electricity, you may claim a tax credit of one-quarter of 10 percent of the cost of the car, costing up to $40,000.

Example

You buy an electric car in 2006 for $30,000. You may claim a tax credit of $750 (1/4 of 10% × $30,000 = $3,000).

Conditions

To claim this tax credit, both of the following conditions must be satisfied:

1. The car must be a qualified electric vehicle, which is one powered by rechargeable batteries, fuel cells, or other portable sources of electricity.
2. You must be the original owner of the car. If you purchase a used electric car, you are not entitled to the credit.

You must reduce the basis of the car by the amount of the credit. For example, if the car costs $30,000 and you claim a credit in 2006 of $750, your basis for purposes of determining gain or loss on a later sale or for claiming business-related deductions becomes $29,250 ($30,000 – $750).

Planning Tips

In addition to the credit, you can claim depreciation on the car if you use it for business purposes. The dollar limits on depreciation for electric cars may be found in IRS Publication 463, *Travel, Entertainment, Gift, and Car Expenses*.

You can elect *not* to claim the credit. You might want to make this election if the car is used in business and you would obtain a greater benefit by claiming bonus depreciation and other deductions for the car.

Pitfall

If you sell or otherwise dispose of the car, you may be subject to recapture, which means you must include some of the benefit realized from the credit in your income.

No credit may be claimed after 2006 unless Congress extends the law.

Where to Claim the Benefit

You figure the credit on Form 8834, Qualified Electric Vehicle Credit, which you attach to Form 1040. You enter the credit on the line in the "Tax and Credits" section of the return marked "Other Credits." Enter the form number "8834" in the space provided for this purpose.

You cannot claim the credit if you file Form 1040A or 1040EZ.

CHAPTER 8

Investing

Putting money aside for that proverbial rainy day is an admirable and necessary goal but it can be a difficult proposition, especially in tough economic times when your paycheck doesn't seem to stretch far enough. Still, savings and investing are essential to your financial well-being, and the tax laws can help you to make the most of your efforts.

This chapter explains:

- Penalty on early withdrawal of savings
- Loss on bank deposits
- Capital losses
- Worthless securities
- Loss on Section 1244 stock
- Margin interest and other investment-related borrowing
- Safe-deposit box rental fee
- Subscriptions to investment newsletters and online services
- Home computer used for investments
- Fees to financial planners
- Amortization of bond premium
- Municipal bonds
- Savings bonds

- Gain on the sale of small business stock
- Gain on empowerment zone assets
- Foreign taxes on investments

For more information, see IRS Publication 514, *Foreign Tax Credit for Individuals*; IRS Publication 525, *Taxable and Nontaxable Income*; IRS Publication 544, *Sales and Other Dispositions of Assets*; IRS Publication 550, *Investment Income and Expenses*; IRS Publication 551, *Basis of Assets*; and IRS Publication 564, *Mutual Fund Distributions*.

Penalty on Early Withdrawal of Savings

Time deposit accounts and certificates of deposit are fixed for a set term. These savings vehicles generally pay a higher rate of interest than money-market and passbook accounts. But if they are cashed in before maturity, a penalty is imposed. The penalty usually is forfeiture of some interest and, in some cases, even principal. The penalty is tax deductible.

Benefit

If you cash in a certificate of deposit (CD) or savings account before its fixed maturity date for any reason (such as you need the money to pay personal expenses or you can obtain a higher interest rate if you move the money), you may be forced to pay a penalty. The penalty is subtracted from the funds you receive.

You can deduct this penalty, which may be a forfeiture of interest and/or principal (if the penalty exceeds the interest), even though you do not itemize your other deductions. In the case of savings certificates with fixed maturities of longer than one year, your deduction is based on the forfeiture of original issue discount (which is nothing more than a way of figuring interest). Regardless of the maturity involved, this deduction is called a penalty on early withdrawal of savings. There is no dollar limit on this deduction.

Conditions

There are no conditions or requirements to meet. As long as you take money out of a savings certificate before the specified maturity date and are subject to a penalty, you can deduct the penalty in full.

Planning Tip

When putting money into time-savings vehicles, such as certificates of deposit, don't extend the investment period beyond the time you *may* need the funds so that you can avoid early withdrawal penalties if you *do* need the money then. Consider splitting your savings into multiple savings certificates with different maturity dates so that you can readily have access to some funds penalty free.

Example

You have $10,000 for savings. Instead of putting $10,000 into a single CD for five years, consider putting only $5,000 in for five years and putting the other $5,000 into a renewable 12-month CD. Each year you know that you can obtain at least $5,000 penalty free. This will also allow some of the funds to be reinvested for higher interest rates should rates rise (but, conversely, you may lose out on your interest rate if rates decline).

Pitfall

You cannot net the penalty against the interest you receive and eliminate the need to separately deduct the penalty. You must report all of the interest on the savings certificate and then separately deduct the early withdrawal penalty.

Where to Claim the Benefit

The forfeited amount is reported to you (and the IRS) on Form 1099-INT if the certificate of deposit is for one year or less, or on Form 1099-OID if the certificate of deposit is for longer than one year. You deduct this amount in the "Adjusted Gross Income" section of Form 1040.

You cannot deduct the penalty if you file Form 1040A or 1040EZ.

Loss on Bank Deposits

During the Great Depression, there was a run on the banks; depositors rushed to withdraw their money, forcing many banks to go under. Today, there are many protections in place (such as state-mandated funding requirements) to ensure the integrity of banks. But despite these protections, some banks still fail. Losses suffered by depositors of failed banks that are not insured by the Federal Deposit Insurance Corporation (FDIC) or funds not covered by FDIC protection may be tax deductible under certain conditions.

Benefit

If your bank goes under and your account is not covered in whole or in part by FDIC (Federal Deposit Insurance Corporation) insurance, you can deduct your loss.

There are different ways to treat your loss (each of which is explained in the next section):

- Bad debt deduction
- Casualty loss
- Ordinary loss

Choose the method that results in the greatest write-off.

Conditions

The conditions for deducting your loss on bank deposits are simple: The bank must be insolvent or bankrupt so that there is no reasonable prospect of recovering your money, and your deposits must not be covered by FDIC or state insurance. Additional conditions and limits, however, may apply to the deduction method you select.

BAD DEBT. You can opt to treat your loss as a bad debt, which is classified for tax purposes as a short-term capital loss (regardless of how long your money was on deposit). This means you can deduct your loss against capital gains. If you do not have capital gains or if these losses are greater than your capital gains, you can only deduct up to $3,000 against your ordinary income. Any unused amount of the loss can be carried forward and used in a future year.

There is one condition for selecting this deduction method: There must be no reasonable prospect of recovery from the insolvent or bankrupt bank. You must wait until the year in which your nonrecovery becomes clear.

The rules for bad debts are explained more fully in Chapter 12.

CASUALTY LOSS. You can opt to treat your loss as a casualty loss, which means you must itemize deductions to claim the loss. The amount of your loss is reduced by $100 right off the top—the $100 subtraction is a feature in the tax law for claiming a casualty loss deduction.

Casualty losses (after the $100 reduction) are deductible only to the extent they exceed 10 percent of your adjusted gross income, another condition in the tax law.

Once you choose the option to treat your loss on bank deposits as a casualty loss, it's irrevocable and must be used for any additional losses you incur from the same financial institution.

You can use this option if you have an estimated loss. You do not have to wait until there is no reasonable prospect of recovery to claim a casualty loss deduction. If, by some reason, you eventually receive some or all of your money, you must report the recovery as income in the year you receive it to the extent your original deduction produced a tax benefit.

This option is *not* open to stockholders of the bank who own more than a 1 percent interest. Similarly, this option cannot be used by the bank's officers or relatives of officers or stockholders.

The rules for casualty losses are explained more fully in Chapter 13.

ORDINARY LOSS. You can opt to deduct up to $20,000 ($10,000 if you are married and file a separate return) as a miscellaneous itemized deduction, which is subject to the 2 percent of AGI floor. The dollar limit applies per institution, not per account. For example, if you have two accounts at the same insolvent bank, each for $15,000, your total deduction is limited to $20,000. But if you have those accounts at two separate insolvent banks, you could deduct a total of $30,000 ($15,000 for each account since this does not exceed the $20,000 per-bank limit) in the same year.

There is one condition for selecting this option: None of your deposits were federally insured.

Planning Tips

If you qualify to select any of the three deduction options, which one should you choose? There is no single answer; it depends on the amount of your loss and your other income. Keep these factors in mind and run the numbers on each of your options.

Choose the bad debt deduction option if your loss can be fully used in the current year (you have capital gains to offset the loss or no more than $3,000 of bad debt in excess of your capital gains). If you suffered a deposit loss years ago but didn't know about it, it may be too late to claim an ordinary or casualty loss but not too late for a bad debt deduction. Generally, you have seven years from the due date of your return for the year of the loss to amend it and report the bad debt deduction.

Choose the casualty loss option if you already have casualty or theft losses for the year that offset the 10 percent of AGI floor.

Example

In 2006, your car was damaged in an accident and you did not have collision insurance. Your loss on this incident was $6,000. You also have an uninsured loss on your bank deposit of $10,000. Assuming your adjusted gross income is $60,000 or less, you can then fully utilize the $10,000 bank deposit loss. But if the bank deposit loss was your only loss for the year, using the casualty loss method means you cannot benefit from the first $6,000 of your $10,000 loss because of the 10 percent of AGI floor.

Choose the ordinary loss option if your loss is under the dollar limit and you already have miscellaneous itemized deductions that offset the 2 percent of AGI floor and are *not* subject to the alternative minimum tax (AMT).

Example

In 2006, you have an uninsured bank loss of $15,000. Your adjusted gross income is $60,000 and you also have $1,200 or more of other miscellaneous itemized deductions. You can fully deduct your $15,000 loss. But if you are subject to the alternative minimum tax, selecting this option may increase your liability because miscellaneous itemized deductions are not deductible for AMT purposes.

But why rely on tax write-offs to make you whole? The best option is to make sure that your deposits are adequately covered by FDIC insurance. Understand your FDIC limits so you don't expose your savings to potential loss, especially when you have accounts in separate institutions that have recently merged or been taken over.

The rules on FDIC coverage and a listing of the banks with this insurance protection may be found at www.fdic.gov. You can also use the Electronic Deposit Insurance Estimator (EDIE) at www2.fdic.gov/edie to see where your bank accounts stand in terms of FDIC coverage.

Pitfall

The biggest problem with bank losses is knowing exactly what your losses really are. You may recover something when the bank's finances are settled, even if it is only pennies on the dollar. Generally the trustees of a troubled bank will give you an estimate of your expected recovery and loss.

Where to Claim the Benefit

If you opt to treat the loss as a bad debt, you must file Schedule D to report the loss. In column (f) of Schedule D, be sure that your loss is entered in parentheses to indicate a loss amount.

If you treat the loss as a casualty loss, you must file Form 4684, Casualties and Thefts, to report the loss, which is then entered on Schedule A.

If you claim the loss as an ordinary loss, you must file Schedule A to report the loss.

Regardless of which option you select, you can claim a loss on bank deposits only if you file Form 1040. You cannot claim the loss if you file Form 1040A or 1040EZ.

Capital Losses

Wouldn't it be great if every investment turned out to be profitable? Unfortunately, this isn't the way things work—despite our best efforts, investments may decline in value. A mere drop in an asset's value isn't a tax loss; there must be an actual transaction that fixes the loss. If a sale produces a loss, it may be tax deductible.

Benefit

In today's uncertain stock market, it's not uncommon to have losses, even if prices had run up considerably during the 1990s. Capital losses are deductible in full (there is no dollar limit) as an offset to your capital gains for the year. If your capital losses exceed your gains, up to $3,000 of capital losses can be used to offset ordinary income, such as salary and interest income. If your capital losses are more than this $3,000 limit, you can carry the excess forward indefinitely to be used in a future year.

Understand what capital losses are so that you can plan wisely to get the greatest tax benefit from your losses. Capital losses generally arise on the sale or other disposition of capital assets, such as stocks, collectibles, or real estate. Your loss is the difference between what you receive on the sale and your adjusted basis in the property (usually what you paid for it).

Example

In 2003, you bought 100 shares of X Corp. for $10,000. In December 2006, you sell those shares for $6,000. You have a $4,000 capital loss ($10,000 basis – $6,000 proceeds on the sale).

There are two classes of capital losses: short-term losses resulting from assets held one year or less and long-term losses resulting from assets held more than one year. As a practical matter, while complex rules govern the order in which capital losses are used to offset different categories of capital gains, in the end capital losses can be used to fully offset capital gains.

Conditions

You must sell or otherwise dispose of an asset to have a deductible loss. A mere decline in the value of an asset you continue to hold does not entitle you to claim a loss. There are exceptions to the disposition requirement (e.g., a bad debt is treated as a short-term capital loss even though the debt is not sold or otherwise disposed of).

As mentioned earlier, the loss must be with respect to a capital asset. And this asset must be held for investment or business purposes. You cannot deduct a capital loss on an asset held primarily for personal purposes (such as your home, personal car, or boat).

Planning Tips

Don't overlook basis adjustments that may increase your loss (by increasing your basis). Take into account:

- Stock dividends you reinvested in the same company.
- Brokers' commissions.
- Acquisition costs (e.g., attorney's fees to handle the purchase of real estate).
- Selling costs (e.g., real estate broker's fees).

At year-end, review your investment portfolio to see if there are capital losses you want to harvest for tax advantage. But always temper your tax planning with investment considerations. Don't sell only to generate losses; let your investment decisions be driven primarily by economics (e.g., you think the investment will never recover or there are better places to put your investment dollars).

Pitfalls

While you may have an economic loss on a transaction, do not automatically assume it qualifies for capital loss treatment for tax purposes. Certain pitfalls may trip you up.

WASH SALE RULE. You cannot claim a loss if you acquire substantially identical securities within 30 days before or after the date of sale. Under this "wash sale rule," you do not lose the loss entirely. Instead, you adjust the basis of the newly acquired securities to reflect the loss you could not take. This will enable you to claim the loss when you later sell the newly acquired securities in a transaction that is not subject to the wash sale rule.

What is a substantially identical security? If you sell Coca-Cola stock at a loss on March 14, 2006, and purchase Coca-Cola stock on April 10, 2006, you are subject to the wash sale rule. But if you sell Pepsi stock at a loss and buy Coca-Cola on these dates, the wash sale rule does not apply because these are different companies and their stocks are not substantially identical securities.

Also, if you sell an IBM bond at a loss on March 14, 2006, bearing an interest rate of 7 percent payable in 2011, and purchase an IBM bond on April 10, 2006, bearing an interest rate of 6 percent payable in 2016, you are *not* subject to the wash sale rule. The differences in the coupon rates and maturities of these bonds make them different securities.

OTHER PITFALLS. You cannot claim a capital loss on the sale or other disposition of all property. Some types of property are not classified as capital assets so they do not qualify for capital loss treatment:

- Business inventory and property held for sale to customers.
- Depreciable business property and rental property.
- Copyrights, literary and musical compositions, letters, or other such property that you created, that you acquired by gift from the persons who created them, or that were created for you.
- Government publications.

If one spouse incurs the capital loss and dies, it can be used only in the year of death. Excess capital losses cannot be carried forward and used by a surviving spouse in a later year.

Also, as mentioned earlier, you may not claim a loss on your personal property, such as on the sale of your residence or personal car. You can claim a loss only on assets held for investment and which are not otherwise excluded from capital loss treatment. While you may view your home as an investment (perhaps your greatest investment), the tax law does not.

Where to Claim the Loss

To claim capital losses, you must file Schedule D to figure the deductible amount. Short-term transactions are entered in Part I of Schedule D; long-term transactions are entered in Part II of Schedule D. Gains and losses are netted in each of these parts and then short-term gains or losses are netted against long-term gains or losses in Part III of Schedule D. Make sure that the amount of any loss entered in column (f) of Schedule D is within parentheses to indicate a loss amount.

You enter the amount of your net capital loss from Part III of Schedule D onto Form 1040.

You cannot claim capital losses if you file Form 1040A or 1040EZ.

Worthless Securities

Investments in a corporation—stocks or bonds—are made with the intention of collecting income and/or making a profit. But some corporations go under and investors are left holding the bag. The tax law allows a deduction for worthless securities.

Benefit

If you hold stocks or bonds issued with coupons or in registered form that become worthless, you can deduct your investment. Worthless securities are treated as becoming worthless on the last day of the year in which they actually become worthless. This date governs whether the loss is treated as a short-term loss (if you held the security no more than one year prior to December

31) or a long-term loss (if you held the security more than one year prior to December 31).

The loss is treated as a capital loss (discussed earlier in this chapter), even though there is no sale involved. However, if the loss relates to Section 1244 stock (discussed later in this chapter), the loss is treated as an ordinary loss up to $50,000 ($100,000 on a joint return).

Conditions

There are two conditions you must meet to write off your investment in worthless securities:

1. The security must have had some value at the end of the prior year.
2. The security must have become *totally* worthless.

VALUE IN THE PRIOR YEAR. To claim a loss in 2006, you must show that the stock or bond had some value on December 31, 2005. Generally, you can learn whether the stock has any value by checking your year-end statements from brokerage firms holding your investment. If you hold publicly traded stock in your own name rather than in the brokerage firm's name ("street name"), check newspapers for December 31 to see if the stock is listed in the financial section (only stock with a value is listed in the papers). For example, Enron stock officially became worthless on November 17, 2004 (so the loss is claimed on December 31, 2004), even though the corporation filed for bankruptcy in 2001.

TOTALLY WORTHLESS. The stock or bond must have *no* value by the end of the year in which you claim the loss. Just because a bond has stopped paying interest or a stock has been delisted does not mean it is totally worthless. Be prepared to present facts showing the security is worthless. You can assume that it is worthless if the company issuing it:

- Goes into bankruptcy that results in a liquidation of the company.
- Ceases to do business.
- Becomes insolvent.

However, don't assume that a security is worthless if the company has plans to reorganize in bankruptcy.

Planning Tips

If you hold a security that is partially but not wholly worthless, sell it to nail down your loss. For example, if you think a company is on the brink of bankruptcy, try to sell the security so that you can fix the loss. Typically, your brokerage firm will buy it for a nominal amount, enabling you to claim a loss for the difference between your basis (usually what you paid for it) and what you received for it.

Bonds not issued with interest coupons or in registered form that become worthless result in a bad debt deduction (discussed earlier under "Loss on Bank Deposits").

You can claim a loss only in the year in which the security becomes totally worthless. But you have seven years to discover that a security has become worthless. This is because the statute of limitations on amending your return to claim the loss for a worthless security is seven years rather than the usual three years from the due date of your return.

Example

In 2006, you discover that a stock you held became completely worthless in 1999. You have until April 16, 2007, to file an amended return for 1999 (which was due on April 15, 2000) to report the loss.

If you are unsure in which year to claim the loss, it is generally advisable to report it in the earliest year you suspect that the worthlessness occurred and then to renew your claim in each subsequent year when the earliest year proves to be incorrect. This requires that you file amended returns to eliminate the loss from the earliest return and report it on a subsequent return.

Pitfalls

Don't let time pass you by. Once the seven-year period for filing an amended return has passed, your loss can never be claimed. Each year, make sure to check on the status of any questionable securities to make sure you don't overlook a loss write-off you are entitled to claim.

The amount you can write off for worthless securities is limited to your basis in the stocks or bonds. Even though you may have witnessed soaring prices only to be followed by the wipeout, you cannot benefit in any way from those record highs; your tax loss is limited to your basis, which is usually what you paid for the securities.

Where to Claim the Loss

You report worthless securities on Schedule D of Form 1040 (in Part I if the securities were held for no more than one year; Part II if they were held more than one year). In columns (c) and (d) write "Worthless." Then, in column (f), be sure to enter the amount of your loss in parentheses.

You cannot deduct a loss for worthless securities if you file Form 1040A or 1040EZ.

Loss on Section 1244 Stock

Typically, losses on stock are treated as capital losses, which are deductible to the extent of capital gains for the year, plus up to $3,000 of ordinary income. But losses on a special type of stock, called Section 1244 stock after the section in the Internal Revenue Code defining it, can be treated as ordinary losses within set limits.

Benefit

If you own stock that qualifies as Section 1244 stock, you can claim an ordinary loss on the sale or worthlessness of the stock. The ordinary loss is limited to $50,000 ($100,000 on a joint return).

Conditions

To be able to treat your loss as an ordinary loss, you must meet the following two conditions:

1. The stock must qualify as Section 1244 stock.
2. The amount of your loss cannot exceed the dollar limit.

SECTION 1244 REQUIREMENTS. The issuing corporation can be a C or an S corporation. The stock can be common or preferred (provided the preferred stock was issued after July 18, 1984). But all four of these conditions must be met:

1. The corporation's equity cannot be greater than $1 million at the time the stock is issued (including amounts received for the stock).
2. The stock must be issued for money or property (other than securities). If you inherited the stock or acquired it for services rendered to the corporation, you cannot treat your loss as an ordinary loss.
3. The corporation must have derived more than half of its gross receipts during the five-year period before your loss from business operations (and not from passive income such as investments, rents, or royalties). If the corporation is in business less than five years, then it must have derived more than half of its gross receipts from business operations in all of its years in existence.
4. You must be the original owner of the stock (you cannot have purchased it from the original owner or someone else).

DOLLAR LIMIT. You can treat only the first $50,000 of the loss as an ordinary loss. The limit on a joint return is $100,000, even if one spouse owned the stock in his or her sole name. Losses in excess of this dollar limit may be treated as capital losses (discussed earlier in this chapter).

Planning Tip

You can claim a Section 1244 loss regardless of how you suffer the loss. Whether you sell your stock at a loss or the company goes under, ordinary loss treatment applies if you meet the conditions discussed earlier.

You (and the corporation) must keep certain records and make them available for IRS inspection if requested. The records should show that the corporation met the qualifications for the stock to be classified as Section 1244 stock. The corporation should keep records on its gross receipts data for five years, and you should keep records on what you paid for the stock. If you don't keep these records, you risk losing your ordinary loss deduction.

Pitfall

If you own stock in an S corporation that holds small business stock, the portion of any loss on such stock passed through to you does *not* qualify as an ordinary loss on Section 1244 stock. Under the technical language of the tax law, only individuals and partnerships can claim Section 1244 losses. Even though S corporations are pass-through entities like partnerships, they are not eligible to claim Section 1244 losses.

Where to Claim the Loss

An ordinary loss on Section 1244 stock is reported on Form 4797, Sales of Business Property, which you attach to Form 1040. This form is used whether the loss arises from the sale of the stock or from it becoming worthless so that no sale takes place.

If the amount of the loss exceeds your dollar limit, you treat the excess loss as a capital loss (discussed earlier).

You cannot claim a Section 1244 loss if you file Form 1040A or 1040EZ.

Margin Interest and Other Investment-Related Borrowing

Interest paid to borrow money for the purpose of making investments is viewed as "investment interest." The tax law sets strict limits on when and the extent to which investment interest may be deductible.

Benefit

You can deduct interest on borrowing that uses your brokerage account as collateral if the money is used for investment purposes. This is called margin interest. You can also deduct interest on other loans used to make investments as an itemized deduction to the extent of your net investment income. If your investment interest is more than your net investment income for the year, you can carry the excess interest forward indefinitely and use it in a future year.

Conditions

There are two important conditions:

1. The funds borrowed must be used for investment purposes.
2. For full deductibility of the interest, you must have net investment income to offset it.

BORROWING FOR INVESTMENT PURPOSES. It is not the source of the borrowing that determines the treatment of the interest but the purpose for which you use the proceeds from the loan. For example, margin interest is not automatically deductible. If you use the loan to buy a personal car, you cannot deduct the margin interest even though the loan arises from your investment account.

If you borrow money to buy stock in a business, interest on the loan is treated as investment interest, not business interest. In contrast, if you buy the assets of a business, the interest is treated as fully deductible business interest, not investment interest limited to the extent of net investment income.

NET INVESTMENT INCOME. Your investment interest is deductible only to the extent of your net investment income for the year. Investment income includes:

- Interest income
- Annuities
- Royalties

Interest from passive activities that is not classified by the activities as "portfolio income" is not treated as investment income. This includes interest on rental real estate or interest passed through to you from investments in limited partnerships or other pass-through entities in which you do not materially participate. Property subject to a net lease is not treated as investment property (it is treated as a passive activity). As a practical matter, you simply look at the Schedule K-1 sent to you by the investment to see how to classify the passed-through interest.

You must reduce investment income by investment expenses for the year to arrive at your net investment income. Investment expenses are expenses directly connected with the production of investment income *after* applying the 2 percent of AGI floor. Examples of other investment expenses are found throughout this chapter. (If you have both investment expenses and miscellaneous itemized expenses, the tax law assumes that the 2 percent floor offsets those other deductions before your investment expenses.)

Planning Tip

You can opt to treat capital gains and/or dividends as investment income. If you make this election, your capital gains and/or dividends are not eligible for preferential tax rates and are instead included as ordinary income.

Generally it is *not* advisable to make this election because doing so effectively converts income that would otherwise be taxed at no more than 15 percent to income taxed at up to 35 percent. But the election can make sense in some situations; only running the numbers can determine when this is so.

Example

You have $3,000 of capital losses for the year and $6,000 of capital gains. You also have investment interest of $3,000 and no other investment income. If you don't make the election, $3,000 of your capital gains is taxed at 15 percent, but you can't deduct any of your investment interest this year. If you do make the election, then your capital losses become deductible against ordinary income so that only $3,000 of your capital gains is exposed to ordinary income, while all of your investment interest becomes deductible.

Pitfall

You cannot deduct interest, regardless of the source of the loan, if you use the money to buy or carry municipal bonds (for example, you need to raise cash and you sell your taxable investments while holding onto your municipal bonds).

Where to Claim the Deduction

You figure your investment interest limitation on Form 4952, Investment Interest Expense Deduction. You then enter the deductible amount on Schedule A, which is filed with Form 1040.

You cannot deduct investment interest if you file Form 1040A or 1040EZ.

Safe-Deposit Box Rental Fee

Where do you store your valuables? There's no tax break for keeping them under the mattress. But if you rent a safe-deposit box, you may be able to deduct your annual costs.

Benefit

If you rent a safe-deposit box in a bank or company specializing in safe-deposit box rentals in order to store your investments, you can deduct the fee as a miscellaneous itemized deduction. The deduction for investment expenses is subject to the 2 percent of AGI floor discussed earlier in this chapter.

Conditions

To claim the deduction, the use of the safe-deposit box must be investment-related. For example, you use the safe-deposit box to store your stock certificates.

If you use it to store your personal items, such as your will, the expense is not a deductible investment expense.

Planning Tip

You can eliminate the need for a safe-deposit box to store your securities and save the rental fee by putting the securities in street name. This means giving physical custody of your stock and bond certificates to your brokerage firm, which then transfers title into its name. You continue to see your interests on your monthly statements.

Pitfall

Claiming a deduction for a safe-deposit box on your return alerts the IRS to the fact that you have investments and/or other property stored away. Are you reporting investment income on your tax return? A negative answer to this question may prompt the IRS to question your deduction for the safe-deposit box.

Where to Claim the Deduction

You report the safe-deposit box rental fee as a miscellaneous itemized deduction on Schedule A of Form 1040.

You cannot claim a deduction for safe-deposit box rental fees as an investment expense if you file Form 1040A or 1040EZ.

Subscriptions to Investment Newsletters and Online Services

Investors need to stay up to date with developments in the economy and the stock market in order to make sound investment decisions. There are many ways to stay current—investment newsletters, magazines, and Web-based services. The cost of keeping on top of financial developments may be tax deductible.

Benefit

If you subscribe to investment newspapers, newsletters, or online services, you can deduct the expenses as a miscellaneous itemized deduction. The deduction for investment expenses is subject to the 2 percent of AGI floor discussed earlier in this chapter.

Conditions

The purpose for the expense must be investment-related. If you are using online services for personal purposes, your outlays are not deductible.

If you use your purchases for both investment and personal purposes, you should allocate your costs and deduct only the portion related to investments.

Example

You pay $240 annually for your online computer access. You estimate that you spend half your time online tracking your investments and the other half pursuing personal interests. You allocate one-half of the expense, or $120, to investment purposes. This is your deductible amount.

Planning Tip

If you pay for multiple-year subscriptions and deduct only a portion of the cost for this year, be sure to keep records so you won't overlook the opportunity to deduct another portion next year.

Pitfall

There is no downside to claiming a deduction for these subscription costs if you are eligible to so do.

Where to Claim the Deduction

You report the costs of investment newsletters and other investment-related expenses as a miscellaneous itemized deduction on Schedule A of Form 1040.

You cannot claim a deduction for these investment-related expenses if you file Form 1040A or 1040EZ.

Home Computer Used for Investments

Home computers can be used for more than just e-mailing relatives across the country, visiting chat rooms on hobby interests, or helping children with homework. Home computers can be used for investment activities, including research and recordkeeping. Depending on how the computer is used, some costs may be deductible.

Benefit

If you buy or lease a home computer to monitor your investments, you can deduct expenses for the computer as a miscellaneous itemized deduction. The deduction for investment expenses is subject to the 2 percent of AGI floor discussed earlier in this chapter.

If you buy the computer, you depreciate the cost of the computer over its recovery period, a fixed time in the tax law (you cannot deduct the entire cost in the year you buy the computer because first-year expensing is a write-off limited to business property, as explained in Chapter 15). The computer is treated as five-year property. However, since the computer is not used more than 50 percent in business (presumably you use it entirely for your investments, or only incidentally for personal purposes), you must use straight-line depreciation.

Example

In 2006, you pay $1,200 for a computer used to track your investments. In 2006, you can claim an allowance for depreciation of $120 (10 percent of $1,200). During each of the next five years you may deduct $240 (20 percent of $1,200). In the sixth year, assuming you still have the same computer, you can again deduct $120 (10 percent of its cost).

If you lease the computer for investment-related purposes, you can deduct your annual lease payments.

Conditions

The use of the computer must be investment-related. If you use it primarily for personal purposes and only incidentally for investment purposes, your outlays are not deductible.

If you use your computer for both investment and personal purposes, you should allocate your costs and deduct only the portion related to investments.

Example

You pay $540 annually to rent a computer. You estimate that you spend half your time on the computer tracking your investments and the other half pursuing personal interests. You allocate one-half of the expense, or $270, to investment purposes. This is your deductible amount.

Planning Tips

You cannot claim first-year expensing for a home computer used for monitoring your investments. Only business assets qualify for the expensing write-off.

If you use a computer for business as well as investment purposes, different rules may apply. See Chapters 14 and 15 for details.

Pitfall

If you qualify to depreciate the computer, you effectively can't opt *not* to claim the write-off. While you do not have to subtract your depreciation allowance, you must reduce the basis of the computer by the depreciation you were entitled to claim. This means that if you later sell the computer, you may have a gain (because of the reduction to basis from depreciation), even though its value has declined.

Where to Claim the Deduction

To claim depreciation, you must file Form 4562, Depreciation and Amortization. You enter your depreciation allowance in Part III of the form. The deductible amount is then entered on Schedule A of Form 1040, miscellaneous itemized deductions. If you lease the computer, lease payments are entered directly on Schedule A.

You cannot claim a deduction for a home computer if you file Form 1040A or 1040EZ.

Fees to Financial Planners

When it comes to investments, it's helpful to turn to experts for assistance. Financial experts may be compensated for their services in different ways. Stockbrokers, for example, are paid through commissions on the investments they sell. But some financial advisers are paid on a fee basis; some receive both fees and commissions. Commissions are not a deductible expense (they are added to the cost basis of the investments purchased). But fees may be deductible.

Benefit

If you consult with a fee-only financial planner who charges for his or her time and advice regardless of the actions you take, you can deduct the fees you pay as a miscellaneous itemized deduction.

Conditions

You can deduct only fees that are separately paid. If you consult with a financial planner who charges you both a fee plus commissions, you can deduct only the fee portion.

If you consult with an attorney who prepares a will for you while providing estate planning advice, you can deduct the portion of the attorney's fee for estate planning services if such amount is itemized on the attorney's invoice.

Planning Tip

Fee-only financial planners charge you an hourly rate or a flat fee for a specific service, such as creating a comprehensive financial plan. If you have the planner monitor your assets throughout the year, you may also be charged a fee based on a percentage of these assets. Usually, fee-only planners are in the best position to give you objective financial advice because they do not stand to gain or lose by your subsequent actions.

Pitfall

If you consult a commission-based financial planner who does not charge you a fee for advice, but includes commissions or charges on investments he or she sells you, you cannot deduct these costs. Instead, add commissions or other costs to the basis of the assets you acquire to reduce your gain (or increase your loss) on a subsequent sale.

Where to Claim the Deduction

You report the fees paid to financial planners as a miscellaneous itemized deduction on Schedule A of Form 1040.

You cannot claim a deduction for fees to financial planners as an investment expense if you file Form 1040A or 1040EZ.

Amortization of Bond Premium

If you buy a bond at a price greater than its stated principal (or face) amount, the excess is called bond premium. You may opt to amortize the premium on taxable bonds; in some cases you *must* amortize bond premium (you don't have any choice).

Benefit

If you buy a taxable bond, such as a corporate bond, you can elect in the year of the purchase to begin amortizing the bond premium. This means that each year you own the bond, you can offset the taxable interest received on the bond by the amortizable premium amount.

Example

In 2006, you buy a $5,000 corporate bond for $5,500. Your bond premium is $500. Assuming the bond has five years left to maturity, you can amortize the $500 premium over five years. This means you can use $100 ($500 ÷ 5 years) to offset interest from the bond.

If you buy a tax-exempt bond, such as a municipal bond, at a premium, you *must* amortize the bond premium. You cannot deduct the amortized premium amount. Instead, you reduce the basis of the bond by the amortization for the year.

Example

Same as the preceding example except the bond is a tax-free municipal bond. If you sell the bond at the end of the third year, the basis in the bond is $5,200 ($5,500 – $300). If the sale price of the bond is $5,200, you have no gain or loss on the transaction. If the price is higher than $5,200, you have a taxable gain; if the price is lower, you have a taxable loss.

Conditions

To amortize bond premium on a taxable bond, you must meet the following two conditions:

1. You elect amortization.
2. You figure amortization using the constant yield method for bonds issued after September 27, 1985 (other amortization methods apply for earlier bond issues). This is a three-step process under which you determine your yield, the accrual periods to use in figuring amortization, and the bond premium. The computation is rather complicated. For more details, see Chapter 3 of IRS Publication 550, *Investment Income and Expenses*.

Planning Tips

Usually it is advisable to elect amortization so you can offset current interest income from the bond. If you do not make the election, you probably will realize a capital loss when the bond is redeemed at par or you sell it for less than you paid for it.

You do not have to elect amortization for taxable bonds held in IRAs or qualified retirement plans. Since the interest is not currently deductible, no offset is necessary.

Pitfall

If you want to amortize bond premium on taxable bonds, you generally must elect to do so by attaching your own statement to the return indicating this choice. The election applies to all taxable bonds you own and to those you buy in later years.

Once you have made your choice, you can't change it unless you receive the written approval of the IRS. To request a change, you must file Form 3115, Application for Change in Accounting Method.

Where to Claim the Deduction

The amortizable amount of premium is not a separate deduction. Instead, it is an adjustment to the interest reported on Schedule B of Form 1040. Report the bond's interest and on the line below it subtract the amortization, noting "ABP Adjustment" next to it.

If the amortization exceeds the amount of interest reported, the excess can be deducted as a miscellaneous itemized deduction on Schedule A of Form 1040. This deduction is not subject to the 2 percent of adjusted gross income floor.

You cannot deduct amortization of bond premium if you file Form 1040A or 1040EZ.

Municipal Bonds

States, local governments, and their agencies raise money to operate through the sale of bonds. They pay interest on the bonds as inducements to investors to buy the bonds (i.e., lend them money). The federal government generally exempts this interest from taxes; there may or may not be any state income tax breaks as well.

Benefit

Interest on municipal bonds is not subject to federal income tax. You may fully exclude this interest from income. There is no dollar limit.

The exclusion applies to both interest on individual bonds and interest from mutual funds holding municipal bonds.

Conditions

Interest is classified as municipal bond interest only if the bond is issued by a state or local government or government agency.

Planning Tip

Interest on municipal bonds may also be exempt from state income taxes. Table 8.1 shows you how the states treat municipal bond interest.

Pitfalls

Municipal bond interest can affect the amount of taxes you pay on your Social Security benefits. Municipal bond interest, while exempt from federal income tax, is taken into account in determining your provisional income, the figure used to fix the taxable portion of Social Security benefits at 85 percent, 50 percent, or zero.

Interest on private activity bonds issued after August 6, 1986, while excluded from income for regular tax purposes, is subject to the alternative minimum tax (AMT). These bonds generally pay a slightly higher interest rate than other municipal bonds. However, if you know you will be subject to AMT, it is advisable when making bond investments to forgo the additional interest in favor of municipal bonds not subject to AMT.

Even though interest on municipal bonds is tax free, gain on the sale of the bonds is taxable. For instance, you purchase a bond at par value and sell it two years later for $2,000 more than you paid. You have a $2,000 gain that is taxable.

Where to Claim the Exclusion

Even though the interest is fully excludable, you are required to report tax-exempt interest on your return. You report this interest on the line provided for it on Form 1040 or Form 1040A.

TABLE 8.1 State Income Tax Treatment of Municipal Bond Interest

State	State Income Tax Treatment
Alaska, Florida, Nevada, South Dakota, Texas, Washington, and Wyoming	No state income tax (so interest on municipal bonds is not taxed)
Alabama, Arizona, Arkansas, California, Colorado, Connecticut, Delaware, Georgia, Hawaii, Idaho, Kentucky, Louisiana, Maine, Maryland, Massachusetts, Michigan, Minnesota, Mississippi, Missouri, Montana, Nebraska, New Hampshire, New Jersey, New Mexico, New York, North Carolina, Ohio, Oregon, Pennsylvania, Rhode Island, South Carolina, Tennessee, Vermont, Virginia and West Virginia	Interest is exempt from state income tax if the bond is issued by the state in which you file your return (or by Puerto Rico, U.S. Virgin Islands, or American Samoa)
District of Columbia, Indiana, North Dakota (if the long form is not used), and Utah	Interest is tax free regardless of the state of issuance
Illinois, Iowa, Kansas, Oklahoma, and Wisconsin	Interest is fully taxable for state income tax purposes regardless of the state of issuance

You do not have to report this income if you file Form 1040EZ. However, you cannot use this form if you have Social Security benefits.

Savings Bonds

United States savings bonds were first sold by the federal government in World War I and again in World War II as a way to raise money. Today, these bonds have become a permanent savings vehicle for the more than 55 million Americans who own them.

Benefit

Tax on the interest on series E, EE, and I bonds can be deferred until the bonds are cashed in or reach their final maturity dates.

Conditions

Deferral is automatic; you don't have to take any action to receive this tax treatment. You simply do not report the interest annually on your return.

Planning Tips

You can opt to report interest on these savings bonds annually instead of using deferral. This option may make sense when the bondholder has little or no other income so that the interest is taxed at a low rate, if at all.

Example

A child receives a series EE bond at her birth with a face value of $1,000. Since these bonds are sold at a 50 percent discount (the $1,000 bond costs only $500), any increase in the bond's value over $500 is treated as interest. If the child has no other income, the interest is effectively tax free provided that an election is made to report the interest annually. This election is made simply by including the interest on a tax return filed for the child. File a return to establish this reporting even though the child is otherwise not required to file because his or her income is below the filing threshold.

The U.S. Treasury has changed the way in which interest on Series EE bonds is computed. Rather than adjusting the interest semiannually, these bonds now pay a fixed rate until redemption or maturity. As a result, Series I bonds may be a better option because their interest rate still adjusts semiannually for inflation.

Interest *may* be tax free if bonds are redeemed to pay certain higher education costs and other conditions are met (see Chapter 3).

Interest is *never* subject to state and local income taxes.

Pitfall

Do not continue to hold a bond beyond its final maturity date. No interest is paid after this date. As of February 2006, the value of unredeemed bonds that had reached their final maturity date was $14 billion. Bonds reach final maturity as follows: 30 years for series EE and I bonds (and E bonds issued from December 1965 through June 1980); 40 years for E bonds issued between May 1941 and November 1965 (the final bond in this series matured November 2005).

In the past, you could have continued deferral beyond a bond's maturity date by rolling it over into a series HH bond. However, these bonds ceased being issued as of August 31, 2004 (previously issued series HH bonds continue to earn interest).

Where to Claim the Benefit

You do not have to report interest if you want to defer it; no special form or schedule needs to be filed.

Gain on the Sale of Small Business Stock

The government wants to encourage investments in small businesses. To do so, it has created certain tax breaks should these investments turn out to be profitable.

Benefit

If you have a gain on the sale of small business stock, you have two options for favorable tax treatment:

1. You can roll over the proceeds into other small business stock to defer the gain. You must reinvest your proceeds from the sale within 60 days of the date of sale to complete the rollover. If you roll over less than all of the proceeds, you must report gain on the portion of the proceeds not rolled over.
2. You can do nothing and exclude 50 percent of the gain from income (called a Section 1202 exclusion). The 50 percent of the gain that is not excluded is subject to a 28 percent capital gain rate (unless your tax bracket is below this rate so that the tax rate is limited to your bracket, which is what you would pay on ordinary income).

Conditions

To qualify for rollover treatment or to exclude 50 percent of the gain from income, the stock must qualify as small business stock and you must meet a holding period requirement.

SMALL BUSINESS STOCK. There are five conditions for qualifying as a small business stock:

1. The issuing corporation must be a C corporation (an S corporation cannot issue small business stock for purposes of rollover or exclusion treatment).
2. The stock must have been originally issued after August 10, 1993.
3. The gross assets of the business cannot be more than $50 million when the stock is issued.
4. The corporation must be an active business (and not a holding or investment company). This requires that at least 80 percent of the corporation's assets are used in the active conduct of a qualified business. A qualified business is one involved in other than the practice of law, medicine, architecture, engineering, health, performing arts, consulting, actuarial science, financial services, brokerage services, banking, insurance, leasing, farming, hotel or motel management, restaurants, or similar businesses.
5. You must have acquired the stock for cash or other property or as pay for services. You cannot treat inherited or gifted stock as small business stock.

HOLDING PERIOD. For rollover treatment, you must have held the stock more than six months before the date of sale.

For the 50 percent exclusion, you must have held the stock more than five years before the date of sale.

Planning Tips

Assuming you qualify for rollover treatment and the exclusion, which one should you use? Generally, if you reinvest in small business stock, opt for the rollover treatment, which allows you to defer your gain. At some future time when you do not reinvest in small business stock in a timely fashion you can use the exclusion.

If you have losses on other investments during the year, you may prefer *not* to use deferral or the exclusion but instead report the gain. Losses can offset your gains to eliminate any tax due on these gains.

Pitfall

If you defer gain on the sale of small business stock, understand that eventually you may pay tax on the gain. You must reduce the basis in the small business stock acquired during the 60-day period by the amount of the deferred gain. When you sell this stock, the reduction will effectively increase your gain.

Example

In 2006, you sell small business stock and acquire new stock within 60 days. The gain from the sale is $10,000. You pay $25,000 for the new stock. Your basis in the new stock is $15,000 ($25,000 – $10,000 deferred gain). Later, when the value of the new stock has increased to $35,000, you sell (and there is no additional deferral or exclusion). At this time you have a taxable gain of $20,000 ($35,000 – $15,000).

Where to Claim the Rollover or Exclusion

If you elect rollover treatment, you must do so by reporting the entire gain on Schedule D of Form 1040, and then on the line immediately below the line on which you reported gain write "Section 1045 rollover" and enter the amount rolled over as a loss (in parentheses) in column (f).

If you exclude 50 percent of your gain, report the entire gain on line 8 of Schedule D, completing all the columns on that line. Then immediately below the line on which you reported gain in column (a) write "Section 1202 exclusion" and in column (f) enter the amount of the exclusion as a loss (in parentheses). If you have net capital gains for the year, then enter the exclusion as a positive number on line 2 of the 28% Rate Gain Worksheet in the IRS instructions to Schedule D.

If you have any gain on the sale of small business stock, you cannot file Form 1040A or 1040EZ.

Gain on Empowerment Zone Assets

There are about 180 empowerment zones, renewal communities, and enterprise communities (EZ/RC/ECs) in the United States. RCs and urban EZ/ECs fall under the jurisdiction of the U.S. Department of Housing and Urban Development (HUD). Rural EZ/ECs are overseen by the U.S. Department of Agriculture-Office of Community Development (USDA-OCD). The designations generally remain in effect through 2009. You can find these designated areas at www.hud.gov/crlocator.

If you invest in government-designated economically disadvantaged areas, any gain you realize on the sale of assets in these areas is eligible for special treatment.

Benefit

If you have a gain on the sale of empowerment zone assets, there are two favorable options that you may qualify for:

1. You can roll over part or all of the gain from empowerment zone assets held more than one year.

2. You can exclude all of the gain from assets held more than five years in a renewal community or the District of Columbia enterprise zone. In effect, you are not taxed now or in the future when you sell these qualified assets.

Conditions

Separate conditions apply to each benefit.

ROLLOVER OF GAIN FROM EMPOWERMENT ZONE ASSETS. There are four conditions to qualify for rollover treatment:

1. Both the assets you sell and the assets you acquire as replacement property must be qualified empowerment zone assets, which are tangible property acquired after December 21, 2000, and used in the zone with you as the original owner, or stock in a domestic corporation or capital or profits interest in a domestic partnership acquired after December 21, 2000, if the business is operated in the zone.
2. You must have held for more than one year the assets that were sold.
3. You must acquire other empowerment zone asset(s) as replacement property. District of Columbia enterprise zone property is not treated as empowerment zone property for this purpose.
4. You must reduce the basis of the replacement property by the amount of postponed gain.

EXCLUSION OF GAIN FROM RC OR DC ZONE ASSETS. There are three conditions for excluding gain:

1. The property must be a renewal community (RC) or District of Columbia enterprise zone (DC zone) asset, which includes RC or DC zone business stock, RC or DC zone partnership interest and RC or DC zone business property (including real or other property integral to an RC or DC zone business).
2. You must have held the RC or DC zone assets for more than five years before the sale.
3. The gain may not be otherwise treated as recapture income or gain from a sale to a related party.

Planning Tips

To determine whether you own property in a qualified zone, see IRS Publication 954, Tax Incentives for Distressed Communities.

If you own a business that employs people in a qualified zone, you may be eligible for a special employment tax credit (see Chapter 15).

Pitfall

The election to postpone gain from empowerment zone assets by making a rollover is irrevocable without IRS consent to change your mind.

Where to Claim the Benefit

To report a rollover of gain from empowerment zone assets, enter on line 8 of Schedule D "Section 1397B Rollover" in column (a) and enter a loss in column (f); enter the gain in Part II of Schedule D.

To report the exclusion of RC or DC zone assets, enter on line 8 of Schedule D "RC or DC Zone Asset" in column (a) and enter a loss in column (f); enter the gain in Part II of Schedule D.

Foreign Taxes on Investments

Investors in foreign companies may pay taxes overseas to other governments. To provide a break so that these investors aren't taxed twice, for federal income tax purposes a deduction or tax credit can be claimed if certain conditions are met.

Benefit

If you hold investments in foreign countries, including stocks or mutual funds, you may pay taxes abroad. You can write off foreign taxes you pay in one of two ways:

1. Deduct the taxes as an itemized deduction.
2. Claim a tax credit for the foreign taxes.

Either way, there is no dollar limit to the benefit you can claim.

Conditions

The foreign tax must be a tax on income similar to U.S. tax. However, you cannot write off any tax imposed by a country designated by the U.S. government as engaging in terrorist activities. These countries are listed in IRS Publication 514, *Foreign Tax Credit for Individuals*.

Planning Tips

Generally, claiming the credit is more valuable than deducting the foreign taxes. The credit reduces your tax liability dollar for dollar. You do not have to be an itemizer if you claim the credit. And, if you do itemize deductions but are subject to a reduction in your itemized deductions because you are a high-income taxpayer, claiming the credit avoids this additional limit.

If you opt to claim the credit and the amount of the credit you can use in the current year is limited because of your tax liability, you can carry the excess credit back to the two preceding years and then forward for up to five succeeding years until it is used up. You can only use a carryback or carryover in a year in which you have income from foreign sources.

You have 10 years in which to change your choice from deduction to credit or credit to deduction. You can file an amended return for a period of up to 10 years to change the treatment of the write-off on your return.

Example

For the past 15 years, you have been claiming a deduction for foreign taxes you paid with respect to a mutual fund. In March 2006, you discover that it would have been preferable to claim the credit. You can amend returns from 1995 onward. The 10-year period for the 1995 return ends on April 15, 2006, 10 years from the due date of the 1995 return.

Pitfalls

You cannot elect to treat some foreign taxes as a deduction while treating others as a credit within the same year. You must opt to use one write-off method for all your foreign taxes. But you can change your choice from year to year.

If you are subject to the alternative minimum tax (AMT) (a shadow tax system to ensure that taxpayers who successfully reduce their regular tax will at least pay some income tax), you lose the benefit of an itemized deduction for foreign taxes, which are not deductible for AMT purposes.

Where to Claim the Deduction or Credit

Foreign taxes you pay on investments are reported to you (and the IRS) on Form 1099-INT or Form 1099-DIV. Use this figure for claiming your deduction or credit.

If you are claiming a deduction for foreign taxes, you must file Schedule A. Your deduction is part of your itemized deductions entered on Form 1040. You cannot claim a deduction if you file Form 1040A or 1040EZ.

If you are claiming the foreign tax credit related to your investments, you may qualify to report it directly on Form 1040 (without having to complete an additional form). This simplified filing option applies if the amount of the foreign tax credit is not more than $300 ($600 on a joint return). You report the credit in the "Tax and Credits" section of Form 1040. You cannot claim the foreign tax credit if you file Form 1040A or 1040EZ.

If your foreign tax credit is more than this limit, you must complete Form 1116, Foreign Tax Credit (Individual, Estate, or Trust), and then follow the filing instructions given earlier.

CHAPTER 9

Travel

We live a highly mobile age—we are always on the go for work, play, or other activities. We travel by car, airplane, train, ship, bus, and taxi. We spend a lot of money annually on getting around. The tax laws can help to defray some of your travel costs in certain situations.

This chapter explains:

- Business travel
- Temporary work assignments
- Conventions
- Medical travel
- Charitable travel
- Educational travel
- National Guard and military reservist travel
- Frequent flier miles

In addition, you will find an explanation of recordkeeping rules for travel expenses as well as some forms you can use to comply with these rules.

For more information, see IRS Publication 463, *Travel, Entertainment, Gift, and Car Expenses*, and IRS Publication 1542, *Per Diem Rates*.

Business Travel

Americans travel quite a lot for business. The costs of travel, including transportation, lodging, and meals, that are related to business may be fully or partially tax deductible if certain conditions are met.

Benefit

Whether you are self-employed or an employee whose company-related travel costs are not covered by an accountable plan, business travel is a deductible expense. As an employee, it can be deducted to the extent miscellaneous itemized expenses exceed 2 percent of adjusted gross income. An accountable plan is a reimbursement arrangement under which you are required to account for your expenses to your employer within a set time and refund to your employer any excess advances or reimbursements.

If, however, your employer has an accountable plan that reimburses you for travel expenses, you are not taxed on the reimbursements so you do not get to deduct the expenses (your employer claims the deduction).

If you are self-employed, the deduction for business expenses is *not* limited by 2 percent of your adjusted gross income. These costs are fully deductible to the extent otherwise allowed. There is no overall dollar limit on what you can deduct.

Conditions

Business travel costs are deductible if they are ordinary and necessary business expenses. In other words, the travel costs must be business-related and not for personal reasons.

Also, as a condition for claiming a deduction, you must maintain good records (discussed later).

EXAMPLES OF BUSINESS TRAVEL EXPENSES

Airfare.

Bus fare.

Car expenses (explained in Chapter 7).

Cab fare.

Convention costs (explained later in this chapter).

Educational travel if work-related (explained later in this chapter).

Fax service charges.

Job-hunting travel costs in the same line of work.

Laundry and dry cleaning during trips.

Lodging.

Lodging taxes.

Meals away from home.

Out-of-town expenses while working on a temporary job assignment (explained later in this chapter).

Subway and train fare.

Telephone calls.

You cannot deduct travel expenses if you are looking for your first job or changing your line of work. For example, if you fly from Los Angeles to Houston to interview for a new position in your same line of work, you can deduct your airfare and local transportation costs as a business expense. But if this travel is for your first job out of college, it is not deductible.

PART-BUSINESS TRIPS WITHIN THE UNITED STATES. If you combine business with pleasure, you can deduct your travel costs, such as airfare, as a business expense if the *primary* purpose of the trip is for business. But you can deduct hotel costs only for the business portion of the trip.

Example

You live and work in New Haven and fly to San Francisco for a five-day business trip. You extend your stay for two extra days to sightsee. You can fully deduct your airfare as a business expense since the primary purpose of your trip is business. Your lodging is deductible only for the five days on business (your two personal days are nondeductible).

If you extend your stay over the weekend to obtain more favorable airfare that requires a Saturday night stay-over, this time is treated as business time, not personal time, even if you spend the weekend on personal activities.

If the primary purpose of your trip is for personal activities, you can deduct only local transportation costs to and from business locations as a business expense.

Example

You live and work in New Haven and fly to San Francisco to attend your niece's wedding. Family activities take up four days of your trip. On the fifth day you see a client and then fly home. Only local transportation costs from your hotel to the client and from the client to the airport are deductible.

PART-BUSINESS TRIPS ABROAD. If you combine business with pleasure on a trip outside the United States, different rules apply to determine if and the extent to which airfare can be treated as a deductible business expense.

If you are an employee who does not have control over scheduling business trips, you can deduct all of your expenses, including airfare, lodging, and 50 percent of meal costs if the primary purpose of the trip is business. Taking some time out to sightsee does not change this result.

If you are a managing executive, a more than 10 percent owner of the business, or a self-employed person with control over scheduling, you can deduct airfare, lodging, and 50 percent of meal costs only if you fall within one of these categories:

- The trip lasts a week or less (not counting the day you left the United States but counting the day of your return).
- The trip lasts more than one week, but less than 25 percent of time (counting both the day of departure and arrival) is spent on personal activities.
- In planning the trip, major emphasis was not placed on personal activities.

If a trip lasts more than one week and you spend 25 percent or more on personal activities (and cannot show that major emphasis was not placed on these activities), then you can deduct only the portion of expenses related to business. This requires that you allocate costs between business and personal time. Divide the total number of days of the trip by the days spent on business activities to find the deductible portion of your costs.

Example

On Sunday you fly from New York to London for a 10-day stay. You spend Monday through Friday on business and the balance of the trip sightseeing. You can deduct one-half of your airfare, lodging, and meal costs as a business expense (10 ÷ 5).

If you have business meetings scheduled before or after a weekend or holiday, you can treat the days in between the meetings as business days, even though you spend the time on personal activities.

PER DIEM RATES. Instead of keeping track of your actual costs for lodging, meals, and incidental expenses away from home on business, you can rely on government-set standard rates. (Incidental expenses include tips for porters, baggage carriers, bellhops, and hotel maids.) You have two options for rates:

1. *Maximum federal per diem rate*—an allowance for lodging and for meals and incidental expenses (M&IE) for travel within the continental United States (CONUS). The rate you use depends on the location you are in and the time of travel. For the period October 1, 2005, through September 30, 2006, the rate for most locations is $99 per day ($60 for lodging and $39 for M&IE). However, higher rates apply in certain locations. For instance, the daily rate for Manhattan for certain times of the year is $290 ($226 for lodging and $64 for M&IE). Federal per diem rates may be found at www.gsa.gov (click on Per Diem Rates).
2. *High-low substantiation rate*—an allowance for meals and incidental expenses for CONUS travel. There are two rates: one for areas designated as "high-cost areas" and one for all other areas within CONUS. For the period October 1, 2005, through September 30, 2006, the daily meal and incidental expenses rate for high-cost areas is $226 ($168 for lodging and $58 for M&IE); the rate for all other areas is $141 ($96 for lodging and $45 for M&IE).

Even though you use a standard per diem rate, you must still apply a 50 percent limitation to the M&IE portion of the allowance. The 50 percent limitation is explained in Chapter 10.

If you incur incidental expenses on any travel day for which you do not have deductible meals, you can deduct these expenses at a flat $3 per day.

Planning Tips

You *must* keep good records of your business travel in order to claim a deduction. The tax law requires substantiation of business travel expenses as a condition of claiming the deduction. You generally need two types of records: written information and documentary evidence such as receipts or credit card statements.

You must note certain information in a diary, logbook, account statement, handheld computer, or other record keeper. The type of information to record and a sample weekly travel expense form that you can use for this purpose are included at the end of this chapter.

If you are an employee whose employer has an accountable plan, you are required to provide recordkeeping information to your employer. If not, you should generally retain these records along with copies of your tax return for at least three years from the date you filed the return on which you claimed a deduction for business travel. This will allow you to back up your deduction if your return is questioned by the IRS.

You do not have to retain receipts for travel costs (other than lodging) of less than $75. Thus, for example, you do not need receipts for taxi fares under $75.

If you fail to maintain the necessary records or if they are destroyed by events beyond your control, such as a flood or fire, you *may* be able to prove your entitlement to a deduction through your own written or oral statement and other supporting evidence. But it may be difficult to establish the full amount of expenses, and you can lose out on a deduction you are otherwise entitled to claim.

In some situations, especially when records are destroyed through no fault of the taxpayer, courts have allowed taxpayers to estimate their expenses. This is called the Cohan rule, named after the famous entertainer George M. Cohan, who convinced a court of his entitlement to a business deduction despite the lack of records.

Pitfall

Generally the cost of commuting to and from work is not deductible; it is a personal expense. This is so even if you are forced to use your car because there is no public transportation or you must travel great distances. You cannot convert nondeductible commuting costs to deductible expenses merely by using your cell phone on business or putting a sign with your business logo on the side of your car. Nondeductible commuting costs include:

- Carpooling expenses, even if you discuss business with your fellow passengers.
- Emergency travel between home and work.
- Travel from a union hall to a job site.

However, there are certain situations in which commuting costs can be treated as deductible business expenses.

- If you incur additional costs to transport tools to and from work you can treat the added cost as a deductible expense.
- You commute to a temporary work location.
- You work from home and claim a home office deduction. The cost of travel between your home and any business location, such as customers' offices, is deductible.
- You work at temporary locations. For example, if you are an accountant or other professional who travels to client work sites for a few days or a week or two, you can deduct the costs of travel between home and these sites as business travel, *provided* you have a regular work office.

Where to Claim the Deduction

If you are an employee whose job-related travel costs are covered by an employer's accountable plan, you do not have to do anything. Reimbursements for this travel are *not* included on your Form W-2. You do not have to deduct anything (your employer claims the deduction for your travel costs).

If you are an employee whose job-related travel costs are *not* covered by an accountable plan, you first figure your deductible travel costs in Part I of Form 2106 or 2106-EZ. Your deductible expenses are then entered on Schedule A of Form 1040.

If you are self-employed, you deduct your business travel costs on Schedule C or C-EZ.

You cannot claim a deduction for business travel expenses if you file Form 1040A or 1040EZ.

Temporary Work Assignments

Not everyone who works does so from a fixed location. Some people are stationed at various work locations for a few days, a few months, or even longer. Living away from home means paying for additional housing and travel expenses between home and work. In recognition of the burden these additional costs can place on workers, the tax law allows what might be viewed as personal expenses to become deductible if certain conditions are met.

Benefit

If you work at a temporary location, your travel costs between home and this location are deductible.

If the temporary location is out of town, you can deduct not only your travel costs but also your living expenses, including lodging and 50 percent of meals. There is no dollar limit on what you can deduct.

Conditions

There are two key conditions for deducting expenses related to temporary work assignments:

1. The assignment must be temporary.
2. You must have a regular place of business to deduct travel costs between home and work or be away from home on business to deduct travel and living costs.

DEFINITION OF TEMPORARY WORK ASSIGNMENTS. For travel expenses to be deductible, the work assignment must be temporary. This means that the assignment is expected to last no more than one year and does in fact end within this time. A work assignment is *not* considered temporary if it is expected to last:

- For more than one year even if it in fact ends within the year.
- For no more than one year but runs beyond this time (although expenses for the period up to one year are deductible in this case).

REGULAR PLACE OF BUSINESS. You must maintain a regular place of business outside of your home, or have a home office that is your principal place of business.

If all of your work takes place at temporary assignments outside of the metropolitan area in which you live, you do not have a regular place of business and cannot deduct your travel costs.

AWAY FROM HOME. You must maintain a tax home from which you are away on business to deduct travel and living costs. Your tax home is your place of employment or business, regardless of where you or your family live. It may be one and the same place if you live and work in the same area.

Example

You live and work in Trenton, New Jersey. You travel to Boston for two weeks of business. You can deduct your travel and living expenses on this trip.

Example

You live in Trenton, New Jersey, and work in Washington, D.C. Washington, D.C., not Trenton, is your tax home. You cannot deduct your travel costs between Trenton and D.C. But if you travel for two weeks to Dallas, Texas, you can deduct your travel costs between D.C. and Dallas, as well as your living costs in Dallas.

If you are constantly on the road, moving from job to job so that you do not work within any particular locality, you may not deduct your living costs. The reason: You are not away from home on business.

Your residence can be treated as your tax home so that if you travel away from home on business your costs are deductible if you meet three conditions:

1. You do *some* work in the vicinity of your residence.
2. You have mortgage expenses or pay rent for the residence while you are on the road.
3. You or a member of your immediate family has lived in the area of your residence for a long time.

If you meet two of the three conditions, you *may* be able to use your residence as your tax home, but if you meet only one condition, you cannot do so. A member of the armed forces who maintains a home cannot treat the home as his or her tax home if he or she has a permanent duty stationed elsewhere.

If you regularly work in two or more locations, your tax home is the area of your *principal* work location. This is usually determined by the time spent in each location, the degree of business activity in each place, what income you receive from each place, where you have your home, and whether either location is temporary. You can't use any one factor to decide which of the two locations is your tax home.

Planning Tips

When you travel away from home, be sure to keep accurate and complete records of your travel and living expenses.

If you are in the armed forces and your ship or squadron is away from your home port or base, you may be able to deduct travel expenses while away. However, you are not treated as being "away" if you are at your permanent duty station or you are a naval officer assigned to permanent duty aboard a ship.

Pitfall

Spouses who live and work in different cities can have different tax homes. Just because they are treated as domiciled within the same place and may vote or file their taxes together, they may be restricted in deducting travel expenses between these locations.

Example

A couple maintains a home in Baltimore, where the husband resides. The wife works in New York City during the week and travels to Baltimore each weekend. Even though Baltimore is the city she considers home, she cannot deduct her travel costs between Baltimore and New York City, nor her living expenses in New York City. Her tax home is New York City, not Baltimore, and she is not traveling on business when she returns to Baltimore each weekend.

Where to Claim the Benefit

If you are an employee whose job-related travel costs on temporary work assignments are covered by an employer's accountable plan, you do not have to do anything. Reimbursements for this travel are *not* included on your Form W-2. You do not have to deduct anything (your employer claims the deduction for your travel costs).

If you are an employee whose job-related travel costs on temporary work assignments are *not* covered by an accountable plan, you first figure your deductible travel costs on Form 2106 or 2106-EZ. Your deductible expenses are then entered on Schedule A of Form 1040.

If you are self-employed, you deduct your business travel costs on temporary work assignments on Schedule C or C-EZ.

You cannot claim a deduction for business travel expenses on temporary work assignments if you file Form 1040A or 1040EZ.

Conventions

Conventions and trade shows are a key way in which businesses can show off their wares, make new connections, and learn about industry developments. To find the best shows to market your products or services, visit www.tradegroup.com/resources/showdirectories.htm. Whether you are an exhibitor or a visitor, your attendance costs may be deductible.

Benefit

You can deduct the cost of attending business conventions, including travel, lodging, 50 percent of meal costs, and attendance fees, even though there is an element of pleasure associated with such activities.

There are restrictions, however, if you attend a convention held outside the North American area or on a cruise ship.

Conditions

You must be able to show that your attendance at the convention has some benefit to your trade or business. This can be shown by comparing the purpose of the convention as stated in its program or agenda with your official job duties or work.

The fact that you are appointed or elected as a delegate to the convention does not, by itself, establish a business benefit.

FOREIGN CONVENTIONS. If the convention is held outside the North American area, you must show that:

- The meeting is directly related to your trade or business.
- It is as reasonable to hold the meeting outside the North American area as in it. Reasonableness is based on the purpose of the meeting and activities taking place, the sponsoring group or organization, and the homes of active members. The North American area includes all of the locations detailed in Table 9.1.

TABLE 9.1 North American Area for Convention Deduction

American Samoa	Johnston Island
Baker Island	Kingman Reef
Barbados	Marshall Islands
Bermuda	Mexico
Canada	Micronesia
Costa Rica	Midway Islands
Dominica	Northern Mariana Islands
Dominican Republic	Palau
Grenada	Palmyra
Guam	Puerto Rico
Guyana	Saint Lucia
Honduras	Trinidad and Tobago
Howland Island	United States
Jamaica	U.S. Virgin Islands
Jarvis Island	Wake Island

CONVENTIONS ON CRUISE SHIPS. If you attend a business convention held on a cruise ship, your business deduction is limited to $2,000 per year, regardless of the cost of the cruise or the number of convention cruises you take. And even this limited deduction can *only* be claimed if all five of these conditions are met:

1. The convention is directly related to your business.
2. The ship is a vessel registered in the United States.
3. All of the ports of call on the trip are in the United States or U.S. possessions.
4. You attach a signed statement to your return that includes the number of days for the cruise, the hours you spent each day devoted to scheduled business activities, and a copy of the program showing the scheduled business activities.
5. You also attach a signed statement by an officer of the organization or group sponsoring the meeting that shows the schedule of business activities each day and the number of hours you attended.

Planning Tip

Keep good records of your expenses at the convention, including a copy of the convention program with notations of the sessions you attended. If the convention has a sign-in book, be sure to sign in at every session.

If the convention is held on a cruise, follow the recordkeeping requirements discussed earlier.

Pitfall

If your spouse or other person accompanies you to the convention, you cannot deduct the expenses of your companion. This is so even if your companion is helpful to you.

However, as a practical matter, there may be no added cost for a second person in your room, so the only extras for your companion are meals and travel. And if you drive to the convention, even extra travel costs are eliminated.

Where to Claim the Deduction

If you are an employee whose job-related travel costs are covered by an employer's accountable plan, you do not have to do anything. Reimbursements for attendance at a business convention are *not* included on your Form W-2. You do not have to deduct anything (your employer claims the deduction for your travel costs).

If you are an employee whose job-related travel costs are *not* covered by an accountable plan, you first figure your deductible convention costs on Form 2106 or 2106-EZ. Your deductible expenses are then entered on Schedule A of Form 1040.

If you are self-employed, you deduct your business convention costs on Schedule C or C-EZ.

You cannot claim a deduction for business convention expenses if you file Form 1040A or 1040EZ.

Medical Travel

The days of doctors' house calls are all but over. To obtain medical assistance, you must go to the providers' sites—doctors' offices, hospitals, clinics, and other facilities. The tax law lets you treat your travel costs for medical purposes as a deductible medical expense.

Benefit

Medical insurance typically does not cover your expenses for getting to and from the doctor or pharmacy or other travel for other medical purposes. These costs are deductible as an itemized medical deduction. This means that the costs of medical travel are added to your other medical expenses, the total of which is deductible to the extent they exceed 7.5 percent of your adjusted gross income.

Conditions

To be treated as qualified medical expenses, the costs of travel must be related to obtaining a diagnosis, cure, mitigation, treatment, or prevention of disease or any treatment that affects a part or function of your body.

Deductible expenses include those paid not only for yourself, but also for a spouse and dependents. Who qualifies as a dependent is explained in Chapter 1.

EXAMPLES OF MEDICAL TRAVEL COSTS

- Ambulance hire.
- Autoette (auto device for a handicapped person).
- Bus, cab, or train fare to see doctors, obtain treatment (including attendance at AA meetings or to the gym if you are obese), or pick up prescriptions.
- Car use to see doctors, obtain treatment (including attendance at AA meetings or to the gym if you are obese), or pick up prescriptions at 18 cents per mile for 2006.
- Conferences (travel costs and admission fees) for medical conferences on an illness or condition suffered by you, your spouse, or a dependent.
- Lodging to receive outpatient care at a licensed hospital, clinic, or hospital-equivalent facility, up to $50 per night ($100 per night if you accompany a sick child).

Planning Tip

Keep good records of your expenditures for medical-related travel.

- For use of your car, note the date, purpose, and odometer reading at the start and end of each trip.
- For other travel costs, retain receipts of all expenses.

Pitfall

You cannot deduct the costs of trips taken for general good health. For example, your car mileage to and from the gym is not deductible if you are there to improve your appearance or maintain general good health rather than to treat a condition such as obesity or high blood pressure.

Similarly, if you fly to Florida each winter to escape the cold of New

Hampshire, you cannot deduct your travel costs, even though the warm climate may be beneficial to your health. You are not traveling for the purpose of obtaining treatment or for some other deductible medical purpose.

Where to Claim the Deduction

Medical travel costs, which are part of itemized medical expenses, are reported in the "Medical and Dental Expenses" section of Schedule A of Form 1040.

You cannot deduct medical expenses if you file Form 1040A or Form 1040EZ.

Charitable Travel

Volunteering for your favorite cause may cost you money; just getting to and from your volunteer activity can be an expense. The tax law lets you deduct your out-of-pocket travel costs incurred for charitable pursuits.

Benefit

If you use your car for charitable purposes, including attending meetings of organizations you serve, you can deduct either your actual car expenses for gas and oil or mileage at the rate of 14 cents per mile (32 cents per mile for Katrina relief). Whichever method you select, you can also write off parking and tolls.

You can also deduct travel expenses, plus meals and lodging, for overnight trips away from home to serve as an official delegate to a convention of a church, charitable, veteran, or other similar organization.

Conditions

You qualify to deduct your car expenses to the extent that the use of your car is for a tax-exempt organization or governmental unit. To see whether the charity you work for is tax-exempt, see Chapter 6.

You qualify for convention-related expenses that you are not reimbursed for if you serve as an official delegate on behalf of a religious, charitable, veteran, or other similar organization.

Planning Tip

Keep track of your mileage and out-of-pocket expenses on behalf of the charity. In a diary or logbook, note the odometer readings for every charity-related trip for which your car is used.

Pitfall

You cannot deduct travel costs to work on a project for a nonprofit organization if there is a significant element of personal pleasure, recreation, or vacation involved.

You cannot deduct travel costs to attend a charity-related convention if you do not serve as an official delegate.

Where to Claim the Benefit

To claim a charitable deduction for your charity-related travel expenses, you must complete Schedule A of Form 1040. Enter your deduction for charity-related expenses in the "Gifts to Charity" section of Schedule A.

You cannot deduct donations if you file Form 1040A or Form 1040EZ.

Educational Travel

Unless you're taking classes online or via television from home or listening to teleconferences, you must travel to a classroom to learn. If the education is job-related, your travel costs may be deductible.

Benefit

Whether you drive across town to take college credits or fly across the country for a continuing education course, you can deduct your travel costs as a miscellaneous itemized deduction if the education is related to your job. For example, if you go to night school to take a computer course to keep you up-to-date for your job, which is working with computers, your travel from work to school and from school to home is deductible.

Education-related travel costs are added to your other miscellaneous itemized deductions, the total of which is deductible to the extent they exceed 2 percent of your adjusted gross income.

Example

In 2006, your adjusted gross income is $80,000. Your miscellaneous itemized deductions are $2,500. Since the first 2 percent of your adjusted gross income, or $1,600, is not deductible, you can write off $900 of such expenses.

Conditions

For educational travel to be treated as a deductible expense, the education you are traveling for must be job-related. This means that:

- You are employed (or self-employed). For example, you cannot deduct as job-related expenses the cost of an undergraduate education.

- You already meet the minimum job requirements for your position, based on employer standards and the laws and regulations of your state.
- The courses maintain or improve your current job skills.
- The courses do not lead to qualification for a new profession.

The rules on job-related education are explained more fully in Chapter 3.

EXAMPLES OF EDUCATIONAL TRAVEL COSTS

- Car expenses from work to school. You can deduct your actual costs or use the standard mileage rate for business travel (44.5 cents per mile in 2006), plus parking and tolls.
- Local transportation expenses (bus, subway, cab, train, or other fare) of going from your job to school.
- Car expenses or local transportation expenses (bus, subway, cab, train, or other fare) of going from school to home, *provided* you are regularly employed and going to school is a temporary endeavor (courses are expected to last no more than one year and do, in fact, end within this time).
- Travel costs away from home to attend a course (transportation to and from the course, lodging, and 50 percent of meals).

Example

You regularly work in New York City and every night for six weeks you take a refresher course. Since the course is temporary, you may deduct your travel expenses between work and school and school and home. It does not matter whether you go directly from work to school; your travel costs from home to school, in either or both directions, are deductible. The same is true if you take the refresher course on Saturday.

Planning Tip

If you are taking a course out of town and spend some time on personal activities, be prepared to prove that the primary purpose of the out-of-town travel was business-related education. This can be done by showing that you spend most of your time attending the course and only a relatively small amount of time on sightseeing or other personal activities.

Example

You travel from Boston, your place of employment, to Las Vegas for a two-day continuing education program. If your total travel is three days, you can confidently show that the primary purpose of your trip is for the education so that your airfare to and from Boston is a deductible travel expense.

Example

Same facts except your trip to Las Vegas lasts seven days. In this case, it may be difficult to show that the primary reason for the trip was job-related education since you spend five of the seven days on personal activities. However, even if the airfare is not deductible, local transportation costs to and from the two-day course are deductible.

Pitfalls

You cannot deduct travel that is educational in nature, even though it may be beneficial to your job. For example, a teacher may not deduct the cost of traveling to a foreign country to see the sights and absorb the culture. However, if the teacher takes courses abroad, then the travel costs become deductible even if the courses are not taken for credit. Decide whether it will save you money to pay for and take a course in order to deduct your travel costs.

If you are away from home for education purposes, you may not deduct travel costs for sightseeing, social visiting, or entertaining while taking the course.

You cannot deduct the cost of traveling to and attending investment seminars, despite how educational and beneficial they may be. The tax law specifically bans this deduction.

Where to Claim the Benefit

If you are an employee, then to claim a deduction for your education-related travel expenses you must first complete Form 2106 or 2106-EZ to arrive at your unreimbursed employee business expenses. This total is then entered on the line provided for it on Schedule A of Form 1040.

If you are a self-employed individual, you enter your education-related travel on Schedule C or Schedule C-EZ.

You cannot deduct education-related travel if you file Form 1040A or Form 1040EZ.

National Guard and Military Reservist Travel

As of February 2005 there were about 700,000 members of the National Guard and military reserve (about 113,000 of whom have been mobilized on active duty).

Benefit

You can deduct your overnight travel costs as an adjustment to gross income rather than as an unreimbursed employee business expense subject to the 2 percent of AGI floor.

Conditions

To claim the deduction, besides the obvious requirement of being a member of the National Guard or in the reserves, you must meet the following three conditions:

1. You must incur the costs to attend a meeting more than 100 miles away from home. You are considered to be away from home if you are away from the permanent duty station long enough to require rest or sleep in order to complete your duties. For naval personnel of a drydocked submarine, your tax home is the area or vicinity of your principal place of employment or shore assignment (not the submarine itself).
2. The costs must relate to overnight transportation, meals, and lodging.
3. The amount of the deductible expenses cannot exceed the general federal per diem rate applicable to the locality to which you travel. You can find these per diem rates at www.gsa.gov (click on Per Diem Rates).

Planning Tip

Keep good records of your travel mileage and expenses to be able to substantiate the deduction you claim.

Pitfall

Only 50 percent of the cost of meals is deductible.

Where to Claim the Deduction

The deduction for travel expenses that meet these qualifications is claimed as an above-the-line deduction in the "Adjusted Gross Income" section of Form 1040.

You cannot claim this deduction if you file Form 1040A or 1040EZ.

Frequent Flier Miles

Whether you travel on business or for pleasure, you can build up frequent flier miles that can be cashed in for fares or upgrades. You can also earn frequent flier miles by charging goods and services to special credit cards that award mileage. Fortunately, there may be no tax cost to you for using frequent flier miles.

Benefit

You are not taxed on the value of frequent flier miles you earn on business travel and use for personal travel. For example, you earn enough points on your business travel throughout the year to receive free tickets for your summer vacation. You are not taxed on the frequent flier miles as they accrue, and you are not taxed when you use them for travel benefits—business or personal. The IRS, for the moment, has given up trying to tax this benefit because it is too difficult to assign a value to it. There is no dollar limit to the amount of this benefit that you can exclude from income.

Condition

To be excludable from income, frequent flier miles can be used only for in-kind benefits, which include free airline tickets or seat upgrades.

Planning Tip

Check on the expiration date of frequent flier miles you have earned so that you can use them up before it is too late.

Pitfall

If you convert frequent flier miles to cash, the cash value of the benefits must be reported as income in this case.

Where to Claim the Exclusion

Since this employee fringe benefit is excluded from income, you do not have to report anything on your tax return. Frequent flier miles earned as an employee are not reported on your Form W-2.

Recordkeeping for Travel Expenses

The tax law requires you to keep records of your travel expenses as a condition for claiming a deduction. Your travel expense records must include the following information:

- *Amount.* The cost of each separate expense for travel, lodging, and meals. Incidental expenses can be totaled in any reasonable category (such as taxi fares). However, if you rely on a per diem rate for lodging, meals, and incidental expenses, you need not record these expenses nor retain receipts for them.

TABLE 9.2 Sample Weekly Travel Expense Record Keeper

Date: From: ________ To: ________

Expense	Sunday	Monday	Tuesday	Wednesday	Thursday	Friday	Saturday	Total
Airlines								
Excess baggage								
Bus								
Train								
Cab/limo								
Tips								
Other costs								
Hotel: Name City								
Breakfast								
Lunch								
Dinner								
Entertainment expenses								

- *Time.* Record the dates you leave and return for each trip and the number of days spent on business.
- *Place or destination.* Note the area of your travel (the name of the city, town, or other destination).
- *Business purpose.* Record the reason for the expense or the benefit to be gained or expected to be gained from the trip.

You can use the recordkeeper in Table 9.2 to record the amount of your travel expenses each week.

In addition to your diary or logbook, you also need documentary proof of your expenses. Usually this means retaining receipts, canceled checks, or other proof of what you pay for your travel expenses. However, you do not need receipts for expenses under $75 (except in the case of lodging, where proof is required regardless of the amount).

CHAPTER 10

Entertainment

Your personal entertainment costs—eating out, going to the movies or a ball game—are not deductible. But there's no law saying you can't combine business with pleasure—and make Uncle Sam foot the bill. It's common business practice to wine and dine customers, clients, and other business associates in the hopes of getting new business or keeping existing business. If you meet certain conditions, you can treat these expenses as deductible even though they may have provided some element of personal pleasure or recreation. But in view of the potential for abusing the write-off option, the IRS looks very closely at entertainment deductions. So be fully prepared to support any of your claims with the necessary proof to back up the positions you take on your tax return.

This chapter explains:

- Meals and entertainment
- Company holiday parties and picnics
- Sporting and theater events
- Home entertainment
- Entertainment facilities and club dues
- Recordkeeping for meals and entertainment expenses
- Gambling losses

For more information, see IRS Publication 463, *Travel, Entertainment, Gifts, and Car Expenses*, and IRS Publication 1542, *Per Diem Rates*.

Meals and Entertainment

Wining and dining is a common business practice in just about every line of work. The government recognizes that this is standard operating procedure, but it doesn't want to underwrite the cost of a three-martini lunch. So the cost of business meals and entertainment may be only partially deductible.

Benefit

In general, your meal costs are nondeductible personal expenses. But if your meal costs are business-related, they are deductible if certain conditions are met. It doesn't matter what time of the day you eat—breakfast, lunch, or dinner. Deductible costs include not only your meal expenses but also those of your guests. If you dine alone, your meal costs are deductible generally only when you are out of town on business.

You may be able to rely on standard meal allowances instead of keeping track of your actual meal costs (standard meal allowances and where to find these amounts are discussed later). Using a standard meal allowance simplifies your recordkeeping requirements.

Assuming you meet the conditions that transform your personal eating costs into a deductible business expense, you are then limited in most cases to writing off only 50 percent of your cost.

Conditions

For meals and entertainment when hosting business associates to be considered a deductible business expense, they must be an ordinary and necessary business expense (meaning a helpful and common practice in your trade or business), that is *either*:

- Directly related to the active conduct of your business ("directly related" test).
- Directly preceding or following a substantial and bona fide business discussion on a subject that is associated with the active conduct of your business ("associated with" test).

Business associates can include employees, agents, partners, your business accountant, your attorney, your insurance agent, your business banker, and suppliers—both established and prospective.

DIRECTLY RELATED TEST. The directly related test entails the conduct of business *at* the meal. There are three different ways in which you can meet the directly related test:

1. Show that the activity is generally related to your business. This means proving that you have more than a general expectation of getting future income or other business benefit (other than goodwill), whether or not such income or benefit ever materializes. Talk business during the meal, or at least have a reasonable intention of doing so.
2. Hold the meal in a clear business setting. Usually, if there are no distractions, just about any location can be considered a clear business setting because it is conducive to business discussions. Restaurants usually meet the bill, but nightclubs may not.

Example

You take a hospitality suite at a hotel where you display your business products. This is considered a clear business setting directly related to your business.

Example

You own a restaurant and give free meals to your supplier. This also is considered a clear business setting directly related to your business.

Example

You meet with several people, including some who are *not* business associates, at a cocktail lounge. This is *not* considered a clear business setting directly related to your business.

3. If your guest is an employee or your independent contractor, you can treat the meal as an expense made for the benefit of the guest as (1) compensation for service or (2) a prize or an award. In either event, the amount of the expense is deductible to you but reported as income to the guest—on Form W-2 as additional compensation to an employee or Form 1099-MISC for an independent contractor (unless payments to the person are less than $600 for the year).

"ASSOCIATED WITH" TEST. Use this test when you are wining and dining in nonbusiness settings (such as nightclubs or dinner theaters) prospective clients, customers, or other business associates in the hope of getting new business or existing associates to engender goodwill that encourages continued business; the meal must come before or after you have conducted a genuine business discussion.

Example

You meet in your office to discuss the renewal of a contract with your supplier. Later that evening you take the supplier out to a nightclub. Since the dinner in this case follows a bona fide business discussion held earlier in the day in your office, you can treat the costs of your meal and the supplier's meal as a deductible business expense.

MEALS AWAY FROM HOME. You can't deduct your meal costs when you eat alone within the general area of your work. For example, if you eat lunch following a sales call on a customer across town, you cannot deduct the cost of the lunch. Or if you work overtime and grab a quick dinner before returning to the office for more work, you can't deduct your meal costs.

To deduct the costs of meals you eat alone, you must meet an overnight-sleep rule. You can only deduct meal costs incurred while away from home on a business trip that lasts longer than a regular workday (but not necessarily 24 hours) and requires you to take time off to sleep (not just to rest) before returning home. Taking a nap in your car on the side of the road does *not* meet the overnight-sleep test.

STANDARD MEAL ALLOWANCE. Instead of keeping track of your actual meal costs away from home, you can rely on government-set standard meal rates for your travel. You have several options for rates:

- *Maximum federal per diem rate*—an allowance for meals and incidental expenses (M&IE) for travel within the continental United States (CONUS). The rate you use depends on the location you are in. For the period October 1, 2005, through September 30, 2006, the rate for most locations is $39 per day. However, higher daily rates—$44, $49, $59, and $64—apply in certain locations. For instance, the daily M&IE rate for Los Angeles and Manhattan is $64.
- *High-low substantiation rate*—an allowance for meals and incidental expenses for CONUS travel. There are two rates: one for areas designated as "high-cost areas" and one for all other areas within CONUS. For the

period October 1, 2005, through September 30, 2006, the daily meal and incidental expenses rate for high-cost areas is $58; the daily rate for all other areas is $45.

- *Meal allowance for transportation industry workers*—an allowance for meals for employees and self-employed persons in the transportation industry. For the period October 1, 2005, through September 30, 2006, the standard daily meal allowance for travel within the continental United States is $52 per day.

Rates may change with the government's fiscal year starting October 1, 2006. For the fourth quarter of 2006, you can use the rates for October 1, 2005, through September 30, 2006, or the new rates that take effect on October 1, 2006. You can find rates for locations you travel to in IRS Publication 1542, *Per Diem Rates*, or at www.gsa.gov (click on Per Diem Rates).

FIFTY PERCENT LIMITATION. Your deductible meal costs, whether entertaining others or dining alone out of town, are usually limited to 50 percent. This 50 percent limit applies whether you are an employee paying unreimbursed expenses or a self-employed individual in his or her own business. It also applies when you claim a standard meal allowance.

Example

Throughout the year you spend $480 on taking clients out to lunch and such costs are not reimbursed by your employer. You can deduct $240 (50 percent of $480) as an unreimbursed employee business expense.

Example

Throughout the year you spend $620 on meals you eat alone while out of town on business, which are not reimbursed by your employer. You can deduct $310 (50 percent of $620).

Because of the 50 percent limitation, it is necessary to allocate the cost of a hotel bill that includes your meals with your room charge—you separate the total cost between the expenses for the room itself and those for meals. Then apply the 50 percent limit to only the meal portion of the bill.

There are some important exceptions to the 50 percent limit. If you are an employee who is reimbursed for meal costs under an accountable plan, the

50 percent limit does not apply—tax-free reimbursement covers all of your meal costs.

For employees who work in the transportation industry and are subject to Department of Transportation (DOT) hours of service limitations, an increased percentage applies to meals consumed away from home. This limit is 75 percent in 2006 and increases to 80 percent starting in 2008.

If you are in business (these exceptions do not have application for employees), the 50 percent limit does not apply to:

- Your employees' meal costs that you pay and treat as additional compensation.
- Reimbursements to independent contractors for meal costs incurred on your behalf.
- Company picnics and holiday parties open to all employees.
- Meals included in advertising or promotional activities. For example, one real estate broker could deduct the cost of meals provided to potential investors attending his promotional seminar.
- Meal costs for you and your staff if meals are sold to the public in the course of your business—for example, if you own a restaurant.
- Food and beverages treated as *de minimis* fringe benefits to your employees. For example, if you provide doughnuts each morning for your staff, you can deduct their entire cost.

LAVISH AND EXTRAVAGANT. There is one more limitation that applies to meal and entertainment costs. They cannot be lavish or extravagant. There is no dollar amount used to make this determination; it depends on the facts and circumstances. If you use common sense and don't go overboard, the costs probably won't be considered lavish and extravagant.

Planning Tip

You may be able to deduct not only the costs for you and the business associate but for spouses as well. For example, if an out-of-town customer brings her spouse to dinner, the cost of meals for the customer, her spouse, and you and your own spouse are deductible expenses.

Pitfall

You cannot convert nondeductible personal eating expenses by taking turns paying for meals with associates or business acquaintances. For example, you can't create an eating circle in which one person picks up the check in rotation in order to deduct costs for the group. If the directly related or associated with test is not satisfied, then no one within the group can pick up the check and write it off.

Where to Claim the Deduction

If you are an employee whose meal and entertainment costs are covered by an employer's accountable plan, you do not have to do anything. Reimbursements for these expenses are *not* included on your Form W-2. You are not allowed to deduct anything (your employer claims the deduction for your meals and entertainment costs).

If you are an employee whose meal and entertainment costs are *not* covered by an accountable plan, you first figure your deductible costs in Part II of Form 2106 or 2106-EZ. You enter your full expenses and the form then imposes the 50 percent limitation. Your deductible expenses are then entered on Schedule A of Form 1040.

If you are self-employed, you deduct your business meal and entertainment costs on Schedule C or C-EZ. You enter your full expenses and the schedule then imposes the 50 percent limitation.

You cannot claim a deduction for meal and entertainment expenses if you file Form 1040A or 1040EZ.

Company Holiday Parties and Picnics

Businesses commonly pay for certain activities to which employees have become accustomed—holiday parties, company picnics, and other annual events. How the costs of these activities are treated depends on which end you are on: Businesses may be able to deduct the costs, while employees who attend them usually aren't taxed on this benefit.

Benefit

If you are an employee, the value of company holiday parties, picnics, and other similar events you attend is treated as a tax-free fringe benefit. You are not taxed on this amount.

If you are a self-employed individual who pays for your company's holiday parties, picnics, or other similar events for your staff, you can deduct the cost of the event. The expense is fully deductible; even though meal costs are involved, they are *not* subject to the 50 percent limitation applied to most other business meal costs.

Conditions

To be a deductible entertainment expense for a self-employed individual, the company event must meet the entertainment expense requirements discussed earlier in this chapter.

Planning Tip

If your spouse or family attends the company event, you are *not* taxed on this benefit, either.

Pitfall

In most cases, you may not be able to deduct the costs you incur to enable you to attend a company event, such as the rental of a tuxedo.

Where to Claim the Deduction

If you are an employee who attends a company event, you are not taxed on the benefit you enjoy. Since the benefit is tax free, it is not reported on your Form W-2 and you do not have to report anything on your return.

If you are a self-employed individual, you deduct the cost of company-provided holiday parties, picnics, or other events as an entertainment expense on Schedule C of Form 1040. Make sure you do *not* apply the 50 percent limitation to these costs.

You cannot claim a deduction for these expenses if you file Form 1040A or Form 1040EZ.

Sporting and Theater Events

Business entertainment at sporting and theater events may be deductible. But because these are such clear recreational activities, strict conditions apply to make them deductible as business expenses. And then only a portion of the cost may be deductible.

Benefit

You can deduct the cost of tickets to sporting and theater events as long as you meet the general conditions for deducting entertainment expenses (discussed earlier in this chapter). Like other entertainment expenses, the cost of tickets is subject to a 50 percent limitation.

Special limits apply in the case of rental fees for skyboxes and private luxury boxes used for multiple events at sporting arenas or stadiums. In this case, your deduction usually is limited to the price of a nonluxury box seat ticket.

There is a special rule for tickets to events that benefit a charitable organization. In this case, your deduction is not limited to the face value of the ticket; you can deduct the full amount of what you pay for the event (which often exceeds the face or fair market value of the ticket) if you meet certain conditions. And the deduction is *not* limited to 50 percent of your costs.

Conditions

For the cost of tickets to sporting and theater events to be considered a deductible business expense, they must be an ordinary and necessary business expense (meaning helpful and common practice in your trade or business), which are either:

- Directly related to the active conduct of your business ("directly related" test).
- Directly preceding or following a substantial and bona fide business discussion on a subject that is associated with the active conduct of your business ("associated with" test).

Assuming you satisfy the directly related or associated with test, then 50 percent of your costs are deductible as entertainment expenses.

These tests, including the 50 percent limitation, are explained in greater detail earlier in this chapter.

SKYBOXES AND PRIVATE LUXURY BOXES. How do you determine whether a skybox seat has been rented for more than one event? Count each game or performance as one event. For example, a skybox for a series of playoff games is treated as having been rented for each of these games. All skyboxes you rent in the same arena, plus any rentals by related persons (your close family members, related corporations, a partnership and its partners, a corporation and partnership with common ownership, or parties who have reciprocal arrangements to share boxes), are taken into account.

Example

You pay $2,000 to rent a 10-seat skybox at your local arena for three baseball games. The cost of a regular nonluxury box seat at each event is $20. You can deduct only $300 ([10 seats × $20] × 3 events = $600, which is then subject to the 50 percent limitation).

TICKETS TO SPORTS EVENTS BENEFITING CHARITY. You can deduct the full cost of what you pay for the events, even if the amount exceeds the actual ticket price, as long as you meet all three of these conditions:

1. The event's main purpose is to benefit a qualified charity. More details on qualified charities may be found in Chapter 6.
2. All of the net proceeds go to the charity.

3. The event uses volunteers to perform substantially all of the event's work.

Example

You pay $100 to enter your business in a golf tournament to benefit your local volunteer fire company at a local golf course where the greens fee is $30. All of the proceeds will be used to buy new fire-fighting equipment. The volunteer firefighters run the event. You can deduct the full $100, not merely the $70 in excess of the normal greens fee (and do not have to apply the 50 percent limitation), assuming your participation is a deductible entertainment expense.

"DIRECTLY RELATED" TEST. The directly related test entails the conduct of business *at* the entertainment event. There are three different ways in which you can meet the directly related test.

1. Show that the activity is generally related to your business. This means proving that you have more than a general expectation of getting future income or other business benefit (other than goodwill), whether or not such income or benefit ever materializes.
2. Talk business during the event, or at least have a reasonable intention of doing so.
3. Hold the event in a clear business setting. Usually, if there are no distractions, just about any location can be considered a clear business setting because it is conducive to business discussions. Sporting or theater events usually do not automatically fit the bill as a clear business setting because of the distractions.

"ASSOCIATED WITH" TEST. In the case of entertaining at sporting events or the theater, you are more likely to use the associated with test than the directly related test. This is because sports arenas and theaters aren't clear business settings. In this case, the event must come before or after you have conducted a genuine business discussion.

Example

You meet in your office to discuss the renewal of a contract with your supplier. Later that evening you take the supplier out to the theater. Since the entertainment in this case follows a bona fide business discussion held earlier in the day in your office, you can treat the costs of your ticket and the supplier's ticket as a deductible business expense.

Planning Tip

If you give business associates tickets to sporting or theater events *and* do not accompany them, you may have a choice on how to deduct expenses. You can treat them as entertainment costs (discussed earlier), which requires that you have bona fide business discussions preceding or following the event.

Alternatively, you can choose to treat the expense as a business gift, the cost of which is deductible up to $25 per gift per year. This deduction is *not* subject to the 50 percent limitation.

Example

Two out-of-town customers spend the afternoon at your office. You give them each theater tickets costing $40 apiece. You do not accompany them to the theater. You can deduct them as an entertainment expense, where your write-off is $40 ($40 × 2 × 50% limitation). Or you can deduct them as business gifts, where your write-off is $50 ($25 limitation on business gifts × 2). Since the gift option results in the larger deduction, you should select this option.

However, since the $25 gift deduction applies on a per-year basis, if you have already made deductible gifts to these customers this year, you can't use the second option and must treat the tickets as an entertainment expense.

You can even change your treatment of the cost at a later time by filing an amended return as long as it is not too late to still do so (generally three years from the time you filed the return).

If you rent skyboxes and your deduction for tickets is limited (as explained earlier), you can also deduct food and beverages as a separate expense. Of course, the separate amount must be reasonable (you can't simply inflate the cost of the food and drinks as a way around the limit on skybox rentals).

Pitfall

As with other entertainment or gift expenses, you are required to keep good records to substantiate your deduction. The failure to do so can cost you the write-off you are otherwise entitled to claim.

Where to Claim the Deduction

If you are an employee whose entertainment costs are covered by an employer's accountable plan, you do not have to do anything. Reimbursements for this expense are *not* included on your Form W-2. You do not have to deduct anything (your employer claims the deduction for your entertainment costs).

If you are an employee whose entertainment costs are *not* covered by an accountable plan, you first figure your deductible costs in Part II of Form 2106 or 2106-EZ. You enter your full expenses and the form then imposes the 50 percent limitation. Your deductible expenses are then entered on Schedule A of Form 1040. If you are treating the cost of tickets as a business gift, do not apply the 50 percent limitation.

If you are self-employed, you deduct your business entertainment costs on Schedule C or C-EZ of Form 1040. You enter your full expenses and the schedule then imposes the 50 percent limit if applicable.

You cannot claim a deduction for entertainment expenses if you file Form 1040A or 1040EZ.

Home Entertainment

Entertainment of business clients, customers, and associates isn't limited to restaurants, clubs, and bars. You can easily conduct your entertaining at home. The cost of home entertainment is deductible within limits if certain conditions are met.

Benefit

If you entertain business clients, customers, or other business associates in your home, you may be able to deduct 50 percent of your costs. Your costs may include food, beverages, paper goods, dishware rentals, and even charges for a maid or bartender to assist you.

Conditions

The same conditions that apply to meals and entertainment costs in general (discussed earlier in this chapter) apply to home entertaining. You must meet the directly related or associated with test and apply the 50 percent limitation. Your expenses cannot be lavish and extravagant.

Planning Tips

This type of entertainment can raise eyebrows with the IRS. Dinners, which are conducive to business discussions, may be appropriate vehicles for business entertaining. It is probably a good idea to limit the guest list to no more than a dozen people. A larger crowd makes it more difficult to demonstrate that you conducted bona fide business discussions in your home.

Events such as pool parties may not easily satisfy the conditions for deductible entertainment costs and probably are not advisable.

Pitfall

You cannot claim a deduction for home entertainment for personal reasons. Parties for personal events, such as a child's birthday party, probably won't satisfy the conditions for deductibility. Even if business associates are invited, it may be difficult to prove that business discussions are carried on (court decisions on these types of events usually have not gone in favor of taxpayers).

Where to Claim the Deduction

If you are an employee whose entertainment costs are covered by an employer's accountable plan, you do not have to do anything. Reimbursements for this expense are *not* included on your Form W-2. You do not have to deduct anything (your employer claims the deduction for your entertainment costs).

If you are an employee whose entertainment costs are *not* covered by an accountable plan, you first figure your deductible entertainment costs in Part II of Form 2106 or 2106-EZ. Your deductible expenses are then entered on Schedule A of Form 1040.

If you are self-employed, you deduct your home entertainment costs for business on Schedule C or C-EZ.

You cannot claim a deduction for home entertainment expenses for business if you file Form 1040A or 1040EZ.

Entertainment Facilities and Club Dues

The "old boy" network is famed as a means of making connections helpful to business. This network, which isn't limited to men, is often found at country clubs, civic organizations, and other associations. The tax law heavily restricts your ability to deduct the costs of belonging to these groups, even though there is a strong business reason for doing so.

Benefit

You may *not* deduct the cost of buying or maintaining entertainment facilities, which include yachts, hunting lodges, fishing camps, swimming pools, tennis courts, hotel suites, company apartments, or homes in vacation areas. This ban applies even if the main reason for the facility is to entertain clients and customers. By law, the cost of entertainment facilities is not deductible.

And you may not deduct the cost of membership in a golf, tennis, swim, or hunting club; an airline club; a hotel club; a business luncheon club; and any other club organized for pleasure, recreation, or social purposes. Again, this ban applies even if there is a strong business element involved.

However, there are two key exceptions to the bans on deducting the cost of entertainment facilities and club dues.

1. You can deduct expenses for food and drinks at the facility when your entertainment meets the conditions discussed earlier in this chapter.

2. You can deduct dues paid to civic or public service organizations, such as Kiwanis, Lions, and Rotary clubs; professional organizations such as medical or bar associations; and chambers of commerce, trade associations, business leagues, real estate boards, and boards of trade.

Conditions

Separate conditions apply, depending on which exception to the ban on entertainment facilities and club dues you are qualifying under.

FOOD AND DRINKS AT FACILITIES. To deduct the costs of food and drinks at entertainment facilities, you must meet the conditions discussed earlier for writing off entertainment costs.

CLUB DUES. You must be able to demonstrate that membership in any of the clubs listed earlier does not have a principal purpose of providing entertainment for members or their guests.

Planning Tips

If you maintain an entertainment facility, you can still write off any costs that would otherwise be deductible.

Example

You own a hunting lodge to which you bring clients and customers. You cannot deduct depreciation on the lodge, nor operating expenses such as utilities, security, and maintenance. But you can deduct real estate taxes and mortgage interest, which are deductible in any event.

If you are a self-employed individual who pays country club dues on behalf of employees, you can turn a nondeductible expense into a deductible one by treating the expense as additional compensation. You then deduct the expense as compensation. This option applies only if the employees use the club for business purposes (not if the employees use the club for personal purposes). You can make this election on an employee-by-employee basis. So, for example, if you are a shareholder-employee, there may not be any net benefit for making this election with respect to your compensation; you are merely shifting the tax from the corporation to you. But you can opt to treat the payment as compensation for your other employees, saving the corporation money.

Pitfall

If your employer pays for a membership on your behalf, your employer may opt to include this benefit in your income (so that it becomes a deduction for the employer). It is reported to you as additional compensation on your Form W-2 and is subject to income tax.

Where to Claim the Deduction

If you are an employee who pays for club dues that are not *barred* (e.g., dues to Rotary Club), you deduct your costs. You first enter these costs in Part I of Form 2106 or 2106-EZ. Your deductible expenses are then entered on Schedule A of Form 1040.

If you are self-employed, you deduct your allowable club dues on Schedule C or C-EZ.

You cannot claim a deduction for allowable club dues if you file Form 1040A or 1040EZ.

Recordkeeping for Meals and Entertainment Expenses

The tax law requires you to keep records of your meals and entertainment expenses as a condition for claiming a deduction. Your meal and entertainment expense records must include the following information:

- *Amount.* Record the cost of each separate expense for meals and entertainment. Incidental expenses can be totaled in any reasonable category (such as taxi fares).
- *Time.* Record the dates of your meals and entertainment.
- *Place.* Note the location of the meals or entertainment. Also note the type of entertainment if it is not apparent.
- *Business purpose.* Record the reason for the expense or the benefit to be gained or expected to be gained from the meals or entertainment. For entertainment, note the nature of the business discussion or activity; whether the entertainment is directly before or after a business discussion; and the date, place, nature, and duration of the business discussion. Identify the persons who took part in both the business discussion and the entertainment activity.

You can use Tables 10.1 and 10.2 to record the amounts of your meals and expenses each week. Enter the details of the expenses in Table 10.1. Then enter the totals in the appropriate spaces provided in Table 10.2.

In addition to your diary or logbook, you also need documentary proof of your expenses. Usually this means retaining receipts, canceled checks, or other proof of what you pay for your meals and entertainment expenses. However, you do not need receipts for any of these expenses under $75.

TABLE 10.1 Sample Weekly Meal and Entertainment Expense Record Keeper—Details

Date: From: ___________ To: ___________

Date	Item	Place	Amount*	Business Purpose	Business Relationship

*You do not have to keep track of amounts for meals if you rely on a standard meal allowance.

TABLE 10.2 Sample Weekly Meal and Entertainment Expense Record Keeper—Summary

Date: From: ___________ To: ___________

Expense	Sunday	Monday	Tuesday	Wednesday	Thursday	Friday	Saturday	Total
Breakfast								
Lunch								
Dinner								
Entertainment expenses								

Gambling Losses

The American Gaming Association estimates that legal gambling is a $78.6 billion industry. Everyone knows that the odds always favor the house, whether it is a casino, race track, or state lottery. The chances of losing far outweigh those of winning. The tax law allows gambling losses to be deductible within limits under certain conditions.

Benefit

You can deduct gambling losses to the extent of your gambling winnings for the year. The losses do not have to result from the same gaming activities that produce the winnings.

If you are not a professional gambler, then gambling losses are claimed as miscellaneous itemized deductions, but they are not subject to the 2 percent of adjusted gross income floor that applies to most other miscellaneous itemized expenses.

If you are a professional gambler who devotes full time to this activity, you

Example

During 2006, you spend $20 every week to play bingo ($1,040 for the year) and you do not win anything. But in December 2006, you win $500 on a state-sponsored scratch-off game, which you declare as income. In 2006, you can deduct $500 of your bingo losses; the other $540 of your gambling losses is not deductible, and cannot be carried forward to offset winnings in a future year.

can treat your losses as a business expense. But even in this case gambling losses are limited to the extent of your winnings.

Conditions

You must report the gambling winnings that equal or exceed your claimed losses for the year. And you must have adequate records or receipts to prove your gambling expenses.

The Tax Court says that gambling winnings can include "comps" given to high rollers by a casino, such as a car, jewelry, and tickets to sporting events.

Planning Tip

Keep track of the amount you gamble throughout the year, since you don't know when in the year you will win. For example, retain all losing lottery tickets as proof of your gambling expenses so you can claim these losses when and to the extent you have winnings for the year.

Pitfalls

Gambling winnings may be reported to you (and the IRS) on Form W-2G, Certain Gambling Winnings. If you claim losses in excess of amounts reported to the IRS, be prepared to show you had other winnings and that you reported these other winnings as income on your return.

Be sure to pay sufficient taxes on winnings to avoid estimated tax penalties. Winnings of $5,000 or more are subject to income tax withholding, but this withholding may not adequately cover your liability; you are entirely responsible for estimated taxes on smaller winnings.

Where to Claim the Deduction

If you are not a professional gambler, you claim a deduction for gambling losses in the space provided on Schedule A of Form 1040.

If you are a full-time professional gambler, you can treat your gambling losses as a business expense. The wages must be placed only for your own account. Gambling losses in this case are reported on Schedule C or Schedule C-EZ of Form 1040. You cannot claim a deduction for gambling losses if you file Form 1040A or 1040EZ.

CHAPTER 11

Real Estate

The vast majority of Americans own real estate, with nearly 70 percent owning their own homes. (Tax write-offs for your main home are discussed in Chapter 4.) But owning a principal residence isn't the only way to invest in real estate. Many individuals also own second homes or invest in rental properties to generate income.

This chapter explains:

- Vacation home
- Home office
- Rentals
- Low-income housing credit
- Rehabilitation credit
- Special breaks for post-hurricane rebuilding
- Deduction for energy-efficient commercial buildings

For more information, see IRS Publication 527, *Residential Rental Property (Including Rental of Vacation Homes)*; IRS Publication 587, *Business Use of Your Home (Including Use by Day-Care Providers)*; and IRS Publication 946, *How to Depreciate Property*. See also *J.K. Lasser's Homeowner's Tax Guide* by Gerald Robinson.

Vacation Home

The rich have traditionally maintained more than one residence, summering in Newport, skiing in Aspen, escaping winters in Miami. But today, second homes aren't limited to the very rich; they are increasingly common among an ever-broadening populace. The tax law offers some tax breaks that help to make ownership of vacation homes more affordable.

Benefit

If you use your vacation home solely for your own personal enjoyment (you don't rent it out at any time during the year), you can deduct all of your real estate taxes and home mortgage interest (if the vacation home is designated as your second home under the home mortgage interest rules in Chapter 4). But, like your personal residence, you can't write off any of the costs of utilities, insurance, or upkeep.

If you rent out a home that you use for part of the year yourself, you may be entitled to certain tax benefits over and above those allowed for pure personal use of the home. The rules that apply to you depend on your rental period and the time that you use the home.

Conditions for Vacation Home with No Rentals

The conditions for deducting real estate taxes and home mortgage interest are explained in Chapter 4.

Conditions for Vacation Home with Rentals

The conditions you must meet and the benefits you are entitled to depend on how long you rent out the home and how long you use it for yourself during the year. There are three categories into which you can fall:

1. Rental of no more than 14 days during the year.
2. Rental of 15 days or more but personal use is for less than 14 days or 10 percent of the days of rental.
3. Personal use is more than 14 days or 10 percent of the total days the home was rented for a fair rental price.

TAX-FREE RENTAL INCOME. If you rent out your home for no more than 14 days during the year, you do not have to report the rental income. There's no dollar limit on this exclusion.

You cannot, however, deduct any expenses related to maintaining the home, depreciation, or any rent you pay. Of course, if you itemize your deductions, you can deduct your mortgage interest if you designate the home as your second residence and your real estate taxes (there is no limit on the number of homes for which you can deduct real estate taxes).

BUSINESS DEDUCTIONS. If you rent out your home for 15 days or more but you personally use the home for less than 14 days or 10 percent of the days of rental, your rental activities are viewed as a business.

Example

You rent out your home for three months and use it for only one week during the year. Since the rental period is more than 15 days (it is actually 92 days) and your personal use is less than 14 days or 10 percent of the days of rental (9 days), you fall within this rule for figuring your deductions from the rental activity.

As such, you must report all of the rental income, but you can deduct all of the expenses related to the rental activity. If your expenses, including depreciation on a home you own, exceed your rents for the year, you can use the loss to offset your income from other purposes.

Personal use of your home includes any day the home is used by:

- You or any member of your family (unless a family member pays a fair rental price).
- Anyone else who pays less than a fair rental price.
- Anyone under a reciprocal agreement that lets you use his or her home.
- Any other person who owns a part of the home (unless it is rented to that person under a shared equity agreement).

You do not have to count your personal use during the year if your home is rented for at least 12 consecutive months.

Example

You move from your home in March 2006 and start renting it in April 2006. Assuming your rental lasts at least until through March 2007, you do not have to count your personal use in 2006.

However, your actual write-offs for the year may be limited by the passive activity loss rules discussed later.

LIMITED BUSINESS DEDUCTIONS. If your personal use is more than 14 days or 10 percent of the total days the home was rented for a fair rental price, you must report all of the rental income. Your deductions are limited to the amount of rents you receive. And the order in which you claim your deductions is carefully orchestrated:

1. Mortgage interest, real estate taxes, and casualty losses are fully deductible. You can claim them even if they exceed your rental income. But you must apply them first against your rental income to determine how much of your other deductions to claim.
2. Operating expenses, such as utilities and maintenance costs, are deductible only to the extent of your rental income after reduction for mortgage interest and so on.
3. Depreciation and other basis adjustments are deductible only to the extent that rental income has not yet been fully offset by the aforementioned deductions.

Example

You own a condo at the shore. You rent it out for June and July. You use it for August. Since your rental is 61 days and your personal use is 31 days, you must figure your deductions using this ordering rule. Assume you receive $6,000 for the two months of rental, and your deductions for the year are $2,000 for interest and $3,000 for taxes. In this case, you can deduct up to $1,000 of operating expenses. Assuming you have at least $1,000 of operating expenses, then you cannot claim any depreciation. Your deductions, in effect, fully offset your rental income so you have no taxable income from your rental activity.

PASSIVE LOSS LIMITATIONS. If the rental of your vacation home is treated as a rental activity (your personal use is less than 15 days but the rental period is more than two weeks), you are subject to the passive loss rules. Generally your deductions related to the rental of your home cannot exceed all of your passive activity income from the year (income from this rental activity plus any other passive activities). (The law calls them passive "losses" but really means deductions in excess of rental income.)

Example

The rental of a vacation home is your only passive activity. Rental income for the year is $6,000, while deductions are $8,000. You can deduct only $6,000 this year.

Passive activity losses in excess of passive activity income can be carried forward and used in a future year when there is passive activity income to offset it. There is no limit on the carryforward period.

There are two key exceptions to the ban on deducting passive losses in excess of passive activity income.

1. You can deduct all carryover losses from a passive activity in the year in which you dispose of your passive activity (e.g., sell your vacation home).
2. You can deduct up to $25,000 of passive activity losses in excess of passive activity income from a rental activity in which you actively participate (e.g., approve new tenants, decide on rental terms, and authorize capital expenditures and repairs). The $25,000 limit is phased out when your modified adjusted gross income exceeds $100,000 and is completely phased out when MAGI reaches $150,000. MAGI for this purpose means AGI without taxable Social Security benefits, the exclusion for interest from U.S. savings bonds used for higher education, the exclusion for employer-paid adoption expenses, and deductions for IRA contributions and student loan interest. You cannot use the $25,000 allowance if you are married and file a separate return.

Example

You are single with MAGI of $135,000. You actively participate in the rental of your condo at a ski resort. Your rental loss in excess of passive activity income is limited to $7,500: $25,000 – 50% of ($135,000 – $100,000).

Planning Tip

If you rent out your vacation home for more than 15 days and use it for less than 14 days or 10 percent of the days of rental, you are *not* subject to the passive activity loss limitations on your deductions if you are considered a "real estate professional." This means:

- More than 50 percent of your personal services during the year are performed in real estate trades or businesses in which you materially participate (e.g., work more than 500 hours for the year, which is 10 hours a week for 50 weeks, or your participation is substantially all of the participation for the activity during the year).

- You perform more than 750 hours of service in real estate trades or businesses in which you materially participate.

Pitfalls

If you rent out your home for more than 15 days but use it for less than 14 days or 10 percent of the rental days, you cannot deduct the portion of home mortgage interest disallowed under the rental loss rules discussed earlier. In this case, since your home ceases to be treated as a personal residence, you cannot itemize any portion of the mortgage interest.

When you sell your vacation home, don't be surprised by the tax impact that can result. Your gain does not qualify for the home sale exclusion (see Chapter 4) because the vacation home is not your principal residence. As long as you own the home for more than one year, your gain is a long-term capital gain.

However, if you rented the home at any time and claimed depreciation on it, you must recapture the depreciation on the sale. This means that gain to the extent of your depreciation is taxed at 25 percent (assuming you are in a tax bracket at or above this rate).

Example

In 2006, you sell your vacation home for a profit of $100,000. You had bought the home in 2001 and claimed depreciation deductions for the rental of the home totaling $2,800. Of the $100,000 gain, $2,800 is taxed at 25 percent, while $97,200 is taxed at 15 percent.

If you realize a loss on the sale of your vacation home, your ability to claim the loss depends on whether or not the home was used for rental.

- If the home was used solely for personal purposes, no loss can be claimed on the sale.
- If the home was used some of the time for rental activities, you cannot claim a loss on the sale.
- If the home was converted solely to rental, you can then claim a capital loss on the sale. The loss is limited to the decline in value after the conversion.

Example

If the home was purchased for $150,000 and has declined in value to $125,000 when you decide to sell it, you can convert it to rental at this time and figure your deductible loss with reference to the $125,000 value. Assume you sell the home after a year on the market for $100,000. Your actual loss is $50,000 ($150,000 – $100,000), but your deductible loss is $25,000 ($125,000 – $100,000). Converting the home to rental means holding the property out for rental, even if you are unsuccessful in your efforts.

Where to Claim the Benefit

If you use your vacation home solely for personal purposes, you deduct your mortgage interest and real estate taxes on Schedule A of Form 1040 (as explained in Chapter 4).

If you rent out your vacation home, you report your rents and expenses in Part I of Schedule E of Form 1040 (unless rental income from your vacation home is tax free).

If you are subject to the passive activity limitations, you must complete Form 8582, Passive Activity Loss Limitations, to determine your deduction limit for the year.

You cannot use Form 1040A or 1040EZ if you have rental real estate activities.

Home Office

The president of the United States works from home, but since he doesn't pay for the costs of the Oval Office, he can't claim any deduction for his home office. But if you work from your home, you may qualify for write-offs if certain conditions are met.

Benefit

If you use a part of your home for business, you may qualify to deduct costs related to the home office, including rent (if you lease your residence) or depreciation (if you own your home), maintenance and utilities, and other expenses. In effect, the personal expenses you are already paying become deductible business expenses, so the home office deduction is a write-off that doesn't require you to pay anything other than what you are already paying.

Generally, you figure your home office deduction by apportioning expenses to that space. The IRS generally wants you to make the apportionment based on square footage. For example, if your home is 2,500 square feet and you use

250 square feet of it for a home office, then generally 10 percent of your home's expenses are part of your home office deduction.

If all your rooms are about the same size, you can opt to make your allocation based on the number of rooms. For example, if you have eight rooms in your home and one is used for business, then one-eighth of your home's expenses are part of your home office deduction.

There are two general categories of deductible expenses—those directly related to the home office and those indirectly related to the home office. The first category includes only costs for the office itself, and these costs are fully deductible; the second category includes costs related to the home in general, and these are deductible to the extent of your allocation.

Example

If you paint the office, it is a direct expense and is fully deductible. If you paint the outside of your home, it is an indirect expense and is deductible to the extent of your allocation. For example, if your allocation to the home office is 10 percent, then 10 percent of the outside paint job is part of your home office deduction.

If you own the home, you can claim depreciation on the portion used as a home office (see later in this chapter under Rentals). Usually, depreciation is figured using a 39-year recovery period on a straight line basis. However, if the office is within property qualifying as residential rental property (e.g., you use one room in your apartment within eight-unit building you own), then depreciation is figured using a 27.5-year recovery period.

Conditions

To be eligible to treat costs related to a home office as a deductible business expense, you must first show that the office is one of the following:

- Your principal place of business.
- A place to meet or deal with patients, clients, or customers in the normal course of your business.
- A separate structure (not attached to your residence) that is used in connection with your business.

Then you must show that you use the home office regularly and exclusively for business. Then, assuming you meet this condition, you must have sufficient income from your home office activity. Finally, if you are an employee, you must satisfy an additional condition; use of the home office must be for the convenience of your employer.

PRINCIPAL PLACE OF BUSINESS. The home office must be the prime location for running your business. The business itself need not be your prime activity; you can claim a home office deduction for a sideline or moonlighting business. Usually prime location means the place where you earn your money. For example, a freelance writer's prime location is her home office.

Your home office is treated as your prime location if it is used for substantial managerial or administrative activities and there is no other fixed location for these activities. For example, an electrician's prime location is the customers' homes where his fees are earned. But if he uses a home office to keep his books, schedule appointments, and order supplies, and he does not have another office, then the home office is treated as his prime location.

PLACE TO MEET OR DEAL WITH CUSTOMERS. You don't have to use your home office as your prime location. You merely have to use it on a regular basis to meet or deal with customers, clients, or patients. Thus, for example, an attorney with a downtown office who uses a home office several times each month to meet with clients qualifies as having a deductible home office.

SEPARATE STRUCTURE. If you have a freestanding garage, barn, greenhouse, or studio that you use in connection with your business, it qualifies as a deductible home office. It does not have to be used as an office or qualify as a principal place of business or a place to meet or deal with customers. For example, a florist with a store in the city who uses a greenhouse on her property to grow orchids can treat the greenhouse as her home office.

EXCLUSIVE USE TEST. You must show that you use the home office space regularly and exclusively for business. There is no minimum amount of time that the office must be used to show regular use. Regular use means more than just occasional use.

For purposes of showing exclusive use, you can't, for example, use the family den as an office by day and a family room by night. A piano teacher was able to show that her living room containing her baby grand piano was her home office; her family never used the room for personal reasons.

You do not have to use an entire room as your office; a portion of a room can qualify. You don't even need to make a physical partition for the space. Just be sure it is used only for business. Furnish it appropriately for your business activity (e.g., a desk, and so on if you run a travel agency business from home).

There is a special rule if you run a day-care business from home (explained in IRS Publication 587, *Business Use of Your Home*).

GROSS INCOME LIMITATION. Your home office deduction cannot be more than your gross income from the home office activity. If you use your home office for a profitable business, this limitation should pose no problem. But if your business is merely a sideline generating modest income or a struggling business, you must check whether this limitation applies to you.

Gross income for purposes of the home office deduction means income from the business activity you run from home.

- If you are self-employed, this is your profit reported on Schedule C.
- If you are an employee, this is your salary earned from the home office.

If you find that gross income is less than your home office deduction, the deduction becomes limited. Your deduction for expenses that would otherwise be nondeductible (such as depreciation and utilities—category 1) cannot exceed gross income from the home office activity, reduced by the business portion of otherwise deductible expenses (such as home mortgage interest and real estate taxes—category 2), plus business expenses not attributable to business use of the home (such as salaries and supplies—category 3). In effect, this rather complex-sounding rule merely orders the categories of deductions you can claim.

Example

In 2006, you run a sideline business from home, showing a profit of $4,500 on Schedule C. Your deductions in the three categories of expenses are $1,200 for category 1, $1,400 for category 2, and $2,200 for category 3. Your category 1 deductions are limited to $900: $4,500 gross income – ($1,400 + $2,200).

If, after going through the computation, you have an unused home office deduction, you can carry it forward indefinitely. The carryforward can be used in any future year in which there is gross income from the same home office activity to offset it. Using the carryforward is permissible even if you are no longer in the same home office.

Example

Same as the preceding example except that at the end of 2006 you relocate to a larger home. You continue to conduct your sideline business from your new home. In 2007, you can use the $300 home office deduction carryforward (assuming your sideline business has sufficient gross income).

CONVENIENCE OF THE EMPLOYER. If you are an employee who works from home, you have an additional condition to satisfy when claiming a home office deduction. As a telecommuter, you must be able to show that use of your home office is for the convenience of your employer (and not simply for your convenience or preference).

Be prepared to show a real need on your employer's part to have you work from home. This can be easily proven when there is no desk space for you at your employer's location. Just getting a letter from your employer stating your home office use is for the employer's convenience is not enough proof for the IRS; the letter must explain *why* it is for the employer's convenience (e.g., no space for you in the employer's location).

Planning Tips

If you were unable to claim the full home office deduction in a prior year due to income limitations, be sure to include any carryover of the home office deduction in your computations for the current year.

If you qualify for a home office, there are some ancillary benefits to consider. Travel to and from your home on business is deductible business travel. In effect, there is no such thing as nondeductible commuting when you have a home office.

Another ancillary benefit concerns depreciation on a computer used in your home office. A computer used in a regular business establishment is not treated as listed property for which you must prove that business use exceeds 50 percent in order to claim first-year expensing or accelerated depreciation. Since the computer is used in a home office, which is treated as a regular business establishment, you are presumed to use it more than 50 percent of the time on business. You do not have to maintain any logs showing the use of the computer.

Pitfalls

You cannot claim a home office deduction if you are an employee who leases the space to your corporation. The tax law specifically bars a home office deduction in this case. However, like any homeowner, you can continue to claim your regular deductions, such as mortgage interest, real estate taxes, and casualty and theft losses.

Not all expenses related to your home office are deductible. The cost of landscaping is not part of a home office deduction. Similarly the expenses of a telephone to a home office are not part of your home office deduction. You cannot deduct the basic service charge for the first line to your home. But the cost of a second phone line or even extra charges on the first line are separately deductible as a business expense that is not part of your home office deduction.

Claiming a home office deduction is often called a red flag, a signal to the IRS to look closely at the deduction. However, if you are entitled to claim the deduction, then by all means do so; just be prepared to back up the position you take on your tax return.

If you own your home, then any depreciation claimed with respect to a home office after May 6, 1997, must be recaptured when your home is sold. Recapture means that this portion of your gain is taxed at a 25 percent rate (assuming you are in a tax bracket at or above this level). You must report your depreciation even if you qualify to exclude gain on the sale of your home; you cannot use the exclusion to offset depreciation recapture.

Where to Claim the Deduction

If you are an employee, you figure your home office deduction on a special IRS worksheet in IRS Publication 587 (you do *not* use the home office deduction form, Form 8829). The amount of your home office deduction is then entered on Form 2106 or 2106-EZ. Deductions from Form 2106 or 2106-EZ are then entered as miscellaneous itemized deductions on Schedule A of Form 1040.

If you are a self-employed individual, you figure your home office deduction on Form 8829, Expenses for Business Use of Your Home.

In either event, you cannot claim a home office deduction if you file Form 1040A or 1040EZ.

Rentals

Becoming a landlord by acquiring real estate and renting it out can be a sound financial activity. There is the possibility of making money both from rental income as well as property appreciation upon an eventual sale. The tax law helps to underwrite the cost of being a landlord, allowing for certain tax deductions. But there are limits on and special rules for write-offs associated with rental properties.

Benefit

If you rent out property, you can deduct your expenses against the rental income. Any loss resulting from having expenses in excess of rental income can effectively be used to offset your other income, such as salary or dividends.

However, losses from rental activities are subject to the passive loss rules that may restrict your deductions for the current year.

Conditions

If you own realty—a single-family home, a condo unit, a multifamily home in which you live and rent out a portion, an office building, a strip mall, or any other property—you can deduct expenses related to the property.

EXAMPLES OF DEDUCTIBLE RENTAL EXPENSES

Advertising to find tenants.

Car expenses to and from the property.

Cleaning and maintenance.

Commissions to real estate brokers when finding tenants.

Depreciation.

Insurance.

Legal and professional fees (but not attorney's fees to buy the property).

Management fees.

Mortgage interest on rental property.

Repairs.

Security system monitoring fees.

Supplies.

Taxes.

Utilities.

PASSIVE LOSS LIMITATIONS. When you rent out property, you usually fall within the passive loss rules (exceptions to these rules are discussed later), then generally your deductions cannot exceed all of your passive activity income from the year (income from this rental activity plus any other passive activities). (The law calls them passive "losses" but really means deductions in excess of rental income.)

Example

The rental of a single-family home in which you do not live during the year is your only passive activity. Rental income for the year is $6,000, while deductions are $8,000. You can deduct only $6,000 this year.

Passive activity losses in excess of passive activity income can be carried forward and used in a future year when there is passive activity income to offset them. There is no limit on the carryforward period.

There are three key exceptions to the ban on deducting passive losses in excess of passive activity income.

1. You can deduct all carryover losses from a passive activity in the year in which you dispose of your income (e.g., sell your vacation home).
2. You can deduct up to $25,000 of passive activity losses in excess of passive activity income from a rental activity in which you actively participate (e.g., approve new tenants, decide on rental terms, and authorize capital expenditures and repairs). The $25,000 limit is phased out when

your modified adjusted gross income exceeds $100,000 and is completely phased out when MAGI reaches $150,000. MAGI for this purpose means AGI without taxable Social Security benefits, the exclusion for interest from U.S. savings bonds used for higher education, the exclusion for employer-paid adoption expenses, deductions for IRA contributions, the deduction for contributions to Archer medical savings accounts, the domestic production activities deduction, the deduction for tuition and fees, and student loan interest. You cannot use the $25,000 allowance if you are married and file a separate return.

Example

You are single with MAGI of $135,000. You actively participate in the rental of your beachfront condo. Your rental loss in excess of passive activity income is limited to $7,500: $25,000 – 50% of ($135,000 – $100,000).

3. You are a real estate professional exempt from the passive loss rules. If you are in the real estate business and want to check whether you are treated as a real estate professional exempt from the passive loss rules, see the instructions to IRS Form 8582.

Planning Tips

Depreciation is a no-cost deduction (you don't spend any dollars to claim the write-off, other than buying the property). How do you figure this valuable write-off called depreciation? It is a deduction *only* for the building (you can't depreciate), so you must allocate the cost of the property between the building and the land.

Example

You buy a single-family home for rental, paying $180,000. You figure that the lot itself would sell for $25,000, so you allocate $155,000 to the house. This is your basis for depreciation.

If you convert personal property to rental property (for example, you move from your home and rent it out), your basis for depreciation purposes is your basis (as figured earlier) or the fair market value of the home at the time of conversion, whichever is less.

Example

You bought your home (exclusive of the land) for $200,000 in 1996. In 2006, you move from it and rent it out indefinitely. The value of the home in 2006 is $300,000. Your basis for depreciation is $200,000, which is the lower of basis or fair market value.

The amount you claim for depreciation is based on the month in which you place the property into service as a rental and the type of realty involved:

- Residential rental property is depreciated over a period of 27.5 years using the straight-line method and a midmonth depreciation convention. Residential rental property is a building for which 80 percent or more of the gross rental income for the year is rental income from dwelling units. So, if you own an apartment building with stores at street level, you must see whether the property meets the 80 percent test.
- Nonresidential property is depreciated over a period of 39 years.

Depreciation is simply your basis multiplied by the depreciation rate from the IRS table. Table 11.1 shows depreciation rates for residential property. Table 11.2 shows depreciation rates for nonresidential property.

If you sublease property—you are a tenant who leases the property to someone else—you cannot claim a depreciation deduction. Depreciation can only be claimed by the owner of the property.

Pitfall

Depreciation claimed on your rental realty is subject to recapture. This means that the gain you realize on the sale is taxed at 25 percent to the extent of depreciation deductions you have claimed. Gain in excess of this amount is taxed at no more than 20 percent (assuming you owned the property for more than one year).

Example

On July 5, 2001, you bought an office building for $250,000 (exclusive of the land). You sell it on July 5, 2006, for $350,000. Depreciation deductions total $31,665. Your gain is $131,665 ($350,000 – $218,335). Of this gain, $31,665 is recaptured and taxed at the 25 percent rate; $100,000 is taxed at 15 percent. Your total tax is $22,916 ($7,916 + $15,000).

TABLE 11.1 Depreciation Rates for Residential Rental Property

Year	Month											
	1	2	3	4	5	6	7	8	9	10	11	12
1	3.485%	3.182%	2.879%	2.576%	2.273%	1.970%	1.667%	1.364%	1.061%	0.758%	0.455%	0.152%
2–9	3.636	3.636	3.636	3.636	3.636	3.636	3.636	3.636	3.636	3.636	3.636	3.636
10	3.637	3.637	3.637	3.637	3.637	3.637	3.636	3.636	3.636	3.636	3.636	3.636

For years 11–28, see IRS Publication 946, *How to Depreciate Property.*

TABLE 11.2 Depreciation Rates for Nonresidential Rental Property (Placed in Service after May 13, 1993)

Year	Month											
	1	2	3	4	5	6	7	8	9	10	11	12
1	2.461%	2.247%	2.033%	1.819%	1.605%	1.391%	1.177%	0.963%	0.749%	0.535%	0.321%	0.107%
2–39	2.564	2.564	2.564	2.564	2.564	2.564	2.564	2.564	2.564	2.564	2.564	2.564

Where to Claim the Deduction

You report your rents and expenses in Part I of Schedule E of Form 1040. If you own a multifamily home in which you live, the portion of mortgage interest and real estate taxes is allocated between Schedule E (for the rental portion) and Schedule A of Form 1040 (for the personal portion of the home).

Example

You own a three-family house and live in one unit. Two-thirds of your mortgage interest and property taxes and all of your rent-related expenses are reported on Schedule E; one-third of your mortgage interest and property taxes are reported on Schedule A.

If you own an interest in rental realty through a partnership or limited liability company, you report your share of rental income or losses on Schedule E (you obtain the amount you must report from a Schedule K-1 that is given to you by the entity).

You must also complete Form 8582, Passive Activity Loss Limitations, to determine your deduction limit for the year under the passive activity rules.

You cannot use Form 1040A or 1040EZ if you have rental real estate activities.

Low-Income Housing Credit

The federal government wants to encourage investments in housing to accommodate low-income individuals. To make such investments attractive to investors, special tax credits have been made available. These credits effectively operate to replace the rental income investors do not receive because of the rent reductions or breaks provided to certain renters because of their income levels.

Benefit

If you invest in low-income housing—to build it or substantially renovate existing structures—you may be eligible for a tax credit each year for a period of 10 years, generally starting with the year the building is placed in service. The amount of the credit depends on whether the building is new and whether any federal subsidies were used for construction or rehabilitation purposes.

The credit is based on 70 percent of the qualified basis of each new low-income housing building placed in service after 1986 or 30 percent of the qualified basis in the case of federally subsidized new or existing buildings. The credit itself is the present value of the 10 annual credit amounts determined as of the last day of the first year of the credit period.

Conditions

You can invest in low-income housing directly, by building the units or rehabilitating existing ones, or by putting money into a limited partnership that does the building or rehabilitating for you. Either way, to qualify for a credit, the building must be considered a low-income housing building.

LOW-INCOME HOUSING BUILDING. Low-income housing does not mean the property must be located in the slums or that the building itself is a tenement. Rather, the tax law requires only that the building offer a certain percentage of the rental units to tenants with income below fixed levels. For example, in the case of housing in suburban areas and smaller towns, the building is considered to be low-income housing if the tenants earn no more than 60 percent of the local median income (although the rule is waived for housing provided to victims of Hurricane Katrina who do not qualify as low-income). How do you know if your building qualifies? You must receive certification from an authorized housing credit agency. The agency allocates the credit to you on Form 8609, Low-Income Housing Credit Allocation Certificate.

The building must have been constructed after 1986; older buildings don't qualify.

Planning Tip

Generally the first year of the credit is the year in which the building is placed in service for low-income housing. However, you can elect to start claiming the credit in the following year just by indicating your election on Form 8609. You may wish to do so if you cannot fully benefit from the credit in the year the building is placed in service (see "Pitfalls" that follow) or if you will have more income to offset in the following year.

Pitfalls

If you dispose of your interest before the end of a set period, you are subject to recapture. This means that part of the benefit you received from claiming the credit is reported as an additional tax you owe in the year of recapture. The building must continue to meet certain requirements for a 15-year period. If not, then your recapture is figured on Form 8611, Recapture of the Low-Income Housing Credit.

You won't benefit from the credit if you are subject to the alternative minimum tax. This credit may not be used to reduce your AMT liability.

Where to Claim the Credit

You figure your credit on Form 8586, Low-Income Housing Credit. The credit is part of the general business credit, which is figured on Form 3800, General Business Credit.

You may also need to figure whether the passive activity restrictions apply to your claiming the credit in the current year. You do this by completing Form 8582-CR, Passive Activity Credit Limitations.

The amount of the credit that can be claimed this year is then entered in the "Tax and Credits" section of Form 1040.

You cannot claim the credit if you file Form 1040A or 1040EZ.

Rehabilitation Credit

Fix it up or tear it down? The tax law provides key incentives for restoring certain older properties. These incentives are tax credits that may be claimed if certain conditions are met.

Benefit

If you spend money fixing up an old building, you may be eligible to claim a tax credit. The amount of the credit depends on the type of building you renovate:

- Certified historic structures—20 percent of your expenditures.
- Buildings built before 1936—10 percent of your expenditures.

There is no overall dollar limit on the credit. However, there are certain limitations that may restrict the amount you can claim in the current year.

Conditions

Only certain buildings are eligible for the credit. They include:

- Historic structures
- Pre-1936 buildings

Regardless of which type of building is involved, you must expend a certain amount on rehabilitation in order to claim a credit.

HISTORIC STRUCTURES. The 20 percent credit applies to both residential or nonresidential buildings (such as industrial and commercial buildings). The only criterion is that the building is a historic structure, which is one that has been recognized by a national or state registry (placed on the National Register of Historic Places or located in a registered historic district and certified by the Secretary of the Interior as being of historic significance to the district).

The National Park Service must certify that your planned rehabilitation of the building is in keeping with its historic status designation.

PRE-1936 BUILDINGS. The 10 percent credit applies only to nonresidential buildings; you cannot claim a credit for fixing up your home or other residential building. In making renovations, you must retain a certain portion of the original structure (this rule prevents you from basically tearing down the old building to put up a new one).

More specifically, at least 75 percent of the external walls must be intact, with at least 50 percent kept as external walls. And at least 75 percent of the existing internal structural framework must be kept in place. One federal court allowed the credit to be claimed for a building that was moved to a new location and then renovated where at least 75 percent of the walls were retained as external walls after the relocation.

MINIMUM REHABILITATION. You can't claim the credit simply for adding a doorbell or making other minor renovations. The credit is limited to expenses of at least a certain amount: $5,000 or your adjusted basis in the building, whichever is greater.

Example

You buy an old building for a cost of $50,000 (exclusive of the land). To claim the credit, you must spend at least $50,000 on renovations (since your basis of $50,000 is greater than $5,000).

The expenditures must be made within a 24-month period. This period is extended to 60 months if the rehabilitation is undertaken pursuant to a written architectural plan and specifications are completed before the rehabilitation begins.

Planning Tips

When shopping for real estate to purchase for investment or business, consider the impact that claiming the credit may have on your fix-up costs. Also explore any federal or state grants that may be available for restoring historic structures (for example, see the Historic Preservation Grants program through the National Park Service at www.cr.nps.gov/hps/hpf/index.htm).

Check to see if there are state income tax credits or other incentives (such as real estate tax abatements) for rehabilitating certified historic structures or other old buildings.

Pitfalls

The tax credit for rehabilitating an old building falls under the passive loss rules. This means that the credit you are otherwise entitled to claim may be limited by passive activity restrictions. For more details, see the instructions to IRS Form 8582-CR, Passive Activity Credit Limitations.

You won't benefit from the credit if you are subject to the alternative minimum tax. This credit may not be used to reduce your AMT liability.

Where to Claim the Credit

You figure your credit on Form 3468, Investment Credit. The credit is part of the general business credit, which is figured on Form 3800, General Business Credit.

You may also need to figure whether the passive activity restrictions apply to your claiming the credit in the current year. You do this by completing Form 8582-CR, Passive Activity Credit Limitations.

The amount of the credit that can be claimed this year is then entered in the "Tax and Credits" section of Form 1040.

You cannot claim the credit if you file Form 1040A or 1040EZ.

Special Breaks for Post-Hurricane Rebuilding

The Katrina Emergency Tax Relief Act of 2005 provides several key tax incentives to encourage rebuilding in the Gulf area devastated by Hurricanes Katrina, Rita, and Wilma. The breaks extend only through the end of 2007 (or 2008 where noted).

PARTIAL EXPENSING FOR DEMOLITION AND CLEANUP COSTS. Costs to tear down or clean up a building that would normally be capitalized can be deducted up to 50 percent.

Also, the deduction that can be claimed for cleaning up so-called brownfields is extended to affected areas (this deduction expired for other locations at the end of 2005).

FIFTY PERCENT BONUS DEPRECIATION. Although bonus depreciation expired at the end of 2004, it has been extended for affected areas. This is an additional first-year deduction equal to 50 percent of the property's basis.

In the case of commercial and residential realty, bonus depreciation can be claimed for property placed in service through December 31, 2008.

REHABILITATION CREDIT. The usual limit on the tax credit for rehabilitating buildings located in affected areas is increased to 13 percent (26 percent for historic structures) through 2008; ordinarily the credit is limited to 10 percent and 20 percent respectively, as explained earlier in this chapter.

LOW-INCOME HOUSING CREDIT. The amount of the credit that can be claimed for qualified housing in the region has been increased for investments through 2008.

Deduction for Energy-Efficient Commercial Buildings

It has been estimated that commercial buildings use one-quarter of all domestic energy consumption. To encourage owners and lessees of commercial property to make certain energy improvements, new tax law allows a special deduction for 2006 and 2007.

Benefit

The cost of energy-efficient property can be deducted up to $1.80 per square foot. A reduced deduction of 60 cents per square foot can be claimed for a building that achieves only partial energy savings.

Conditions

To qualify for the full deduction, the addition of energy-efficient property must help a commercial building achieve a 50 percent energy savings as compared with similar property that meets benchmarks set by the Standard 90.1-2001 of the American Society of Heating, Refrigerating, and Air Conditioning Engineers and the Illuminating Engineering Society of North America (www.ashrae.com). The savings is measured by the reduction in cost (not in the actual units consumed). Cost is determined on a fuel-neutral basis (e.g., without regard to whether the building is heated by gas, oil, or electricity) by reference to the Standard and not on the basis of the owner's actual costs.

The partial deduction (60 cents per square foot) is allowed for a building that fails the 50 percent energy-savings requirement but meets a lesser standard.

The deduction applies to improvements made to:

- The interior lighting system.
- The heating, cooling, ventilation, and hot water systems.
- The building envelop (exterior).

The building owner must obtain certification of a plan to reduce overall energy costs before installing the property. There are various ways to satisfy the certification requirement, including use of approved software to calculate energy consumption.

Planning Tip

Check for state tax incentives for making energy improvements. Many states provide deductions and/or tax credits for these improvements.

Pitfall

The basis of the property must be reduced by the amount of any deduction claimed. This will have the effect of reducing allowable depreciation for the property.

Where to Claim the Deduction

The deduction is a business expense reported by the building's owner or lessee on the proper tax return.

CHAPTER 12

Borrowing and Interest

With the prices of things rising, jobs tight, and investments performing weakly, it seems that every paycheck is stretched to the limit. We often choose or are forced to rely on credit to pay for the things we want or need. Whether you are a borrower or a lender, you may be eligible for tax breaks with respect to loan activities.

This chapter explains:

- Home mortgage interest
- Student loan interest
- Investment-related loans
- Business interest
- Accrued interest on bond purchases
- Below-market loans
- Bad debts
- Loan forgiveness

For more information, see IRS Publication 550, Investment Income and Expenses.

Home Mortgage Interest

If you are a homeowner repaying a mortgage, you can deduct the interest portion of your payments. There is no dollar limit on how much interest you can deduct. However, the law limits the amount of borrowing you can take into account in figuring your deductible interest on loans taken after October 14, 1987.

- For acquisition indebtedness to buy, build, or substantially renovate your home: $1 million.
- For home equity debt, which is a loan other than acquisition indebtedness secured by your home (such as a home equity line of credit): $100,000.

In effect, you can deduct all of the interest on up to a total amount of debt of $1,100,000 ($1 million acquisition indebtedness plus $100,000 home equity debt).

Home mortgage interest is deductible only as an itemized deduction; you cannot deduct the interest if you use the standard deduction.

For more details on deducting home mortgage interest, see Chapter 4.

Student Loan Interest

When you are repaying student loans, you may be able to deduct up to $2,500 of interest annually. The deduction is an adjustment to gross income so you can claim it even if you do not itemize your other deductions and simply use the standard deduction.

The ability to deduct student loan interest depends on your modified adjusted gross income (MAGI). If your MAGI is too high, you cannot claim this benefit.

For more details on deducting student loan interest, see Chapter 3.

Investment-Related Interest

You can deduct interest paid on loans used to buy or carry investments to the extent of your net investment income received (such as interest income). If your investment interest paid is more than your net investment income for the year, you can carry the excess interest forward indefinitely and use it in a future year. There is no overall dollar limit on this deduction.

You can deduct investment-related interest only if you itemize your deductions. You cannot claim a deduction if you use the standard deduction.

You cannot deduct interest on a loan used to buy tax-exempt securities, such as municipal bonds or muni-bond funds.

For more details on deducting investment-related interest, see Chapter 8.

Business Interest

Business in many cases runs on other people's money. Loans are used to start up a company, buy equipment, and pay operating expenses. Loans used for business come in all sizes—fixed loans for a set term, revolving lines of credit, or even basic credit card charges for purchases made. Fortunately, whatever type of business loan is involved, interest on the loan may be fully deductible.

Benefit

If you borrow money for business—by taking out a loan or charging a business purchase to a credit card on which you finance the payments—you can deduct the interest in full against your business income. There is no dollar limit on this deduction.

Condition

The source of the loan does not govern the treatment of the interest. Deductibility depends on what you use the proceeds for. If you use the proceeds for business—for example, to acquire a sole proprietorship—then interest is considered fully deductible business interest.

Interest on a loan used to buy shares in a corporation is viewed as investment interest, not business interest. Interest you pay on tax deficiencies related to your business (for example, a deficiency related to Schedule C of your sole proprietorship) is not deductible. This interest is treated as personal interest, not business interest.

Planning Tip

If you guarantee a loan made to your corporation, you can deduct interest on the loan as business interest, but only when and to the extent you are called upon to do so because the corporation cannot make the payment.

Pitfalls

You cannot deduct business interest that is otherwise required to be capitalized, such as construction period interest. In effect, you cannot deduct interest during the construction period. Construction period interest is added to the basis of the property.

If you borrow money from your corporation, the interest you pay back to the corporation is *not* automatically business interest just because of your relationship to the lender. Again, the treatment of interest depends on what you use the proceeds for. For example, if you borrow money from your corporation to take a vacation, the interest is nondeductible personal interest.

Where to Claim the Deduction

Self-employed individuals who pay business interest deduct these payments on Schedule C or C-EZ of Form 1040.

You cannot deduct business interest if you file Form 1040A or 1040EZ.

Accrued Interest on Bond Purchases

In the financial world, bonds are bought and sold in the secondary market: After an initial offering, they trade among investors at their current values. But when trades are made between interest payment dates, which is common, bond buyers pay for the interest that is actually received by the bond sellers; the interest is included in the cost of the bond. The tax law allows for a correction of this situation by allowing bond sellers a deduction.

Benefit

If you buy a bond between its interest payment dates, some interest may be included in the purchase price that doesn't belong to you. That interest is payable to the bond seller even though it is reported as payable to you. To correct this inequity, you can effectively deduct the accrued interest. This is not a tax deduction in the true sense of the word. Rather, you are allowed to make a subtraction that amounts to the same thing.

Condition

This subtraction applies only if you are a bond purchaser and there is accrued interest on the bond you buy. This occurs only when the purchase takes place between the bond's interest dates (typically twice a year).

Planning Tips

When purchasing a bond, you can ask your stockbroker about interest dates on the security. Knowing the interest dates will apprise you of whether there will be any accrued interest to deal with when you file your return.

If you *sell* a bond with accrued interest, you do not subtract it from interest income. Instead, you reduce the sales proceeds by the amount of accrued interest belonging to the purchaser (which reduces your gain or increases your loss). For example, if you sell a bond for which you paid $9,500 at $10,000 and have accrued interest of $180, you reduce the proceeds by this amount. As a result, your gain is $320 ([$10,000 proceeds–$180 accrued interest]–$9,500 basis).

Pitfall

Do *not* simply subtract from the interest reported to you on Form 1099-INT the accrued interest you paid when you purchased a bond. Netting the interest in this manner can trigger an examination of your return because your reporting does not match the information sent to the IRS on Form 1099-INT. Instead, follow the reporting instructions below.

Where to Claim the Benefit

Generally, you do not have to complete Part I of Schedule B of Form 1040 unless your interest income is over $1,500. However, you must do so, regardless of your total interest, if you want to deduct the accrued interest you paid on a bond purchase.

In Part I of Schedule B of Form 1040, report the full amount of interest shown on Form 1099-INT. Then, after entering any other interest you received, create a subtotal line reflecting the total of all entries. On the line immediately below the subtotal, write "Accrued interest" and enter the amount of accrued interest that you paid the seller. Subtract this amount from the subtotal and enter the result on line 2 of Part I of Schedule B.

You cannot effectively deduct accrued interest if you file Form 1040A or 1040EZ.

Below-Market Loans

In today's low-interest environment—the federal funds rate at which banks borrow is currently just 1 percent—it's hard to imagine that borrowers would bother to devise strategies for avoiding interest payments. But when rates were higher it was common for business owners to borrow from their companies and for children to borrow from parents at little or no interest, realizing a considerable economic benefit. The tax law took note of this benefit, creating the below-market interest rate rules. Under these rules, phantom interest may be created for lenders and phantom interest deductions for borrowers. While the interest may be phantom, the income from this interest can be very real.

Benefit

If you lend money to or borrow from a relative, friend, or your business at no interest or at highly favorable low interest rates, there may be some tax issues to consider. Depending on who the parties are, the amount of the loan, and the interest rate charged, these results can ensue:

- *Gift loans up to $10,000.* Gift loans, compensation-related loans, and shareholder-corporation loans up to $10,000 have no consequences to the parties. No interest deduction can be claimed with respect to any interest that is not actually paid.
- *Gift loans in the range of $10,000 to $100,000.* No interest deduction can be claimed with respect to any interest that is not actually paid if the borrower's investment income is no more than $1,000.
- *All other loans.* In addition to interest actually paid, a deduction can be claimed for below-market interest (assuming that it is deductible interest). This is the interest that should have been charged, based on the

government's applicable federal rate (AFR) for the term of the loan. The lender must report a like amount of income. However, the lender may be able to offset the income by deducting the forgiven interest in some way.

Example

You borrow $20,000 from your corporation interest free for five years. Assuming the AFR for this term is 3 percent at the time the loan originates, your annual interest deduction is $600 for each of the five years that the loan is outstanding (3% of $20,000). If the corporation treats the forgiven loan as compensation, you must report $600 as compensation. From the corporation's standpoint, it picks up $600 interest and deducts $600 compensation.

Keep in mind that even if you have imputed interest from a below-market loan, it may not necessarily be deductible. It depends on what you use the loan proceeds for. If you use the funds to buy stocks, for example, you can treat the imputed interest as investment interest (discussed earlier in this chapter). But if you use the funds to pay off your personal credit card debt or take a vacation, you cannot deduct the imputed interest; it is nondeductible personal interest.

Condition

Whether a loan falls within the below-market loan rules depends on the rate of interest, if any, fixed when the loan originates. Loans fall into three basic categories:

1. Short-term: three years or less.
2. Mid-term: over three but not over nine years.
3. Long-term: over nine years.

If the loan is payable on demand (there is no fixed term), then the interest rate used for a loan outstanding for the entire year is a blended rate announced by the IRS each July (4.71 percent for 2006).

Each month the IRS publishes AFRs. You can check the AFRs monthly at www.irs.gov/taxpros/lists/0,,id=98042,00.html.

Planning Tip

When arranging loans between family or other related persons, keep the below-market loan rules in mind. With today's historic low interest rates it is easy to keep loans from falling subject to the rules by charging the minimum AFR. But even if no or lower interest is charged so that income results, the arrangement may still be desirable.

Pitfall

If you are the lender of a below-market loan that does not meet the gift loan or other exemption rules, you have to report interest income even though you not actually receive any payments.

Where to Claim the Benefit

If you are exempt from the below-market loan rules, do not report anything on your return. If you are a borrower subject to the below-market loan rules, you can deduct your interest payments if such interest is otherwise deductible. For instance, if the interest qualifies as investment interest, deduct it on Schedule A of Form 1040 (see Chapter 8 for more details about deducting investment interest).

Bad Debts

Lenders never loan money with the expectation they won't be repaid. They expect to collect interest during the term of the loan and recoup the amount of principal in the loan. But reality shows that some borrowers default. Taxwise, lenders may be able to write off these bad loans under certain conditions.

Benefit

If you loan money to someone who fails to repay you, you can claim a loss for the outstanding balance. The conditions for writing off the loss and the manner in which the loss is treated for tax purposes depend on the type of bad debt involved. There are two types:

1. Business bad debts, which are debts arising in the course of business. For example, your business is on the accrual method of accounting and fails to receive payment on an accounts receivable; this is a business bad debt. Loans made to protect your salary are treated as business bad debts. Business bad debts are fully deductible as ordinary losses against business income.
2. Nonbusiness bad debts, which are any other type of debts. For example, you loan money to your friend to buy a car and your friend fails to repay the loan; this is a nonbusiness bad debt. Nonbusiness bad debts also include loans that you make to protect your investments and uninsured bank deposits (explained in Chapter 8). Nonbusiness bad debts are deductible as short-term capital losses.

Condition

You must satisfy four conditions in order to deduct a bad debt loss:

1. It is a valid debt.
2. There was a debtor-creditor relationship.

3. The loan was made from your after-tax income or capital.
4. You must show that the debt has become worthless.

VALID DEBT. Your right to repayment must be enforceable and cannot depend on some future occurrence. For example, if the loan violates state usury laws, the debt cannot be deducted when it goes unpaid.

If you own a corporation and make loans to it, be sure that the arrangement is truly a loan and not merely an advance of capital. If the corporation is thinly capitalized (there is just too much debt compared with equity), the IRS may view a supposed loan to the corporation as an advance of capital.

DEBTOR-CREDITOR RELATIONSHIP. You must prove that there was a debtor-creditor relationship. In the context of a business loan, there is usually no issue.

But when you lend money to family or friends, there is the question of whether you are truly lending the money or really making a gift of it.

If you guarantee a loan made to someone else who defaults, you can claim a bad debt deduction when you make the payment *if* it is a business bad debt or a nonbusiness bad debt made to protect an investment. No deduction can be claimed for making good on your guarantee of a loan for personal reasons, such as a favor to a relative or friend.

LOAN FROM AFTER-TAX INCOME OR CAPITAL. If, like most individuals, you are on the cash basis of accounting, you cannot treat nonpayments of salary, rents, or fees owed to you as bad debts. Since you never reported the income (under the cash method you report as income only what you receive), you cannot claim a bad debt deduction for nonpayment.

Example

You are a consultant on the cash method of accounting. You complete a job for which you are owed $2,500. You never recover your fee because the client has gone out of business. You cannot deduct this amount as a bad debt because you never reported the consulting fee as income. While this may seem unfair because of the time and effort you put into the work, the tax law does not view you as having sustained a loss.

WORTHLESSNESS. You must show that the debt will never be repaid. If the debtor has gone out of business or filed for bankruptcy, this is a good indication that there is little hope of recovery. Show any steps you have taken to recover on the debt, such as suing for it in court or turning it over to a collection agency. You do not actually have to sue if this action would be futile because you would be unable to collect on a judgment.

In the case of nonbusiness bad debts, you must show that the debt is entirely worthless; a partially worthless bad debt cannot be claimed in this case.

To fix the year of worthlessness, show that the debt had some value on December 31 of the prior year to the year in which you believe the debt became worthless. Then show the identifiable event that leads you to conclude the debt is worthless.

You do not have to wait until the debt is due in order to claim a bad debt deduction if you know that it has already become worthless. You claim the deduction in the year it becomes worthless, not the year in which it is due.

Planning Tips

Whenever you make a loan, be sure to put all of the terms of the loan in writing. This will accomplish a couple of things: It will make the borrower aware of when and how much you expect to be repaid, and, in the case of default, you will have the proof that the arrangement was truly a loan and not a gift.

It's not always easy to tell when a debt has gone bad. You have seven years in which to file an amended return for the year in which the bad debt became worthless in order to make a claim for a refund. The filing period generally runs seven years from the due date of the return for the year of worthlessness.

Example

In June 2006, you discover that a loan you made to a friend became totally worthless in 2003. You have until April 15, 2010, to file an amended return for 2003 to report the nonbusiness bad debt.

Pitfalls

You cannot claim a bad debt deduction for unpaid child support. For example, if your former spouse owes you $10,000 in back child support, you cannot write this off as a bad debt. The reason: You do not have any basis in the debt so, for tax purposes, you do not have a loss (even though you surely have an economic loss).

Also, you cannot take a nonbusiness bad debt for any debt owed to you by a political party or committee.

If you deducted a bad debt in a prior year and to your amazement you receive repayment now, you must include the amount in income. But inclusion is required only to the extent that the deduction in a prior year reduced your tax in that year.

Where to Claim the Benefit

A business bad debt that you make in the course of your business is reported as a deductible item on Schedule C of Form 1040. But if you are a shareholder-employee with a loan to your corporation that has gone sour, determine whether it is a business bad debt or a nonbusiness bad debt. A business bad debt in this situation is only deductible as a miscellaneous itemized deduction subject to the 2-percent-of-AGI floor.

A nonbusiness bad debt is reported as a short-term capital loss in Part I of Schedule D of Form 1040. In column (a), enter the name of the debtor and

"Statement attached." On your own statement, which you attach to your return, include:

- A description of the debt, including the amount, and the date it became worthless.
- The name of the debtor and any business or family relationship between you.
- The efforts you made to collect the debt.
- Why you believe the debt is now worthless.

You cannot deduct your bad debts if you file Form 1040A or 1040EZ.

Loan Forgiveness

Usually, when a lender allows a borrower to pay less than the outstanding loan balance, the borrower has taxable income. However, in some special situations, loan forgiveness is not taxed.

Benefit

Certain debt forgiveness is tax free. This includes student loan interest canceled in exchange for certain public service and debt discharged while you are insolvent (when your liabilities exceed the fair market value of your assets) or through a bankruptcy proceeding.

For individuals whose principal residence was located in the core disaster area of Hurricane Katrina, as well as those who suffered an economic loss because of this disaster, personal debt forgiven by a government agency or financial institution on or after August 25, 2005, and before January 1, 2007, is tax free.

Condition

Student loan cancellation that is tax free requires public service to be performed under the direction of a governmental unit or tax-exempt organization.

Planning Tips

A price adjustment for an item purchased on credit is not taxable cancellation of debt.

Except in the limited circumstances where cancellation of debt is tax free, before accepting a lender's offer to reduce your loan balance (e.g., reduction of your home mortgage), consider the tax cost of the resulting income to you.

Pitfall

Taxable cancellation of debt is reported to you and the IRS on Form 1099-C, Cancellation of Debt.

Where to Claim the Benefit

If loan forgiveness is tax free, you do not have to report it on your return.

CHAPTER 13

Insurance and Catastrophes

No one likes to think about bad things happening, but happen they do, as seen in the Gulf region due to Hurricanes Katrina, Rita, and Wilma. Natural disasters, accidents, illnesses, and now terrorist activities and war all present serious personal and financial threats that can become reality. When faced with such catastrophes, insurance may carry you just so far, with economic losses outstripping your insurance recoveries. But you may be able to mitigate your financial losses by certain tax write-offs.

This chapter explains:

- Casualty and theft losses
- Disaster losses
- Special tax breaks for hurricane victims
- Disaster relief payments
- Damages
- Disability coverage
- Accelerated death benefits
- Legal fees
- Appraisal fees

Losses to your bank deposits are discussed in Chapter 8. For more information, see IRS Publication 547, *Casualties, Disasters, and Thefts (Business and*

Nonbusiness), and IRS Publication 584, *Casualty, Disaster, and Theft Loss Workbook (Personal-Use Property).*

Casualty and Theft Losses

Things happen beyond man's control, such as hurricanes and wildfires, that damage or destroy property. If there is insurance it may only partially cover the loss. The tax law allows a deduction for losses resulting from a casualty event or theft. But strict rules apply to limit the amount of the write-off. Special rules relating to casualty losses that apply to victims of Hurricanes Katrina, Rita, and Wilma are discussed later in this chapter.

Benefit

If you suffer property damage due to a casualty or theft that is not fully covered by insurance, you may be able to deduct your loss as an itemized deduction. There is no overall dollar limit on the amount you can deduct. Your itemized deduction is *not* subject to the overall reduction in itemized deductions for high-income taxpayers (explained in the Introduction).

The amount of your loss, however, is limited to the decrease in the value of property from the casualty or its adjusted basis (usually your cost), whichever amount is smaller. ***Rule of thumb:*** For property that appreciates in value, your loss is usually based on your adjusted basis; for property that declines in value, your loss is usually based on the decrease in value. Any casualty or theft loss must be reduced by insurance or similar recoveries.

Example

Your car is damaged in an accident and you do not have collision coverage. Before the accident, your car was worth $8,000. After the accident it was worth only $2,000. Your adjusted basis for the car (what you paid for it) was $19,000. Your casualty loss is the decrease in value of $6,000 ($8,000 – $2,000), which is less than the car's adjusted basis of $19,000.

Example

You bought a painting several years ago for $2,500 that was valued at $25,000 before it was stolen (you did not have any insurance). Your loss is limited to your adjusted basis of $2,500, which is lower than the loss in value of $25,000.

Conditions

To deduct a loss relating to your personal property, such as your home or car, you must meet all four of these conditions:

1. The loss must result from a casualty event or theft.
2. You must have proof of the casualty loss or theft.
3. You must reduce your loss by any insurance or other reimbursements.
4. The amount of your loss must exceed certain limits if the loss is to personal items (there are no such limits for business losses).

CASUALTY EVENT. A casualty is a sudden, unexpected, or unusual event, such as an earthquake, explosion, fire, flood, hurricane, storm, or tornado. Generally, deciding whether an event qualifies as a casualty is not too difficult. But when damage or loss results from something that is progressive in nature, you can't claim a deduction because it is not a casualty.

Example

If the pipes in your house burst because of freezing and the water damages your carpeting, you have suffered a casualty loss. But if the pipes leak because of corrosion over time, the resulting water damage to your carpeting is not due to a casualty and you can't deduct the loss.

THEFT EVENT. For tax purposes, a theft includes any unlawful taking of your money or property. Thefts include burglary, embezzlement, larceny, and robbery.

If you lose money through extortion, kidnapping, threats, and blackmail, these are considered thefts for tax purposes if you meet both of the following conditions:

1. The taking is illegal under local law.
2. It is done with criminal intent.

PROOF OF YOUR CASUALTY LOSS OR THEFT. You must show all four of these conditions for a casualty loss:

1. The type of casualty, such as hurricane damage to your home.
2. The date of the casualty.

3. The connection between the casualty and your loss (that is, that your loss is the direct result of the casualty event).
4. That you are the owner of the property. If you lease property, you cannot claim a casualty loss; this right belongs only to the owner *unless* you are contractually obligated to return the property in the same condition (in effect, you bear the risk of loss).

For a theft, you must show all three of these conditions:

1. When you discovered that your property was missing.
2. That your property was stolen through a robbery, embezzlement, or otherwise.
3. That you are the owner of the property.

INSURANCE REIMBURSEMENTS. If you carry proper insurance coverage, you may have little or no loss for tax purposes. You cannot create a tax loss by *not* submitting an insurance claim to which you are entitled. If you do not submit a claim for a covered loss, you cannot claim a casualty loss deduction, even for the portion of the loss not covered by insurance.

Example

You have insured an item for $10,000 for which you paid $12,000; it is now worth $15,000. If the item is totally destroyed in a casualty and you do not submit an insurance claim because you do not want the premiums increased on your other property or for any other reason, you cannot deduct any loss. You cannot even deduct the $2,000 that you would have been entitled to had you made the claim and received the full coverage.

What if you have made a claim but have not received any reimbursement from the insurance company by the end of the year? File your return using an estimate of what you expect for reimbursement.

If you receive more in a later year than you had estimated, report the additional insurance recovery as "Other income" on your return for that later year (do not file an amended return for the year of the casualty event) to the extent you received a tax benefit from the deduction you should not have claimed. (Whether you realized any tax benefit is a difficult determination for which you may need to consult a tax expert.)

Example

In 2006, you suffer a casualty and figure your loss deduction based on the assumption you will receive $10,000 from the insurance company. In 2007, you receive a check from the insurance company for $12,000. On your 2007 return, report $2,000 as "Other income."

If you later receive *less* than you had estimated, you need to file an amended return to increase your loss deduction.

$100 LIMIT. You must reduce each loss from a personal casualty or theft event by $100 (business losses are not subject to this limitation). The dollar reduction applies per event (not per item lost or damaged in the event). Thus, you figure your loss separately for each item but then apply only one $100 reduction per event.

Example

On June 1, 2006, you are robbed of $1,000 cash plus jewelry you just purchased for $8,000 (assume your loss is not covered by insurance). Your loss for tax purposes is $8,900 ($1,000 + $8,000 – $100).

If you are unfortunate enough to suffer two such losses in the same year, you must reduce your loss for each event by $100 (effectively, your total losses are reduced by $200).

TEN PERCENT OF AGI LIMIT. You can deduct personal casualty and theft losses only to the extent that the total of all such losses for the year exceeds 10 percent of your adjusted gross income (business losses are not subject to this limitation).

Example

You determine that the unreimbursed damage to your home from a tornado is $8,400 (after reducing your loss by the $100 limit). If your adjusted gross income for the year is $75,000, you can deduct $900 ($8,400 – 10% of $75,000). If your adjusted gross income is $84,000 or more, you cannot claim any casualty loss deduction.

Losses that cannot be claimed because of the 10 percent limit are lost forever; you cannot carry forward the unused amount.

Planning Tips

How do you determine the decrease in value? There are a few alternatives:

- Obtain an appraisal. Use a qualified appraiser to determine the value of the property before and after the casualty (the tax treatment of appraisal fees is discussed later in this chapter).
- Use the cost of repairs or restoration as the measure of loss. You can rely on this cost if the repairs are necessary to bring the property back to its precasualty condition, the amount spent is not excessive, and the value of the property after the repairs is not more than it was before the casualty.
- If the loss involves your car, you can use various online valuation services to determine the value of your car, including Hemmings (www.hemmings.com), Kelley Blue Book (www.kbb.com), and NADA Appraisal Guides (www.nadaguides.com).

If you are married and one spouse suffers a casualty loss (for example, an expensive uninsured piece of jewelry is stolen), it may be advisable to file separate returns. This is so where the spouse with the lower AGI suffers the loss. The lower AGI may entitle the spouse to a deduction that would otherwise be blocked because of the couple's combined AGI. Of course, other factors must be taken into account when filing separate returns, such as eligibility to claim other tax benefits that require filing a joint return.

Review your insurance coverage carefully to understand what it does and does not cover. You may be able to expand the coverage under your existing policy. Or you may need to obtain other coverage (for example, flood insurance if you are located within a flood zone). In some cases, you may not be able to obtain coverage because it is just not sold or the premiums are prohibitive. For example, even though federal legislation has provided underwriting guarantees to carriers for claims due to terrorist attacks, many major carriers are simply not covering such events.

Pitfalls

Not all losses related to a casualty are deductible. You cannot deduct your personal living expenses in temporary housing when a casualty event forces you out of your home. You cannot deduct cleanup costs from the casualty.

Your deduction is limited to your economic loss from the casualty or theft. You cannot recoup anything related to sentimental value.

Example

Your wedding album is ruined during a fire in your home. The pictures cost a few hundred dollars, which is the limit of your tax loss, even though their value to you may have been priceless.

Where to Claim the Deduction

You must file Form 4684, Casualties and Thefts, to report the loss and figure the amount of the deduction. The deduction is then entered on Schedule A of Form 1040.

You cannot claim a deduction for casualty or theft losses if you file Form 1040A or 1040EZ.

Disaster Losses

Disaster losses are losses to property within areas designed as disaster areas qualifying for federal disaster assistance. From a tax perspective, disaster losses are a type of casualty loss—the way in which you figure the loss is the same but the year in which it can be claimed may be different.

Benefit

If you suffer property damage or loss because of a disaster—a storm, wildfire, earthquake, or other event declared by the president to be eligible for federal disaster relief—you can claim a disaster loss. A disaster loss is a type of casualty loss with this difference: You can deduct it in either the year of the loss or the prior year. Having the option of claiming the deduction for the prior year may give you an immediate infusion of cash (a tax refund) to use to rebuild from the disaster.

Like ordinary casualty losses, there is no dollar limit on the amount you can claim as a disaster loss. And your reduction for a disaster loss is not subject to the overall reduction of itemized deductions for high-income taxpayers (explained in the introduction).

Whether or not you qualify for a disaster loss deduction, you may be able to exclude from income certain disaster relief payments you receive as a result of a disaster (discussed later in this chapter).

Conditions

In addition to meeting *all* of the conditions for claiming a casualty loss deduction (discussed earlier in this chapter), there are two additional conditions:

1. The loss must occur within a federally designated disaster area.
2. You must act within set time limits if you want to claim the loss on the return for the prior year.

DISASTER AREAS. The loss must result in an area designated by the president as qualifying for federal disaster relief. Generally, you will know that the designation has been given and probably already have had contact with the Federal Emergency Management Agency (FEMA). If you are unsure, you can check on designations at www.fema.gov. The IRS also publishes an annual list of federal disaster areas (for example, in 2005 there were dozens of designated disasters nationwide for storms, flooding, earthquakes, and fires).

TIME LIMITS. You can claim the loss on the return for the year of the disaster, which gives you plenty of time to amass the information needed to establish your loss when completing your return.

But if you want to claim the loss on a return for the prior year, you must act no later than one of the following dates:

- The due date (without extensions) for filing your return for the tax year in which the disaster actually occurred.
- The due date (with extensions) for filing the return for the preceding year.

Example

In 2006, you have a disaster loss that you want to claim on a 2005 return. You usually have until April 16, 2007, to file an amended return for 2006 to report the disaster that took place in 2006.

You have 90 days in which to change your mind and revoke your choice by returning to the IRS any refund or credit you received. If you revoke your choice before receiving a refund, you must return the refund within 30 days after receiving it in order for the revocation to be effective.

Planning Tips

Which year should you claim the loss—the year of the disaster or the prior year? Generally, choose the year in which you have a lower adjusted gross income threshold for figuring your loss.

If your home and its contents are damaged or destroyed in a disaster, figure the loss separately for the home and for the furnishings.

If you are living in a federal disaster area, you may be entitled to certain tax breaks, even if you don't qualify to claim a disaster loss (you might be fully compensated by insurance or might not have had any loss). For example, you may be subject to a one-year postponement of tax deadlines, including the due date for filing returns and making IRA contributions. The IRS may also abate the interest and penalties on underpayment of income tax for the length of any postponement of tax deadlines.

Pitfall

Just because you suffer property damage during a disaster does not automatically mean you have a tax loss. You can even have a tax *gain* as a result of a disaster (for example, where insurance or other recoveries exceed your basis in the property). You need to work through the numbers to determine whether and to what extent you have a tax loss.

Where to Claim the Deduction

You must file Form 4684, Casualties and Thefts, to report the disaster loss and figure the amount of the deduction. The deduction is then entered on Schedule A of Form 1040.

You cannot claim a deduction for disaster losses if you file Form 1040A or 1040EZ.

If you are claiming a disaster loss for the prior year for which you have not yet filed a return (for example, in January 2007 you have a casualty loss that you report on your 2006 return to be filed in April 2007), write at the top of the return "DISASTER LOSS." If you are claiming a disaster loss for the prior year for which you have already filed a return, you must file an amended return, Form 1040X. At the top of the return write "DISASTER LOSS."

Special Tax Breaks for Hurricane Victims

Hundreds of thousands of individuals suffered through Hurricanes Katrina, Rita, and Wilma, many losing homes and personal possessions. If you lost property in one of these catastrophic events, you may be eligible for special tax breaks. The usual limitations on casualty losses discussed earlier in this chapter do not apply to losses arising from Hurricanes Katrina, Rita, and Wilma. This means that the $100 floor and the 10 percent of AGI limit are waived for these losses. More specifically, these limitations to not apply for casualty losses incurred in:

- Hurricane Katrina disaster area after August 24, 2005.
- Hurricane Rita disaster area after September 22, 2005.
- Hurricane Wilma disaster area after October 22, 2005.

If you have been displaced from your home and received housing through your employer or from an unrelated person, you are not taxed on this benefit. Your employer and the unrelated person who took you in may be eligible for a tax break.

Also, you may not have to report any income from the cancellation of indebtedness (explained earlier in this chapter).

Disaster Relief Payments

When disaster strikes, the federal government may provide needed assistance. The Federal Emergency Management Agency (FEMA) steps in to provide grants and other assistance to affected individuals and businesses. (For more information about disaster assistance, check www.fema.gov.) To avoid adding insult to injury, certain government assistance can be received tax free.

Benefit

You are not taxed on disaster relief payments you receive from federal agencies or charitable organizations to cover personal expenses. There is no dollar limit on the amount you can exclude from income. Your exclusion does not depend on your income or need.

Conditions

Only "qualified disaster relief payments" are excludable. These include payments, regardless of the source, for the following reasonable and necessary expenses:

- Personal, family, living, or funeral expenses incurred as a result of a presidentially declared disaster.
- Expenses incurred for the repair or rehabilitation of a personal residence due to a presidentially declared disaster (whether you own the home or rent it as a tenant).
- Expenses incurred for the repair or replacement of the contents of a personal residence due to a presidentially declared disaster.

Grants under the Disaster Relief and Emergency Assistance Act are excludable from income, but you cannot deduct a disaster loss to the extent you are reimbursed for it by the grants. Cancellation of all or part of a federal disaster loan is also considered reimbursement for a loss (it reduces your casualty loss deduction).

Disaster relief mitigation payments are also excludable from income. These are payments made under the Robert T. Stafford Disaster Relief and Emergency Assistance Act or the National Flood Insurance Act for hazard mitigation of your property.

Planning Tip

If you are the victim of a disaster, be sure to check with your local authorities as well as with FEMA to see whether there are any grants or relief payments you may be entitled to.

Pitfall

Disaster relief payments for business-related expenses, lost wages, or unemployment compensation may not be excluded from income and are fully taxable.

Where to Claim the Benefit

Since qualified disaster relief payments are not taxable, you do not have to report them on your return.

Damages

An average of 20 million lawsuits are filed in the United States each year to redress wrongs, such as medical malpractice claims and breach of contract. The tax law allows only certain types of damages to receive favorable tax treatment.

Benefit

If you receive compensatory damages for personal *physical* injury, you can exclude your recovery. For example, if you recover for a medical malpractice incident that affected your body, the damages are tax free. There is no dollar limit on the amount you can exclude from income.

There is a special exclusion for persons who were persecuted by the Nazis. They can exclude *all* amounts received as restitution payments for their ordeal. The exclusion applies to:

- Heirs or estates of such persons who suffered on the basis of their race, religion, physical or mental disability, or sexual orientation.
- Restitution payments for assets that were lost or stolen before or during World War II.
- Life insurance issued by European insurance companies immediately before and during the war.
- Interest earned on escrow accounts and funds established in settlement of Holocaust victim claims.

Damages arising out of the purchase of property are treated as a recovery for injury or damage to a capital asset. As such, damages are tax free to the extent of your basis in the property.

Example

You buy land for $100,000. After the sale you learn it is contaminated and sue the seller, who settles with you for $25,000. You are not taxed on these damages. They serve to reduce your basis in the land to $75,000.

If you receive damages for any other reason, including punitive damages for physical injury or any type of damages for personal injury that is not physical, the damages are fully taxable. Nonphysical personal injuries for which damages are taxable include injury to reputation, discrimination, and back pay.

Conditions

To claim the exclusion for damages, the award must relate to some physical injury or sickness. Damages for emotional distress are excludable only if they are attributable to a physical injury or sickness and compensate you for related medical expenses.

The damages must be compensatory, meaning that they aim to make you whole from your loss (covering medical expenses, etc.). Punitive damages are not tax free, even if they relate to physical injuries.

The damages award can be a negotiated settlement or an award fixed by a court.

Planning Tip

If an action involved both physical and nonphysical injury aspects, be sure that the complaint allocates the degree of injury to each part.

Example

Suppose you are injured in a car accident in a state that does not have a no-fault law. You sue for $75,000 for personal injuries and $25,000 for damage to your car. You settle with the other party for $40,000. Of this amount, three-quarters or $30,000 relates to personal injuries and is tax free; $10,000 relates to property damage and is taxable.

Pitfalls

If you receive interest on an award for physical damages, you are taxed on the interest even though the award itself is tax free.

If you obtain a recovery under a contingent fee agreement with your attorney, you must include the *entire* award in income if such awards are taxable (e.g., defamation actions). How you treat the attorney's fees depends on the nature of the action (see Chapter 16).

Where to Claim the Benefit

Since damages for personal physical injury are excludable from your income, you do not have to report them on your return.

If you receive damages for personal injuries that are not physical (for example, for libel), they are taxable and must be reported as "Other income" on Form 1040. You cannot file Form 1040A or 1040EZ if you have taxable damages.

Disability Coverage

Between the ages of 35 and 65, three out of 10 working people become disabled for 90 days or longer; one in five people becomes disabled for five years or longer before age 65. To protect against this possibility, it is advisable to carry disability insurance. The tax law does not treat disability coverage in the same way as medical insurance; special rules apply that *may* allow a deduction for premiums.

Benefit

Disability benefits you receive under a policy on which you paid the premiums are tax free. There is no dollar limit on the amount of disability benefits you can exclude from income. If your employer paid the premiums on a policy that you are now collecting on, the benefits are taxable to you. If you and your employer shared the cost of premiums, you must allocate the benefits accordingly; you can exclude only the portion that relates to *your* payments.

Disability coverage under Social Security is treated for tax purposes in the same way as Social Security retirement benefits—they may be wholly excludable or included in income in the amount of 50 percent or 85 percent of benefits, depending on your income. Generally, the payment of disability benefits under Social Security ends once you attain your full retirement age (for example, 65 years and six months for someone born in 1940). At that time you start receiving Social Security retirement benefits.

Condition

Tax-free treatment applies to benefits paid under a policy for which you paid the premiums with after-tax dollars. Tax-free treatment also applies to these types of disability payments:

- Disability pensions from the Department of Veterans Affairs.
- Pensions for combat-related injuries or injuries from a terrorist attack.
- Disability pensions for anyone who has injuries resulting from terrorist attacks after September 10, 2001.

Planning Tips

If your employer gives you the choice between accepting employer-paid disability coverage or paying for such coverage yourself, you may prefer to pay for it so that benefits will be tax free if you become disabled. While your employer's payment of disability insurance premiums may be tax free to you, the price for this benefit is taxability of any disability payments you later receive.

If you are totally and permanently disabled and receive little or no Social Security benefits, you may be eligible for a tax credit called the credit for the elderly and disabled.

Pitfall

If you retire on disability and receive a lump-sum payment for accrued annual leave, you cannot exclude this payment; it is fully taxable as additional compensation.

Where to Claim the Benefit

If you are entitled to exclude disability payments you receive, you do not have to report them on your return. In this event, it does not matter whether you file Form 1040, 1040A, or 1040EZ.

Taxable disability payments received before age 65 are reported on your return as compensation (use the same line you would for reporting salary, wages, etc.).

To determine the portion of Social Security disability payments that are excludable from income, complete the worksheet for Social Security benefits in the instructions to Form 1040. Ignore the words "Retirement Benefits" on this worksheet and enter your disability benefits in substitution. You must file Form 1040 to report the taxable portion, if any, of your disability payments from Social Security (report Social Security disability payments on the line in the "Income" section of Form 1040 used for Social Security benefits).

Accelerated Death Benefits

A life insurance policy may provide more than just death benefits. In some cases it can be used to provide funds during the insured's lifetime. The tax law treats the proceeds during life, called accelerated death benefits, the same as postdeath payments (that is, tax free) if certain conditions are met.

Benefit

Accelerated death benefits are an insurance company's payment of some or all of the death benefits under a life insurance policy on account of terminal or chronic illness of the insured. Viatical settlements involve the selling of a cash-value life insurance policy to a company in the business of buying such policies. Accelerated death benefits and viatical settlement proceeds received by a terminally ill individual are tax free.

Such payments to a person who is chronically ill can be excluded in full to the extent used to pay long-term care costs; per diem payments in excess of care costs are excludable only up to a set dollar limit per day ($250 in 2006).

Conditions

Tax-free treatment of accelerated death benefits and viatical settlement proceeds apply for someone who is terminally ill. This means you have a condition or illness that is expected to result in death within 24 months of certification by a physician. The exclusion applies without regard to the use of the benefits or proceeds.

To qualify for favorable treatment as a chronically ill individual, you must be certified by a licensed health-care practitioner that, within the preceding 12 months, you are unable to perform for a period of at least 90 days two or more of the following activities:

- Eating.
- Toileting.
- Bathing.
- Dressing.
- Continence.
- Transferring (such as getting in and out of bed).

A person also qualifies as chronically ill if certified as requiring substantial supervision for one's own health and safety because of cognitive impairment (for example, the person has Alzheimer's disease).

For a chronically ill individual, excludable amounts must be used to pay long-term care expenses. These are necessary diagnostic, preventive, therapeutic, curing, treating, mitigation, and rehabilitative services, as well as personal care services. The services must be provided under a plan of care prescribed by a licensed health-care practitioner (which includes a doctor, registered nurse, or licensed social worker).

Planning Tip

When shopping for life insurance, inquire about accelerated death benefit options under the policy. You want to have as many options as possible, even if you never need to use them.

Pitfall

Generally, it is not advisable for someone who is terminally or chronically ill to use life insurance proceeds to cover lifetime care expenses. The purpose for which the policy was originally purchased, such as the care of surviving family members or the payment of funeral expenses and estate taxes, is frustrated by such use. Thus, using a life insurance policy for lifetime needs is usually a last resort for paying care expenses.

Where to Claim the Benefit

If accelerated death benefits or viatical settlement proceeds are excludable, they are not reported on the return.

Legal Fees

In most cases there is no requirement that a lawyer be used to bring a lawsuit or conduct other types of business. But it is usually advisable to use an expert to protect your rights. Of course, this assistance may not come cheaply. Whether you can deduct legal fees depends on the type of activities involved.

Legal fees are discussed in Chapter 16.

Appraisal Fees

When property is damaged or destroyed, how do you know the true extent of the economic loss? Typically you must rely on experts who can assess your unique situation. Experts, called appraisers, generally charge for their services. Fortunately, the tax law allows you to deduct appraisal fees if certain conditions are met.

Benefit

If you pay fees to an appraiser in order to determine the amount of a casualty, disaster, or theft loss, you may deduct the appraisal fees as a miscellaneous itemized deduction. You do *not* include appraisal fees as part of the loss.

The deduction is part of miscellaneous itemized expenses, which are deductible only to the extent the total exceeds 2 percent of your adjusted gross income. There is no dollar limit on the deduction for appraisal fees.

Conditions

There are no specific conditions to meet in order to deduct your appraisal fees. Simply retain proof of this cost (keep it with copies of your tax return).

Planning Tip

Find the right appraiser for the item for which you are claiming a loss. For example, if your home is damaged by a storm, use a qualified real estate appraiser to assist in determining your loss.

In general, to find a qualified appraiser, see:

- American Society of Appraisers (www.appraisers.org).
- Foundation of Real Estate Appraisers (www.frea.com).
- International Society of Appraisers (www.isa-appraisers.org).

Pitfall

If your miscellaneous itemized deductions do not exceed 2 percent of your adjusted gross income, you do not receive any benefit from the write-off of appraisal fees. In effect, the deduction is lost forever.

Where to Claim the Deduction

You claim the deduction for appraisal fees as a miscellaneous itemized deduction on Schedule A of Form 1040.

You cannot claim the deduction if you file Form 1040A or 1040EZ.

CHAPTER 14

Your Job

Your job not only is what occupies the majority of your time during the greater part of each week and, hopefully, provides satisfaction; it also gives you a paycheck and perhaps other benefits. While your earnings are taxable in most cases, some of the fringe benefits may be tax free.

In order to earn that paycheck, you may have to expend your own dollars on various things. Fortunately, you may be able to deduct your out-of-pocket job-related costs.

This chapter explains:

- Job-hunting expenses
- Dues to unions and professional associations
- Work clothes and uniforms
- Subscriptions to professional journals and newsletters
- Work tools and equipment
- Miscellaneous job-related expenses
- Home office deduction
- Prizes and awards
- Performing artists

- State and local government officials paid on a fee basis
- Repayment of supplemental unemployment benefits
- Jury duty pay turned over to your employer
- Impairment-related expenses
- Military benefits
- Fringe benefits
- Personal reemployment accounts (PRAs)
- Income earned abroad

Job-related moving expenses are discussed in Chapter 4. Employment-related travel and entertainment expenses are explained in Chapter 9.

For more information, see IRS Publication 3, *Armed Forces' Tax Guide*; IRS Publication 535, *Business Expenses*; and IRS Publication 587, *Business Use of Your Home*.

Job-Hunting Expenses

In today's tight job market, it may take considerable time and effort to land a new position. The costs incurred in this endeavor may be deductible if certain conditions are met.

Benefit

The cost of searching for a new job in your same line of work is deductible as a miscellaneous itemized deduction. There is no dollar limit on the amount of this deduction. You can claim the deduction whether or not a new job is found.

Miscellaneous itemized deductions can be claimed only to the extent they exceed 2 percent of your adjusted gross income (the 2 percent of AGI floor).

If your employer or former employer pays for certain job placement costs, you are not taxed on this benefit. For example, if you are laid off and your employer provides outplacement services (including office space and resume preparation), this benefit is tax free.

Condition

The only condition for claiming this deduction is that your search relate to the same line of work you are currently or most recently in. For example, if you are an out-of-work programmer seeking a job as a programmer, this is considered to be in the same line of work. But if you are looking for a job in teaching, something you did 10 years ago, this is a new line of work.

If you are just out of college seeking your first full-time job in your field, you cannot deduct job-hunting expenses. If you are seeking work in a new line of business, you cannot deduct job-hunting expenses. If you are out of work for a long time, the IRS may question whether your job-hunting expenses are deductible.

Example

You leave your job when your first child is born, returning to the workforce when she enters kindergarten. Your job-hunting expenses in this case would probably *not* be deductible because of the five-year period since your last job, even if you are searching for employment in the same line of work that you left.

EXAMPLES OF JOB-HUNTING EXPENSES

- Employment agency fees.
- Postage and supplies.
- Resumes.
- Telephone costs.
- Travel costs (for example, an out-of-town trip to interview for a job).

Planning Tip

Keep track of your job-hunting costs to support the amount of the deduction you claim.

Pitfalls

You cannot deduct job-hunting expenses for your first job. This is so even if you do find employment. The reason: Since you are not yet an employee, job-hunting expenses cannot be work-related as yet.

You cannot deduct job-hunting expenses that relate to a new line of work. For example, you are a teacher who attends law school in the evening. You cannot deduct job-hunting expenses to find a job as an attorney.

If you pay an employment agency fee to obtain a job and deduct this amount in the year of payment only to be reimbursed by your new employer in the following year, you must report the reimbursement as income to the extent that the deduction provided you with a tax benefit. Do not file an amended return for the year in which you claimed the deduction to back the deduction up.

Where to Claim the Deduction

If this is your only unreimbursed employee business expense, the deduction for job-hunting expenses is included with miscellaneous itemized deductions and entered directly on Schedule A of Form 1040. If you have other employee business expenses, you must complete Form 2106, Employee Business Expenses, or Form 2106-EZ, Unreimbursed Employee Business Expenses, to report your employee business expenses; the total amount is then entered on Schedule A of Form 1040.

You cannot deduct job-hunting expenses if you file Form 1040A or 1040EZ.

Dues to Unions and Professional Associations

According to the U.S. Department of Labor, Bureau of Labor Statistics, there were about 15.7 million union members nationwide in 2005. In addition, millions of professionals belong to trade or professional associations. The cost of this membership generally is deductible.

Benefit

Dues you pay to unions or professional associations are deductible. The dues are treated as a miscellaneous itemized deduction. Miscellaneous itemized expenses are deductible only to the extent they exceed 2 percent of adjusted gross income (the 2 percent of AGI floor).

There is no dollar limit on the amount of dues you can deduct each year.

Condition

Dues that you pay to a union or a professional association are deductible if they are ordinary and necessary business expenses (helpful to your job).

EXAMPLES OF DEDUCTIBLE PAYMENTS TO UNIONS

- Dues.
- Initiation fees.
- Mandatory payments for unemployment benefits (required as a condition for remaining in the union).
- Monthly service charges to nonunion members.

EXAMPLES OF DEDUCTIBLE PAYMENTS TO PROFESSIONAL ASSOCIATIONS

- Chamber of commerce if it is conducted to advance the business interests of its membership.
- Community booster club dues conducted to attract tourists and settlers to your locality.

- Professional societies if you are a salaried accountant, attorney, doctor, teacher, or other professional.
- Stock exchange if you are a securities dealer.
- Trade association dues if the association is conducted to further the business interests of its membership.

Planning Tip

Check to see what benefits you may be entitled to because of membership in a union or trade or professional association. The savings you can realize on member benefits may well exceed the cost of dues.

Pitfall

Just because funds are collected by your union or payments relate to your union does not automatically mean they are deductible. You may not deduct the following types of payments:

- Assessments for a construction fund to build union recreation facilities.
- Campaign costs for running for union office.
- Mandatory contributions to a union pension fund applied toward the purchase of an annuity (you are treated as having purchased the annuity and cannot deduct your cost).
- Voluntary payments to a union unemployment benefit or strike fund.

Where to Claim the Deduction

If this is your only unreimbursed employee business expense, the deduction for dues to unions and professional associations is included with miscellaneous itemized deductions and entered directly on Schedule A of Form 1040. If you have other employee business expenses, you must complete Form 2106, Employee Business Expenses, or Form 2106-EZ, Unreimbursed Employee Business Expenses, to report your employee business expenses; the total amount is then entered on Schedule A of Form 1040.

You cannot deduct dues to unions and professional associations if you file Form 1040A or 1040EZ.

Work Clothes and Uniforms

Everyone wants to look his best on the job. But only certain types of workers can deduct the cost of work clothes, provided certain conditions are met.

Benefit

The costs of work clothes and uniforms are deductible. They are treated as a miscellaneous itemized deduction. Miscellaneous itemized expenses are deductible only to the extent they exceed 2 percent of adjusted gross income (the 2 percent of AGI floor).

There is no dollar limit on the amount you can deduct for work clothes and uniforms.

If your employer provides you with a clothing allowance, you can exclude this amount from your income as long as you are required to substantiate your purchases to your employer (for example, provide your employer with receipts showing how you spent the allowance). If you spend more than the substantiated amounts, you can treat the excess costs as a deductible expense, provided you satisfy the following conditions.

Conditions

There are two conditions for deducting the cost of work clothes and uniforms; you must satisfy both conditions:

1. You are required to use such wear to keep your job. Generally, these include items necessary to keep you safe and enable you to perform your job, such as protective clothing, steel-tip shoes, eye goggles, and protective gloves.
2. The clothing is not suitable for ordinary street wear. The fact that your job requires you to wear expensive clothing is not a justification for deducting your costs; if the items can be worn off the job, the costs are not deductible. Similarly, those involved in many types of sports cannot deduct warm-up clothing and similar clothing that is suitable for wear off the job.

EXAMPLES OF PROFESSIONALS HAVING DEDUCTIBLE WORK CLOTHES AND UNIFORMS

- Airline pilot.
- Bakery salesperson (uniform with company label).
- Baseball player.
- Bus driver.
- Cement finisher (gloves, overshoes, and rubber boots).
- Civilian faculty member of a military school.
- Commercial fisherman (protective clothing such as oilskins, gloves, and rubber boots).
- Dairy worker (rubber boots, white shirts, trousers, and cap for inside use).

- Dance instructor (jazz shoes).
- Doctor (scrubs).
- Electrical worker (coveralls and protective gear).
- Entertainer (theatrical clothing used solely for performances).
- Factory foreman (white coat with company name and "foreman" designation).
- Factory worker (safety shoes).
- Firefighter.
- Hospital attendant (clothes used only on the job with patients having contagious diseases).
- Jockey.
- Letter carrier.
- Meat cutter (special white shoes).
- Musician (formal wear).
- Paint machine operator (high-top shoes and long leather gloves).
- Plumber (special shoes and gloves).
- Police officer.
- Railroad conductor.
- Reservists (uniform costs in excess of military allowances for clothing prohibited from wearing off duty).
- Roughneck for oil drilling company (protective clothing).

Planning Tip

In addition to a deduction for clothes and uniforms, you can also write off costs of cleaning, laundering, and alterations for such items.

EXAMPLES OF DEDUCTIBLE CLEANING EXPENSES

- Clothing in need of daily laundering.
- Clothing viewed as a hazard if not freshly pressed (baggy clothing could become caught in machinery).
- Meat cutters required to wear clean work clothes.
- Shoeshines for military-like shoes worn by pilots only with uniforms.

Pitfall

The fact that your union or your position requires you to wear certain items does *not* make their costs deductible. For example, painters in the painters' union may be required to wear white bib overalls, but this does not make the cost of the overalls deductible.

Where to Claim the Deduction

If this is your only unreimbursed employee business expense, the deduction for work clothes and uniforms is included with miscellaneous itemized deductions and entered directly on Schedule A of Form 1040. If you have other employee business expenses, you must complete Form 2106, Employee Business Expenses, or Form 2106-EZ, Unreimbursed Employee Business Expenses, to report your employee business expenses; the total amount is then entered on Schedule A of Form 1040.

You cannot deduct expenses for work clothes and uniforms if you file Form 1040A or 1040EZ.

Subscriptions to Professional Journals and Newsletters

It has been estimated that information in the world now doubles every two years. How can you keep up with developments affecting your job or profession? Journals, newsletters, magazines, and online subscription sites help to provide needed information for your work, the cost of which may be deductible.

Benefit

The cost of subscriptions to professional journals and newsletters are deductible. This applies to print as well as online versions. The cost is treated as a miscellaneous itemized deduction. Miscellaneous itemized expenses are deductible only to the extent they exceed 2 percent of adjusted gross income (the 2 percent of AGI floor).

There is no dollar limit on the amount you can deduct for subscriptions to professional journals and newsletters.

Conditions

The subscriptions must be an ordinary and necessary expense of your job or profession. For example, an accountant who subscribes to tax newsletters, such as *J.K. Lasser's Monthly Tax Letter*, can treat the cost as a deductible job expense.

Planning Tip

You may be able to save on subscription costs by opting for online or fax versions of newspapers and newsletters instead of receiving them by mail.

Pitfall

If you pay for multiyear subscriptions, under a so-called 12-month rule you cannot deduct subscription costs that cover a period of more than 12 months or the 12-month period ends on or before the last day of the income year following the year in which the payment was incurred.

Example

In July 2006, you take out a one-year subscription to a trade journal. Because the period does not exceed 12 months, you can deduct the entire payment in the year you make it. But if you take out a three-year subscription, you can deduct only six months for the three-year subscription in 2006, 12 months in 2007, 12 months in 2008, and six months in 2009.

Where to Claim the Deduction

If this is your only unreimbursed employee business expense, the deduction for professional journals and newsletters is included with miscellaneous itemized deductions and entered directly on Schedule A of Form 1040. If you have other employee business expenses, you must complete Form 2106, Employee Business Expenses, or Form 2106EZ, Unreimbursed Employee Business Expenses, to report your employee business expenses; the total amount is then entered on Schedule A of Form 1040.

You cannot deduct expenses for professional journals and newsletters if you file Form 1040A or 1040EZ.

Work Tools and Equipment

Tools of the trade don't always come with the job. Sometimes it's up to you to provide them. When you do, the tax law lets you write off their cost under certain conditions.

Benefit

The cost of work tools is deductible. The cost is treated as a miscellaneous itemized deduction. Miscellaneous itemized expenses are deductible only to the extent they exceed 2 percent of adjusted gross income (the 2 percent of AGI floor).

There is no dollar limit on the amount you can deduct for work tools. The question you must decide is *when* to claim the write-offs: the year of the purchase or over a set number of years based on the recovery period of the tools. The answer depends on the useful life of the tools. If a tool has a useful life of no more than one year, you can simply deduct its cost in full in the year of purchase. But if it has a longer useful life, you must depreciate its cost or elect first-year expensing.

Conditions

You must show that the tools or equipment are an ordinary and necessary expense of your job. This means that you need the tools or equipment to do your job properly and your employer does not provide such items. Merely obtaining a letter from your employer stating that the item is required does not, by itself, prove your necessity; include the *reason* why it is required (e.g., safety).

Example

You are a salesperson and purchase a laptop to make sales presentations at customer locations. You cannot make sales presentations without the computer and your employer does not provide you with a laptop. In this instance, the laptop may be deductible. But if the laptop is merely helpful (e.g., you keep notes for yourself), a deduction is not allowed, even though it is used on the job.

EXAMPLES OF DEDUCTIBLE WORK TOOLS AND EQUIPMENT

Camera, watch, and gun of a federal investigator.

Cellular phones.

Computers and laptops.

Personal digital assistants (PDAs) and handheld PCs, such as the PalmPilot or BlackBerry.

Tools of your trade (e.g., for plumbing or electrical work, painting and plastering, or woodworking).

Planning Tip

Ask whether your employer can supply you with the necessary tools for your job, eliminating your need to make the purchase, since the 2 percent of AGI floor may bar you from claiming any deduction if you make the purchase.

Pitfall

If you use the tools or equipment for personal purpose in addition to job-related use, only the portion of the cost related to the job is deductible. For example, if you use a computer for work (and show it is required for you to do your job) but also use it on your off time, allocate the cost of the computer between job and personal use.

Where to Claim the Deduction

If this is your only unreimbursed employee business expense and the work tools have a useful life of no more than one year, the deduction for work tools is included with miscellaneous itemized deductions and entered directly on Schedule A of Form 1040. If you have other employee business expenses, you must complete Form 2106, Employee Business Expenses, or Form 2106-EZ, Unreimbursed Employee Business Expenses, to report your employee business expenses; the total amount is then entered on Schedule A of Form 1040. If tools have a useful life of more than one year, you must file Form 4562, Amortization and Depreciation, to figure depreciation on the tools. Depreciation is explained in greater detail in IRS Publication 946, *How to Depreciate Property.*

You cannot deduct expenses for work tools and equipment if you file Form 1040A or 1040EZ.

Miscellaneous Job-Related Expenses

Not every expense related to a job fits neatly into a set category. But just because you can't find a specific rule for the expense doesn't mean you can't claim a deduction for it. Various types of miscellaneous job-related expenses can be deductible if certain conditions are met.

Benefit

Just about any type of expense related to your job that can be viewed as ordinary and necessary may be deductible. These miscellaneous job-related expenses are treated as a miscellaneous itemized deduction. Miscellaneous itemized expenses are deductible only to the extent they exceed 2 percent of adjusted gross income (the 2 percent of AGI floor).

There is no dollar limit on the amount you can deduct for miscellaneous job-related expenses.

Conditions

The expense must be an ordinary and necessary expense of your job. Generally this means that the item must be appropriate and helpful to your particular job or position.

No deduction can be claimed if the expense is really a company expense that you voluntarily make.

EXAMPLES OF DEDUCTIBLE MISCELLANEOUS EXPENSES

- Breast implants of an exotic dancer that made her the abnormal size of 56N.

- Laboratory breakage by a research scientist.
- Office decorations. In one case an office manager purchased his own furniture when the company moved to new quarters and the Tax Court allowed him to depreciate the cost of the furniture, which was appropriate and helpful to his image as a successful manager.
- Politician's expenses in excess of a government allowance for such costs as employee salaries, office rent, and supplies. The expense is allowable whether the position is full-time or part-time.
- Private airplane operating costs of a salesman whose territory, covering six states, was not near commercial airports (even though expenses were large in relation to his compensation).
- Repayment of layoff benefits upon being rehired (essentially payments required as a condition of reemployment).
- Stockbroker's repayment to his firm for a client's loss that the firm made good on due to his trading errors.

Planning Tip

If you claim a deduction that is out of the ordinary, be prepared to support your deduction not only with proof of the cost but also with reasoning on why the cost is deductible.

Pitfall

Not all seemingly ordinary and necessary job-related costs are deductible. Even though the expense may have some relation to the job, it may be primarily a nondeductible personal expense. Here is a roundup of cases in which taxpayers lost their claimed deductions:

- Campaign costs of running for union presidency.
- Currency loss on converting a U.S. paycheck into foreign currency of a government employee stationed abroad.
- Donations to political parties in order to secure a job.
- Gifts to superiors.
- Haircuts by a pilot required to keep his hair short and neat at all times. The same results apply to service personnel and to secretaries' coiffures.
- Health club membership, even if the job requires physical fitness (for example, a police officer could not deduct membership fees).
- Insurance premiums withheld from pay to cover disability insurance.
- Makeup for a television newsman.
- Pension fund assessments.

Where to Claim the Deduction

If this is your only unreimbursed employee business expense, the deduction for miscellaneous job-related expenses is included with miscellaneous itemized deductions and entered directly on Schedule A of Form 1040. If you have other employee business expenses, you must complete Form 2106, Employee Business Expenses, or Form 2106-EZ, Unreimbursed Employee Business Expenses, to report your employee business expenses; the total amount is then entered on Schedule A of Form 1040.

You cannot deduct miscellaneous job-related expenses if you file Form 1040A or 1040EZ.

Legislative Alert

Congress is considering an extension to the deduction for teachers who pay for classroom supplies. The deduction of up to $250 expired at the end of 2005.

Home Office Deduction

According to the International Telework Association and Council (ITAC), in 2003 there were about 23.5 million employees who work at least one day from home (and another 23.4 million self-employed teleworkers and the numbers continue to grow). Those who work from home may be eligible to deduct some of their housing cost as a job expense as long as they meet certain conditions.

Benefit

If you telecommute or use a portion of your home as an office for your job, you may be entitled to deduct expenses related to that portion of your home, including rent (if you are a tenant) or depreciation (if you are a homeowner), utilities, insurance, and maintenance.

The home office deduction is treated as a miscellaneous itemized deduction. Miscellaneous itemized expenses are deductible only to the extent they exceed 2 percent of adjusted gross income (the 2 percent of AGI floor).

There is no dollar limit on the amount you can write off as a home office deduction.

For a further discussion of the home office deduction, see Chapter 15.

Conditions

Employees have a unique requirement to be eligible for a home office deduction: The home office must be used for the convenience of your employer.

Convenience of the employer does not mean that your employer just supports your preference to work from home. Rather, it usually means that your employer *needs* you to work from home (for example, there is no office space at the company's location). Simply obtaining a letter from your employer stating that your home office use is for the convenience of the employer generally is not sufficient to prove your employer's convenience; the letter must explain the reason why use of a home office is for the employer's convenience (e.g., space considerations).

Planning Tip

Discuss your work arrangement thoroughly with your employer so you'll know whether you satisfy the condition for eligibility. If you do, then ask your employer for a letter stating that working from home is for the employer's convenience and add the employer's reason why (for example, there is no desk space for you at the company office).

Pitfall

You cannot claim *any* home office deduction if you lease the space to your employer. Mortgage interest, real estate taxes, and casualty losses otherwise deductible by any homeowner continue to be deductible even if you rent space to your employer; only utilities, insurance, maintenance, and other office-related costs are not deductible. You must, of course, report as income any rent you receive from your employer.

Where to Claim the Benefit

You figure your home office deduction on a worksheet contained in IRS Publication 587, *Business Use of Your Home* (you do *not* use Form 8829 for this purpose; only self-employed individuals complete that form).

If this is your only unreimbursed employee business expense, the deduction for home office expenses is included with miscellaneous itemized deductions and entered directly on Schedule A of Form 1040. If you have other employee business expenses, you must complete Form 2106, Employee Business Expenses, or Form 2106-EZ, Unreimbursed Employee Business Expenses, to report your employee business expenses; the total amount is then entered on Schedule A of Form 1040.

You cannot claim a home office deduction if you file Form 1040A or 1040EZ.

Prizes and Awards

Recognition for a job well done is always appreciated. When it is accompanied by a monetary item, it may be valued even more. Taxwise, a prize or award may be tax free under very limited circumstances.

Benefit

If you receive certain prizes or awards *other than cash*, you can exclude the amount you receive from income. These include awards of tangible personal property, such as the proverbial gold watch, given as awards for length of service or safety achievements, and your employer is permitted to deduct the awards. However, other prizes and awards are fully taxable.

Conditions

Generally, your ability to exclude employment-related prizes and awards depends on your employer's ability to deduct the payments. But you don't have to be the company's comptroller to determine this; the company will report to you the tax treatment of the award on your Form W-2.

Just to give you some idea of the extent of what you can exclude, your employer's deduction depends on whether the award is part of a qualified award plan. If yes, then up to $1,600 may be given to the same employee during the year. If the award it not part of a qualified award plan, then the annual limit per employee is $400.

Planning Tip

If you receive a valuable prize or award that is *not* tax free, your employer will automatically withhold income taxes on the payment (at the flat rate of 25 percent). If this withholding is not enough to cover your estimated tax requirements, ask your employer to withhold an additional amount.

Pitfall

If you win a sales or other contest on the job and receive a prize, such as a vacation, you can decline the award to avoid taxation on the benefit. If you accept the prize, you generally are taxed on the value of the benefit.

Where to Claim the Benefit

Prizes and awards that are tax free need not be reported on your tax return.

Performing Artists

Actors, singers, dancers, comedians, and other performing artists can deduct the same job expenses as any other worker. But the tax law provides a special rule on *how* to claim deductions.

Benefit

If you are a performing artist with income below a set amount, you can deduct your employment-related expenses as an adjustment to gross income rather than as a miscellaneous itemized deduction. This means that your employment-related expenses become fully deductible; they are not subject to the 2 percent of AGI floor (discussed earlier in this chapter).

Conditions

You must meet all of the following three conditions to treat your job-related expenses as an adjustment to gross income rather than as an itemized deduction:

1. You have two or more employers in the performing arts during the year with at least $200 of earnings from at least two of them.
2. Your expenses from acting or other services are more than 10 percent of your gross income from such work. For example, you spend $8,000 during the year on voice lessons and earn $22,000 doing voice-overs and other jobs in the performing arts. Since $8,000 is more than 10 percent of $22,000, you meet this condition.
3. Your adjusted gross income from all sources (not just performing arts) is no more than $16,000.

SPECIAL RULE FOR MARRIED INDIVIDUALS. You must file a joint return if you are married, unless you live apart from your spouse for the entire year.

If both you and your spouse work in the performing arts, you figure the two-employer requirement and the 10 percent requirement separately for each of you. Compare your personal employment-related expenses to the money you earn from performing arts jobs.

For purposes of your adjusted gross income, the $16,000 applies to your *combined* AGI.

Planning Tip

As with any other type of expense, it is vital to keep good records of your job-related outlays. Retain receipts for lessons you take. Use a diary or other record keeper to note travel expenses and other items.

Pitfall

Even one dollar of adjusted gross income over the $16,000 limit means your expenses can be deducted only as a miscellaneous itemized deduction subject to the 2 percent of AGI floor. If you anticipate AGI of about this amount, weigh carefully the after-tax cost of accepting work that puts you over the limit.

Example

You earn $15,000 from your work in acting, have expenses of $7,000, and meet the other conditions for treating your expenses as an adjustment to gross income. This means your AGI after the deduction becomes $8,000. But if you have $1,000 more of AGI, your expenses are deductible in excess of $320, so your write-off is limited to $6,680. The $1,000 of additional income nets you only $680 ($1,000 – $320 lost deduction).

Where to Claim the Benefit

You figure your deductible work-related expenses on Form 2106 (or Form 2106-EZ if eligible). Your total amount is then entered on the line for this item in the "Adjusted Gross Income" section of Form 1040.

State or Local Government Officials Paid on a Fee Basis

Not every bureaucrat is a regular employee on the government's payroll. Some government employees are paid under a contract arrangement. Those who are can write off their related employee expenses in a special way.

Benefit

If you are an employee of a state or local government and are paid in whole or in part on a fee basis, you can deduct the businesses expenses related to these services as an adjustment to gross income rather than as a miscellaneous itemized deduction.

Conditions

The only conditions for treating your business expenses as an adjustment to gross income are:

- You are an employee of a state or local government.
- You are paid in whole or in part on a fee basis.

Planning Tip

If you are a state or local government employee, ask to arrange partial compensation on a fee basis (for example, related to a specific government project) to create an above-the-line deduction for your job expenses.

Pitfall

There is no downside to treating these business expenses as an adjustment to gross income.

Where to Claim the Deduction

You figure your deductible work-related expenses on Form 2106 (or Form 2106-EZ if eligible). Your total amount is then entered on the line for adding up your adjustments to gross income in the "Adjusted Gross Income" section of Form 1040; there is no specially labeled line for this deduction. On the dotted line alongside the total adjustments to gross income write "FBO" to indicate that the deduction is for a fee basis official.

Repayment of Supplemental Unemployment Benefits

While unemployed, you may receive benefits in addition to regular state unemployment benefits. These "supplemental" benefits may have to be repaid once you obtain employment. If so, you may be able to write them off, either as a deduction or as a tax credit, if certain conditions are met.

Benefit

If you are required to repay supplemental unemployment benefits in order to qualify for trade readjustment allowances, you can claim a deduction for the repayment as an adjustment to gross income, even if you do not itemize your other deductions.

In some cases you may even be eligible for a tax credit (instead of a deduction) for your repayments.

Conditions

To claim the deduction, you must be required to repay supplemental unemployment benefits that you included in income in a prior year. The deduction is designed to wipe the slate clean; you already paid tax on the benefits when you received them and now you are entitled to a deduction to reduce your income, effectively backing out the benefits.

To claim a credit, your repayment must exceed $3,000. Then figure your credit by recomputing the tax you would have paid had you *not* received the repaid amount in the initial year, and compare the tax with what you actually paid.

Planning Tip

If you have repaid supplemental unemployment benefits in order to qualify for trade readjustment allowances, you may also be eligible for a tax credit

Example

In 2005, you received supplemental unemployment benefits and your tax bill was $3,800. In 2006, you repay $5,000. You recompute your 2005 tax, eliminating the $5,000 from income. Without this income you would have paid $2,774. Therefore your credit is $1,026 ($3,800 – $2,774).

for health insurance coverage under COBRA or state insurance programs. For details, see Chapter 2 for details on the health insurance credit for eligible recipients.

Pitfall

You cannot choose to file an amended return for the year in which the supplemental unemployment benefits were originally paid to subtract your later repayment. Your only choice in handling the repayment is to deduct it or, if eligible, claim a tax credit in the year of repayment.

Where to Claim the Benefit

If you are claiming the deduction, enter the amount of your repayment in the "Adjusted Gross Income" section of Form 1040; there is no specially labeled line for this deduction. On the dotted line alongside the total adjustments to gross income write "subpay TRA" to indicate that the deduction is for repayment of unemployment benefits due to trade readjustment allowances.

If you opt to treat repayments exceeding $3,000 as a tax credit, enter the credit as another payment in the "Payments" section of Form 1040. Write in "IRC 1341" to indicate the type of credit you are claiming.

Jury Duty Pay Turned Over to Your Employer

Jury duty is a civic duty that is hard to avoid. If you are called to serve, you are paid a nominal amount that is taxable income. But if you also receive your regular wages from your employer and must hand over your jury duty pay, you can claim a deduction for the income you don't get to keep.

Benefit

If you receive your regular pay while serving on jury duty and turn over your jury duty pay to your employer, you can claim a deduction for this action as an adjustment to gross income, even if you do not itemize your other deductions. This deduction is intended to offset your having to include the jury duty pay in income. There are no dollar limits on this deduction.

Condition

You must be required by your employer to turn over jury duty pay as a condition of receiving your regular compensation.

Planning Tip

Ask your employer whether you can keep your jury duty pay and simply receive your ordinary compensation in excess of this amount so that you reduce your FICA taxes (and your employer saves a like amount in FICA taxes).

Example

Your regular daily pay is $150. Assume you serve on a jury for five days and receive $40 per day. If your employer pays you only $110 and allows you to retain the $40, you save $15 in taxes ($40 × 5 days × 7.65% rate for Social Security and Medicare taxes).

Pitfall

Don't overlook this deduction for jury duty pay, especially if you receive it early in the year. It's easy to forget about it since payments of less than $600 are not reported to you on an information return from the government.

Where to Claim the Deduction

If you are claiming a deduction for jury duty pay turned over to your employer, enter the amount in the "Adjusted Gross Income" section of Form 1040; there is no specially labeled line for this deduction. On the dotted line alongside the total adjustments to gross income write "jury pay" to indicate that the deduction is for the amount of jury duty pay that you turned over to your employer.

Impairment-Related Expenses

Having a disability may necessitate certain additional expenses in order to work. The tax law recognizes this added cost and allows these work-related expenses to be deductible under a special rule.

Benefit

If you suffer from a physical or mental impairment and you must incur special expenses to enable you to work, you can deduct these impairment-related expenses as an itemized deduction. This deduction is *not* subject to the 2 percent of AGI floor discussed earlier with respect to certain other employment-related expenses.

There is no dollar limit on this deduction. The deduction may be claimed without regard to the amount of your income.

Conditions

To be eligible for the deduction, you must meet both of the following conditions:

1. You have a physical or mental disability that results in a functional limitation of employment that substantially limits one or more major life activities.
2. You must pay the expenses in order to work. For example, if you require an attendant at work so you can perform your job, your cost for these services is a qualified expense.

EXAMPLES OF IMPAIRMENTS. Any one of these impairments entitles you to deduct job-related expenses without regard to the 2 percent of AGI limit:

- Blindness.
- Deafness.
- Impairment limiting your ability to perform manual tasks.
- Inability to speak or walk.

Planning Tip

You may be able to avoid paying some or all of your work-related expenses due to your impairment (no cost to you is better than a deductible one). Under the Americans with Disabilities Act (ADA), your employer must provide reasonable accommodations to enable you to perform your job duties. This may include special equipment or assistance. For more information about benefits to which you may be entitled by the ADA, visit www.usdoj.gov/crt/ada/adahom1.htm.

Pitfall

You cannot claim a double deduction for the same expense, so if you treat some impairment-related costs as a job expense you cannot also deduct them as a medical expense. For example, Braille books for your work are an impairment-related job expense and also qualify as a deductible medical expense, but if you treat them as a job expense you cannot also deduct them as a medical expense.

Where to Claim the Deduction

You must complete Form 2106, Employee Business Expenses, or Form 2106-EZ, Unreimbursed Employee Business Expenses, to report your impairment-related expenses along with other unreimbursed employee business expenses. The total amount is then entered as a miscellaneous itemized deduction *not* subject to the 2 percent of AGI floor on Schedule A of Form 1040.

You cannot deduct impairment-related expenses if you file Form 1040A or 1040EZ.

Military Benefits

Serving your country in the military won't make you rich. But it may entitle you to a variety of benefits and other assistance. The tax law looks favorably on those in the service by allowing tax-free treatment for a long list of benefits.

Benefit

If you are a member of the armed forces, including the National Guard and the reserves, you may be entitled to certain benefits because of your job status.

EXAMPLES OF TAX-FREE BENEFITS

- Adjustments in pay to compensate for losses resulting from inflated foreign currency.
- Benefits under the Servicemembers' Group Life Insurance.
- Combat pay.
- Death allowance for burial services, gratuity payments to survivors up to $5,000, and travel of dependents to burial sites.
- Death benefit payable to family members for those killed in combat ($100,000 in 2006; additional $150,000 for those who died between October 1, 2001 and May 11, 2005).
- Defense counseling payments.
- Disability pay.
- Dislocation allowance (intended to partially reimburse expenses such as lease forfeitures, temporary living costs in hotels, and other expenses incurred in relocating a household).
- Dividends on GI insurance.

- Education, training, or subsistence allowances paid under any law administered by the Veterans Administration (VA) (deductible education costs must be reduced by the VA allowance).
- Family allowances for education expenses of dependents, emergencies, evacuation to a place of safety, and separation.
- Housing allowances (Basic Allowance for Housing, Variable Housing Allowance, temporary lodging expense allowance, and a moving-in allowance intended to defray costs such as rental agent fees, home security improvements, and supplemental heating equipment associated with occupying leased space outside the United States).
- Interest on dividends left on deposit with the VA.
- Living allowances (Basic Allowance for Subsistence).
- Medical or hospital treatment.
- Payments to former prisoners of war.
- ROTC educational and subsistence allowances.
- Survivor and retirement protection plan premium payments.
- Travel allowances for annual round-trip for dependent students, leave between consecutive overseas tours, reassignment in a dependent-restricted area, and transportation for you or your dependents during ship overhaul or inactivation.
- Uniform allowances.

Condition

There are no specific conditions for claiming these benefits; you are entitled to them if you are a member of the armed forces.

Planning Tips

If you receive a Basic Allowance for Housing, you can still deduct your mortgage interest and real estate taxes on your home, even though you pay these expenses with your BAH.

Military personnel can treat tax-free combat pay as earned income for purposes of making contributions to a traditional or Roth IRA. This special break, created by the Heroes Earned Retirement Opportunities (HERO) Act, allows you to go back to 2004 and 2005 to make contributions up to the IRA limits in those years. For 2004, the basic limit was $3,000, with a $500 catch-up contribution for those age 50 and older; for 2005, the basic limit was $4,000, with a $5,000 catch-up contribution. You have until May 28, 2009, to make IRA contributions for 2004 and 2005.

Military personnel can also treat tax-free combat pay as earned income for purposes of the earned income credit (see Chapter 1).

For purposes of the home sale exclusion for gain on the sale of a principal residence, military personnel have a 10-year period (in place of a five-year period) in which to have owned and used the home as their main home (see Chapter 4).

Pitfall

Nearly half the states tax military retirement pay, so check with your state for details.

Where to Claim the Benefit

Benefits that are excludable need not be reported on your return.

Fringe Benefits

Wages or salary is only one aspect of remuneration for working. Your job may entitle you to a wide range of benefits, called perquisites ("perks") or fringe benefits. Many of these benefits are fully or partially tax free.

Benefit

If your employer pays for certain benefits, you may be able to exclude from your income some or all of these items. In many cases, however, tax-free treatment does not apply if you are an employee of an S corporation in which you own more than 2 percent of the stock.

There are various limitations and conditions for different fringe benefits, many of which are discussed in other chapters in this book (see Table 14.1).

You may be unaware of certain fringe benefits because you do not have to sign up for them as you would for, say, health coverage or a retirement plan, and they are not reported on your annual Form W-2. These fringe benefits include:

De minimis (minimal) fringe benefits. These are items so modest that accounting for them would be an administrative burden on your employer. For example:

- Birthday cakes.
- Doughnuts, coffee, and soda.
- Occasional personal long-distance calls.
- Occasional lunch or dinner money.

TABLE 14.1 Fringe Benefits in 2006

Type of Benefit	Dollar Limit on Exclusion	Other Limitations	For More Details See Chapter
Accident and health plans	None (except for long-term care benefits)		2
Achievement awards	Up to $1,600 ($400 for nonqualified awards)		
Adoption assistance	$10,960	Income limitations	1
Athletic facilities	None		
De minimis (minimal) benefits			
Dependent care assistance	$5,000		1
Educational assistance	$5,250		3
Employee discounts			
Employee stock options			
Free parking	$205/month		
Group term life insurance	$50,000		
Lodging on business premises			
Meals on business premises for convenience of employer			
Meals—*de minimis*			
Moving expense reimbursements		50-mile distance test and 39-week employment test	4
No-additional-cost services			
Transit passes	$105/month		
Working condition benefits			

- Photocopying.
- Postage on personal items once in a while.
- Tickets bought by the company for sporting or entertainment events.

Caution: Some companies have a policy *against* personal phone calls or other personal use of company property (e.g., photocopying) and such use can be considered a theft, so ask about your employer's policy on this matter.

Employee discounts. Typically, these are limited to 25 percent to 30 percent of the cost of goods such as store merchandise (usually 20 percent of the cost of services such as dry cleaning).

No-additional-cost services. These are items for which your employer does not incur any additional cost when you use them. For example:

- Flights for airline employees and their families on a standby basis.
- Hotel rooms for hotel workers when there is a vacancy.

Working condition fringe benefits. These include expenses that would be deductible as an unreimbursed employee business expense on your return if you, rather than your employer, had paid for them. For example:

- Dues to professional or trade associations.
- Subscriptions to work-related publications.
- Travel, entertainment, and meals.
- Work-related continuing education courses.

Conditions

Different fringe benefits have different conditions and limitations. Table 14.1 contains a survey of various fringe benefits that are excludable, including any other limitations that may apply, and references where appropriate to the chapter in which you will find an additional explanation.

Planning Tip

If a fringe benefit is tax free, it may also be exempt from Social Security and Medicare (FICA) taxes. Table 14.2 shows which benefits are exempt from Social Security and Medicare taxes.

Pitfall

Employees in an S corporation who own more than 2 percent of the stock cannot exclude the following types of fringe benefits from income:

- Accident and health benefits.
- Achievement awards.

TABLE 14.2 Benefits Exempt from Social Security and Medicare (FICA) Taxes

Benefit	FICA Taxes
Accident and health benefits	Exempt (except to S corporation shareholders owning more than 2 percent of the stock)
Achievement awards	Exempt up to $1,600 ($400 for nonqualified awards)
Adoption assistance	Not exempt
Athletic facilities	Exempt
De minimis benefits	Exempt
Dependent care assistance	Exempt up to $5,000

- Adoption assistance.
- Lodging on the business premises.
- Meals furnished for the employer's convenience.
- Moving expenses.
- Transportation benefits (free parking and transit passes). However, transit passes up to $21 per month can be excluded if the value of the passes is not more than this amount (if more, then all of the benefit is taxable; you cannot exclude the $21 per month).

Certain benefits payable to highly compensated employees (generally executives and other highly paid workers, even those who are not S corporation shareholders) are not excludable. These benefits include:

- Self-insured medical reimbursement plans.
- Dependent care assistance if the program favors these employees.
- Employee discounts.
- No-additional-cost services.

Where to Claim the Benefit

Tax-free fringe benefits need not be reported on your return. Many fringe benefits are listed on your Form W-2, with any necessary reporting requirements included in the instructions to the form.

Income Earned Abroad

Working abroad does not relieve citizens of their obligation to file U.S. tax returns and pay taxes here. But to make things easier for those working overseas, the tax law lets a limited amount of income be received tax free each year as long as certain conditions are met.

Benefit

If you live and work abroad, you are not taxed on up to $82,400 of foreign earned income. If you are married and both you and your spouse have foreign income, you may each be eligible for an exclusion. If your foreign earned income is more than $82,400, you are taxable only on amounts in excess of $82,400.

This exclusion is not automatic; you must elect it.

Conditions

To qualify for the foreign earned income exclusion, you must meet two conditions:

1. Your tax home is in a foreign country.
2. You meet either a foreign residence test (you live abroad for an uninterrupted period that includes one full year) or a physical presence test (you live abroad for 330 days during a 12-month period).

You can apply the exclusion only to foreign earned income, not to other types of foreign income.

FOREIGN EARNED INCOME. You must have income from the performance of personal services. This includes:

- Allowances from your employer for housing or other expenses.
- Bonuses.
- Business profits tied to the performance of services.
- Commissions.
- Professional fees.
- Rents and royalties tied to the performance of services.
- Salaries.
- Value of an employer-provided car or housing.
- Wages.

The earned income must be received no later than the year after the year in which you performed the services.

If you qualify under the foreign residence or physical presence test for only part of the year, you can prorate the exclusion. Proration is made on a daily basis.

Example

On January 1, 2005, you move to England and reside there until you move back to the United States on July 1, 2006. Since you have satisfied the foreign residence test and you lived abroad in 2006 for 181 days, you can exclude 181/365 of $82,400 or $40,861.

If you receive payment this year for foreign earned income earned last year, you can exclude this amount this year to the extent that you did not use up your exclusion in the prior year.

Example

In 2005, you earned $75,000 but were paid only $70,000, which you excluded. In 2006, you earn $82,000 and receive the $5,000 for 2005 services. In 2006 you can exclude a total of $84,440 ($5,000 for 2005 pay because you did not use up your 2005 exclusion of $80,000, plus $82,400 exclusion for 2006). You are taxable on $2,000 of your 2006 earnings.

Not all foreign income is eligible for the exclusion. Nonqualified payments include:

- Alimony.
- Annuity income.
- Capital gains.
- Dividends.
- Gambling winnings.
- Interest income.
- Pensions.
- U.S. government pay (if you work for the government and are stationed abroad, your pay is not tax free).
- Value of tax-free meals or lodging.

If, while you are living abroad, you receive pay for services you earned in the United States, you cannot exclude this income.

If you work in Antarctica, you cannot exclude your income (Antarctica is not considered a foreign country by the IRS).

Planning Tips

What happens if you haven't met the foreign residence or physical presence test by the time your return is due? You cannot claim the exclusion before you have met either test, but you have a choice:

You can ask for a filing extension if you expect to meet either test within the extension period.

Example

Your return for 2006 is due June 15, 2006, but you request a filing extension to October 16, 2006, because you expect to satisfy the 330-day test in July 2007, so that you can claim the exclusion on your 2006 return.

Alternatively, you can file your return to report the foreign earned income and then file an amended return to claim the exclusion once you satisfy either test.

Example

Same as the preceding facts except that you won't satisfy the 330-day test until after October 16, 2007. You file your 2006 return and pay tax on the foreign income. Once the test is met, you file an amended return to receive a refund.

Once you make the election to exclude foreign earned income, it remains in effect for subsequent years unless you revoke it. You revoke the election by attaching a statement to your return indicating revocation.

Weigh carefully whether you want to revoke the election to claim the foreign earned income exclusion. Following a revocation you may not use the exclusion for five years unless the IRS grants you permission to do so. The IRS may grant permission under these circumstances:

- You return to the United States for a period of time.
- You move to a different foreign country that has different tax rates.
- You change employers.
- There is a change in the tax law of the foreign country in which you reside.

Pitfalls

If you elect to exclude your foreign earned income, you may not deduct any expenses related to such income.

You cannot base a contribution to an IRA or a Roth IRA on excludable foreign earned income.

You cannot claim the foreign tax credit or a deduction for foreign taxes related to excludable foreign earned income. In fact, if you had claimed the foreign earned income exclusion in the past and claim a foreign tax credit this year, you have effectively revoked your election to claim the exclusion. You cannot claim the exclusion for at least five years unless the IRS grants you permission to claim the exclusion.

Under a new "stacking rule," excluded foreign income is taken into account in figuring the tax rate you pay on income that is taxable.

You cannot claim the foreign earned income exclusion with respect to earnings from any country subject to U.S. government travel restrictions, such as Cuba. Countries subject to travel restrictions may be found at www.state.gov/travel.

Where to Claim the Benefit

To elect the foreign earned income exclusion, file Form 2555, Foreign Earned Income, which you attach to Form 1040. You can used a simplified Form 2555-EZ, Foreign Earned Income Exclusion, if your foreign wages are no more than $80,000, you do not have any foreign self-employment income, and you do not claim the foreign housing exclusion or deductions for foreign housing, moving, or business expenses.

You cannot claim the foreign earned income exclusion if you file Form 1040A or 1040EZ.

CHAPTER 15

Your Business

The United States is an entrepreneurial country—it is the American dream to own your own business, and millions already do. It has been estimated that there are now more than 25 million business owners. Most expenses related to running a business are deductible, but timing issues and limitations may come into play. The tax rules for your business apply whether you operate a full-time or a sideline business. This chapter deals primarily with business deductions for a sole proprietor who files Schedule C (or, for farming, Schedule F). Of course, many rules discussed in this chapter apply to partnerships, limited liability companies, and corporations.

This chapter explains:

- Start-up costs
- Equipment purchases
- Payment for services
- Supplies
- Gifts
- Hobby losses
- Self-employment tax deduction
- Home office deduction

- Farming-related breaks
- Domestic production activities deduction
- Other business deductions
- Other business credits
- Net operating losses

Retirement plans for self-employed individuals are discussed in Chapter 5.

For more information, see IRS Publication 15, *Circular E, Employer's Tax Guide*; IRS Publication 225, *Farmer's Tax Guide*; IRS Publication 334, *Tax Guide for Small Business*; IRS Publication 535, *Business Expenses*; IRS Publication 536, *Net Operating Losses*; IRS Publication 587, *Business Use of Your Home*; and IRS Publication 946, *How to Depreciate Property*. Also see *J.K. Lasser's Small Business Taxes 2007*, by Barbara Weltman.

Start-up Costs

The term "start-up" has a very specific meaning for tax purposes. When you think of the start-up phase of a business, you typically think about the first few years of operation when the business gets going. But for tax purposes, start-up means that period of time just *before* you actually focus on the business you then begin. It is the period in which you are looking for a business to go into.

Benefit

When you decide to start a business, you may incur certain costs. Usually, these costs are viewed as capital expenditures that are not currently deductible. But you can deduct up to $5,000 of start-up costs in the year the business begins. If start-up costs exceed $5,000, the balance can be amortized (deducted ratably) over 180 months.

If start-up costs exceed $50,000, the $5,000 deduction limit is reduced dollar for dollar by the excess over $50,000. If start-up costs exceed $55,000, no immediate deduction is allowed; such costs can be amortized over 180 months.

Conditions

Start-up expenses include costs related to deciding *whether* to go into business and *which* business to buy or start. This is referred to as the "whether and which" test.

EXAMPLES OF START-UP COSTS

- A survey of potential markets.
- Advertisements for the opening of the business.
- An analysis of available facilities, labor, and supplies.

- Salaries and fees for consultants and executives.
- Travel and other expenses incurred to get prospective distributors, suppliers, and customers.

Expenses incurred after the start-up phase that relate to starting the business cannot be amortized; they must be capitalized (added to the cost of the business).

Example

You find a business you want to purchase and ask your accountant to review the company's books. Then you ask your attorney to draw up a contract of sale. Since you have already identified a particular business, you are beyond the start-up phase for tax purposes and accountant's and attorney's fees cannot be currently deducted or amortized as part of start-up expenses; they are simply part of the basis (cost) of your business, along with the purchase price of the company.

Planning Tips

Remember to keep track of your annual deductible amount so you don't overlook the write-off opportunity in the coming years.

If you sell your business before the end of the amortization period (assuming your start-up costs were not initially fully deducted), you can deduct any unamortized amount in the final year of business.

The same $5,000 deduction limit and 180-month amortization period applies to certain other expenses you may incur in forming a business: incorporation costs and partnership organizational costs. Like start-up costs, make sure that the items fit within the write-off category and then apply the $5,000 deduction limit and 180-month amortization rule.

Pitfall

Start-up costs are limited to expenses incurred *before* you begin operations. Once you have passed the start-up phase, which means you've identified the business or type of business you'll start, you can no longer include expenses in your pot of start-up expenses.

Where to Claim the Benefit

Report the amortizable amount of your start-up costs on Schedule C (or Schedule F) as "Other expenses." If you have more than one expense, you must list each of them in the space provided for this on Schedule C (or Schedule F).

You cannot claim a deduction for start-up expenses if you file Form 1040A or 1040EZ.

Equipment Purchases

It usually takes more than just your brains and hard work to make a business run. You need equipment, from technology-based items (e.g., computers and cell phones), to furniture (e.g., desks, file cabinets, and chairs), to industry-specific items (e.g., carpentry tools and heavy machinery). For tax purposes, all of these items are viewed as "equipment" for which special tax treatment may be claimed. Today, the tax law encourages investments in equipment as a means of spurring the economy by allowing an immediate deduction for purchase costs if certain conditions are met.

Benefit

You can deduct as an ordinary business expense amounts you pay for equipment used in your business. However, tax law dictates when and how much of your cost you can deduct. Two sets of rules come into play:

1. *First-year expensing*. Up to $108,000 can be deducted in the year the equipment is placed in service. Higher dollar limits apply for equipment placed in service in the New York Liberty Zone and the Gulf Opportunity Zone; a lower dollar limit applies for vehicles weighing more than 6,000 pounds.
2. *Depreciation*. A percentage of the equipment's basis is deducted over a set term (a recovery period fixed for various types of assets). There is no dollar limit on depreciation.

There is an additional tax break for businesses in the Gulf Opportunity Zone (the Gulf coast region declared a disaster because of Hurricane Katrina). They can claim an additional first-year deduction, called bonus depreciation, for 50 percent of the cost of the equipment. This break runs only through 2007.

Conditions

Equipment purchases are not limited to machinery; the term "equipment" includes just about any type of property other than real estate.

EXAMPLES OF EQUIPMENT

- Answering machine
- Bookshelves
- Cars (see Chapter 7)
- Cell phones
- Computers
- Copiers
- Desk accessories
- Desk chairs

- Desks
- Farming equipment (see later in this chapter)
- Fax machines
- File cabinets
- Floor models and displays
- Machinery
- Musical instruments for musicians
- Printers
- Signs
- Software purchased off-the-shelf
- Telephones
- Tools of your trade
- Trucks (see Chapter 7)
- Vacuum cleaner

Different conditions apply to the different ways in which you can write off equipment purchases. You can combine these write-offs to maximize your deduction.

Example

In June 2006, you purchase a machine costing $150,000 (assume the machine is classified under the tax law as five-year property). You can deduct a total of $116,400 ($108,000 + $8,400):

First-year expensing of $108,000.

Regular depreciation of $8,400 ([$150,000 – $108,000] × 20%).

The rules on depreciation are quite complex, and a complete discussion is well beyond the scope of this chapter. Here you will gain an overview of the rules that apply. To learn more, see IRS Publication 946, *How to Depreciate Property*.

Conditions for First-Year Expensing

There are three basic conditions for claiming first-year expensing:

1. You must elect it.
2. Your total equipment purchases for the year cannot exceed a set dollar amount.
3. Your taxable income must at least equal your expense deduction.

ELECTION. You must elect to claim first-year expensing (also referred to as a Section 179 deduction because of the section in the Internal Revenue Code governing the deduction).

EQUIPMENT PURCHASES. To qualify for the election, your total equipment purchases for the year cannot exceed a set dollar amount. For 2006, you can claim the $108,000 expensing deduction only if your total purchases are no more than $430,000. The dollar limit phases out on a dollar-for-dollar basis so that no expensing deduction can be claimed if total purchases exceed $538,000.

TAXABLE INCOME. Your first-year expensing deduction cannot be more than the taxable income from the active conduct of a business. Taxable income for this purpose means your net income (or loss) from all businesses you actively conduct. If you are married and file a joint return, your spouse's net income (or loss) is added to yours. Taxable income also includes Section 1231 gains and losses (from the sale of certain business property) and salary or wages from being an employee. Taxable income must be reduced by the deduction for one-half of self-employment tax and net operating loss carrybacks and carryforwards.

Example

You own a sole proprietorship that shows a $5,000 profit for the year, and your deduction for one-half of self-employment tax is $383. Your spouse works as an employee with a salary of $50,000. Your taxable income for purposes of figuring your first-year expensing deduction is $54,617 ($5,000 – $383 + $50,000).

Conditions for Depreciation

Depreciation is a method for recovering your investment in property over a period of time fixed by law, called a recovery period. You apply a set percentage (based on the property's recovery period) to the property's basis (generally its cost) to arrive at your annual deduction. These percentages may be found in IRS Publication 946.

Example

In 2006, you place in service a copier machine (five-year property) for which you do not claim any first-year expensing. Assume the cost of the machine is $8,000. Your depreciation percentage for the year that five-year property is placed in service is 20 percent, so your depreciation deduction is $1,600 ($8,000 × 20%).

Different types of property are classified by their recovery periods:

- Three-year property, such as taxis, tractors, racehorses over two years old when placed in service, and breeding hogs.
- Five-year property, such as cars, trucks, copiers, assets used in construction, and breeding and dairy cattle.
- Seven-year property, such as office fixtures and furniture, fax machines, assets used in printing, assets used in recreation (e.g., billiard tables), and breeding horses and workhorses.

There are also 10-year, 15-year, and 20-year types of property as well as realty (27.5 years for residential realty and 39 years for nonresidential realty such as office buildings, strip malls, and factories).

CONVENTIONS. Special depreciation rules, called conventions, come into play to determine your write-offs for the year.

- For property other than realty, a midyear convention makes a hypothetical assumption that the property has been placed in service in the middle of the year. As a result of the midyear convention, five-year property is depreciated over six years.
- For property other than realty, a midquarter convention applies. If you place in service more than 40 percent of all your equipment purchases for the year in the final quarter of the year, a special rule dictates the amount of depreciation you can claim for each item placed in service during the year. This special rule is called a midquarter convention and generally operates to limit write-offs (although in some cases it may enable you to take greater deductions than under regular depreciation rules).
- For realty, a midmonth convention assumes that the property has been placed in service in the middle of the month it is actually placed in service. The midmonth convention is built into the depreciation rate tables applied to realty.

Planning Tips

The amount of your write-offs does not depend on whether you pay cash for the equipment or finance your purchase. If, for example, you finance your purchase, you may wind up deducting more in the first year than you pay out of pocket.

Example

In December 2006, you buy a machine for $25,000, financing it over five years at 8 percent interest. In 2006, you can claim a first-year expensing deduction of $25,000, even though you have not yet paid a penny.

Decide whether to make the first-year expensing election. Generally, if your current income is modest but you expect it to increase in coming years, it may be preferable to forgo the deduction now in favor of using it against future income that would otherwise be taxed at higher rates.

Pitfalls

Special rules apply to so-called "listed property," which includes cars, computers and peripherals not used at a regular business establishment, and cell phones. You cannot use first-year expensing or accelerated depreciation *unless* business use of a listed property item is more than 50 percent of total use.

Example

You buy a cell phone that is used 75 percent for business and 25 percent for personal purposes. Since business use exceeds 50 percent, you can use first-year expensing or accelerated depreciation for the portion of the phone (75 percent of its purchase price) used for business.

If you sell or cease using property for which first-year expensing has been claimed, you *may* be subject to recapture. This means you're required to report a portion of the previous write-off as income in the year of the disposition of the property. Discuss this rather complicated matter with a tax adviser.

Where to Claim the Deduction

You figure your deduction for equipment purchases on Form 4562, Depreciation and Amortization. You enter the amount of your deduction on the line provided for this write-off on Schedule C (or Schedule F).

If you are claiming depreciation this year on an item placed in service in a prior year and you do not have any new items to report, you do not have to file Form 4562. Simply attach your own schedule to the return showing the amount of depreciation you are claiming this year.

You cannot claim a deduction for equipment purchases if you file Form 1040A or 1040EZ.

Payment for Services *(Provision expired 12/31/05. Extension expected for 2006.)*

You may not be able to do it alone and may therefore need to hire employees to work for your business. The costs of wages, salaries, bonuses, and other payments are deductible if certain conditions are met.

Benefit

Amounts you pay to individuals who provide services to you are deductible as ordinary expenses against your business income. Such payments fall into two general categories:

1. Wages and compensation to employees.
2. Fees and payments to independent contractors.

There are no dollar limits on the amount you can deduct for payments for services.

In addition to a deduction for wages and compensation to employees, you may be eligible to claim a tax credit for a portion of these payments.

Conditions

There are several conditions for determining how much to deduct for payments to workers:

- It must be determined whether the worker is an employee or independent contractor.
- Amounts paid must be reasonable.
- Payment must relate to work actually performed.
- Payments must be made in a timely fashion.

WORKER CLASSIFICATION. First you must determine whether workers are your employees or independent contractors. The key reason for making the distinction is the obligation to pay employment taxes—Social Security and Medicare (FICA) taxes, federal unemployment insurance (FUTA), and state unemployment and other payroll taxes. If you are the employer, you are responsible for the employer's share of taxes as well as withholding income taxes and the employee's share of FICA. If your worker is an independent contractor, then he or she is responsible for employment taxes.

Generally, worker classification as an employee or independent contractor is based on control. If you control when, where, and how work is to be performed, the person is your employee regardless of what label you may attach. If the person is in his or her own business and provides services to you, the person usually is treated as an independent contractor.

REASONABLE PAYMENTS. Compensation paid to your employees must be "reasonable." There's no set dollar amount. Reasonable depends on many factors, including job responsibilities, education level, and location of the business. Payments to yourself as a sole proprietor are not treated as deductible compensation because you are not an employee.

Payments paid to independent contractors must also be reasonable.

PERFORMANCE OF WORK. You can deduct only payments for work actually performed. Generally, this poses no problem for your rank-and-file employees. But if you put family members on the payroll, the IRS may look closely at the relation between their wages and work performed. Keep track of the hours they worked and the tasks they performed as proof they earned the compensation you paid.

TIMELINESS OF PAYMENT. You can deduct only payments you actually make (if you are on the cash method of accounting for your business). If you are on the accrual method, payments to rank-and-file employees must be made no later than two-and-a-half months after the close of the year (e.g., by March 15, 2007, for compensation earned in 2006). (Different rules apply to payments to shareholders in C and S corporations.)

Planning Tip *(Provision expired 12/31/05. Extension expected for 2006.)*

Compensation paid to certain employees may entitle you to claim a tax credit (more details may be found later in this chapter). These include:

- Work opportunity credit for workers within several targeted groups.
- Welfare-to-work credit for certain long-term welfare recipients.
- Empowerment zone credit for workers within designated areas.
- Indian employment credit for workers on Indian reservations.
- Social Security tax credit on certain tips for workers in restaurant and tavern businesses.

Pitfall

If your workers are employees, you are responsible for employment taxes. This requires you to withhold federal and, if applicable, state income taxes from their wages, as well as the employee share of FICA tax. You must also pay the employer share of FICA as well as FUTA and state employment taxes. If you fail to pay over these taxes in a timely fashion, you may be personally liable for them.

Where to Claim the Deduction

You report the deduction for compensation to employees on the line designated as "Wages" on Schedule C of Form 1040. Wages are reduced by employment tax credits you claim (listed earlier in "Planning Tip"). You report payments to independent contractors on the line marked "Commissions and fees" of this schedule.

For farming-related activities, the deduction for wages to employees is reported on the line marked "Labor hired" on Schedule F of Form 1040. Wages are reduced by employment tax credits you claim. You report payments to independent contractors on the line marked "Customer hire" of this schedule.

Employment tax credits to which you may be entitled are figured on the following forms:

- Work opportunity credit: Form 5884.
- Welfare-to-work credit: Form 8861.
- Empowerment zone credit: Form 8844.
- Indian employment credit: Form 8845.
- Social Security tax credit on certain tips: Form 8846.

Supplies

To paraphrase Benjamin Franklin, for want of a paper clip your business may be lost. Despite predictions of a paperless society, most businesses use reams of paper and other supplies every year. The tax law allows a full write-off for the cost of ordinary supplies as long as certain conditions are met.

Benefit

Office supplies (including paper, pens, tape, and toner replacements) and cleaning supplies (such as detergent, paper towels, and sponges) are deductible against your business income. There is no dollar limit on this deduction.

Supplies that are part of your inventory are *not* currently deductible; they are part of the cost of goods sold.

Conditions

For supplies to be currently deductible, they must be ordinary and necessary business expenses. They cannot be items with a useful life of more than one year. If they have a longer useful life, they are treated as equipment (discussed later in this chapter).

EXAMPLES OF DEDUCTIBLE SUPPLIES

- Binders and presentation material.
- Boards and easels.
- Business cards.
- Cleaning supplies.
- Diskettes, CDs, and zip disks.
- Filing and storage material.
- Ink cartridges and toners.

- Labels, envelopes, and shipping material.
- Paper clips, tape, and staples.
- Paper, pads, and notes.
- Pens, pencils, and markers.
- Replacement parts (which are not part of inventory).
- Rubber stamps.
- Small wares of restaurants and taverns (e.g., glassware, paper or plastic cups, dishes, pots and pans, and bar supplies).
- Stationery.
- Trash bags.

Planning Tips

From a nontax standpoint, it may not make economic sense to load up on supplies even though you can deduct them. You are incurring costs now that could be paid later.

While the cost of supplies generally is deductible, it is a good business practice to economize on purchases. Look for discounts and special business incentives from such office supplies companies as:

- Office Depot (www.officedepot.com)
- Office Max (www.officemax.com)
- Staples (www.staples.com)

Pitfall

Supplies that are part of your inventory are *not* separately deducted. Instead, they are included as part of your cost of goods sold.

Where to Claim the Benefit

Report supplies used in your business on the line provided for this item on Schedule C (or Schedule F) of Form 1040. You do not have to complete any additional form or schedule for this purpose.

You cannot deduct business supplies if you file Form 1040A or Form 1040EZ.

Gifts

Gifts generally are given because of personal feelings without any expectations or strings attached. But business gifts usually are motivated by gratitude for some business activity or hope for future business activity. In recognition of this fact, the tax law allows a deduction for business gifts, but only in very limited amounts.

Benefit

You may wish to bestow some gratuitous benefit on employees, customers, dealers, distributors, or other business relations. You can qualify for a deduction for business gifts, but the amount you can deduct is limited. Generally, you cannot deduct more than $25 per gift for any person each year. The dollar limit applies even if you attempt to make an indirect gift (for example, you give the gift to a company that is intended for the eventual personal use of a particular person).

Conditions

To claim a deduction for business gifts, you must meet both of the following conditions:

1. Dollar limit.
2. Substantiation.

DOLLAR LIMIT. The deductible amount of the gift cannot exceed $25 per person per year. The dollar limit does not include incidental costs, such as wrapping, insuring, or shipping the gift.

Example

You give a new vendor a gift that cost you $60. You paid $10 more to insure and ship it. You can deduct $35 ($25 of the $60, plus incidental expenses of $10).

In determining your $25 annual limit, you do not have to count any gifts of nominal value ($4 or less) with your company name imprinted on them that you distribute to a number of clients or customers (e.g., calendars at Christmastime).

SUBSTANTIATION REQUIREMENTS. You must show the cost of the gift, a description of the gift, the date it was given, and to whom. You must also state the reason for the gift (such as the business to be gained from making it). This information should be recorded on an expense log or business diary.

In addition, you must have evidentiary proof of the expense, such as a canceled check or receipt for the item.

Planning Tips

Gifts to your employees are *not* subject to this $25 limit because payments to them usually are treated as compensation (discussed earlier in this chapter).

As long as regular compensation plus any purported gifts are reasonable, the total is deductible as compensation.

Certain items can be treated as gifts, such as an entertainment expense, which is *not* subject to the $25 limit. You have the option of using this treatment if you give tickets to the theater or a sports event and do *not* attend the event yourself. In making the choice, keep in mind that the entertainment deduction is subject to a 50 percent limit (without regard to a dollar amount).

Example

You buy your best customer tickets to a local golf tournament for $80. Assuming you do not attend, you are better off treating the ticket as an entertainment expense so you can deduct $40 (50% of $80), rather than as a business gift, which would be deductible at only $25.

If you treat the ticket as a business gift, you have three years in which to change your mind and file an amended return to report the ticket as an entertainment expense.

If you give food or a beverage intended to be consumed by your customer or other businessperson, you *must* treat the item as a gift (you do not have the choice to treat it as an entertainment expense).

Pitfall

You must substantiate your business gifts in order to support your deduction. If you fail to meet full substantiation requirements, your deduction is lost. For example, merely retaining a receipt for the gift is not sufficient; you need to note all the information listed earlier as full substantiation for the gift.

Where to Claim the Deduction

You report the gifts as "Other expenses" on Schedule C (or Schedule F) of Form 1040. If you have more than one such expense (for example, in addition to business gifts, you are deducting environmental cleanup costs), you must list each type of expense in the space provided (or on your own attachment if more space is required).

You cannot deduct any business gifts if you file Form 1040A or 1040EZ.

Hobby Losses

When does a hobby become a business? The tax law says this happens when you are profitable. In effect, if you lose money you bear the cost entirely, but if you make money the government shares in your good fortune. You can deduct losses from activities that might be viewed as hobbies only under certain conditions.

Benefit

If you do not have a profit motive for running an activity—especially one involving some element of personal recreation or pleasure, such as coin collecting or dog breeding—then your expenses are deductible only to the extent of your income from the activity. The hobby loss rule acts as a limitation on your deductions—dictating how much you can deduct and where to claim the deduction for your business expenses.

Hobby losses are treated as miscellaneous itemized deductions, which are deductible only to the extent they exceed 2 percent of adjusted gross income.

Conditions

You want to avoid application of the hobby loss rule so that your business expenses in excess of business income are deductible. If your business is unprofitable year after year, the IRS may question whether you are in it for a profit or are merely trying to deduct the costs of a hobby.

To avoid the hobby loss rule, you must be able to demonstrate that you are in the activity to make a profit. Of course, this is a subjective determination based on your reasonable expectations and beliefs. But certain objective criteria are used to show you really mean business. No single factor is determinative; the more you can muster, the better off you will be:

- You run the activity in a businesslike manner (e.g., keep good records separate from your personal activities and have a business bank account, telephone, stationery, and other indications of a business).
- You put in substantial time and effort.
- You depend on income from the activity for your livelihood (if you have other sources of income, this tends to show the activity is merely a hobby).
- You consult with advisers to make the business profitable.
- You have profits in some years (the bounty in your good years can support a profit motive).
- You expect to see a profit from the appreciation of assets used in the activity.

Planning Tips

You can opt to rely on a presumption that you are in the activity for a profit—opting for this presumption delays any IRS inquiry about your activity. You are presumed to be in an activity for profit if you make a profit for at least three of the first five years you are in business (two out of seven years if the activity is breeding, training, showing, or racing horses).

To use the presumption, you must file Form 5213, Election to Postpone Determination as to Whether the Presumption Applies That an Activity Is Engaged In for Profit. The form can be filed with the first return for your activity; it must be filed within three years of the due date of the return for the first year of the activity.

Of course, the downside to making this election to postpone inquiry into your activity is that you are extending the statute of limitations under which the IRS may question your deductions. Generally the IRS has only three years, but filing Form 5213 means they have five years—and you can expect to have your returns examined at the end of the five-year period.

If you make the election but fail the presumption, you are not precluded from arguing you really had a profit motive, even though you had losses in many years. One of the key ways to show a profit motive is to have a written business plan spelling out how you expect to make the activity profitable and when you anticipate that this will occur.

Pitfall

The hobby loss rule applies to individuals, including partners and members of limited liability companies; it does not apply to C corporations. In the case of pass-through entities, the determination of a profit motive is made at the entity level (for example, you might be in a partnership to make a profit but it is up to the partnership to prove it has a profit motive).

Where to Claim the Benefit

If you are subject to the hobby loss rule, you report your income from the activity as other income in the "Income" section of Form 1040 and expenses from the activity as miscellaneous itemized deductions on Schedule A of Form 1040. You cannot claim any hobby loss deduction if you file Form 1040A or 1040EZ.

Self-Employment Tax Deduction

Self-employed individuals pay both the employer and employee share of Social Security and Medicare taxes. But self-employed persons are treated as their own employers to the extent they are permitted to deduct the employer share of these taxes.

Benefit

If you pay self-employment tax on your net earnings from self-employment, you can deduct one-half of the liability as an adjustment to gross income, even if you do not itemize your other deductions.

Conditions

Self-employment tax is the employer and employee share of Social Security and Medicare taxes figured on your net earnings from self-employment. As long as you show a profit in your self-employment activities, you owe self-employment tax and can deduct the portion representing the employer share (one-half of the total tax).

Planning Tip

To figure your deduction, simply look at Schedule SE, Self-Employment Tax, the form used to figure your self-employment tax. The last line of the short or long form of Schedule SE allows you to figure your deduction by multiplying your self-employment tax by 50 percent.

Pitfall

The deduction for one-half of your self-employment tax is *not* a business expense, but a personal one. It does not reduce your profits on which you pay income and self-employment taxes.

Where to Claim the Benefit

You report the deduction on the line provided in the "Adjusted Gross Income" section of Form 1040. No separate form or schedule is required for this purpose.

Home Office Deduction

The number of home-based businesses is put between 18 million and 38 million; exact figures are not available because the U.S. Census Bureau failed to question whether full-time employees also had home-based businesses. Whatever the number, the cost of operating an office from home may be deductible as long as certain conditions are met. The term "home office" isn't limited to clerical space; it can include a workshop, greenhouse, artist studio, or any other area of a home used for business.

Benefit

Whether you work exclusively at a home-based business or operate a sideline business from home, you may be able to deduct a portion of your housing costs, including depreciation if you own your home or rent if you lease it, plus utilities, insurance, maintenance, and other related costs. The deduction serves to offset your business income.

There are two types of expenses related to a home office:

1. Indirect expenses (the portion of the general expenses of running your home).
2. Direct expenses (costs incurred solely in your home office).

Example

You paint the outside of your home for $8,000. If your home office is 10 percent of your home, then $800 of this cost is an indirect expense. If you paid $800 to paint the home office itself, it is entirely deductible (no allocation is required) because it is a direct expense.

In the case of indirect expenses, you must allocate them between the residence and office portion of the home. Usually home office space for purposes of making an allocation is figured on a square footage basis (e.g., if your home is 2,400 square feet and you use 240 square feet as a home office, then 10 percent of your indirect expenses become part of your home office deduction).

Conditions

To claim a home office deduction, you must meet all three of these conditions:

1. Principal place of business or other acceptable use.
2. Regular and exclusive use.
3. Gross income requirement.

PRINCIPAL PLACE OF BUSINESS OR OTHER ACCEPTABLE USE. Your home office must be one of the following:

- Your principal place of business, which is generally the place at which you conduct your business and generate income from the business activity. This includes using your office for substantial administrative or managerial activities for which you have no other fixed location.
- A place to meet or deal with clients, customers, or patients in the normal course of your business.
- A separate structure (such as a freestanding garage) that is used *in connection with* your business.

REGULAR AND EXCLUSIVE USE. The portion of your home used for business must be used for this purpose regularly and exclusively. This means that you can't use your den as an office by day and a family room by night.

You do not need to use an entire room or physically partition space within a room; you only need to devote whatever space you use for business entirely for this purpose.

GROSS INCOME REQUIREMENT. Your home office deduction cannot exceed gross income from the home office activity. Gross income for this purpose generally means your profits reported on Schedule C (or Schedule F) from the activity for which the home office is used.

If you have a bad year, your deduction may be limited (the ordering of what expenses you can claim is figured by following the line-by-line instructions to Form 8829, Expenses for Business Use of Your Home).

If after applying this ordering of deductions you still have unused expenses, you can carry forward this unused amount. There is no time limit on this carryfoward. You can use it when you have income *from the same activity that generated the deduction*, whether or not you are still in the same home at the time of earning that income.

Example

In 2005, your sole proprietorship in the landscaping business reported a loss so that your $2,300 home office deduction could not be claimed. In 2006, your landscaping business becomes profitable enough to allow you to deduct the $2,300 carryforward (plus any home office deduction for 2006). You could still deduct the $2,300 even if you moved to a new residence in 2006.

Planning Tips

Claiming a home office deduction entitles you to certain ancillary benefits:

- Travel to and from your home for business is deductible (there's no such thing as commuting when you have a home office).
- A computer used in the home office is *not* treated as listed property (you do not have to track the business use of the computer in order to claim first-year expensing or accelerated depreciation as discussed earlier in this chapter).

Claiming a home office deduction does *not* taint your opportunity to exclude gain on the sale of your home. The tax law allows you to claim a home sale exclusion of up to $250,000 ($500,000 on a joint return) for the *entire* home (see Chapter 4 for more details).

Pitfall

When you sell your home, you must recapture any depreciation claimed after May 6, 1997, on your home office. Recapture means that the amount becomes taxable at the rate of 25 percent (assuming you are in a tax bracket higher than 25 percent).

Where to Claim the Benefit

You figure the home office deduction on Form 8829, Expenses for Business Use of Your Home. The deduction is then entered on Schedule C (or Schedule F) of Form 1040 on the line provided for it.

If this is the first year in which you are claiming a home office deduction for a home you own, you must also complete Form 4562, Depreciation and Amortization, to figure the depreciation allowance for the year. In future years, you do not have to complete this form if you do not place any new property in service; you simply attach your own statement to the return showing how you figured the depreciation allowance entered on Form 8829.

You cannot claim a home office deduction if you file Form 1040A or 1040EZ.

Farming-Related Breaks

According to the U.S. Department of Agriculture, there were more than 2.10 million farms in the United States in 2005. Farming is considered a type of business and is therefore entitled to deductions available to any other business. But the tax law provides special breaks just for farms.

Benefit

If you operate a farm or farming activity, many of your costs are deductible against your farming income. In addition to any business expense you could claim in a nonfarming business, you may be entitled to special write-offs. Generally, there are no dollar limits on your farming-related deductions.

Some benefits payable to farmers may be tax free. And some expenses paid by farmers may qualify for a tax credit.

Conditions

Like other business expenses, farming-related deductions must be ordinary and necessary expenses.

EXAMPLES OF FARMING-RELATED DEDUCTIONS

- Chemicals.
- Conservation expenses for soil and water.
- Custom hire (machine work).
- Feed purchased (there are limits on how much you can deduct for feed to be consumed beyond this year).
- Fertilizers and lime.
- Freight and trucking.
- Gasoline, oil, and other fuel.

- Ginning.
- Hired labor (reduced by any employment-related tax credits discussed earlier in this chapter).
- Insect sprays and dusts.
- Seeds and plants purchased.
- Storage and warehousing.
- Tying materials and containers.
- Veterinary and breeding fees and medicine.

Planning Tips

Some payments to farmers may be tax free. These include:

- Cost-sharing payments under The Conservation Reserve Program (CRP).
- Soil and water conservation assistance payments under a special federal program, which may run as high as $50,000.
- Agricultural management assistance program payments.

In addition to deductions for farming expenses, you may be eligible for certain tax credits related to farming. These include:

- Credit for federal excise tax paid on kerosene used in your home for heating, lighting, and cooking.
- Credit for federal excise tax paid on gasoline, special motor fuels, and compressed natural gas used on a farm for farming purposes.
- Credit for federal excise tax on fuels used in running stationary machines, for cleaning purposes, or in other off-highway vehicles.

You can claim the credits on your return or claim a refund of the excise taxes you already paid. The credits and your options on claiming them are explained in more detail in IRS Publication 225, *Farmer's Tax Guide*.

Pitfall

Not all farming-related expenses are deductible. You may not deduct your personal living expenses, such as taxes, insurance, and repairs to your home.

Where to Claim Farming-Related Deductions

Report the deduction on the line provided for it on Schedule F of Form 1040. If there is no specific line for the type of deduction you are claiming, list it in the space provided for other expenses (attach your own explanation or description of the expense if not self-explanatory).

You cannot deduct farming-related expenses if you file Form 1040A or Form 1040EZ.

Domestic Production Activities Deduction

If your business makes something in the United States, whether it's by manufacturing, agriculture, mining extraction, construction, filming, software development, or certain other approved activities, you can claim a deduction that effectively reduces the tax rate you pay on your business profits. The best part of the deduction: You don't have to spend any separate money to get it (you are entitled to it because of your activities).

Benefit

You may deduct 3 percent of the net income from qualified domestic production activities. The deduction for individuals is claimed as a subtraction after you have figured the other deductions in the adjusted gross income section of your return.

Conditions

There are several conditions to claiming this deduction:

- Derive income from a qualified activity.
- Meet a W-2 limit.
- Meet an adjusted gross income limit.

QUALIFIED DOMESTIC ACTIVITY. You must derive the net income from a qualified activity, which includes:

- Selling, leasing, or licensing items manufactured, produced, grown, or extracted in the United States in whole or significant part (see safe harbor below).
- Selling, leasing, or licensing films produced in the United States.
- Construction in the United States Construction includes both erection and substantial renovation of residential and commercial buildings (but not cosmetic activities, such as painting).
- Engineering and architectural services relating to a construction project performed in the United States.
- Software developed in the United States, regardless of whether it is purchased off-the-shelf or downloaded from the Internet. The term *software* includes video games. But, with some de minimis exceptions, the term does not include fees for online use of software, fees for customer support, and fees for playing computer games online.

Under significant part safe harbor, you are treated as conducting activities in the United States if labor and overhead costs incurred in the

United States for the manufacture, production, growth, and extraction of the property are at least 20 percent of the total cost of goods sold of the property.

Net income is figured by reducing gross receipts from qualified domestic activities by expenses allocated to these receipts. Under a de minimis rule, if less than 5 percent of total gross receipts is derived from nonqualified domestic production activities, you do not have to make any allocation; all gross receipts are treated as attributable to qualified domestic production activities.

If there is a service element in the activity, allocate gross receipts between the qualified activity and the services. However, no allocation is required if the gross receipts relate to a qualified warranty and other gross receipts from these services are 5 percent or less of the gross receipts from the property.

W-2 LIMIT. The deduction cannot exceed 50 percent of your business's W-2 wages paid in the calendar year for domestic production activities. W-2 wages includes both taxable compensation and elective deferrals (e.g., employee contributions to 401(k) plans).

ADJUSTED GROSS INCOME LIMIT. The deduction cannot exceed your adjusted gross income.

Planning Tips

In order to increase your W-2 limitation, consider hiring employees rather than using independent contractors. Weigh the added cost of employment taxes against the tax savings derived from the higher production activities deduction because of additional W-2 wages.

If you are an owner of a pass-through entity (partnership, limited liability company, or S corporation), your share of the business's qualified production activities income and W-2 wages are reported on your Schedule K-1.

Pitfalls

You cannot claim the deduction if you lease or license property to a related party.

You cannot claim the deduction for the sale of food or beverages prepared at a retail establishment. However, if a business both manufactures food and sells it at a restaurant or take-out store, income and expenses can be allocated so that those related to manufacture and wholesale distribution qualify for the deduction. Thus, in the so-called "Starbucks" situation, roasting and packaging coffee beans could qualify, but selling the beans or brewed coffee at their stores would not.

Where to Claim the Deduction

The production activities deduction is figured on Form 8903, Domestic Production Activities Deduction, and is reported in the "Adjusted Gross Income" section of Form 1040. First report all of the other deductions in this section; then enter your production activities deduction (subject to the adjusted gross income limitation).

You cannot claim the deduction if you file Form 1040EZ or Form 1040A.

Other Business Deductions

Not every expense fits neatly into a business deduction category. The tax law provides a catchall deduction rule, referred to as the ordinary and necessary expense rule, under which an expense can be written off as long as certain conditions are met.

Benefit

A variety of miscellaneous expenses you incur in your business are currently deductible against business income.

Condition

The only condition for deductibility of miscellaneous expenses is that they are ordinary and necessary for your business. "Ordinary" means that they are usual. "Necessary" means they are helpful and appropriate.

EXAMPLES OF OTHER BUSINESS DEDUCTIONS

- Advertising costs—promotional costs as well as goodwill advertising to keep your name in the public eye.
- Asbestos removal.
- Banking fees.
- Depletion for certain oil, gas, and mineral as well as timber properties.
- Dues to professional and trade associations.
- Environmental cleanup costs—expenses to restore property to its precontamination condition.
- Insurance (for self-employed health insurance see Chapter 2).
- Intangibles (e.g., goodwill and covenant not to compete) that are acquired (must be amortized over 15 years).
- Interest on borrowing (for example, financing of equipment purchases).

- Leasing costs for equipment.
- Licenses and regulatory fees paid annually to state or local governments.
- Merchant authorization fees for credit card payments.
- Moving equipment and machinery.
- Rent for office and other business-related space.
- Repairs to keep property in working order (if repairs add to the value or usefulness of the property, the cost must be capitalized).
- Repayments of income reported in prior years. ***Note:*** If the amount of repayment is more than $3,000, you may be able to take a tax credit in lieu of a deduction to obtain a greater benefit from the write-off.
- Shipping and postage.
- Storage and warehousing.
- Subscriptions (see Chapter 14).
- Telephone. If you operate your business from a home office, the basic service charge of the first line to your home is not deductible. But this ban does not apply to additional charges, such as business long-distance calls and the cost of a second business line. The monthly cost of cell phone use is deductible (treatment of the purchase of a cell phone is discussed earlier in this chapter).
- Utilities. Gas, electric, water, and other charges are deductible. If you claim a home office deduction, the treatment of these charges is discussed earlier in this chapter.

Planning Tip

As with all business expenses, keep good records, including receipts, canceled checks, and bills of sale.

Pitfall

Not all expenses you incur in your business are deductible. The tax law specifically prevents you from writing off certain expenses, even though they may be ordinary and necessary to your business.

EXAMPLES OF NONDEDUCTIBLE EXPENSES

- Bribes and kickbacks—even if customary or common business practice, if they are in violation of the law. For example, an insurance broker who pays a "referral fee" to car dealers who refer customers to him cannot deduct the fee because the car dealers are not licensed to sell insurance.

- Club dues for clubs organized for pleasure, recreation, or any other social purpose. Exceptions to this rule are discussed in Chapter 10.
- Demolition expenses to raze a building. These costs are added to the basis of the land on which the building was demolished.
- Fines and penalties.
- Interest on a business-related tax deficiency.
- Lobbying expenses to influence legislation. ***Exception:*** Up to $2,000 of in-house costs for influencing legislation and communicating directly with a covered executive branch official can be deducted.

Where to Claim the Deduction

Deductible miscellaneous business expenses are reported on Schedule C (or Schedule F) either on the line provided for the type of expense (e.g., "Advertising" on Schedule C) or as "Other expenses." If you have more than one such expense, you must list each type of expense in the space provided (or on your own attachment if more space is required).

Other Business Credits

Not every business expense is treated as a deductible item. Some expenses qualify as tax credits that can be used to reduce tax liability on a dollar-for-dollar basis.

Benefit

Other expenses you incur in your business may entitle you to a tax credit, which reduces your taxes dollar for dollar. In Table 15.1 you will see a listing of tax credits, the forms you use to figure them, and where the credits are discussed in this book.

Conditions

Each credit has its own conditions. However, many of the credits are part of the general business credit, which acts as an overall limitation on these credits. The limit for the general business credit is your regular tax liability (after credits other than those that are part of the general business credit), plus any alternative minimum tax liability, minus whichever of the following is larger:

- Tentative AMT from Form 6251.
- Twenty-five percent of your regular tax liability (after other credits) over $25,000.

TABLE 15.1 Tax Credits

Tax Credit	IRS Form	For more information, see Chapter:
Alcohol fuels credit	6478	15
Alternative fuel vehicle refueling credit	8911	
Alternative motor vehicle credit	8910	
Biodiesel fuel credit	8864	
Credit for contributions to certain community development corporations	8847	
Credit for employer-paid Social Security and Medicare taxes on certain tips received by employees of food and beverage establishments	8846	15
Credit for employers affected by Hurricane Katrina, Rita, or Wilma	5884-A	
Credit for wages paid in an empowerment zone	8844	15
Disabled access credit	8826	
Distilled spirits credit	8906	
Employer-provided child care facilities and services	8882	
Energy efficient home credit	8908	
Enhanced oil recovery credit	8830	
Indian employment credit	8845	15
Investment credit (including rehabilitation property credit)	3468	11
Low-income housing credit	8586	11
Low sulfur diesel fuel production credit	8896	
Marginal well oil and gas production credit		
New markets credit	8874	
Nonconventional source fuel credit	8907	
Orphan drug credit	8820	
Railroad track maintenance credit	8900	
Renewable electricity production credit	8835	
Research credit	6765	
Small employer pension plan start-up costs credit	8881	
Welfare-to-work credit	8861	15
Work opportunity credit	5884	15

Planning Tip

Credits in excess of the general business credit limitation can be carried back one year and forward for up to 20 years until they are used up. Be sure to keep track of carryfowards so you do not fail to claim credits to which you may be entitled.

Pitfall

A special limitation applies to tax credits related to passive activities. See Chapter 11 for more details.

Where to Claim the Credits

Figure the credits on the forms specified for each one. Then, if required, complete Form 3800, General Business Credit, to figure the overall limitation on certain credits.

The credits are entered in the "Tax and Credits" section of Form 1040. You cannot claim these business credits if you file Form 1040A or 1040EZ.

Net Operating Losses

Not every business can be profitable year in and year out. What happens if your business suffers a loss from its operations that effectively wipes out more than your tax liability for the year? You may then have what is called a net operating loss. You may be able to use this loss to reduce taxes in prior and/or future years.

Benefit

If your business expenses for the year outweigh your income, your loss may give rise to a net operating loss (NOL) that can be used to offset income in other tax years. Such loss can be carried back to offset income in prior years (producing an immediate tax refund); unused amounts can be carried forward to offset future income. There are limits on the carryback and carryforward years.

The net operating loss deduction is not an additional loss deduction. Rather it is the result of having deductions exceed your business income and applying this excess against income in other years.

Conditions

You must determine whether having a loss in your business for the year results in a net operating loss. You have an NOL if your adjusted gross income is a negative figure. But adjusted gross income for purposes of an NOL does not include certain deductions you are otherwise allowed to take. When figuring your NOL, increase your adjusted gross income by all of the following that apply to you:

- IRA deduction.
- Alimony deduction.
- Net capital losses (capital losses in excess of capital gains).
- Self-employed person's contribution to a qualified retirement plan.

While this computation may sound complicated, you need only follow the line-by-line instructions to Form 1045, Application for Tentative Refund, to see how you adjust your income and determine your net operating loss.

CARRYBACK AND CARRYFORWARD PERIODS. The years to which you carry the loss backward and forward depend on the year in which the NOL arises.

- NOLs arising in tax years beginning before August 6, 1997, and after 2002: three years back; 15 years forward.
- NOLs arising in tax years beginning after August 5, 1997, and before January 1, 2001: generally two years back and 20 years forward. However, small businesses with average annual gross receipts of $5 million or less during a three-year period can use a three-year carryback for NOLs arising from federally declared disasters. For farmers and ranchers, as well as individuals and businesses in the disaster areas created by Hurricane Katrina, Rita, or Wilma, there is a five-year carryback. For NOLs arising from product liability, there is a 10-year carryback.
- NOLs arising in 2001 and 2002: five years back and 20 years forward.

Planning Tips

You can obtain a quick refund from an NOL carryback, money you can put into your business or use for any other purpose. To obtain a quick refund file Form 1045, Application for Tentative Refund, with the IRS. Usually you'll receive your refund within 90 days of filing the form.

Alternatively, you can obtain a refund by filing an amended return, Form 1040X.

You can elect to forgo the carryback and simply carry the NOL forward until it is used up. This election makes sense if you expect to be in a higher tax bracket in coming years than you were in prior years. Keep in mind, however, that tax rates are declining over the next several years.

Another reason to forgo the carryback is to avoid drawing attention to a prior year in which you may have taken a questionable tax position.

If you make the election to forgo the NOL carryback, it applies for alternative minimum tax purposes as well.

Be sure to keep track of NOLs arising in different years, especially since they may be subject to different carryback and carryforward periods.

Pitfalls

An NOL carryback does *not* allow you to refigure your self-employment tax and obtain a refund of that tax.

Net operating losses that are not used up within the carryforward period of 20 years are lost forever.

Where to Claim the Deduction

There is no special form required to be used in figuring a net operating loss. As a practical matter, you can figure your NOL on Schedule A of Form 1045.

A net operating loss is reported as a negative income item; it is not a direct offset to your business income. For example, if your net operating loss carryforward is $4,400, enter –4,400 on the "Other income" line in the "Income" section of Form 1040.

CHAPTER 16

Miscellaneous Items

There are some tax benefits that simply defy classification so they cannot be included in any other chapter. You may be entitled to claim them nonetheless.

This chapter explains:

- State and local income taxes
- State and local sales taxes
- Certain federal taxes
- Tax preparation costs
- Tax audits
- Legal fees
- Gifts you receive
- Inheritances
- Life insurance proceeds
- Estate tax deduction on income in respect of a decedent
- Government benefits
- Alternative minimum tax

For more information see IRS Publication 525, *Taxable and Nontaxable Income*, and IRS Publication 529, *Miscellaneous Deductions*.

State and Local Income Taxes

Individuals in all but seven states (Alaska, Florida, Nevada, South Dakota, Texas, Washington, and Wyoming) and the District of Columbia may be subject to income taxes (those in New Hampshire and Tennessee have an income tax on interest income and dividends only). There may also be income taxes on the local level. These taxes are deductible for federal income tax purposes if you itemize deductions.

Benefit

If you pay state and local income tax, through withholding or estimated tax payments, you can deduct the total amount as an itemized deduction. There is no dollar limit to this deduction.

Conditions

There are no conditions for claiming this deduction. Whatever amount you pay is deductible, provided you itemize your deductions. Withholding from wages is reported on Form W-2.

You may not deduct your state and local income tax if you opt to deduct state and local sales taxes, explained next.

Planning Tips

You may increase your deduction for state income tax for 2006 by prepaying the fourth installment of estimated tax. Generally, the fourth installment for 2006 is due on January 15, 2007. This fourth installment would normally be deductible for federal income tax purposes in 2007. However, you can pay it before the end of the year to increase the deduction for 2006.

Do not forget to add to your 2006 payments any 2005 state and local estimated taxes that were paid in January 2006.

Pitfall

Do not prepay state income tax if you are subject to the alternative minimum tax (AMT). State income tax is not deductible for AMT purposes, so prepaying effectively wastes the deduction.

Where to Claim the Deduction

The deduction is claimed on Schedule A of Form 1040. There is no special form or worksheet needed to figure your deduction.

You cannot claim this deduction if you file Form 1040A or 1040-EZ.

State and Local Sales Taxes *(Provision expired 12/31/05. Extension expected for 2006.)*

There are over 7,000 state and local sales tax jurisdictions throughout the United States. The amount of tax you pay depends on how much you buy each year and the state (or states) in which you live. The deduction for state and local sales taxes can be claimed only if you itemize deductions and you do not deduct state and local income taxes.

Benefit

You can deduct state and local sales taxes paid during the year as an itemized deduction. You can claim your actual payments based on receipts for purchases or rely on an IRS table in the instructions to Schedule A of Form 1040. There is no dollar limit to this deduction.

Conditions

There are no conditions for claiming this deduction. Whatever amount you pay (or the figure for your state of residence, income level, and number of exemptions claimed on your return) can be deducted. "Income" for purposes of the IRS tables is based on total available income, which is taxable income increased by nontaxable items such as tax-exempt interest; veterans' benefits; nontaxable combat pay; workers' compensation; nontaxable part of Social Security and Railroad Retirement benefits; nontaxable part of IRA, pension, or annuity distributions (but no rollovers); and public assistance payments.

As mentioned, you may not deduct state and local sales taxes if you opt to deduct state and local income taxes.

Planning Tips

You can increase the deduction from the IRS tables by state and local general sales taxes paid on the following items *only*:

- Car
- Motorcycle
- Motor home
- Recreational vehicle
- Sport utility vehicle
- Truck
- Van
- Off-road vehicle
- Leased motor vehicle

You can also add in sales taxes paid on an aircraft, a boat, a mobile home, a prefabricated home, or home building materials as long as the tax rate is the same as the general sales tax rate.

If you live in more than one state you must allocate the deduction found in the IRS tables for the number of days you lived in that state. For example, if you lived in Arizona for six months and New Jersey for six months in 2006, your total deduction for state and local sales taxes is one-half of your amount from the table for Arizona and one-half of your amount from the table for New Jersey.

Just because you live in a state in which you pay income taxes, do not assume that that deduction will be larger than the one for state sales tax. You may have a higher sales tax deduction if you fall into any of the following situations:

- A retiree whose income is primarily from Social Security benefits, certain types of annuities and pensions, and interest on Treasury securities.
- A self-employed individual who had a bad year.
- A family with a large number of exemptions.
- A person who was laid off from a job.
- A disabled worker who receives nontaxable state disability and workers' compensation payments.

Pitfall

State and local sales taxes are not deductible for alternative minimum tax (AMT) purposes, so claiming the deduction can trigger or increase your AMT liability.

Where to Claim the Deduction

The deduction is claimed on Schedule A of Form 1040. Be sure to check the appropriate box on the schedule to indicate that you are claiming a deduction for general sales taxes.

Certain Federal Taxes

Most federal taxes you pay, such as income taxes, are not deductible. But there are some deductible federal taxes:

- One-half of self-employment tax (see Chapter 15).
- Estate tax paid on income in respect of a decedent (see Chapter 16).

Also, in 2006 you can claim a refund of federal excise tax paid on long-distance telephone service after February 28, 2003 and before August 1, 2006. This benefit is reported as an excess tax payment on your return. You can claim the actual amount of taxes paid or rely on an IRS standard amount. You may be required to complete Form 8913.

You can claim this refund whether you file Form 1040EZ, Form 1040A, or Form 1040. Individuals whose income is below the amount required to file a return can also obtain a refund by filing Form 1040EZ-T.

Tax Preparation Costs

The cost of tax return preparation and filing can be a few dollars for mailing a return by certified mail or hundreds of dollars in professional fees. Fortunately, whatever you spend may be deductible.

Benefit

Whatever way you prepare your personal federal and, if applicable, state income tax returns each year, you can deduct your expenses as a miscellaneous itemized deduction. Such deduction can be claimed only to the extent the total exceeds 2 percent of your adjusted gross income.

The cost of tax preparation for returns for your business or rental activities is deductible as a business expense against your business income.

There is no dollar limit on what you can deduct for tax preparation costs.

Conditions

There are no set conditions for writing off the cost of preparing and filing your tax returns; whatever you pay is a deductible expense.

EXAMPLES OF TAX PREPARATION COSTS

- Books on taxes and tax preparation (including the cost of this book).
- Online (electronic) filing fees.
- Tax preparation software (such as TurboTax).
- Tax preparer fees (such as H&R Block charges and accountants' fees).

Planning Tip

To minimize your tax preparation costs, see if you qualify for free online preparation and filing through a commercial software company. You can learn about eligibility requirements at the IRS web site (www.irs.gov and click on *e-file*).

Pitfall

Be sure to claim tax preparation costs in the right year.

Example

In April 2006, you pay an accountant to prepare and file your 2005 returns. Your deduction for these tax preparation costs is claimed on your 2006 return.

Where to Claim the Deduction

You report your tax preparation costs for personal returns as a miscellaneous itemized deduction on Schedule A of Form 1040.

You report tax preparation costs related to your business or investment properties on the appropriate form: Schedule C, Schedule E, or Schedule F of Form 1040.

You cannot claim any deduction for tax preparation costs if you file Form 1040A or 1040EZ.

Tax Audits

The law does not require professional representation during the course of a tax audit; taxpayers can represent themselves. But it is common practice to use knowledgeable tax professionals during an audit, especially if the dollars at stake justify the cost of their professional fees. Fortunately, whatever you spend on these fees may be deductible. Alternatively, you may be able to get the government to pay for them if certain conditions are met.

Benefit

Fees to pay to your accountant or attorney to assist or represent you in a tax audit are deductible as a miscellaneous itemized deduction, which is subject to the 2 percent of adjusted gross income floor. There is no dollar limit on how much you can deduct for your audit costs.

If you contest an IRS audit and substantially prevail, you may be able to recover attorney's fees and costs if the IRS's position was not substantially justified. Generally, your recovery of attorney's fees is limited to a set dollar amount ($160 per hour in 2006).

Conditions

The conditions for deducting your audit costs are the same as those discussed earlier in this chapter with regard to tax preparation costs. The following conditions relate to recovering your costs from the government.

In order to recover your out-of-pocket costs for contesting an IRS audit through the administrative level as well as in the courts, you must meet all five of these conditions:

1. You exhaust administrative remedies.
2. You substantially prevail against the IRS.
3. The IRS position is not substantially justified.
4. Your request for reimbursement is reasonable.
5. You meet net worth requirements.

EXHAUST ADMINISTRATIVE REMEDIES. This means you must proceed through the IRS appeals process and cooperate at every level. You cannot unreasonably delay the proceedings.

SUBSTANTIALLY PREVAIL AGAINST THE IRS. This means you must win on the key issue or issues or the amount of tax involved. Once you satisfy this requirement, you are entitled to a recovery unless the IRS can show that it was substantially justified in pursuing the case.

THE IRS POSITION NOT SUBSTANTIALLY JUSTIFIED. The IRS position is substantially justified if it is reasonable. The IRS is presumed *not* to be reasonable if it fails to follow Treasury regulations and IRS rulings, procedures, notices, announcements, and private letter rulings. Of course, this is only a presumption that the IRS is free to rebut. In deciding whether the IRS position is substantially justified, a court may consider whether the same IRS position has already been rejected in a federal appellate court.

REASONABLE REIMBURSEMENT. You can recover only reasonable administrative costs of proceeding within the IRS and reasonable litigation costs, such as expert witnesses, court costs, and attorney's fees, in a court action. Attorney's fees generally are limited to a fixed rate per hour ($160 in 2006). However, a higher rate may be granted in special circumstances, such as the limited availability of local tax expertise.

NET WORTH REQUIREMENTS. Even if you meet all of the previous four conditions, you cannot recover anything related to your personal taxes unless your net worth is no more than $2 million. The $2 million limit applies separately to each spouse. The net worth limit is measured at the time the action begins.

If the recovery relates to your business as a sole proprietorship, you cannot have a net worth over $5 million or more than 500 employees.

Planning Tip

To make a claim for reimbursement of reasonable administrative costs, you must make an application for the amount to the IRS before the 91st day after the date on which the IRS mailed you its final decision. If the IRS denies your claim for payment, you must then petition the Tax Court within 90 days from the date the IRS mailed you its denial.

Pitfall

You may not recover any attorney's fees if you represent yourself (pro se). You can, however, recover any other reasonable costs, such as photocopying and postage, as well as travel costs to meet with the IRS (at 44.5 cents per mile for 2006).

Where to Claim the Deduction for Audit Costs

You report your audit costs related to your personal taxes as a miscellaneous itemized deduction on Schedule A of Form 1040.

You report audit costs related to your business or investment properties on the appropriate form: Schedule C, Schedule E, or Schedule F of Form 1040.

You cannot claim any deduction for audit costs if you file Form 1040A or 1040EZ.

If you successfully recover attorney's fees and other costs from the government, you do not have to report this income. It is tax free to you.

Legal Fees

William Shakespeare said, "Let's kill all the lawyers." But when a person today wants to right a perceived wrong, he or she usually turns to a lawyer for assistance. The cost of this help, which can be very steep, can be deducted only in certain circumstances.

Benefit

Legal fees you pay for actions that include discrimination are deducted as an adjustment to gross income. Legal fees for certain other personal matters are deductible as miscellaneous itemized deductions, which are subject to the 2 percent of adjusted gross income floor.

Legal fees related to your business that meet deductibility conditions are ordinary and necessary business expenses that offset business income.

Condition

To be deductible, legal fees must relate to your business, the production of income (which includes, for example, the receipt of taxable alimony or a taxable award), or income taxes.

EXAMPLES OF DEDUCTIBLE FEES. Fees related to these matters can be deducted:

- Action to keep your job, win a promotion, or fight discrimination.
- Estate planning advice.
- Personal injury actions other than for physical illness or injury, (e.g., defamation suits).
- Marital actions in which you seek alimony.
- Social Security benefits contest (assuming your benefits are partially taxable, then that portion of legal fees is deductible).
- Tax actions, including return preparation and audits. Legal fees related to tax advice are also deductible.

To deduct legal fees as an adjustment to gross income, the claim must be for unlawful discrimination (such as age discrimination on the job), claims against the federal government under Subchapter III of Chapter 27, Title 31, of the U.S. Code, and a private cause of action under the Medicare Secondary Payer statute.

Planning Tip

When engaging an attorney for representation, be sure you fully understand the fee arrangement. For example, even in a contingency fee arrangement (in which you owe no money if you do not recover anything), you may owe the attorney money to cover expenses, such as photocopying and postage, in addition to any portion of the award.

Pitfall

Not all legal fees are deductible. Some nondeductible legal fees may be capitalized (added to the basis of property), so that they will, in effect, be recovered when the asset is disposed of.

Example

You buy investment property for $100,000 and pay $5,000 in legal fees. You cannot deduct the fees, but you can add them to the basis of the property. Assume that a few years from now you sell the property for $150,000. Your gain is $45,000 ($150,000 – [$100,000 + $50,000]). In effect, you have reduced your gain for tax purposes by the $5,000 in legal fees you added to the property's basis.

EXAMPLES OF NONDEDUCTIBLE FEES. Fees related to these matters cannot be currently deducted:

- Acquisition of an asset, including a home or a business (the fees are added to the basis of the asset).
- Obtaining child support.
- Defending title to property.
- Marital actions in which you are required to pay alimony or make a property settlement (or actions in which you receive a property settlement), other than amounts related to tax advice.
- Name change.
- Personal injury actions involving physical injury or illness.
- Will preparation.

You cannot deduct legal fees which are part of miscellaneous itemized deductions for alternative minimum tax (AMT) purposes. This means that if you have claimed a large write-off for regular tax purposes, the deduction of legal fees might trigger or increase your AMT liability.

Where to Claim the Benefit

You report deductible legal fees paid for personal matters other than discrimination claims as a miscellaneous itemized deduction on Schedule A of Form 1040.

You report legal fees related to discrimination claims in the "Adjusted Gross Income" section of Form 1040. Write "UDC" on line 36 to indicate that you are deducting legal fees for an unlawful discrimination claim.

You report deductible legal fees related to your business or investment properties on the appropriate form: Schedule C, Schedule E, or Schedule F of Form 1040.

You cannot claim any deduction for legal fees if you file Form 1040A or 1040EZ.

Gifts You Receive

Whether your birthday gift is a tie, a set of golf clubs, or a check for $25,000, you usually can treat the gift as tax free for income tax purposes. The gift doesn't have to relate to a special occasion, such as Mother's Day or an anniversary, and it doesn't have to come from a relative. All you need is for the transfer to be a true gift and not something else (such as disguised compensation).

Benefit

Gifts you receive from just about anyone are tax free. Gifts can be in cash or property. There is no dollar limit on the amount of gifts you can exclude from income each year.

Important: Your income tax treatment is separate and distinct from the gift tax rules imposed on the gift's giver (the donor). Thus, the fact that a donor can make gifts free from gift tax only up to a set dollar amount per person per year ($12,000 in 2006) does not affect your receipt of the gift. Even if the donor exceeds this limit your receipt is still entirely tax free for income tax purposes.

Condition

To be treated as a tax-free gift, the transfer must be made with donative intent (a substantive view toward making a gift) and the recipient cannot pay any consideration for receiving it. In most cases, it is entirely clear that a transfer of property is intended as a gift. There are two key situations, however, in which the transfer may not be entirely clear and tax-free treatment is not assured:

1. Where money is really intended as a loan rather than a gift (see Chapter 12 for rules on distinguishing between a gift and a loan, especially when the parties are related).
2. Where money or property is given to employees (see "Pitfalls").

Planning Tip

When you receive a gift of property, be sure to obtain from the donor the following information needed to determine your gain or loss when you later dispose of the property:

- *The donor's basis.* If the basis of the property at the time of the gift was at least equal to its value at that time, then your basis becomes the donor's basis. If the gift's value was less than its basis at the time of the gift (the property had declined in value), then your basis for purposes of determining gain is the donor's basis, but your basis for determining loss is the value of the gift at the time it was made to you. It is possible under the right circumstances that because of these special basis rules you may realize neither a gain nor a loss when you sell the gift.

- *The donor's holding period.* You can add to the time you own the property all of the donor's holding period. For example, assume the donor purchased stock on July 1, 2003, and gives you the shares on May 1, 2006. If you sell those shares on May 15, 2006, your gain or loss is *long-term* gain or loss because the shares are considered to have been held for more than one year (the holding period begins with the donor's holding period).

Starting in 2010, a donor who is required to file a gift tax return must provide you with the following information within 30 days after the gift tax return's due date (generally April 15 of the year after the year of the gift):

- The name, address, and telephone number of the person required to file the tax return.
- The information specified in the gift tax return (a description of the gift and its value at the time of the gift).

If the donor fails to provide you with this information, he or she can be subject to a $50 penalty.

Pitfalls

Money or items received from your employer that are labeled as gifts may, in fact, be nothing more than additional compensation. Small items, such as a holiday turkey or ham, are tax-free gifts to you. But gifts of *any* cash or cash equivalents (such as gift certificates) and more expensive items (such as golf clubs) are considered taxable compensation, not tax-free gifts.

Income earned on a gift is taxable (unless such income is also tax-free income).

Example

You receive a gift of $10,000. The receipt of the gift is tax-free to you. You use the money to buy a Treasury bill: interest on the investment is taxable to you. If you use the money to buy a municipal bond, however, the interest on the investment is tax free (because municipal bond interest is tax free).

Where to Claim the Benefit

Since gifts are tax free, you do not have to report them on your return.

Inheritances

Whether you inherit your uncle's gold watch or your mother's entire million-dollar estate, you are not taxed on this inheritance. There are no limits to the amount you can inherit tax free.

While the receipt of an inheritance is always tax free, some inheritances may produce taxable income later on. For example, if you inherit a $100,000 traditional IRA, you are not immediately taxed on the inheritance; there's no tax as long as the funds remain in the IRA. However, as you start to withdraw funds from the IRA, you are taxable on this amount. Fortunately, you are entitled to claim a tax deduction for any federal estate tax attributable to this taxable income, called income in respect of a decedent (IRD), which is explained later in this chapter.

Benefit

Inheritances you receive are tax free. There is no dollar limit on the amount of an inheritance you can exclude from income.

In addition to tax-free treatment for an inheritance, you may also be entitled to a tax deduction from the estate. This occurs when an estate is not settled immediately but operates, receiving income and incurring deductions for income tax purposes. The estate becomes a taxpayer until the affairs of the estate are settled. If the estate's income tax total deductions in its last year are more than its gross income for that year, then beneficiaries who succeed to the estate's property can claim a deduction. This is a one-time deduction that can be claimed only in the year in which, or with which, the estate terminates, whether the year of termination is a normal tax year or a short tax year. The executor of the estate should supply any necessary information to enable you to claim a deduction. The deduction can be claimed only as a miscellaneous itemized deduction subject to the 2 percent of AGI floor.

Condition

There are no conditions on the tax-free receipt of an inheritance other than the fact you receive the inheritance on account of the death of a person. Inheritances include amounts paid to you under a will, or by the state's rules of intestacy (if the person died without a will), jointly owned property you receive in full when your co-owner dies, and other amounts you receive as a named beneficiary (for example, a person's pension benefits left to you as the designated beneficiary).

Planning Tips

When you inherit property, your basis becomes the value of the property for estate tax purposes (generally the property's value on the date of death). This is called a "stepped-up basis." Also, you automatically have a long-term holding period, regardless of how long the decedent owned the property before death or how long you hold it after you inherit it.

Example

On January 15, 2007, you inherit 100 shares of X Company from a decedent who purchased them on November 15, 2006, at $10,000. On the date you inherit them, they are worth $12,000. Two weeks later, you sell them for $13,000. You have a long-term capital gain of $1,000 ($13,000 – $12,000).

Pitfalls

If you anticipate an inheritance and sell your right to receive it, the proceeds you receive are taxable as ordinary income. This is so even though you would have received tax-free income had you waited for the inheritance itself.

If you are named as the executor, administrator, or personal representative of an estate, payment of fiduciary fees to you are *not* tax-free inheritances (even if you are also an heir to the estate).

Income earned on an inheritance is taxable (unless the income is also tax-free income—see the earlier example under "Gifts"). Income includes amounts on assets that previously have gone untaxed, such as traditional IRAs and annuities.

Example

You are named as the beneficiary of your father's IRA. When he dies, there is $100,000 in the IRA. Your inheritance of this IRA is tax free. However, since your father never paid income tax on the funds, you must do so under the minimum distribution rules for IRAs (explained in IRS Publication 590, *Individual Retirement Arrangements*). You are taxable when and to the extent you take withdrawals from the IRA.

Where to Claim the Benefit

Since inheritances are tax free, you do not have to report them on your return.

If you are entitled to deduct the estate's deduction from its final year, report the deduction as a miscellaneous itemized deduction subject to the 2 percent of AGI floor on Schedule A of Form 1040.

You cannot claim this deduction if you file Form 1040A or 1040EZ.

Life Insurance Proceeds

The beneficiary of a life insurance policy generally can receive the proceeds free from income tax. There is no requirement that the beneficiary be related to the insured (the person on whose life the insurance is based), and there is no limit on the amount of proceeds that can be received tax free.

Benefit

Life insurance proceeds you receive on account of the death of the insured are tax free to you. There is no dollar limit on the amount you can receive tax free.

Condition

To be tax free, life insurance proceeds must be payable on the death of the insured. The insured may be the same person as the owner of the policy or may be someone else.

Planning Tip

Life insurance proceeds can be used during the insured's life on a tax-free basis under certain conditions. The treatment of accelerated death benefits is explained in Chapter 2.

Pitfalls

If you leave insurance proceeds with the insurance company, interest you receive is taxable. (Only surviving spouses of someone who died before October 23, 1986, can exclude the first $1,000 of interest each year.)

If you paid any consideration for the life insurance policy, then you are taxable on the proceeds. You are treated as having paid consideration if you become the policy owner and there is an outstanding loan on the policy.

Example

A mother has a $100,000 life insurance policy against which she has borrowed $10,000. She gives the policy to her daughter (receipt of the policy is a tax-free gift to the daughter). Shortly thereafter the mother dies and the daughter collects $90,000 ($100,000 face value of the policy minus the outstanding loan of $10,000). The daughter is taxed on the $90,000.

Where to Claim the Benefit

Since life insurance proceeds received on account of the death of the insured are tax free, you do not have to report them on your return.

Estate Tax Deduction on Income in Respect of a Decedent

It has been estimated that there is about $3 *trillion* of unclaimed deductions for federal estate tax payable with respect to income items included in the estate because heirs are simply ignorant of this deduction opportunity. If you inherit something on which you must pay income taxes because the person who left you the inheritance never did, then you may be eligible for this special deduction. To claim this special deduction, certain conditions must be met.

Benefit

If you inherit a traditional IRA, annuity, or other income in respect of a decedent (IRD) and must report income from this inheritance, you may be eligible for an itemized deduction for the portion of federal estate tax related to this property. This itemized deduction is *not* subject to the 2 percent of adjusted gross income floor. There is no dollar limit on this deduction.

Conditions

To claim this deduction, the IRA, annuity, or other income in respect of a decedent (any income that the decedent earned before death but was not taxable to him or her at that time) must have been part of an estate that was subject to federal estate taxes. If the estate is under the estate-tax exemption amount ($2 million in 2006), then there is no estate tax to contend with. State estate or inheritance taxes are not deductible.

Examples of IRD:

- Accounts payable to self-employed business owners on the cash basis.
- Benefits from 401(k) and other qualified retirement plans.
- Damage awards from lawsuits.
- Deferred compensation.
- Health Savings Accounts.
- Interest on U.S. savings bonds that has been deferred.
- Royalties.
- Survivor annuities.
- Traditional IRAs.

Assuming there has been federal estate tax paid on income in respect of a decedent, then figure the portion of the estate tax deductible in the current year. If, for example, you withdraw *all* of the IRA funds, then *all* of the estate tax related to this asset is deductible this year.

Example

In 2006, you inherit a $2.5 million estate consisting of realty worth $2 million and a traditional IRA worth $500,000. Assume the federal estate tax on the decedent's estate is $400,000. Twenty percent of this amount ($500,000 ÷ $2,500,000), or $80,000, is your deduction for the portion of federal income tax on the IRA distribution.

If you withdraw *all* the IRA funds this year, you can claim an itemized deduction for *all* of the federal estate tax attributable to this income, which is $80,000. If you withdraw only some of the funds, then you must allocate the $80,000 accordingly. For example, if you take 10 percent of the $500,000, then you can deduct $8,000 (10% of $80,000).

The calculation on the portion of estate tax can become complex when only part of the IRA is withdrawn within the year. A full explanation of how to figure this deduction may be found in IRS Publication 559, *Survivors, Executors, and Administrators.*

Planning Tips

This deduction is often overlooked. If you inherited an IRA and have not been claiming the deduction every year in which you report a distribution from the account, consider filing amended returns for all open tax years. You generally have three years from the due date of the return to file an amended return. This means you may be able to file for the prior three years and obtain tax refunds for each year.

When you receive an inheritance of IRD, be sure to ask the executor for information about estate taxes so you can figure your deduction. Find out about the amount of federal estate tax, the total estate, and what portion of it is the IRD you inherited.

Pitfall

There is no downside to claiming this deduction where allowable.

Where to Claim the Deduction

Generally, you report this deduction as a miscellaneous itemized deduction on Schedule A of Form 1040. It is *not* subject to the 2 percent floor. However, when the income in respect of a decedent is long-term capital gain (such as an installment payment on a sale made before the decedent's death), the deduction is not claimed separately but rather treated as an expense of sale. This means you still get the benefit of the deduction, but in the form of a reduction of the gain you report.

You cannot claim this deduction if you file Form 1040A or 1040EZ.

Government Benefits

Individuals may receive payments from the federal and/or state government for a variety of reasons. In many cases these benefits may be received entirely tax free.

Benefit

Most government payments can be received tax free; they are excludable without regard to their amount or your income.

If you must repay Social Security benefits in excess of annual benefits received, you may deduct the excess amounts as a miscellaneous itemized deduction to the extent total itemized deductions exceed 2 percent of adjusted gross income.

Condition

As a practical matter, many types of government benefits are payable to individuals whose incomes are below the level at which a tax return must be filed and taxes are owed. Most government benefits or payments are tax free. Any taxable amounts usually are reported to you on an information return:

- Form RRA-1099, Payment by the Railroad Retirement Board.
- Form SSA-1099, Social Security Benefit Statement.
- Form 1099G, Certain Government and Qualified State Tuition Program Payments.

EXAMPLES OF TAX-FREE GOVERNMENT BENEFITS

- Black lung benefit payments.
- Crime victim payments from a state fund for this purpose.
- Disaster relief and disaster mitigation grants (see Chapter 13).
- Energy conservation subsidies paid by public utilities.
- Federal Employees' Compensation Act (FECA) payments for personal injury or sickness (including death benefits to beneficiaries).
- Federal income tax refunds.
- Foster care provider payments (see Chapter 1).

- Foster Grandparents Program payments for supportive services or reimbursement for out-of-pocket expenses.
- Grants for homes designed for wheelchair living of disabled veterans.
- Grants for motor vehicles for veterans who have lost their sight or the use of their limbs.
- Historic preservation grants under the National Historic Preservation Act.
- Holocaust victims restitution (see Chapter 13).
- Interest on insurance dividends left on deposit with the Department of Veterans Affairs.
- Military benefits (see Chapter 14).
- Mortgage assistance payments under Section 235 of the National Housing Act (the homeowner cannot deduct interest paid by this assistance).
- Nutrition Program for the Elderly food benefits.
- Peace Corps payments for housing, food, utilities, and clothing.
- Retired Senior Volunteer Program (RSVP) payments for supportive services or reimbursement for out-of-pocket expenses.
- SCORE payments for supportive services or reimbursement for out-of-pocket expenses.
- Senior Companion program payments for supportive services or reimbursement for out-of-pocket expenses.
- State income tax refunds if you did not itemize deductions in the year to which the payments relate.
- Supplemental Security Income (SSI).
- Survivor benefits of deceased public safety officers (policy and law enforcement officers, firefighters, chaplains, and rescue squad and ambulance crew members).
- Volunteer tax counseling for the elderly (TCE) reimbursements for transportation, meals, and other expenses.
- Volunteers in Service to America (VISTA) volunteers living expense allowances.
- Welfare benefits.
- Winter energy cost reduction payments to qualified individuals.
- Workers' compensation benefits.
- Work-training program payments from state welfare agencies (as long as the payments, exclusive of extra allowances for transportation or other costs, do not exceed public welfare benefits otherwise receivable).
- World Trade Center relief grants to families (but not to businesses).

Planning Tips

Social Security benefits may be fully or partially tax free, depending on your filing status, the amount of Social Security benefits, and other income, including tax-exempt interest. (The same rules apply to equivalent Railroad Retirement benefits.) Table 16.1 shows the portion of benefits excludable from income. The income threshold includes total income plus tax-exempt income and one-half of Social Security benefits.

Example

In 2006, you are single with income from wages and taxable interest of $18,000. You also receive $12,000 in Social Security benefits and $1,000 of tax-exempt interest, with no adjustments to gross income. Since total income ($18,000 + 50% of $12,000 + $1,000) does not exceed $25,000, none of your benefits are included in income; they are tax free.

This explanation of the taxation of Social Security benefits is a brief overview that does not include many nuances to be taken into account. For more complete information about excluding Social Security benefits, see IRS Publication 915, *Social Security and Equivalent Railroad Retirement Benefits*.

If Form SSA-1099 shows a negative number (the benefits you are required to repay for any reason exceed your annual benefits), you may deduct the negative number as a miscellaneous itemized deduction to the extent total miscellaneous deductions exceed 2 percent of adjusted gross income. If the negative number exceeds $3,000, you may qualify to figure tax for the year in a special way (see "Repayment of Supplemental Unemployment Benefits" in Chapter 14).

Pitfalls

Just because a payment comes from the government does not automatically mean it is tax free. Some government payments are taxable.

TABLE 16.1 Income Threshold for the Excludable Portion of Social Security Benefits

	100% Excludable	50% Excludable	15% Excludable
Married filing jointly	Up to $32,000	Over $32,000 but not over $44,000	Over $44,000
Married filing separately	—	—	Automatically applies
Other taxpayers	Up to $25,000	Over $25,000 but not over $34,000	Over $34,000

EXAMPLES OF TAXABLE GOVERNMENT BENEFITS

- Alaska Permanent Fund dividend income.
- Election precinct officials' payments.
- Jury duty pay.
- Peace Corps payments for leave allowances, readjustment allowances, and termination payments.
- State lottery winnings.
- Unemployment compensation.

Where to Claim the Benefit

Those government benefits that are tax free do not have to be reported on your return.

Alternative Minimum Tax

The alternative minimum tax (AMT) is a parallel tax system that exists to ensure all taxpayers pay at least some tax, even if they can reduce their regular tax through legitimate deductions. You pay AMT to the extent it exceeds your regular tax. Throughout this book you have seen many examples of items that receive different tax treatment for regular tax and AMT purposes.

Benefit

You can claim an AMT exemption that may eliminate or at least minimize your AMT liability. For 2006, the exemption for married persons filing jointly is $62,550; for single taxpayers the exemption amount is $42,500. For married persons filing separate returns, the exemption amount is only $31,275.

Conditions

There are no conditions for claiming this exemption. Simply apply the correct one for your filing status.

Planning Tip

Even if the exemption amount does not eliminate AMT liability, you can use various personal tax credits to reduce this liability. These include, for example, the dependent care credit, education credits, and the retirement saver's credit.

Pitfalls

The tax credit for purchasing a hybrid vehicle cannot be used to offset AMT. The exemption amounts are scheduled to decline in 2007 to $45,000 on a joint return and $33,750 for singles unless Congress extends the 2006 limits.

Similarly, after 2006, nonrefundable personal credits that can be used to offset AMT are limited to the adoption credit, child tax credit, and mortgage certificate credit.

Where to Claim the Exemption

The exemption is claimed on Form 6251, Alternative Minimum Tax—Individuals, which is attached to Form 1040. If you are required to complete this form, you cannot file Form 1040A or 1040EZ.

APPENDIX A

Items Adjusted Annually for Inflation

Law changes are one important way in which write-off amounts and restrictions on them change each year. But another, less obvious way is adjustments to certain amounts and limits reflecting cost-of-living changes. Not all items subject to adjustment actually change each year, but the list of the items subject to change continues to grow.

To help you plan your taxes for the future, it's helpful to know that certain limits affecting exclusions, deductions, and credits are raised in step with increases in the cost of living (although some items may be adjusted downward if the times demand it). The following exclusions, deductions, and credits are subject to annual adjustments for inflation.

adoption assistance programs the maximum dollar amount and AGI phaseout range.

adoption credit the maximum dollar amount and the AGI phaseout range.

Archer medical savings accounts the definition of a high-deductible plan (i.e., the range for an annual deductible) and the limit on out-of-pocket costs.

benefits limit for defined benefit plans the dollar limit on benefits under these plans for which contributions are figured on an actuarial basis.

child tax credit the value used in determining the refundable credit.

compensation on which qualified retirement plan deductions are based the amount of compensation or self-employment income taken into account in figuring deductions for plan contributions.

contribution limit for profit-sharing and other defined contribution plans the dollar limit on deductible contributions to these plans.

contribution limit for SEPs the dollar limit on deductible contributions to these plans.

dollar limit for depreciation and first-year expensing on luxury cars the maximum deduction for depreciation or first-year expensing for cars and light trucks weighing no more than 6,000 pounds.

earned income credit the earned income amount, the maximum amount of the credit, and the AGI phaseout range.

first-year expensing limit dollar limit on amount of equipment that can be expensed as well as the taxable income limit.

foreign earned income exclusion the dollar amount that can be received tax free for performing services abroad.

Health Savings Accounts annual deductibles for high-deductible health plans.

Hope and lifetime learning credits MAGI phaseout range.

insubstantial benefits from charities dollar limit on what constitutes insubstantial benefits (ignored when figuring charitable contribution deductions).

interest exclusion on savings bonds AGI phaseout range.

interest on student loans AGI phaseout range.

long-term care premiums dollar limit on annual contributions treated as deductible medical expenses.

low-income housing credit amounts used to calculate the state housing credit ceiling.

overall limit on itemized deductions MAGI threshold at which limit applies.

payments received under long-term care policies or accelerated death benefits daily dollar limit excludable without regard to long-term care expenses or terminal illness.

personal exemption dollar amount.

refundable entrance fee to a continuing care facility dollar threshold below which such fee is exempt from the imputed interest rules.

Social Security wage base for FICA and self-employment tax limit on income taken into account in figuring the Social Security portion of FICA and self-employment tax.

standard deduction dollar amount.

standard mileage rate for business travel the cents-per-mile rate may be increased or decreased.

standard mileage rate for medical or moving the cents-per-mile rate may be increased or decreased.

transportation fringe benefits dollar limit on excludable free parking, monthly transit passes, and van pooling.

APPENDIX B

Checklist of Nondeductible Items

Unfortunately, not everything you spend your money on gives rise to a tax deduction. Most of your personal expenses, such as food, clothing, and recreation, are nondeductible items. The tax law also specifically bans certain write-offs. Of course, in some cases, while a deduction may be banned as a general rule, there may be circumstances under which it becomes deductible (so check throughout the book for exceptions to the general rule).

The IRS has identified a number of scams (the IRS calls them the "Dirty Dozen") in which sharp promoters incorrectly advise taxpayers to claim certain types of write-offs. Here are some types of write-offs that the IRS cautions taxpayers against claiming:

- *Trust deductions for personal expenses.* Promoters tell taxpayers to transfer their assets to trusts and have the trusts deduct the cost of food, clothing and other personal expenses. *Personal expenses, other than those explained throughout the book, are not deductible.*
- *"No gain realized" deduction.* Like the claim of right doctrine, promoters tell taxpayers to claim a miscellaneous itemized deduction on Schedule A equal to their adjusted gross income. *There is no such deduction.*
- *Zero returns.* Promoters instruct taxpayers to enter all zeros on the return (rather than reporting their actual income items). *Income must be reported unless there is a specific tax rule for exemption or exclusion.*

- *Slavery reparations.* Promoters suggest that African-Americans can claim a deduction or credit for reparations. *There are no such reparations and no such allowable deduction or credit.*
- *Home-based businesses.* While there is a deduction allowed for legitimate home-based businesses, promoters tell taxpayers to fictitiously create a business run from home so that a deduction will be allowed. *Fake businesses do not support real deductions.*
- *Shared earned income credits.* Promoters tell taxpayers that they can "share" dependents in order for multiple taxpayers to claim the earned income credit with respect to the same dependents. *Only eligible taxpayers can claim the earned income credit and only one credit is allowed for each dependent.*

Here is a listing of other items you may not deduct.

At-risk, losses in excess of.

Attorney's fees on buying a home.

Bank fees, such as monthly checking fees on a personal account.

Bar examination fees.

Blood donations.

Bribes.

Burial fees.

Car expenses for personal use of the car.

Child support payments.

Club dues for recreational, social, and athletic clubs.

Commuting expenses.

Compensation to housekeepers and other domestic employees.

Cosmetic surgery.

Country club membership.

Credit card interest incurred for personal expenditures.

Debts belonging to another person that you pay.

Demolition costs.

Disability insurance premiums.

Education costs for your child's primary and secondary school.

Elective deferrals to 401(k) and similar plans.

Estimated tax penalties.

Expenses of earning tax-exempt income.

Federal income tax.

Fifty percent of meal and entertainment costs for business.

Fines.

Funeral expenses.

Gambling losses in excess of winnings.

Gift tax.

Gifts you make to family and friends.

Health spa expenses.

Hobby losses.

Interest on loans to buy or carry tax-exempt securities.

Investment seminars.

IRA contributions by participants with AGI over set limits.

Job-hunting costs for a first job.

Kickbacks.

Life insurance premiums.

Lobbying expenses (other than in-house expenses up to $2,000).

Losses from the sale of your home, furniture, car, and other personal items.

Losses on sales to related parties.

Lost or misplaced cash or property.

Lunches with coworkers.

Over-the-counter medications.

Partially worthless securities.

Passive activity losses in excess of passive activity income.

Penalties.

Personal disability insurance premiums.

Personal interest (such as credit card interest).

Personal living expenses (such as food, clothing, rent, and utilities).

Points paid to refinance a home mortgage.

Political contributions.

Professional accreditation fees.

Property settlements when dissolving a marriage.

Reimbursed expenses you receive under an accountable plan.

Repairs to your home or personal car.

Repayment of loans.

Rollover contributions.

Roth IRA contributions.

Sales tax.

Social Security and Medicare (FICA) taxes.

Spousal travel costs.

State inheritance taxes.

Stockholder meetings, expenses of attending.

Tax penalties.

Telephone line (basic service charges of first residential line to home).

Title insurance.

Toiletries.

Travel as a form of education.

Voluntary alimony payments.

Voluntary unemployment benefit fund contributions.

Wash sale losses.

Index